Qualitative Research in Social Work

D0062737

Qualitative Research in Social Work

Edmund Sherman and
William J. Reid
Editors

Columbia University Press
New York

Columbia University Press
New York   Chichester, West Sussex

Copyright © 1994 Columbia University Press

Library of Congress Cataloging-in-Publication Data

Qualitative research in social work / Edmund Sherman and William J.
  Reid, editors.
      p.   cm.
  Includes bibliographical references and index.
  ISBN 0–231–08033–6 (pbk.)
      1. Social service—Research—Methodology.   I. Sherman, Edmund A.
  II. Reid, William James, 1928–
HV11.Q28   1994
361.3′072—dc20   93–23421
                                                                  CIP

☯

Casebound editions of Columbia University Press books are
printed on permanent and durable acid-free paper.

Printed in the United States of America
c 10 9 8 7 6 5 4 3 2 1
p 10 9 8 7 6 5 4 3 2 1

Contents

Preface

This book is the first of its kind that is aimed at providing a broad range of qualitative research approaches for application to social work problems and practices. Although some of these approaches have been available in the social science literature they have not been addressed to the problems of primary concern in social work. Some of the approaches to be presented here are new to the social sciences as well.

The book addresses the current needs and interests of a wide range of social workers, including practitioners, researchers, academics, administrators, and students in the MSW and doctoral programs. It provides a range of alternative research approaches that social work practitioners and researchers are likely to find more promising and compatible with their professional experience than the more traditional quantitative approaches are. As such, these approaches are designed to better capture the context, complexity, and change processes that characterize actual social work practice.

The contributors to this book consist of nationally renowned researchers, scholars, and practitioners who are at the forefront of the development and application of the qualitative methods they will elucidate and illustrate here. Therefore social work researchers will be particularly interested in these offerings, but this interest should go well beyond researchers to all social workers who wish to find alternative ways of evaluating, testing and gaining knowledge about their own practice and to social work educators who can incorporate many of these offerings in their research, policy, and practice courses.

A number of individuals and organizations provided valuable support and assistance in the preparation of this book. We would like to thank Dr. David M. Austin, chair of the National Association of Social Workers Task Force on Social Work Research for his support and the support of the Task Force in this venture. Thanks also to Dr. Juan Ramos, special project officer, National Institute of Mental Health, and to the institute for its financial support in the planning, correspondence, and preliminary writing stages of this project.

Two Ph.D students in the School of Social Welfare of the University at Albany, Janet Myers and Karen Rich, were particularly helpful in providing valuable editorial assistance. Our appreciation also to Jean D'Alessandro for handling the voluminous correspondence associated with the preparation of this book and to B. J. Kelly, who assisted in much of the typing of the manuscript.

Finally, we would like to express our thanks to the School of Social Welfare of the University at Albany and particularly to its dean, Lynn Videka-Sherman, who provided the editors and a number of the authors with the various supports they needed to make their contributions to this book.

ONE

Introduction: Coming of Age in Social Work—The Emergence of Qualitative Research

Edmund Sherman and William J. Reid

Qualitative research has had an uneven history and delayed development as compared with the relatively continuous and progressive growth and maturation of quantitative methods in social work research. For this reason it has not played as much of a role as it could have in the testing and development of social work knowledge.

Qualitative research can be defined simply as research that produces descriptive data based upon spoken or written words and observable behavior. And qualitative methods can be defined as procedures for identifying the presence or absence of something, or describing the amount of something in words, in contrast to quantitative methods, which involve numerically measuring the degree to which some feature is present. Deciding what to count as a unit of analysis is essentially a qualitative and interpretive issue that requires judgment and choice in the development of themes, categories, classifications, and typologies from data collected in naturalistic situations, rather than in the experimental or otherwise controlled conditions common to quantitative procedures.

The elements of judgment, choice, interpretation, and naturalistic situations are actually coterminous with the major elements of direct practice in social work. Indeed, we could justifiably say that the case study method described by Mary Richmond (1917) in *Social Diagnosis* is a legitimate form of qualitative research. The case study has been defined as an in-depth form of research that may focus on a person, a cultural incident, or a community (Patton 1980). Certainly, the in-depth study involved in "social diagnosis" could be construed as applied qualitative research in which research findings guide intervention. In fact, many of the articles in social work journals of the 1920s, 1930s, 1940s, and 1950s consisted of clinical case studies.

Hollis (1949) carried the case study method even further in her study of 100 families who received casework services from eleven different family agencies. Her method relied on the written word in that the study was dependent upon caseworker records that were analyzed after treatment was completed. This amounted to a systematic content analysis of the case records to determine, among other things, the applicability of certain classifications or topologies of casework treatment to family counseling for marital conflict.

However, soon after the publication of Hollis's study the quantitative study of casework was begun at the Community Service Society that culminated in the publication of *Measuring Results in Casework* (Hunt and Kogan 1950). Joseph McVickar Hunt and Leonard S. Kogan, the directors of this project, were research psychologists. They were thus representative of the tradition of social and behavioral scientists carrying out social work research, a tradition that began with the large social surveys of the pre-World War II decades and the evaluative studies of social work services through the 1960s into the 1970s.

The methodology of these scientists was, of course, quantitative, but even when a few qualitative studies of social work were undertaken in the 1960s they were done by social scientists. This was true of Polsky's (1962) use of the ethnographic method of participant observation in *Cottage Six,* his study of delinquent boys in residential treatment. It was also true of Mayer and Timms (1970) in their qualitative study using client interviews (spoken word) to obtain working class impressions of casework in *The Client Speaks.*

However, as more and more social workers obtained research training and experience (under the tutelage of the social scientists) in master's and doctoral degree programs it was perhaps inevitable that a number of them would choose to supplement their largely quantitative research repertoires with qualitative methods. Some even looked to the humanities in such disciplines as literature, philosophy, and linguistics. Literature could provide ways of studying narrative structure, biography, and autobiography that could inform methodology in case studies. Philosophy not only could provide epistemological and ontological justification for qualitative research but also through phenomenology it could provide a method for the study of phenomena that is highly commensurable with grounded theory, ethnography, and other qualitative approaches to research. Similarly, linguistics, through applied semantics, could provide techniques for analyzing communications between clients and social workers as a form of discourse or conversation.

The need for increased knowledge and application of qualitative methods by social work researchers arose for a number of reasons. There was a recognition that the controlled and reductive procedures of quantitative research tended to selectively ignore much of the context of any study and thereby miss significant factors in the situation that more holistic qualitative observation and description might identify. There was also a recognition that the study and analysis of what goes on in the actual process of practice had been shortchanged in favor of measurable outcomes. Further, a need existed for more knowledge about the interactive and subjective experience of the client in the clinical change process. Here, narrative and discourse methods of analysis with a focus on meaning rather than measurement could help. Additionally, a heuristic approach to the study of clinical process could not only help return the case study to its former state of prominence but also provide new and alternative leads for assessment and intervention that are not contained in current theories or models of practice.

There is also a concern that the "bottom line" numbers of quantitative evaluation have tended to denude the findings of much of the richness and complexity of what goes on and what has been accomplished in any program or intervention. Therefore, qualitative research becomes necessary to capture and recapitulate that richness and complexity through its descriptive methods.

Finally, it became evident to many social work researchers that a need existed to address these shortcomings with a combination and integration of qualitative and quantitative methods. Qualitative methods would no longer be seen as just the "soft," exploratory steps to "hard" research but would in fact be seen to enhance the validity of our research endeavors in the ways described in this book. So it seems most appropriate that the growing number of social work researchers with these concerns should be represented in a volume such as this at this time. The qualitative methods these researchers put forward to address the concerns noted above are described in the essays that follow.

AN OVERVIEW OF QUALITATIVE METHODS

In this section we review the major qualitative methods presented in the book. In the course of discussing each method, we refer to relevant essays in the book, which include not only those in part 1 but also others that may elaborate or illustrate its use.

Ethnographic Methods

Cultural anthropology has relied heavily on qualitative field research methods from its beginnings up through the present. The emphasis of its methods is on immersion in and participant observation of cultures and societies in the naturalistic settings for the purposes of description and understanding. In many ways this emphasis is very congenial to field research in various forms of social work practice, because casework in clients' homes as well as group work and community organization in their neighborhoods seem to invite such an approach to research. Therefore, it is rather remarkable that social work practice research opted much more quickly and thoroughly for the quantitative methods from sociology and psychology than for the qualitative methods from anthropology. This is currently changing, however, as attested to by several essays in this volume.

Goodson-Lawes, in her paper, using her experience and illustrations from work with Mexican and Vietnamese newcomers to the United States, describes the kind of stance and preparation the researcher (and practitioner) needs to undertake for sound participant observation as an ethnographic method. She describes and delineates the particular relevance and application of the family studies method of Oscar Lewis for social work research and draws implications for practice with immigrant families.

Although anthropologists originally developed ethnographic methods for the understanding of non-Western cultures, their relevance for American and nonimmigrant cultures is made abundantly clear in papers by Weissman and by Sands and McClelland. Weissman describes how the social work administrator can make use of ethnographic methods to create a learning environment in his or her agency. Sands and McClelland describe their research on communication patterns of interdisciplinary teams assessing children for possible mental retardation/developmental disability. They make a most important distinction between *emic* ("insider") and *etic* ("outsider") perspectives in such ethnographic research. They note that the etic approach is "external or "alien" in that the researcher's perspective is from outside the culture and studies it comparatively according to a preexisting system of knowledge or theory about other cultures. The emic approach is called "internal" or "domestic" because its perspective is more from the subjective or inside experience of the culture and persons under study and what is discovered is related to that culture as a whole rather than cross-culturally. As he discusses the relevance of ethnographic methods and critical inquiry for social work practice research, Goldstein clearly opts for the emic perspective and he provides a clear-cut example of its application in the context of school social work with Puerto Rican students. Another example is presented by Davis and Srinivasan in their ethnographic study of a battered woman's shelter in which they elicit the perspectives of the residents to show how the behavior of the staff was unwittingly (and ironically) creating another form of oppression in the residents' lives.

In her commentary, Fortune discusses two broad applications of ethnographic methods to social work: the use of ethnographic tools to enhance practice skills and the development of knowledge about social work settings and the cultures of client populations through ethnographic studies. Although she underscores the fit between ethnography and social work practice, as other authors do in the book, she also draws attention to areas in which fit is lacking. For instance, ethnographers are content with understanding; social work practitioners must transform their understanding into action.

Heuristic Methods

Perhaps one reason social work did not look earlier to anthropology and its ethnographic methods was that the profession was concurrently engaged in the development of its own indigenous method of studying the lives of clients in the context of their homes and communities. Indeed, the fulcrum of past and present social work practice, i.e., person-in-situation, arose from this type of study, as exemplified in *Social Diagnosis*. Heineman Pieper, in her paper, calls for a return to the "robustness of *naturalistic research*" in which experienced practitioners can systematically study clinical practice in its full complexity without altering it for research purposes ("interventionist" research). She calls for its renewed use, not to replace interventionist research, but to enhance the possibilities of new discovery in clinical practice. To do this she proposes the heuristic paradigm, which, in contrast to scientism, conceptualizes science more broadly as a systematic inquiry into some aspect of reality that is communicated in a way that will allow an interested person to make an informed evaluation of the process of inquiry and its conclusions. Thus heuristic research in social work would encourage the individual practitioner to discover, without primary concern for the constraints of verification and corroboration, through methods that enable further exploration of promising leads and developments in the practice process.

Tyson explicates the heuristic paradigm further in her paper and discusses its application to naturalistic evaluations of child treatment. She then provides illustrations of the application of the heuristic approach to the treatment of a six-year-old boy and at the close of her paper offers a concise summary of heuristic guidelines for naturalistic single-case evaluation in general.

Grounded Theory Methods

Another qualitative approach that is particularly promising for the development of indigenous social work theory and knowledge is the grounded theory approach developed by Glaser and Strauss (1967). It is an approach and set of methods for discovering theories, concepts, hypotheses, and propositions directly from data rather than from a priori assumptions, other research, or existing theoretical frameworks. Thus, it is phenomenological in that it attempts to go directly to the empirical data without preconceptions or prestructuring of data collection procedures on the basis of prior theory or research from the social and behavioral sciences or even social work itself. That is why it is so promising for developing theory and knowledge about contemporary social work. It also tends to be more naturalistic and noninterventionist, in line with the concerns just raised by Heineman Pieper and separately by Tyson.

Gilgun in her essay describes how well grounded theory methods fit into the process of direct social work practice, so well that they fit like "hand into glove." She then describes these methods and demonstrates the relevance of the grounded theory approach to the development of practice knowledge. She describes several social work studies, including her own, that utilized grounded theory methods. One of them was Belcher's (1988) study of homeless persons with chronic mental illness.

Belcher presents a more detailed description himself of the methods and procedures of his project in his paper. His research relied heavily on the constant comparative method from the grounded theory approach, in which the researcher makes continual comparisons within and across cases or incidents and returns to those cases for analysis at a higher level of abstraction and understanding based on knowledge gained from the prior steps. This iterative process enabled him to inductively and empirically discern three stages of homelessness that add to our understanding of the process of social drift among the homeless.

Mizrahi and Abramson, in their study of social worker and physician collaboration, also relied on constant comparative method. Additionally, their approach highlights how tightly interwoven the processes of data collection, coding, and analysis are in the application of that method. They used the method both to develop codes for specific variables and to gain understanding of broader conceptual issues and themes. On the basis of these processes Mizrahi and Abramson were able to derive a typology of social worker/physician collaboration that has much descriptive power and that has potential application to other interdisciplinary relationships.

An additional application of grounded theory is provided by Bernstein and Epstein. In their view grounded theory is "an apt analog for administrative practice because of its suitability for capturing the reality and complexity of that work." They see the "grounded administrator" as one who is successful in discovering grounded theory and who can use it effectively to understand agency processes. When the work of these authors is related to the ethnographic approach of Weissman's referred to above, it becomes apparent that qualitative methods can serve as important tools in administrative practice as well as research.

Narrative Methods

Personal or self-histories told by clients to social workers has been an integral part of casework practice since its inception. However, this preliminary case history or anamnesis was seen as just that—data or information gathered for a psychosocial assessment *preliminary* to actual casework intervention. As Cohler makes clear in his essay, this life story can and does have functions that go far beyond assessment or diagnosis. As he notes, the life history constitutes the presently recounted record of the personal past, ordering and making sense of lived experience, and it is recounted in the form of a story that must be coherent within terms generally accepted within the culture.

The predominant form in our culture is a narrative, i.e., a story that has a plot, a beginning, a middle, and an end. The kind of plot and the structure of the narrative can be crucial for, as Sartre (1964) noted, each person "tries to live his life as if he were recounting it." Certainly, practitioners often become aware of the self-fulfilling prophesies inherent in the way clients tell their life stories, or narratives, or how fractionated, lacking in cohesion, and problematic their narratives are. Consequently, more and more practitioners are using "narrative coherence" as a therapeutic tool— that is, helping a client create a coherent personal life story. Laird, in her article, makes clear how important it is for practitioners and researchers to allow clients to tell their life stories without inhibiting their reconstructions of the past. This is particularly important in family therapy where personal narratives and discussion of them by family members can be revealing of current interaction, past and present conflicts, and the history of family dynamics. It is necessary to allow for and facilitate full narrative conversation and to avoid prematurely imposing a structure that curtails understanding by the family, by the practitioner, and by the researcher.

In her article Martin describes and illustrates the value of the oral history method of obtaining life narratives from elderly African Americans that can contribute to our understanding of the history of oppression and the life forces that enabled them to overcome the effects of oppression and to "get over." Oral history allows uneducated and even illiterate persons as individuals, or in families or small groups, to narrate their life stories. By this means some of the history of culturally disadvantaged and oppressed groups in this country can be reconstructed.

Discourse Analysis

Since discourse is basically conversation or verbal interchange, discourse analysis is the formal and systematic study of this interchange. Linguists are concerned with the function and structure of the interchange so as to identify the structural principles of interpretation, production, and sequencing. The methods they have developed can be of considerable value for the analysis of dialogue in clinical practice.

This is in fact what Chambon does in her essay. She shows how these methods can be applied in the form of dialogical analysis of clinical case materials. As she makes clear, the concern in clinical discourse is not just with the client's narrative (telling) but also with the exchange (talking) and the interactive and interpretive process that goes on between client and worker. She presents a segment of therapeutic dialogue to illustrate a number of tools from linguistics that can be used to analyze the therapeutic process.

Nye, in her article, not only discusses the application of discourse analysis methods but also provides a single case study that illustrates their application in considerable detail. She also shows a useful coding scheme for discourse ratings and a quantitative analysis of the composition of the sessions based on the ratings, which can reflect change over time. Then, in his essay, Sherman proposes and illustrates a framework from change process research in which to capture and provide more data on both the client's and the worker's role in the dialogical and external change processes within and across treatment sessions.

Discourse analysis can be seen as a new addition to the long tradition of research on the processes of clinical social work (Fortune 1981). In recent years there has been a movement toward use of a combination of quantitative and qualitative methods as well as a growing emphasis on examining both intervention processes and client change during treatment. This new research thrust, referred to as "change process research" (Reid 1990; Rice and Greenberg 1984) incorporates methods of discourse analysis as well as other methods presented in this book.

Among other things, qualitative methods enable researchers to depict the subtle and intricate processes of intervention and change that occur during treatment—processes that quantitative techniques may be able to identify but cannot adequately portray. Nye's account of a client's development of self-analytic skills during her therapy provides an excellent example of this kind of application.

QUALITATIVE APPROACHES TO EVALUATION

At the beginning of this introductory paper we noted some of the current dissatisfactions with "bottom line" numbers used in quantitative evaluations of effectiveness and the outcome of social work interventions. This dissatisfaction applies to single case evaluations as well as to the evaluation of programs and policies. In this section we consider what qualitative methods can contribute to both kinds of evaluation.

Case Evaluation

Ruckdeschel writes from the perspective of an instructor who teaches qualitative methods to social work students, two of whom are his co-authors. He indicates how difficult it is to engage the interest of either students or practitioners in evaluation, given the instrumental and measurement approach proposed by social work research texts. He chooses instead to emphasize the "value" meaning of the term *evaluation*. He sees evaluation as the process of finding the value, which is the first and perhaps most important phase of the research in either the classroom or the field. With this focus two of his former students, Earnshaw and Firrek, provide two case studies, respectively, that illustrate the qualitative approach they learned and applied. In the process they also provide excellent examples of thick description, a method of capturing and reporting the interactional and situational processes in a rich, dense, and detailed manner.

Lang, in her paper, compares the cycles of data processing for knowledge building of qualitative research with the data processing for action in social work practice. She provides a clear description and a diagram of how these cycles differ and then proposes the adoption of the qualitative research methodology of data processing and expands it in a way that makes it capable of being used for action purposes. This, she feels, can integrate the qualitative research methodology with practice methodology by defining a new route from which intervention can be derived, which in turn holds promise for the development of theory in practice. However, Dean and Stern, in their separate articles, show how unrealistic it is to expect practitioners to fulfill knowledge-building research functions while at the same time engaging in the reflexive and responsive kind of process required in clinical practice.

These essays and others in this book have implications for practitioners as evaluators of their own practice. During the past two decades a considerable literature has emerged on the use of quantitative methods in own-practice evaluation (Bloom and Fischer 1982; Hudson 1982; Jayaratne and Levy 1979; Tripodi and Epstein 1980; Videka-Sherman and Reid 1990). Practitioners have been enjoined to be "practitioner-researchers" who might use quantitative single-case designs to evaluate their own practice as well as contribute to knowledge. In addition various quantitative techniques that might be used to enhance assessment and treatment processes have been identified, including methods of obtaining behavioral baselines, standardized instruments, and client self-monitoring devices.

The paper on single-case evaluation, as well as others, explore the much neglected qualitative side of the practitioner's use of research methods. A common theme in these papers is the fit between qualitative approaches and social work practice. Similarities between qualitative research and direct practice are drawn in separate essays by Gilgun, Goldstein, and Lang. As these authors argue, direct practitioners can function as participant observers who can collect and analyze essentially qualitative data about their clients in a way that could enhance their practice without disrupting it.

Policy and Program Evaluation

The application of qualitative methods to program and policy evaluation moves us to a different research level, but some of the issues raised in single-case evaluations carry into the larger arena of policy and programs. For example, Ruckdeschel's point that the first dictionary definition of "evaluate" is "to find the value" is central to Bogdan and Taylor's "positive approach" to qualitative and policy research. They make explicit what the value assumptions are in their approach, and using this approach they purposely evaluate programs that appear successful in order to learn how the success was achieved. By contrast, in conventional evaluations the purpose is to learn whether the programs are successful without the values underlying the (usually quantified) criteria of success being of central concern in the analysis.

Qualitative methodology provides a way of depicting social work programs and policies in a penetrating and holistic manner. The investigator as the "human instrument" is critical here. To study such phenomena comprehensively and in depth, there is need for a human intelligence to gather together myriad data from diverse sources: managers, staff, clients, archives, and so on, and to derive patterns and relationships from the data. The investigator needs to have the flexibility to follow leads as they arise and to zero in on what appears to be important. To be sure, quantitative approaches may be able to provide more precise and systematic data on specific variables, such as particular outcomes, but these approaches fall short because they must concentrate on a limited number of variables and may have difficulty in discerning relations among the many factors at work. The numbers they provide usually do not give one a comprehensive picture of what a particular program or policy really looks like.

Several of the papers provide illustrations of qualitative studies of programs and policies. Johnson carried out an investigation of virtually all the institutional and community programs in one geographic area in Sweden. His study involved 135 hours of formal and casual discussions with both patients and staff in eight programs. A number of issues in service delivery, such as conflict between social and biological perspectives and lack of social supports for patients, were explored in depth.

Rapp, Kisthardt, Gowdy, and Hanson conducted a quantitative study to determine factors accounting for success in the eight mental health agencies in Kansas that were producing the best results in respect to hospitalizations, independent living, and vocational status. Analyses of such variables as size of budget and length of program operation produced no meaningful findings. The investigators then tried a qualitative approach, which involved nondirective interviews with managers, staff, and consumers of the agencies. From the data the researchers were able to identify four principles of management that were common to the more successful programs.

Pulice describes a qualitative approach to program evaluation that is oriented to the various constituency groups upon which the program impacts. He provides a case example of an evaluation to identify constituencies in a multilevel, geographically and socioeconomically diverse program for the mentally ill in a large state mental health system. The study involved identifying the various levels (e.g., central, regional, county, agency) in this complex state system and developing a taxonomy of constituency groups associated with each level. Semistructured interviews were held with members of these groups to determine the role of each group in the system (e.g., insiders vs. outsiders) and to obtain its perspective on the impact of the program. As this study illustrates, methods proposed can "give voice" to the usually unheard constituencies that are a part of large-scale programs.

Rodwell and Woody provide an interesting new qualitative approach to program and policy evaluation based on constructivist theory in their paper. Constructivism is the view that entities or objects exist in socially and personally constructed forms and contexts and that any knowledge or "truths" about these entities cannot adequately be known independently of these constructions and contexts. They accept constructivist assumptions that "the nature of reality is multiple, constructed, holistic; that generalizations are not possible or desirable owing to the context and time-bound nature of reality." This means that a constructivist evaluation has to be sensitive (holistically) to the context, to the views or "constructions" of the key parties (and constituencies per Pulice, above), and to the interactional effects of the evaluation process itself. Rodwell and Woody then provide an example of a constructivist evaluation of a child guidance clinic, which illustrates a number of approaches that are sensitive to these elements and issues.

Witkin makes a critical point in his essay when he states that "the conceptual models and methods used by evaluators often form a powerful context (the methodological context) that affects the implementation and interpretation of evaluation." He adds that this context is imposed by the evaluator, but it is usually implicit and overlooked. He notes that Bogdan, Taylor, Pulice, Rodwell and Woody in their own ways demonstrate that evaluation is contextual, and he then shows how their methods (methodological contexts) affect the implementation and interpretation of their evaluations.

These studies, as well as those by Johnson and by Rapp, Kisthardt, Gowdy, and Hanson, illustrate well how qualitative approaches can capture key dimensions of complex programs and policies. Although the results may be subject to the biases of both informants and researchers, they are nevertheless of an order that quantitative approaches simply cannot match. The trade-off is often between a set of reasonably precise but only marginally informative numbers and interesting but contestable generalizations—an argument for integrated and complementary use of qualitative and quantitative methods in evaluations of programs and policies.

APPLICATIONS TO TYPES OF CLIENT POPULATIONS AND SETTINGS

As the papers in this book amply illustrate, qualitative methods have a broad range of application to the diverse settings and populations encompassed by social work. We have already seen how ethnographic and narrative methods can be used to elicit the perspectives of disadvantaged, oppressed, and alienated people—populations of central concern to social workers. Part 3 presents applications to two fields of practice—child and family and mental health. Maluccio and Fein examine the importance of agency context in doing both quantitative and qualitative research in child welfare settings and present principles for creating a supportive context. Carlson argues that agency context has greater salience for qualitative than quantitative research and presents additional guidance for researchers in coping with agency environments. The other application in the child and family field (Davis and Srinivasan), as well as applications in the field of mental health (by Johnson and by Rapp, Kisthardt, Gowdy, and Hanson), have been considered in relation to evaluation methods. Finally, Mullin discusses how qualitative methods can facilitate study of the "new paradigm" in the rehabilitation of mentally ill persons.

The setting applications presented in part 3 are, of course, only some of those considered in the book. Davis and Rodwell and Woody provide additional examples in the child and family field. To the qualitative studies of mental health agencies in part 3 can be added Pulice's research. Use of qualitative methods in health settings can be found in essays by Mizrahi and Abramson and Bogdan and Taylor.

INTEGRATION AND EPISTEMOLOGY

The relation between quantitative and qualitative approaches has become a leading issue in research methodology. Much of the epistemological controversy that has appeared in the social work literature during the past decade has concerned the relative values of these two approaches. The quantitative–qualitative interface is addressed in many of the articles of this volume. The papers in part 4 examine this interrelationship in depth, at both the epistemological (paradigmatic) and methodological levels.

Paradigmatic Level

To understand the debate concerning the commensurability of quantitative and qualitative methods, it is important to distinguish between two levels of discourse: the paradigmatic and the methodological. At the paradigmatic level one is concerned with the philosophical basis of research methods— their rationales and justifications. At the methodological level, attention is given to how the methods are used in doing research.

At the paradigmatic level the same method may be justified in divergent ways by different paradigms, thus producing conflict at that level. For example, in one paradigm the observations of an expert observer may be regarded as inherently more trustworthy than they would be in another paradigm. Clashes at this level may be difficult to resolve.

Our authors offer some approaches to resolution, or at least accommodation. Harrison argues that a resolution is possible through "relativism and reflexivity." A researcher who makes use of both can see the world from the standpoint of different paradigms (relativism) but at the same time can achieve a personal integration of these paradigms through the processes of metacognition, that is, through "thinking about one's perceptions and ideas." Reid and Orcutt separately call for pragmatically determined common standards that can be used to evaluate research methods and products regardless of differences in paradigmatic justification. Hartman advocates mutual tolerance for and acceptance of our "many ways of knowing"; Imre supports this position and stresses the importance of listening to one another as a way of understanding and accepting paradigmatic differences.

Methodological Level

At the methodological level, two kinds of integration are possible. One kind may be thought of as "between-studies" integration. Here the question becomes, What kind of approach, quantitative or qualitative, might be most appropriate for a particular kind of study? For example, using a heuristic paradigm, Heineman Pieper and Tyson separately suggest that the approach used should provide the best fit to the questions without assumptions that one is superior to the other. Making use of Cook's (1985) principle of multiplism, Reid advocates successive use of both kinds of methods to examine the same question. In effect applying this principle, Rapp, Kisthardt, Gowdy, and Hanson show how a qualitative study yielded useful findings to a particular question that had failed to respond to a quantitative approach.

A second kind of integration might be thought of as "within study." At this level quantitative and qualitative methods are used in combination within the same piece of research. Generally the two methods are used in complementary fashion—for instance, qualitative methods may portray complexities and nuances that cannot be adequately depicted by quantitative data, or quantitative methods provide more precise estimations of magnitude—e.g., frequencies—that are not possible in qualitative approaches. Our authors offer many examples. Nye and Sherman, in separate papers, use qualitative techniques to interpret quantitative measures of client discourse. In his change process study, Loneck used qualitative methods to identify variables for statistical modeling. Davis uses both kinds of methods to achieve triangulation in her study of a family treatment model. Toseland's article gives examples from his own research practice of how qualitative methods were used to investigate statistical patterns in different data sets. In one of these instances qualitative inquiry in turn informed additional quantitative analysis. Bernstein and Epstein suggest that the idea of within-study integration can be extended to a social worker's practice. They show how a grounded theory approach can help an administrator make sense out of the many kinds of information that he or she must cope with.

As these examples suggest, our authors overwhelmingly endorse the principle of methodological integration. What is more, they break new ground in showing how it can be done.

References

Belcher, J. R. 1988. Rights versus needs of homeless mentally ill persons. *Social Work* 33: 398–402.

Bloom, M. and J. Fischer. 1982. *Evaluating Practice: Guidelines for the Accountable Professional.* Englewood Cliffs, N.J.: Prentice Hall.

Cook, T. D. 1985. Postivist critical multiplism. In W. R. Shadish and C. S. Relchardt, eds., *Evaluation Studies. 12.* Newbury Park, Calif.: Sage.

Fortune, A. E. 1981. Communication processes in social work practice. *Social Service Review* 55: 93–128.

Glaser, B. and A. Strauss. 1967. *The Discovery of Grounded Theory.* Chicago: Aldine.

Hollis, F. 1949. *Women in Marital Conflict: A Casework Study.* New York: Family Service Association of America.

Hudson, W. W. 1982. *The Clinical Measurement Package.* Homewood, Ill.: Dorsey Press.

Hunt, J. M. and L. S. Kogan. 1950. *Measuring Results in Casework.* New York: Family Service Association of America.

Jayaratne, S. and R. Levy. 1979. *Empirical Clinical Practice.* New York: Columbia University Press.

Mayer, J. E. and N. Timms. 1970. *The Client Speaks: Working Class Impressions of Casework.* New York: Atherton Press.

Patton, M. Q. 1980. *Qualitative Evaluation Research.* Newbury Park, Calif.: Sage.

Polsky, H. 1962. *Cottage Six: The Social System of Delinquent Boys in Residential Treatment.* New York: Wiley.

Reid, W. J. 1990. Change-process research: A new paradigm? In L. Videka-Sherman and W. J. Reid, eds., *Advances in Clinical Social Work Research.* Silver Spring, Md.: NASW Press.

Rice, L. N. and L. S. Greenberg, eds., 1984. *Patterns of Change: Intensive Analysis of Psychotherapy Process.* New York: Guilford Press.

Richmond, M. 1917. *Social Diagnosis.* New York: Russell Sage Foundation.

Sartre, J. P. 1964. *The Words.* Greenwich, Conn.: Fawcett.

Tripodi, T. and I. Epstein. 1980. *Research Techniques for Clinical Social Workers.* New York: Columbia University Press.

Videka-Sherman, L. and W. J. Reid, eds., 1990. *Advances in Clinical Social Work Research.* Silver , Md.: NASW Press.

I

Qualitative Methods in Contemporary Social Work

ETHNOGRAPHIC
METHODS

TWO

Ethnicity and Poverty as Research Variables: Family Studies with Mexican and Vietnamese Newcomers

Julie Goodson-Lawes

Social work research (and practice) with ethnic and immigrant groups is intrinsically problematic. Social workers and social science researchers tend to come from a middle-class, ethnically "mainstreamed" background, which can cause a rift of understanding and confidence in dealing with often poor ethnic minorities. While most social workers would agree that it is important to approach such a client or research subject with an open, nonjudgmental mind, this belief does not translate easily into actual suggestions for interpersonal behavior or interpretation of results. Qualitative research can begin to fill the need for a social work knowledge base that offers insight into actual worker/client relationships across ethnic, class, and gender lines. To do this, social work researchers must learn from practitioners one of the clinician's basic tenets: that trusting, caring human interaction is an integral part of the therapeutic relationship. It should play a similar role in the research relationship.

Only by conducting such humane, seemingly subjective research can social workers learn, for example, about the tangled causes of persistent poverty, the complex effects of racism, or the manifold needs of new arrivals to this country. Quantitative research, by its very disinterested nature, often leaves subjects—especially those who are culturally distinct from the investigators—bewildered, alienated, and even hostile or afraid. In contrast, qualitative research is more personal, interactive, and less intimidating for the research subject. Below I describe an intensive ethnographic method known as family studies, wherein investigators establish relationships of trust and confidence with entire families. I spent one year carrying out such family studies with Mexican immigrant and Vietnamese refugee families in San José, California (1990). On the basis of this research, I suggest that such studies are an ideal vehicle for social welfare practice research—not only for the information they reveal but also for their clinical implications.

Family studies require the development of an intensive relationship between the researcher and the researched that allows each party to act as both giver and receiver of information and human support. Because of the reciprocity involved in this type of qualitative research, typical research (and practice) pitfalls due to power differentials are less likely to develop. Thus, family studies are a perfect addition to the repertoire of those searching to understand the complexity of human situations—such as those that daily confront the clinical social worker and society as a whole.

QUANTITATIVE DATA GATHERING AMONG RECENT IMMIGRANTS

It is no secret that members of poor ethnic minority and immigrant groups are often considered "hard to reach," whether as clients or as subjects of social science research (Arevalo and Minor 1982; Brown, Oliver, and Klor de Alva 1985; Devore and Schlesinger 1981; Gibson 1983; Green 1982; Hopps 1982; Hopps and Tripodi 1983; Lloyd 1978). Since these groups are also more likely to be among America's poor, cultural disparities combine with economic and class differences to confound well-meaning social service workers as well as to frustrate needy individuals. The difficulty with using quantitative methods across such cultural and class lines is twofold. First, can the investigator devise a questionnaire or test that asks the correct questions correctly (i.e., that ask what the investigator really wants to know); and second, does the subject feel able to answer honestly and fully (to tell what the investigator really wants to know)? The reticence common among many ethnic groups when answering surveys or taking part in testing is not arbitrary. Rather, it is indicative of a major weakness in the quantitative method, a weakness that is magnified with each cultural and economic disparity between investigator and investigated.

Of Ethnic Groups and Errors

Some typical—but critical—barriers to information gathering among ethnically distinct groups are translation difficulties, literacy problems, intimidating agency settings, and simple yet significant cultural mistakes on the part of the interviewer (i.e., misunderstanding a lack of eye contact, refusing proferred hospitality, or being overly familiar). All these issues have been discussed in handbooks on ethnic-sensitive social work practice (See, for example, Devore and Schlesinger 1981). More difficult to address, however, are the innumerable obstacles that derive from the alien nature of quantitative research forms per se. Even for the native-born, most encounters with quantitative instruments take place under stressful conditions such as applying for a job, paying taxes, or asking for government subsidies. Among the majority of the world's population, surveys and tests are totally outside the realm of one's normal experience. This is especially true for rural or uneducated peoples entering the United States as immigrants, who often first confront questionnaires and surveys within the bureaucratic maze of immigration and naturalization services.

As I worked with both groups of newcomers, several salient categories emerged as the roots of research errors. This list is not all-inclusive but at least is indicative of the complexity of the research relationship.

1. Mistrust/fear.   When one is working among immigrants, ethnic groups, or the poor, mistrust, fear, and anger are often the prevalent reactions to any information gathering or intervention. This is particularly true if the investigator is associated (or perceived to be associated) with a government or social-service institution. These reactions are generally based on very real concerns about exploitation and abuse at the hands of authority figures. Mistrust and fear can lead to absolute refusals to take part in investigations or to false or misleading answers.

2. Answering what is perceived to be wanted.   If the interview subjects do not withdraw because of mistrust and fear, they may respond in an opposite manner with an overwillingness to please. Often as the result of a feeling of indebtedness, or simply rooted in a tradition of hospitality and friendliness, many clients try very hard to please their interviewers. Such "overcompliance" is a common pitfall that is especially heightened when the investigator is believed to represent a link to desired goods and services.

3. Shame.   Shame in answering survey questions honestly and directly is certainly not limited to ethnic groups, but the cultural misunderstandings that are rampant whenever we attempt to cross cultural barriers add to the probabilities that the investigator will unwittingly ask questions that cause the subject embarrassment or discomfort. Rather than refuse to answer the question, the subject is likely either to develop an excuse for not responding or to answer the question inaccurately. This situation is compounded when the interviewer and interviewed have different statuses, according to gender, class, race, and culture.

4. Joking. An often neglected aspect of data collection is the possibility of a subject's joking or, more precisely, making fun of the interviewer. Although we researchers tend to take our research seriously (counting on it, as we do, for career advancement and funding), there is virtually no reason for our informants to do so. Most ethnographers admit to being made sport of, at least occasionally, while conducting fieldwork. There is little to suggest that survey takers or test givers would escape such treatment. After all, such methods are functionally gullible.

5. Good intentions. Answers to survey questions often have more to do with the good intentions of those surveyed than with the reality of their lives. Particularly for families dealing with the stresses of living in a new country, racism, poverty, and intergenerational conflict, the gap between what they want to do and actually do, or what they want to believe and actually believe, may be broad. Because good intentions combine with feelings of shame over not having fulfilled certain obligations, answers to such questions may fail to reflect a realistic situation.

6. Inadequacy of a question. Often what appears to be a simple question to middle-class sensibilities is anything but for ethnic minorities. A response to a query about monthly income, for example, may invoke a complex web of part-time incomes of different family members, income from selling fruit and popsicles on weekends, income from helping another family make cheese once every two to three weeks, extra money brought in by giving haircuts and permanents to neighborhood women, or occasional childcare or sewing. And all this may change every month as family composition changes, a new immigrant arrives, a boarder is taken in, extra opportunities arise for informal work, etc. In short, the questions we ask are often overly simplistic and, in essence, the wrong ones.

These categories need not be mutually exclusive; on the contrary, all six can and do emerge, certainly within a single survey, and at times within a single question. For example, I was visiting a Mexican neighbor family one afternoon when a survey taker from a local health clinic came to ask ''a few questions.'' The survey taker's ultimate goal was to develop a profile of the health status of the local Spanish-speaking population and to understand why a clinic located in this predominantly Mexican neighborhood was not used more by the nearby community. When he asked this question directly, it was met with polite responses of how nice the clinic looked and excuses for not using it more. Yet as someone who had lived in the neighborhood for several months and who often acted as chauffeur and escort to the clinic, I saw the reasons clearly: the local people were accustomed to receiving most of their health care from village curers who came to their home, distributed vitamins and herbs, sometimes administered injections and dietary admonitions, and generally relied on personal trust for the healer/patient relationship.

In contrast, the clinic was a sterile, cold building that was unclearly marked; there was no obvious desk to walk up to and begin asking questions; the only sign was one at the front door advising that those who had filed for amnesty needed to have their number with them—a sign understood by many to mean that only those eligible for amnesty need approach the clinic for services; the reception staff were professional and efficient but were perceived as cold and unfriendly; and women with children typically had no transportation or child care. It is true that most Mexicans, even from the most isolated towns, have dealt with formal urban health care services for serious illnesses and that such hospitals are not very different from this local clinic. However, one grave difference is evident: when Mexicans are in Mexico they are not, by simple reason of birthplace, considered to be illegal, whereas in many parts of California they are. It is extremely difficult for one to cope with the alien health care setting while feeling sure that one may be deported at any time.

The answers to many of the clinic's questions could have been discovered easily and quickly; a single trip to the clinic with a typical client (where the investigator is assumed to be a friend or family member of the client and thus receives no special treatment) would have reaped a wealth of such information. Spending time with people under informal circumstances, noting what takes place, and accepting with an open mind whatever situations and ideas emerge (only later developing conclusions) are what is known in anthropology as "participant observation." In a sense, participant observation allows the researcher to develop questions *after* exposure to relevant information. It is a simple yet complex method and eminently useful for overcoming precisely the types of cross-cultural, cross-class, and even cross-gender misunderstandings outlined above.

THE ETHNOGRAPHIC SOLUTION

Participant observation, or the qualitative method known as "ethnography," is fundamental to anthropology. It was developed as a method for understanding foreign peoples and cultures at a time of global discovery and interaction on a massive scale. One of the founders of the field, Bronislaw Malinowski, asserted that to truly understand how native populations thought and saw the world, one needed to live with them for extended periods of time (Malinowski 1922). Besides allowing anthropologists to witness and take part in the details of everyday life, such long-term fieldwork transforms researchers into students of their cultural "informants." As they enter the field, these investigators are effectively seen by the host culture as babies, lacking in such basic understanding as how to feed themselves, how to take part in social situations, and how to look after their own best interests.

Fieldworkers must take several steps to gain legitimacy in the eyes of a group of people who have no real reason to trust an outsider. They must learn to speak the language; they must gain at least nominal social status to be taken seriously; they must develop sufficient social skills to be accepted, if not as a native, at least at an admissible level. The "normality" of the ethnographer's presence in a community is heightened by complete participation in daily life and constant observation of others' interactions and actions (see Spradley 1980 for a complete discussion of the techniques of participant observation). Because the intent of ethnography is to comprehend, without judgment, alien ideology, ritual, behavior, and social structure, one of the most important aspects of such fieldwork is that the investigator's attitude not be "loaded" before entering the field. Ethnography seeks to understand the meaning of actions, events, and physical objects for the people who are teaching us, rather than what they mean to us directly.

In addition to participant observation, ethnography can include such techniques as proxemics, mapmaking, kinship charts, formal and informal interviews, collection of life histories, review of personal documentation, analysis of folklore, and administration of surveys. In fact, some ethnographers use a great many quantitative methods, including demographic statistics, detailed questionnaires, and testing devices (Johnson 1978). The use of such methods in addition to participant observation allows the investigator to obtain information from a greater number of people than can be investigated intensively, and the use of both methods can serve as a validity check of one's information. Both quantitative and qualitative methods, after all, are subject to the many difficulties discussed in the preceding section of this essay; misunderstandings, miscommunication, and misleadings are aspects inherent in any human interaction. However, the intensity and longevity of the ethnographic experience are such that contradictions in verbal statements and day-to-day actions can be duly noted. In fact, the discovery that an informant has given false information is, in itself, an extremely important fact, for these inconsistencies are often more telling than conscious proclamations.

Because participant observation discourages the researcher from taking information at face value, the subtleties and inconsistencies in human life can be uncovered. As Kirk and Miller (1986) succinctly state when describing the ethnographic approach:

> This "method" is unusually sensitive to discrepancies between the meanings presumed by investigators and those understood by the target population. Indeed, this is one reason that qualitative research has been such a dominant method in the anthropological study of exotic populations, where it is quite apparent that the investigator makes assumptions about meanings, situations, and attributions at his or her own risk.   (Kirk and Miller 1986:30–31)

While this is true for so-called exotic populations, it is at least equally applicable to communities within our own borders: groups that function according to different cultural rules than those of the majority, whether for historical, socioeconomic, or national origin reasons. Though the ethnographic method has traditionally been used for research with foreign, non-Western, nonurban populations, attention has increasingly turned to studies in the United States, Europe, and urban areas of the Third World. Ethnography in these settings requires the same skills as mentioned above, even while it is carried out in the researcher's own society.

To adapt the ethnographic method to complex urban nations, anthropologists have studied organizations, the workplace, the marketplace, schools, or other public places where community interaction is frequent and structured (Kottak 1982). While such highly delimited studies offer a great deal of insight into social interactions in specific environments, the "wholeness" of human life is often lost in these restricted settings. How does the researcher in a society such as the United States find a manageable research sample that reflects complex lives? Family studies offer one solution.

Family Studies

Family studies take advantage of a manageable unit of analysis while investigating an effective microcosm of the many aspects of an individual's life. The family is the perfect intersection of the public and the private, where the private (i.e., interpersonal relationships) is inexorably linked to the public (i.e., obtaining food, clothes, and supplies, interacting with the children's schools, finding health care, supporting employed family members). In other words, the family infrastructure molds, resists, and makes possible an individual's interaction with the public superstructure.

As Oscar Lewis, an anthropologist who championed the family studies method several decades ago, states:

> The intensive study of families has many methodological advantages. Because the family is a small social system, it lends itself to the holistic

approach of anthropology. The family is a natural unit of study. . . . More-over, in describing a family we see individuals as they live and work rather than as the averages and stereotypes implicit in reports on culture patterns. In studying a culture through the intensive analysis of specific families we learn what institutions mean to individuals. . . . Whole family studies bridge the gap between the conceptual extremes of culture at one pole and the individual at the other; we see both culture and personality as they are interrelated in real life.   (Lewis 1959:17)

It is also a context in which women and children, often not visible or powerful in the public realm, play vital roles.

Family studies, in general, require a very simple research method: spending time with a family. Ideally, this includes actually moving into a household and taking part in everyday life, applying to the family unit the same ethnographic steps as outlined above, such as learning the language, taking part in daily life, and becoming a normal presence in the home. As in all ethnography, events, reactions,emotions, and interactions are re-corded in carefully detailed journals. This generalized participant observa-tion is expanded by Lewis, who suggests the following techniques for the study of family life.

1. The application of conceptual categories used in the study of entire communities to a single family. In other words, collecting data under such topical headings as material culture, social relations, or religious activities.

2. The "Rashomon"-like technique of collecting autobiographies from everyone in the household, including especially one's experi-ences within the family, and comparing them. This provides numer-ous indirect views of family dynamics and serves as an important validity check for family history and events.

3. The intensive study of a particular problem or event and the family's reaction to it. This is usually dependent upon happenstance, such as the birth of a child, a serious illness or death of a family member, or financial crises or windfalls. Although such events cannot always be foreseen, if an investigator spends a great deal of time with a family over an extended period, events typically arise without prov-ocation.

4. The detailed observation and recording of a typical day in the life of a family. Though Lewis himself often spent months with single families, his technique of describing their lives and experiences through the heuristic device of a single "day in the life" was very effective. Lewis justifies this technique by declaring that "the day universally orders family life" and that its use made otherwise intan-

gible stories and information concrete and immediate to the reader.   (Lewis 1959:17–18; Lewis 1950)

In 1966 Lewis elaborated on this final point (#4). An investigator asks informants in the family to reconstruct the previous day, repeating this process for a week or more. This process achieves several ends. First, the differing perspectives of family members are noted; second, the information may include events that the investigator did not witness; and third, the informant's sensitivity to "important" family interactions or events is heightened (Lewis 1966:xxi).

Finally, Lewis compiled lists of a family's material possessions and their provenance. Through this, he could identify social and economic supports, as well as establish the economic status and social power of the family relative to others in the community. The same method can be applied to food acquisition and other intangible supplies such as legalization papers.

Family studies, completed by following these guidelines but always open to the unexpected and the serendipitous nature of the course of human life, can indeed yield a more accurate and complex profile of the intimate lives and everyday needs of specific populations. A trip to a modern U.S. supermarket with a recently arrived Vietnamese family, for instance, demonstrates in a very direct way the bewilderment and alienation felt by those who do not understand how to enter the automatic doors, much less how to collect unfamiliar groceries and take them to the front counter to pay. Even among urban Vietnamese, cultural misunderstandings are rampant; accustomed to paying in cash and offering bribes for services, a Vietnamese father gave a large sum of money to the repairperson who came to fix the heater in his rented apartment, not realizing that the landlord would send a check to the heating company later. Time spent with a Mexican family, on the other hand, provided insights on being terrorized by the threat of deportation and abuse by local police and on the lack of technological sophistication of a rural people who often found telephones new and mysterious contraptions. I also discovered that the Mexican immigrants I knew often felt intimidated by and mistrustful of Chicanos (second- and third-generation Mexican Americans), even though these served as their main link to bilingual social services and education.

FAMILY STUDIES AND SOCIAL WORK RESEARCH

Social workers and psychologists will recognize many of these family studies techniques as consistent with—or in many cases analogous to—those used in clinical practice with families. Indeed, as I spent time with these immigrant families coping with life in their new country, I was frequently impressed with the "casework" nature of my role within the household. While on several levels I became part of the family, I was nonetheless the resident expert in the strange ways of the world in the United States and served as everything from legal advocate to health care educator, to translator, to homework tutor. While I provided assistance to the families I was with, however, they were helping me in turn by patiently answering my endless questions, tirelessly explaining their feelings and actions, and consistently including me in family activities.

Despite what appears to be a natural matching of skills and interests, social work has not taken sufficient advantage of ethnographic methods in general and family studies in particular.

Our own bewilderment, not only as researchers but also as a society as a whole, with respect to the factors that cause and perpetuate poverty and racism among certain sectors can be addressed only through a methodology that recognizes the complexity of human interaction as well as the profundity of human need. While quantitative methods are irreplaceable for many large-scale studies and for statistical data gathering, a commitment to the breadth of individual experience in clinical work requires an equally fervent pledge to pursue such scope through appropriate research techniques. Qualitative methods can meet this goal.

REFERENCES

Arevalo, R. and M. Minor. 1982. *Chicanas and Alcoholism: A Sociocultural Perspective of Women.* San José, Calif.: San José State University.

Brown, L., J. Oliver, and J. Klor de Alva. 1985. *Sociocultural and Service Issues in Working with Hispanic American Clients.* Albany: State University of New York at Albany.

Devore, W. and E. Schlesinger. 1981. *Ethnic-Sensitive Social Work Practice.* St. Louis: Mosby.

Gibson, G., ed. 1983. *Our Kingdom Stands on Broken Glass.* Silver Spring, Md.: NASW Press.

Green, J. W. 1982. *Cultural Awareness in the Human Services.* Englewood Cliffs, N.J.: Prentice Hall.

Hopps, J. and T. Tripodi. eds. 1983. Research on people of color [special issue]. *Social Work Research and Abstracts* 19, no. 4.

Johnson, A. 1978. *Quantification in Cultural Anthropology.* Palo Alto, Calif.: Stanford University.

Kirk, J. and M. L. Miller. 1986. *Reliability and Validity in Qualitative Research.* Beverly Hills: Sage.

Kottak, P., ed. 1982. *Researching American Culture.* Ann Arbor: University of Michigan Press.

Lewis, O. 1950. An anthropological approach to family studies. *American Journal of Sociology* 55: 468–75.

Lewis, O. 1959. *Five Families*. New York: Basic Books.

Lewis, O. 1966. *La Vida*. New York: Random House.

Lloyd, G. A. 1978. *The Culture and Politics of Social Work*. San José, Calif.: San José State University Press.

Malinowski, B. 1922. *Argonauts of the Western Pacific*. London: Routledge.

Spradley, J. 1980. *Participant Observation*. New York: Holt, Rinehart and Winston.

THREE

Emic and Etic Perspectives in Ethnographic Research on the Interdisciplinary Team

Roberta G. Sands and Marleen McClelland

Although ethnography was conceived by anthropologists as a way of understanding non-Western cultures, increasingly ethnographers have been "doing ethnography" in American cultures. The relevance of such applied ethnography to social work is evident in Stack's (1974) ethnography of welfare mothers, Estroff's (1981) work on the PACT program for the severely and persistently mentally disabled, and Gleason's (1989) ethnographic study of the institutionalized developmentally disabled. Like social scientists in other disciplines, social workers are beginning to engage in ethnographic research and to describe their methods and findings in professional journals (e.g., Curtis 1990; Fiene 1990; Sands 1989, 1990).

Two concepts that have guided anthropologists in their ethnographic research are "emic" and "etic." Loosely defined, *emic* refers to the folk or indigenous perspective whereas *etic* encompasses external concepts that the ethnographer brings to the research enterprise (Agar 1986). When social scientists engage in ethnographic research in American cultures with which they share folk knowledge, unanticipated questions are raised about what is emic and etic and the utility of these concepts in ethnographic research.

The purpose of this paper is to examine emic and etic perspectives within an ethnographic research study of interdisciplinary team processes at a center in which children were evaluated for possible mental retardation/developmental disabilities. The teams that were observed represented eleven disciplines and consisted of seasoned professionals (many with university affiliations) and student interns. The researchers were also professionals—one a social worker, the other a physical therapist.

THE EMIC/ETIC DISTINCTION

The terms *emic* and *etic* were coined by the linguist Kenneth Pike (1954), who extracted them from the terms *phonemic* and *phonetic*, respectively. Phonemics refers to sound units that are recognized as distinct and meaningful in a particular language (O'Connor 1973). On the other hand, phonetics refers to the science of speech sounds that occur across languages, the range of which can be represented in a universal system of transcription, such as the International Phonetic Alphabet (Crystal 1971). As Pike moved from an analysis of pronunciation units to an entire language, he realized that meaningful units existed not only within verbal data but also within nonverbal behavior (Pike 1954, 1967). Recently, Pike (1990) explained that the linguistic terms were abbreviated to reflect this notion. Thus, the etic perspective refers to "generalized statements about data" (Pike 1954:8) that are constructed by the analyst on the basis of cross-cultural knowledge, whereas the emic perspective refers to patterns that appear in a particular culture. Pike (1954) described the etic approach as "external" or "alien," for the researcher is positioned outside the culture and compares one culture with others according to a preexisting system of knowledge; and the emic approach as "internal" or "domestic" because what is discovered about a particular culture is related to that culture as a whole (10). Pike affirmed (1954) that no rigid dichotomy exists between the two perspectives, that both foster understanding, and that one approach can be transformed into the other. The differing interpretations of these concepts by Pike and Harris are juxtaposed in the recent volume, *Emics and Etics—The Insider/Outsider Debate* (Headland, Pike, and Harris 1990).

In this paper *emic* and *etic* are defined as insider and outsider perspectives, respectively. The researchers are assuming that neither the participants (traditionally viewed as "insiders") nor the researchers (traditionally viewed as "outsiders") can maintain purely emic or etic perspectives. On the contrary, both participants and researchers move along a continuum of emic and etic perspectives that are constantly changing. What becomes critical is how the ethnographer acknowledges these transitory positions and represents them in the ethnographic report. For the researchers, then, the emic/etic constructs will become a heuristic device for investigating both the process and product of ethnography and its theory–method relationship (Zaharlick and Green 1990).

THE RESEARCH STUDY

The ethnographic research study that is the basis for this paper looked at communication patterns among team members who were assessing children for possible mental retardation/developmental disabilities at an outpatient child evaluation center. During a year, the researchers observed, audio-taped, and took field notes of thirty-one preassessment team meetings of two teams representing eleven disciplines. The disciplines included were special education, psychology, social work, pediatrics, physical therapy, adapted physical education, occupational therapy, nursing, language/com-munication, audiology, and nutrition, but only four of these (social work, psychology, language/communication, and pediatrics) were represented on both teams. During each preassessment team meeting, a new case was described and presented to the team, whose members collaborated in the development of a plan that would guide discipline-specific and joint evalua-tions of the child. In addition to observing these preassessment planning meetings of the team, the researchers observed and videotaped complete evaluations of five of the thirty-one cases from the time of the initial preassessment team meeting through discipline-specific and joint (interdis-ciplinary) evaluations and a postassessment team meeting followed by a team conference with parents. Other sources of data were the case records and interviews with the participants. (For a more thorough discussion of the theory and methods employed, see Sands 1990.)

In the fieldwork of this study, the researchers entered an environment in which they shared the language (English) with the persons they were observing and professional cultures with some members. As social worker and physical therapist, the researchers shared cultural knowledge with their counterparts on the team (emic perspective). Moreover, each of them had previous work experience as a team member in other interdisciplinary settings (health and mental health). Thus, the researchers had some precon-ceived ideas, expectations, and categorical knowledge about interdisciplin-ary teamwork (etic perspective).

EMIC/ETIC ISSUES IN THE FIELD

In the course of conducting this study, the researchers came to realize that neither the emic nor the etic perspective remained fixed in relation to time and person. Accordingly, it was found that persons who appeared to be insiders were outsiders; such outsiders sometimes changed their positions from outsiders to insiders while others remained outsiders; although the researchers were presumed to be outsiders, in some respects they had inside knowledge; and the insider perspective may be shared with a subgroup of participants but not others. Examples of how these issues emerged are presented next.

Insiders/Outsiders as Insiders

Becoming an insider. One of the research questions posed in this research was, "How do professionals and professionals in training learn about becoming a team member?" Fortuitously, a month after the study began, a new social worker joined the team (cf. Sands 1989). Subsequently, the social worker/researcher began to look closely at the process in which a newly hired social worker became socialized as a team member. Initially this new employee's knowledge of the local culture and the specific application of her role was close to that of the observers; that is, it was etic. In comparison with her colleagues on the team, she was closer to an outsider than an insider, but during the study she made a transition from relative outsider to relative insider.

During the first few months of her employment, she was "coached" by the team coordinator and other team members about how to participate in preassessment planning team meetings. The new social worker came to know that she was responsible for identifying potentially problematic issues within the families of the children assessed at the center. Furthermore, she was expected to describe these issues in behaviorally specific language. At first the new social worker had difficulty distinguishing between what the team called problem "descriptors" (the specific family issues) and "objectives" (what was to be accomplished in the social worker's psychosocial evaluation). When she stumbled over phrases, she was corrected by the team coordinator, who made statements such as "That'll be your objective. . . . Here we're trying to get to the problem." Sometimes the social worker was encouraged to use terms that the social worker/researcher recognized as specific to the social work culture in that setting (e.g., *internal/external supports*). On other occasions, the new social worker asked specific questions of the "inside" insiders about how they conduct interdisciplinary assessments. In the early months of her employment, the tacit rules became focal (Petrie 1976) so that at a later time they could be used tacitly. As the new social worker, a relative outsider, gained access to the rules and expectations of the culture, she and the social worker/researcher came closer to acquiring an emic perspective.

During the last six months of the yearlong observation period, the same social worker supervised several social work trainees in this setting. When asked to participate at team meetings, students encountered difficulties with wording that were similar to those she had initially. The social worker was observed coaching the students in language that closely resembled language the team coordinator and other professionals used when they were socializing her. It appeared that at this point the new social worker was in a relatively inside position whereas the students were outsiders.

Remaining relatively outside. Observations of students support the position of students as relative outsiders. Although students were expected to participate as insiders in team meetings and to perform discipline-specific assessments (e.g., psychological testing), they were not fully accepted as integral members of the team. Professional staff did most of the talking at team meetings; students spoke primarily when they were asked. On one occasion, a new group of students took up most of the seats at the team meeting table—leaving the professionals to sit at the periphery. The professionals' discomfort at occupying less desirable seats was revealed at the next meeting of the team, at which time the students were asked to move. Similarly, a member of the team made a comment to one researcher that was critical of the students for taking up the choice seats at the table. The dynamics surrounding seating position symbolize the team's perception that students, as learners, were on the periphery of being insiders.

Insiders among insiders. Within the child evaluation center, each discipline represented another 'inside' group. Frequently terminology specific to one discipline needed to be explained to the group. At one meeting, a psychological test form was the subject of considerable discussion, as the group asked specific questions about its scoring techniques. At other times, little or no explanation of specific terminology was offered or solicited. For example, a pediatrician asked whether a child had "dysmorphic features," after which he said, "You know, when you look at him, is he a funny-looking kid?" Later the pediatrician offered as an objective for the official record his intention to pursue an evaluation of "dysmorphic features." Likewise, when one member changed the term for his evaluation from *adapted physical education* to *psychomotor*, the unusual language was noted but not questioned as appropriate or not. Certain professions overlapped in their evaluative measures and these commonalities provided yet another insider/insider perspective.

Insiders/Outsiders as Outsiders

The position of researchers as outsiders became ambiguous when they observed representatives of their respective and related disciplines on the team. The researchers had inside knowledge of the concepts, tools, procedures, and language of their own professions but were outsiders to other professions. The two different disciplines represented by the research team (social work and physical therapy) stimulated the asking of certain questions.

The missing insider. The most salient instance of researcher (outsider) as insider occurred during observation of a team meeting in which the center's physical therapist was not present. Team members representing other disciplines discussed the child's gross motor problems in vague, generalized terms such as *clumsy, bumps into walls,* and *immature.* The physical therapist/researcher considered these descriptions possible attempts to convey what is called proprioception, an awareness of one's own body movement. Such difficulties hold clear implications for specific physical therapy evaluative tests. The occupational therapist and adapted physical education members of the team who were present identified issues that were appropriate to the case and to their respective disciplines. Nevertheless, their evaluation reports did not address proprioception and their results were inconclusive. The physical therapist/researcher's insider perspective revealed what was *excluded* as well as included. But the social worker/researcher as "outsider" to the profession of physical therapy did not recognize the significance of this omission. For the research, however, it introduced further inquiry into how the team perceived and differentiated among physical therapy, occupational therapy, and adapted physical therapy. Follow-up questions posed to representatives of the various disciplines revealed how the team used these three "motor" disciplines interchangeably, despite disparate theoretical frameworks and criteria for evaluation. If the physical therapist had not joined the research team, these questions would not have been asked.

Further questions about missing perspectives were raised for the researchers when they realized that each of them had a different understanding of some of the terminology used in team meetings. Even though a major concern was with how the team used and understood terminology, the participation of researchers with different professional orientations made clear how researchers function as research instruments. The research focus is a selective process in that "the perceptual system of the observer is the first tool used by the observer and that this tool is influenced by the observer's own goals, biases, frame of reference, and abilities" (Evertson and Green 1986:164). In this study the researchers' diverse frames of reference became apparent during debriefing discussions about their observations. The researchers believe that their individual insights and perspectives enriched the research. Furthermore, they think that it would have been even more productive to have had additional disciplines represented in the research team. It was theoretically consistent with research on the interdisciplinary process to reflect on the effects of perspective on observation and on the presentation of results.

Insider in relation to other observers. The research center in which this project took place was accustomed to having observers. Staff and students observed each other's assessments of children from observation rooms, looking through one-way mirrors. Moreover, parents could watch their children's evaluations from the observation room. When observing and videotaping from these rooms, the researchers were observing assessments together with persons who were subjects of other observations. Indeed, there were times when interactions that occurred in the observation room were as germane to the study as the interactions on the other side of the one-way mirror.

Co-observing gave the researchers access to the insider perspectives of parents (emic), who made comments to nearby observers about how to interpret their children's responses to psychological tests. During one psychological examination in which the psychologist had difficulty understanding a child's speech, the child's mother explained what the child was saying to the observers. In this case, the psychologist appeared to be struggling to understand the child's response, "turtle," to an ambiguous picture in a projective test. The child repeatedly uttered "tu'l" and then explained that it was like a house with feet underneath. Still unable to understand the child, the psychologist entered the observation room to ask the mother what the child meant. The observers who sat adjacent to the mother had the benefit of "inside" knowledge about the child's language before the psychologist did.

The experience of co-observing raised questions for the researchers about whose emic or inside perspective was under consideration. There were many participants in the culture observed—the representatives of the various disciplines, students, administrators, parents, children, visitors from community agencies, and the team as a whole. Identifying the perspectives among varied perspectives that were relevant to the research sharpened the focus of the study.

IMPLICATIONS OF EMIC/ETIC PERSPECTIVES FOR RESEARCH

This research illuminated how difficult it is to make clear distinctions between emic and etic perspectives in theory and practice. Neither emic nor etic phenomena held their shape consistently. Instead the researchers noted a fluctuation from moment to moment and gradations between categories. Rather than presume the enduring existence of either, the researchers raised questions for ethnography. Central to these is the theory-method relationship. For this interdisciplinary study, having researchers from different professions reinforced the researchers' concern over what counts as interdisciplinary communication. This influenced the study's focus as well as its methodology.

Questions remain for the ethnographer to determine the purpose of the study and then to decide how emic and/or etic perspectives will support or constrain that purpose. In this way the emic/etic issue becomes a heuristic device to guide decision making about the research process. The distinctions between emic and etic become useful to the extent that they make principled decisions explicit for the researcher.

The researcher makes additional decisions regarding presentation of emic and etic perspectives. Zinn (1979), for example, proposes that the researcher who is a member of a culture being studied brings distinct advantages to the study but needs to make his or her background and values explicit in reporting. Erickson (1979) would concur that bias is not the issue but "selection of bias—or theoretical frame appropriate to the problems at hand" (5). To the extent that the researcher makes the theoretical framework or etic perspective explicit, the audience can assess the sources of knowledge.

In this study of the interdisciplinary team, emic and etic perspectives did not hold a consistent shape. It became clear that the emic (insider) perspective is relative to the culture as a whole, as exemplified by the new social worker's process of moving toward an inside position over time whereas the students appeared to remain relatively outside the insiders. In some cases the researchers or researchers together with parents had inside knowledge that team members did not have, raising questions about whose emic is focal to the study. Despite the shifting nature of the concepts and the complexity of their application, the researchers found the concepts useful. As they grappled with what was emic and what was etic, whose emic was important, and the place of their own professional knowledge in the study, they were able to refine the study, identify problematic issues, and pursue fruitful lines of inquiry. Even though the distinction between the terms was often ambiguous, examination of emic and etic perspectives clarified relative positions within the group, position change over time, and divergent perspectives.

Issues of emic and etic, the insider and outsider perspectives, pervade ethnographic work. Neither definition nor usage conveys clear distinctions between the terms. Even more troublesome is the preservation of either perspective through methodology. What makes the ethnography cogent is evidence that the researcher understands the anthropological assumptions underlying the terms, has made thoughtful connections between this issue and the topic or question under study, and has made purposeful decisions regarding the impact that etic or emic choices have on data collection, analysis, and presentation. As this interdisciplinary study exemplifies, the importance of emic and etic lies in the new questions they raise and in the continuation of the dialogue.

REFERENCES

Agar, M. H. 1986. *Speaking of Ethnography*. Beverly Hills, Calif.: Sage.

Curtis, P. A. 1990. An ethnographic study of pregnancy counseling. *Clinical Social Work Journal* 18: 243–56.

Crystal, D. 1971. *Linguistics*. Middlesex, England: Pelican.

Erickson, F. 1979. On standards of descriptive validity in studies of classroom activity. Occasional Paper no. 16. East Lansing, Mich.: Michigan State University, Institute for Research on Teaching.

Estroff, S. 1981. *Making It Crazy: An Ethnography of Psychiatric Clients in an American Community*. Berkeley: University of California Press.

Evertson, C. and J. Green. 1986. Observation as inquiry and method. In M. C. Wittrock, ed., *Handbook of Research on Teaching*, pp. 162–213. New York: Macmillan.

Fiene, J. I. 1990. Snobby people and just plain folks: Social stratification and rural, low-status, Appalachian women. *Sociological Spectrum* 10: 527–39.

Gleason, J. J. 1989. *Special Education in Context: An Ethnographic Study of Persons with Developmental Disabilities*. Cambridge, England: Cambridge University Press.

Headland, T. N., K. L. Pike, and M. Harris, eds. 1990. *Emics and Etics: The Insider/Outsider Debate*. Newbury Park, Calif.: Sage.

O'Connor, J. D. 1973. *Phonetics*. Middlesex, England: Pelican.

Petrie, H. G. 1976. Do you see what I see? The epistemology of interdisciplinary inquiry. *Journal of Aesthetic Education* 10: 29–43.

Pike, K. L. 1954. *Language in Relation to a Unified Theory of the Structure of Human Behavior*. Part I: preliminary edition. Santa Ana, Calif.: Summer Institute of Linguistics.

Pike, K. L. 1967. *Language in Relation to a Unified Theory of the Structure of Human Behavior*. Rev. 2d ed. The Hague: Mouton.

Pike, K. L. 1990. On the emics and etics of Pike and Harris. In Headland, Pike, and Harris, eds., *Emics and Etics: The Insider/Outsider Debate*, pp. 28–47. Newbury Park, Calif.: Sage.

Sands, R. G. 1989. The social worker joins the team: A look at the socialization process. *Social Work in Health Care* 14: 1–15.

Sands, R. G. 1990. Ethnographic research: A qualitative research approach to study of the interdisciplinary team. *Social Work in Health Care* 15: 115–29.

Stack, C. B. 1974. *All Our Kin*. New York: Harper and Row.

Zaharlick, A. and J. L. Green. 1990. Ethnographic research. In J. Flood, J. Jensen, D. Lapp, and J. Squire, eds., *Handbook of Research in Teaching the English Language Arts*. New York: Macmillan.

Zinn, M. B. 1979. Field research in minority communities: Ethical, methodological and political observations by an insider. *Social Problems* 27: 209–19.

FOUR

Ethnography, Critical Inquiry and Social Work Practice

Howard Goldstein

The purpose of this essay is to make evident the natural affinity that exists between the forms of qualitative investigation called ethnographic research and the character of social work practice; critical inquiry serves as the bridge between the two. Because research is typically seen as a procedure separate from practice, my inclination, almost reflexively, was to perpetuate this distinction by first outlining the methods or procedures of these modes of inquiry and then showing their applicability to the functions of practice.

It quickly occurred to me that this plan would only contradict the fundamental proposition that this paper intends to express. Essentially, it affirms that, within certain definitions, doing practice and studying practice are variations on a similar humanistic theme and process. In this view, ethnography and critical inquiry share common philosophical assumptions and similar procedures with the traditions of social work practice in how we understand people and their predicaments and find meaning in their thoughts, language, behaviors, and life circumstances. Thus, this essay is more concerned with establishing the foundations for effective practice research than it is with the "how-tos" of qualitative inquiry. A rapidly growing collection of texts and articles (Goldstein 1981) on qualitative methods is becoming available to the interested researcher.

The artificial separation that exists between inquiry and action is the result of the long-standing positivist philosophy that has dominated research in social work. The criteria of this doctrine, which include objectivity, control, and concreteness, create a distance between the reflective, open-ended, and often ambiguous processes that characterize our work and the human problems of living. Such tensions between inquiry and action are gaining recognition in other allied fields.

QUANTITATIVE AND QUALITATIVE MODES: A COMPARISON

Since most things are known in comparative terms, in the current state of the art, any mention of a qualitative orientation to knowledge gathering often weighs this approach against the methods of quantitative research.

Both forms of research are assets in the endeavor to expand knowledge and comprehension. Given that social work's concern is with social ills, quantitative findings, also in metaphorical terms, provide us with a topographic map of sorts, an index, or perhaps a meteorological forecast; in effect, these studies give us a set of social facts that describe the lay of the land of social problems, useful frequencies and categories, and some calculations about what lies ahead.

But these findings have little to say about the unique case and how we ought to think about it. The limits of quantitative methods or any approach that calls for the objective measurement of observed behavior are reached once the line is crossed into the narrative or textual realm of human experience. In this reality we encounter the nonobjective, sometimes irrational, and usually elusive intimations of intention, values, morals, hopes, and other sentiments. If, in practice, we intend to keep the dialogue going, our duty would be to fathom the meaning—and there may be many meanings—embedded in the client's narrative. We would need to take an intersubjective and interpretive disposition of mind, one that is responsive to the nature of idiom, culture, symbols, and antecedent circumstances concurring within the context of relationship. Here we are not technicians generating data; we are people, as in any other human relationship, engaged in reconstructing meaning.

What I have described thus far is the essence of *constructivism,* a dialogical process of meaning-seeking and understanding that occurs between people, whether they are joined in a professional relationship or in ordinary but earnest discourse. If constructivism usefully accounts for the way human beings create their respective versions of reality so as to negotiate or just plain muddle their way across the social terrain, then it would also serve as a relevant mode of inquiry for practice and its meaning-laden substance. As Schwandt (1990:258–76) observes, constructivism offers two related paths of inquiry. The first is the ontological path that cuts across the local, immediate, and specific experience—that is, how things are or appear to be: this we call ethnography. The second is the moral and political path involving values and beliefs that may be open to change and growth, to how things might become: this is called critical inquiry. For our purposes, I want to show that where ethnography is related to research about practice, critical inquiry has much to say about what practice is all about.

ETHNOGRAPHY AND SOCIAL WORK PRACTICE

On referring to the parallels between ethnography and social work practice I have to first qualify what kind of practice I am talking about. I am speaking about approaches to practice that correspond with the humanistic tradition of social work. And by "humanistic" I mean a way of working with people that at least affirms the importance of relationship and process, that is open-ended, and that resists the tendency to categorize or otherwise reduce the human experience to variables or classifications. In these terms, both ethnography and humanistic practice strive to appreciate the human experience as it is lived, felt, and known by its participants. Both search for the meanings, patterns, themes, and rhythms that shape the flow and process of being. Both recognize that understanding requires sensitivity to the contextual, temporal, and cultural complex in which the event is implanted and from which meaning derives. Both use an emergent and adaptable design for inquiry. "Use of self," a familiar social work precept, is also common to both since the investigator and the practitioner alike are the inductive instruments who, through the process of interpretation, discover and generate meaning. And finally, both deal with the text of persons' lives in its moral, narrative, and dramatic forms. Together, these features add up to what Imre (1991:198–200) calls "good knowing" or knowing based on moral responsibility about what is accepted as knowledge, what we do with it, and its implications for others.

To be sure, ethnographic inquiry would not be particularly valuable to practitioners who have settled for a particular framework or scheme for defining their clients and their problems. For others who are more receptive to the ambiguous nature of the human state, ethnography offers what Bruner (1990:35) calls a "folk social science," a bottom-up and inside-out way of knowing life in action. A folk social science tells how things really are, how they came to be, or should be from the perspectives of those living their lives or, in Geertz's (1983:58) terms, how "in each place, people actually represent themselves to themselves and to one another."

Ethnographic studies give new meaning to the venerable social work precept, "person-in-situation," by disclosing the down-to-earth and graphic nature of what it is like to be a real person in a vital situation. Thus, the results of studies of, for example, critical incidents in practice, patterns of interaction, adaptations, life styles of "deviant" groups, the use or nonuse of services, life histories, or communities and cultures inevitably exceed our expectations, our assumptions and stereotypes, and the limits posed by the parochial restraints of our own knowledge and experience. What is to be expected is the discovery of the unexpected. An example of ethnographic research will not only cast light on these ideas but also anticipate the nature of critical inquiry and the role of the social worker as researcher.

ETHNIC WARRIORS: A STUDY OF PUERTO RICAN YOUTH

As a school social worker, Marsiglia (1991) was long troubled about the high dropout rate and low achievement of his Puerto Rican students despite the many efforts of the school system to remedy this problem. Finding little in empirical findings that explained this problem and basing his study on his experience of working with these youngsters, he elected to inquire into their ethnic identity, into their perceptions of the extent of their assimilation into American society, and into how their identities might be related to school achievement. In accord with his practice approaches with these students, Marsiglia used the naturalistic setting of the school group for purposes of participant observation and interviewing. Immediately, one of the unanticipated consequences of this mode of inquiry was the eagerness of the students to contribute to the advancement of knowledge and the sense of pride and self-worth that accompanied their participation.

As often happens in qualitative research, the findings did not fall into neat, exclusive categories. Altogether, the central identifier that gave the students the true sense of being Puerto Rican was "el idioma," their language that distinguished them from other students. Yet their identity was extremely problematical. The students wrestled with a painful existential choice: if they held to their "idioma"/culture, they faced alienation by the majority group; conversely, assimilation meant to them the loss of refuge their ethnic group provided against what they saw as a hostile, uncaring society.

Marsiglia discovered that Puerto Rican identity was not one thing. Moved by their personal narratives, he found that identity could take several forms. Students he named the "warriors" were those who had a strong identity, were low achievers, and were fighters who protected their peers. The "lawyers" were bilingual, with low identity and high achievement. The "poets" spoke Spanish in its purest form, untouched by inner-city culture and dialects. "Traders" were like chameleons who maintained both identity and the ways of the majority group. Altogether, the researcher questioned the validity of the assimilation process as a means of advancement in society.

Even this example, a meager digest of the actual study, almost Byzantine in its complexities, shows how ethnography functions as a net that captures and reveals what might otherwise be fleeting or obscure expressions of self. Such renditions are the powerful but often unformed ideological premises and principles, morals and values, myths and spiritual burdens that shape the client's identity and purpose. Identity was the driving force in this study of the Hispanic youth.

Clearly, ethnography is a mode of inquiry that directly informs social work practice; as I argue shortly (and as some readers may recognize), social workers really "do" ethnography when they strive to know and understand their clients, not according to some grand theory or universal framework, but phenomenologically, from the inside out. The findings of ethnographic research, unlike the statistical inferences of empirical studies, do not have to be translated for their application to practice; the language of ethnography is the language of practice, both voices echoing the natural human experience.

Consider again this example of ethnographic research. These insights about ethnicity, derived from the perspective of members of a particular culture, are not necessarily accepted as generalizable "truths"; rather, they instruct the practitioner to set aside bias and preconception about any client's cultural identity and to be humbly attentive to its many variations and meanings. Derived not from speculation but from the grounded nature of the practice experience, the findings of ethnographic inquiry can lead to a growing theoretical blueprint for practice as well as to the building stones, the tacit and intrinsic understandings that fashion what we ordinarily call practice wisdom.

CRITICAL INQUIRY AND SOCIAL WORK PRACTICE

Critical inquiry is the medium that draws research and practice into a dialogical partnership: each informs the other in useful ways. As the second expression of the constructivist paradigm, critical inquiry shares with ethnography the assumption of multiple realities, each socially and personally created. As observed, where ethnography centers on the ontological nature of the lived experience (knowledge of what is), critical inquiry is directed to the moral and political equation of the lived experience (knowledge for what ends). The generative aim is the same but with the added purpose of inducing new awareness and fruitful change.

The assumption that the "what is" of being is coupled with anticipations of "what might be" draws the ethnographic attitude and critical inquiry into a closer harmony. The latter, guided by sensitivity and ethical regard, probes beliefs—ideological, moral, mythological, political, or spiritual—that support and justify one's behavior, intentions, and goals. Like the Puerto Rican youth one usually does not question one's beliefs—about oneself, one's relationships, or community. They are assumed to be givens, personal verities that are often absorbed from one's culture and that, together, shape the necessary story for one's existence. Critical inquiry is therefore fastened on the possible ways these beliefs may lead to "false consciousness" or erroneous ideologies that distort the lived experience (Schwandt 1990:268). In practice, it is through conversation—dialogue and critical reflection—that the partners (worker and client) search for an increase in self-knowledge, the reduction of illusions, the restoration of meaning, or the alleviation of injustice and discrimination.

Among the historical roots of critical inquiry as a medium of change are Marxist dialectics. Contemporary variations can be found in the writings and work of Freire (1973) and the conscientization movement, in Schön's conception of reflective practice (1983), or in the feminist movement and the many other efforts aimed at "consciousness raising" by many minority and marginal groups in our society.

Thus, social work practice in its natural form can also be understood as a form of critical inquiry. If we strip away the elaborate and sophisticated overlays of theory and technique that the profession has, over the years, assembled over and around its functions, I believe we will find that traditional practice, in accord with the precept of the person-in-situation, is in sympathy with the fundamental intentions of critical inquiry. Or as Wilkes speaks about practice:

> The people we meet are real in themselves and the question is not "how can I shape and control the other person?" but "how can I see that person as he or she really is?" This is not the approach of a technician with a bag of tools, methods, and strategies, all set to repair a poorly operating machine. Nor is it the approach of the social engineer who believes him- or herself to have at his or her disposal the expertise for straightening out the problems of social existence. Rather, it is an approach that calls for humility, patience, an attitude of respect towards the world, and an awareness of its infinite mystery and complexity.   (1981:88)

THE PRACTITIONER AS RESEARCHER

As a prelude to the proposal that the talents of practice are transferable to the procedures of qualitative research, let me offer a capsuled version of the argument developed thus far.

Ethnography and critical inquiry as forms of qualitative research share a pedigree with the design and motif of social work practice. Both qualitative research and practice are based on similar philosophical and ethical principles: the understanding of an unfamiliar social world requires the inquirer, to some extent, to become part of that world. Paraphrasing Van Maanen (1986:5), both employ procedures for "counting to one"—that is, deciding, based on judgment and choice, what is to count as a unit of analysis and interpretation. Both require imagination and creativity in the pursuit of understanding and meaning. Both are prepared to grapple with ambiguity and uncertainty about where things will end up. Learning from mistakes is a given in this quest: misunderstanding illuminates what needs to be understood. In short, both the qualitative researcher and the practitioner depend on similar talents, especially the ability to read and make sense of the dynamics unfolding within a particular social context—the texts of lives at a moment in time expressed within special human circumstances. In a manner of speaking, social workers do ethnography when they cross the threshold of prescribed social convention and, with ethical regard, enter the enigmatic cultural world of the client. This is a world whose meanings are shaped by ambiguous beliefs, patterns, relations, and rituals. Even as meaning and intention slowly surface, critical inquiry is already in process: when the worker merely asks "What does it mean?" or "How does it work?" or "Where does it come from?" or "What does it do for you?" the possibilities for fresh thinking and questioning about previously unquestioned assumptions are already set in motion.

If this argument holds any merit, one could contend that at least some social work practitioners are natural constructivists who would find that doing qualitative research is an extension of or a variation on their own themes in their work with people. Quite possibly, they can be effective researchers. The next question is, Should they do this kind of research?

The received or traditional view of research considers research and practice as separate vocations or specializations. This model of research assigns to the specialist the job of studying professional activities to identify variables that have predictable effects. Results of these studies are published in journals with the assumption that practitioners will, first of all, read these reports and then translate these findings for use in their own practice. Eisner (1990:97–98) wryly observes that this model echoes the model of research in agriculture where the outcomes of agronomists' and botanists' studies are cataloged by agricultural-extension agents, then carried to farmers who implement this knowledge in raising their crops. That the *t* test was first used to determine the effect of fertilizer on the growth of corn gives us an interesting analogy to ponder.

This is, of course, a top-down orientation to research policy: researchers create knowledge—typically in propositional and statistical forms—and pass it down to practitioners who are then supposed to do things differently and better. By no means should this conventional approach be discarded. But what also needs to be considered is the critical need for action or practice-oriented research (Atkin 1989). This can be achieved by workers actually involved in practice within their own local contexts. Practitioners need to know about the vagaries and processes of practice in fundamental ways that differ, as Eisner puts it, "from the kind that will get an assent from three referees reviewing a manuscript submitted for publication to a learned journal" (98).

For these operational reasons alone, social work practitioners who have the necessary constructivist and interpretive talents should be doing their own research. Above all, they are best equipped to generate insights about an area that strongly deserves more intensive study: clients' perceptions of the helping experience as exemplified by previous research illustrations. Such practice-oriented research can be carried out both in formal and informal ways and pursue understanding of local or unique practice questions as well as problems of broader significance. Some examples: A special policy or program installed by an agency and generally accepted as "how we do things here" may have overtones of abrasiveness or liability and therefore call for the input of the consumer. Likewise, even a limited inquiry into "what am I doing that is helpful?" can be productive and enlightening.

Several benefits accrue from such endeavors beyond the insights and knowledge gained. For one thing, qualitative research invites the impressions and reactions of the users of services, probably one of the most underrepresented group of consumers. Unlike other enterprises that depend on forms of "market research," the programs and policies social services initiate or the techniques and models that practitioners apply are assumed to have some relevance only for the vulnerable clients on whom they are imposed. Even when questionnaires or other "objective" measurement devices are used, they can ask only what the researcher wants to know; they cannot always anticipate what the client wants to tell. The study of parents' reactions to child protective services clearly affirms clients' willingness to share their opinions. And not the least, the outcomes of such inquiries will contribute to what we call "practice wisdom," the kind of tacit knowledge and understanding that obtains from the peculiar immediacy of the relationship in process.

As a last word, it is important to add another reason for some social workers to engage in research for themselves and for the profession as a whole. Knowledge that is not handed down or delivered by an external specialist in abstract forms but that is gleaned from the experience of practice itself has intrinsic values. It not only enriches the quality of practice but also enhances the professional status, talents, and artistry of the practitioner. Increased status occurs when practitioners are relieved of the role of the passive consumer of an outside expert's investigations and take on the responsibility for researching and documenting their own activities— what they know best and what they deem as significant. And within the constructivist model, the interpretive, critical, and reflective talents that enrich both research and practice also reinforce and strengthen one another in a helical fashion. The insights gained from research may be applied to practice and vice versa.

In many ways, these complex ideas about the relationship between research and practice are really a matter of common sense. Those of us who do or have done social work practice "know"—perhaps in vague or unformed terms—that practice combines inquiry and artistry in its attempt to make sense of the moral, value-laden, spiritual, and other elusive and often untidy dimensions of living. As such, it resists the ambitious attempts to reduce the flow of the practice experience into piecemeal variables and discrete categories. Well-developed forms of qualitative research such as ethnography and critical inquiry readily articulate the nature of practice, generate useful knowledge about practice, and create a bridge between practice and research that allows the traffic of knowledge, wisdom, and counsel to flow in both directions.

REFERENCES

Atkin, M. 1989. Curriculum action research: An American perspective. Paper presented at the meeting of the American Educational Research Association, San Francisco.

Bruner, J. 1990. *Acts of Meaning*. Cambridge, Mass.: Harvard University Press.

Eisner, E. W. 1990. The meaning of alternative paradigms for practice. In E. G. Guba, ed., *The Paradigm Dialog*, pp. 88–104. Newbury Park, Calif.: Sage.

Freire, P. 1973. *Pedagogy of the Oppressed*. New York: Seabury Press.

Geertz, C. 1983. *Local Knowledge*. New York: Basic Books.

Goldstein, H. 1981. Qualitative research and social work practice: Partners in discovery. *Journal of Sociology and Social Welfare* 18: 101–21.

Imre, R. 1991. What do we need to know for good practice? *Social Work* 36: 198–200.

Marsiglia, F. F. 1991. The ethnic warriors: Ethnic identity and school achievement as perceived by a group of selected mainland Puerto Rican students. Unpublished doctoral dissertation. Case Western Reserve University.

Schön, D. A. 1983. *The Reflective Practitioner: How Professionals Think in Action*. New York: Basic Books.

Schwandt, T. R. 1990. Paths to inquiry in social disciplines: Scientific, constructivist, and critical theory methodologies. In Guba, ed., *The Paradigm Dialog*, pp. 258–76. Newbury Park, Calif.: Sage.

Van Maanen, J. 1986. Introduction. In M. H. Agar, ed., *Speaking of Ethnography*, p. 5. Newbury Park, Calif.: Sage.

Wilkes, R. 1981. *Social Work with Undervalued Groups*. London: Tavistock.

FIVE

The Administrator as Ethnographer and Cartographer

Harold H. Weissman

Mintzberg has divided administrative work into a number of discrete roles: figurehead, leader, liaison, information disseminator, spokesperson, entrepreneur, disturbance handler, resource allocator, and negotiator (In Gortner, Mahler, and Nicholson 1987:316–17) In carrying out these roles a manager has three questions to answer: what is happening, how do I understand it, and what actions are open to me?

Ethnography has been defined as the objective ways of studying the subjective experience of the objective (Bogdan 1991). As such, managers are ethnographers, for answers to the first two of the above-listed questions require ethnographic skills. Administrators must understand the meaning of objective organizational events and how their subjective interpretations of these events may differ from those of a variety of constituencies. Without such understanding they are in a poor position to evaluate the consequences of the actions open to them.

As ethnographers, administrators use a variety of qualitative as well as quantitative methods. Although detailing the quantitative methods is beyond the scope of this paper, it is in harmony with Harrison's perspective on the inevitability of the integration of quantitative and qualitative methods in social welfare and organizational research.

On the qualitative side, participant observation is an obviously important technique, as are in-depth interviews, critical incident analyses, feedback techniques, and a foundation in grounded theory. Examples will be given to illustrate the utility of such methods, yet the main intent of the paper is to suggest that while an administrator uses qualitative methods, they are used in a way that differs significantly from standard ethnographic practice.

Analysis is a useful precursor to action, and yet administrators must be able to set the conditions and change the context for action; otherwise they would in the main be reactors. In terms of ethnography administrators must affect the meaning and interpretation others give to events.

Administrators move out of the role of ethnographers and become cognitive mapmakers, social cartographers, creators, and charters of organizational symbols, patterns, and settings (Peters 1978). They partially create and make visible the mental maps that guide peoples' work.

THE USES OF ETHNOGRAPHY

It has been said that the beginning of wisdom is doubt. For an administrator too much doubt can be immobilizing and too little doubt can be blinding. An ethnographic approach can help an administrator steer between these shoals.

Ethnography can help managers understand the expectations people have of them: a board can have one view, a certain department another, and a professional group of staff another. These assumptions represent ''the values that precede the assumptions that people make about what is good and bad, the unseen values for whose sake people, programs, policies and organizations live and die'' (Quinn 1988:42). Many long-simmering organizational conflicts have at their core different views of the appropriateness of management behavior; one violates a moral order at one's peril.

The essence of an ethnographic stance is the back and forth of collecting data (whether by observation, questioning, survey, etc.), making tentative judgments and hypotheses, collecting more data, then revising provisional ideas, then collecting more data, etc. As such, ethnography can provide the glue to make administrators' skills of expediting, planning, organizing, directing, and coordinating maximally effective as they sniff out potential conflicts, constraints, risks, and opposing motivations.

SOCIAL CARTOGRAPHY

Administrators are not researchers. They are paid to act and often must act with insufficient information. Only unusually inexperienced administrators think that they simply act. What they must do is often to set the conditions that make action possible. Arguments have to be developed, support must be secured, resistance neutralized to the extent possible, contingency plans developed, accountability mechanisms set up, and the like.

In this the search or debate is not simply about the most effective way to do things but in many cases is related to how to avoid undesirable courses of action—how to create degrees of freedom or the space for action between which feasible experiments or action can take place.

The process of pursuing a specific goal and the process of identifying and avoiding noxiants are qualitatively different modes of action that impact organization and environment in very different ways. When one pursues a specific goal one orients action toward a fixed point of reference and in the process narrows one's understanding of and interest in the environment to suit these specific concerns. As a result, relationships with the environment are usually seen and manipulated in an instrumental way.

In contrast, a strategy based on the avoidance of noxiants involves a choice of limits and constraints rather than a choice of ends, creating degrees of freedom that allow meaningful direction to emerge. Cybernetics suggests that this basic principle could be usefully applied to help organizations learn and evolve. (Morgan 1986:106–7)

Administrators attempt to set the conditions for action by promoting certain values, principles, rules, processes, sentiments, and goals. In so doing they have to ensure that others take the meaning that they intend from their statements or activities.

A cartographer is a mapmaker of the physical world. The physical world is slow to change, and as such in most cases one map should in great measure look like another map. The social world is quite different.

Cognitive maps of a particular situation can differ dramatically depending on one's professional background, gender, race, organization role, etc. Yet these are for limited use of administrators to simply document the differing cognitive maps of their staff. These maps have to be brought into some type of alignment or at least enough of an alignment so that effective action can take place.

Around many issues differences of opinion and judgment exist. Good administrators know this, listen carefully, weigh arguments, and make judgments accordingly. They are aware that the debate over one substantive issue will have an effect on other debates as precedents are set, goals are reinforced, and favored approaches are acknowledged.

What they may not know is that in these debates over explicit issues, an implicit world of attitudes, values, beliefs, and meanings exists that is constantly being reinforced or changed.

> It is a world of contested concepts. Its activities go to the heart of moral and political questions about rights and duties, freedom and fairness . . . the

effectiveness of social work intervention may have legitimately different meanings. . . . Social work does not always consist of distinct, easily identifiable units. Many intervention methods will be used in different ways, with different degrees of skill, with multiple purpose and different categories of client . . . the apparently sanitizing and disciplined language of objectives can be illusory . . . when the objective is to care and console or to delay deterioration tangible outcomes are harder to find . . . under the heading of objectives, social work may often be about creating potentialities rather than final states or outcomes.   (Cheetham 1991:18–19)

In such situations, what are the facts? Majone (1989) suggests that "values and opinions count a great deal in evaluation not only because of the ambiguity of the outcomes of practice—the difficulty of assigning specific causes to particular effects, of measuring outputs, and assessing unintended consequences, of distinguishing between flawed conceptions and failures of implementation—but even more because of inescapable disagreements about the kind of evaluative criteria that are meaningful, fair, or politically acceptable in a given situation (168)." Debate and mutual persuasion are required. For a sophisticated discussion of the limitation of outcome evaluation, see Majone (1989:172–82).

What distinguishes an administrator who is concerned about cognitive maps from one simply concerned about substantive issues is the former's desire to make explicit the dynamics of debate, clarifying the nature of arguments, the nature of judgment, the approach to risk, how various meanings evolved. The focus is on both the long-term and present ability to come up with good ideas.

In a sense, by explicitly acknowledging the necessity of dialogue and debate and opening up discussion about the structure and process of debate—for example, how the debate should be carried out, what structures are conducive to a useful debate, who should be involved in the debate, who the crucial stakeholders are and how their views can be heard, how the debate shall be judged, and what makes for reliable and valid arguments—the organizational terrain becomes more malleable.

Social life is part contradiction, disagreement, and paradox, so it has to be argued. While much of what we do seems to be done without thought, or almost instinctively, behind these actions a set of background thoughts rests on a structure of beliefs, assumptions, and experience that account for our actions (Paul 1990:64).

Ultimately all of this must be made explicit as the debate revolves around substantive issues. Cognitive mapmakers institute metathinking or double-loop learning about the debate—a process of questioning the relevance of operating norms (Morgan, 1986:89). And, by so doing, through exposing their own thoughts to scrutiny, they serve as powerful models for others to do the same.

Yet raising issues for discussion and debate does not necessarily lead to better understanding or more effective action. Individuals or groups do not simply learn from experience, or, to put it differently, they may in fact mislearn from experience, i.e., come to erroneous conclusions and reinforce their preexisting errors (Feldman 1986). Cognitive theorists use a variety of terms to describe how human beings process information, e.g., *schemas, scripts, implicit theories, story lines,* etc. The essence of all these concepts is that we all structure or organize our thoughts to comprehend or understand. Our prior thoughts about a particular topic are organized and any new thought is in some way connected to the existing schemas or implicit theories.

As such, context is crucial in understanding both what is rational and what will be done with information and knowledge. Awareness of a problem and even a potential solution alone do not guarantee action in organizations for any number of reasons: fear of consequences, lack of resources, internal opposition, and conflicting goals, among many others.

In most organizations considerable disagreement arises about any number of issues, mirroring clashing values and interests. When these issues do not become subjects for thought and understanding, they create a good deal of anxiety that distorts rational processes. Hirschhorn (1988) suggests that when people face uncertainty and feel at risk they create social defenses that narrow their range of experience and understanding just when it should be expanding. Through psychological processes of splitting, projection, and introjection we create a social world that is incongruent with the needs of task completion. Psychological boundaries are set up that violate pragmatic boundaries based on tasks, simply to reduce anxiety (Hirschhorn 1988:32).

In such a context feedback will not automatically operate in a cybernetic way to ensure effectiveness. It is quite likely to generate more anxiety and uncertainty unless organizational structures and mechanisms are designed to contain such distortions.

Those psychological forces that create distortions are abetted by bureaucratic structures.

> Organizational goals, objectives, structures and roles create clearly defined patterns of attention and responsibility . . . information and knowledge rarely flow in a free manner, so that different sectors of the organization often operate on the basis of different pictures of the total situation, and can pursue subunit goals almost as ends in themselves, unaware of or disinterested in the way they fit the wider picture.   (Morgan 1986:89)

In addition the desire of most staff and administrators in bureaucracies to protect themselves from looking bad results in covering up mistakes, creating the impression that things are fine when they are not, and in engaging in "group think," among other evasive maneuvers.

When these cognitive barriers are added to the psychological and bureaucratic barriers, they make up an impressive set of obstacles that must be overcome if learning is to take place in social agencies. Any attack on these obstacles by administrators must begin with a general approach to creating organizations as contexts for learning, whose creation should be a long-term goal. To make this happen, the skills of a cognitive mapmaker must be joined to the skills of an administrator.

THE LEARNING ORGANIZATION

While it is true that a crisis provides an opportunity and rationale for organizations to do things differently, a greater challenge is to create an organization that routinely seeks to learn while it acts. First such an organization requires stability.

Weick and Boudon (1986:121) draw attention to the need for time for reflection and planning. In this context stability is crucial. Staff turnover can logically limit the potentiality of organizational learning just as it might increase such a potential by bringing in new people and ideas. Yet the former is more likely, given the nature of organizational controls.   -

Stability must be a staff concern as well as an administrative concern. The organizational strain between survival and goal attainment cannot be allowed to devolve into "the staff is unrealistic" or "all the administration cares about is money." The posturing that occurs in such an environment is antithetical to learning. The responsibility for survival and goal attainment must be shared.

Second, while organizational elites have the major responsibility for creating a learning context, they cannot conceptualize themselves as the teachers and the staff as students. At least as it pertains to clients, staff members are better situated to learn from experience and are more likely to be able to teach the administrator. In addition, since the purpose of learning in agencies is to act better, resistance to change is less likely in a situation where everyone "owns" the new knowledge.

Some evidence attests that the most consistently effective managers view action as an opportunity for learning or reflection. They search actively. They act to see responses and consequences to actions and then make judgments about plausible courses of actions. These managers seem much more prone to engage in a recursive pattern of thinking and action (McCall and Kaplan 1985:111). These are not distinct but part of a cycle of activity that enriches both with the understanding of the past and suggests ways of moving into the future. These managers practice a type of action research. In so doing, they are most likely guided by the commonsense desire not to make things worse (111). Though admirable as an approach, the danger here is that they will not ensure that others learn as well.

In an experimental or learning-oriented social agency, managers are not the only ones who must do the learning. Staff members at all levels must be involved. Yet such involvement can threaten power and status structures and differentials. Generally people at the top are valued for their expert knowledge, and if this is open to question, authority structures might become unstable.

Many have suggested participatory styles of management as a cure for this problem. Yet the problem is more subtle and complex. The administrative elites of a social agency are not the only people who have a stake in professional traditions and practices. Thus for learning to take place, tradition has to be valued as much as innovation.

Learning does not simply happen out of the blue—potential new knowledge or ideas are always evaluated in terms of what is already known. In organizational life, the desire to do better cannot be hitched to the idea that no collective wisdom exists. An organizational self-image of experimentation and innovation cannot be constructed on a foundation of cynicism and negation (Mitchell, Rediker, and Beach 1986:300–3).

What is needed are ways of institutionalizing both tradition and change. The use of organizational symbols and rituals is important in this process (Martin 1988:233). While much attention has been given recently to the problems of "group think" in organizations, what is suggested here is that as much attention now must be given to the problems attendant to "new think."

One important way to insure that a destructive opposition between tradition and innovation does not devolve into defensiveness and anxiety through the psychological processes of projection and splitting, noted earlier, is to consciously attempt to give staff a gestalt of the total organization, its functions and roles. How does an organization do this without creating chaos? Peters and Waterman (1982) suggest that excellent corporations manage it by selective use of loose-tight controls. They place tight controls on a very few, carefully selected values (for example, IBM's emphasis on service to the customer) and give a lot of freedom in other spheres (quoted by McCall and Kaplan 1985:112).

Yet no matter how desirous staff and administrators are of establishing a learning environment in an agency, this will be extremely difficult to accomplish without the support of their funding sources and those oversight agencies that hold them accountable. Setting standards and holding agencies accountable for them does not necessarily promote learning. Rigid standards tend to limit flexibility (Weissman 1980:47–50). The modus operandi can become hiding errors, manipulating records, and a host of other self-protective maneuvers (Brodkin 1986:41–48).

An experimental agency represents a culture captured by the phrase "this is the way things are done around here." This culture comprises a set of values, shared beliefs, and social processes that maintain the integrity of the organization (Mitchell, Rediker, and Beach 1986:309). Many different authors have specifically spoken about these aspects of culture as they pertain to organizational learning.

Openness and reflectiveness need to be valued especially as they lead to the "acceptance of error and uncertainty as an inevitable feature of life in complex and changing environments" (Morgan 1986:91). The desire to hide mistakes has to be countered. Trial-and-error learning has to be normative.

A learning environment should recognize the importance of exploring differing viewpoints. Many of the problems social agencies face are multidimensional. In such situations,

> managerial philosophies are required that recognize the importance of probing the various dimensions of a situation, that allow constructive conflict and debate between advocates of competing perspectives. In this way issues can be fully explored, and perhaps redefined so that they can be approached and resolved in new ways. This kind of inquiry helps an organization absorb and deal with the uncertainty of its environment rather than trying to avoid or eliminate it.   (Morgan 1986:92)

What is implied but seldom made explicit in much of the discussion of how to make agencies open to new ideas is the inevitability of debate about programs, policies, and procedures. How to conduct these debates is a crucial strategic decision in planning for an open agency, for debate and dialogue are the essence of such an entity.

A number of values related to debating or arguing the merits of particular courses of action need to be institutionalized. Such values include among many others: exercising fairmindedness, legitimating intellectual humility and the suspension of judgment, and honoring intellectual courage, integrity, and perseverance (Paul 1990:189). To make such values normative in an agency, the administrator as social cartographer has to give careful attention to socialization processes, supervisory practices, the symbolism attendant to organizational events and rituals, and staff evaluation procedures.

Another focus of attention relates to the correctness of the reasoning (Feldman 1986:270). This will require all involved to have the ability to assess arguments and disparities as well as specific structures that accept the fact that in organizational life various sources of distortion of information will exist—political, perceptual, structural, etc.

A number of authors have suggested purposively creating alternative sources of information, encouraging divergent views such as by institutionalizing a role such as "devil's advocate," eliminating layers of hierarchy and many of the middle people in communication, and consciously engaging in counterbiasing (Gortner 1987:188–89).

Yet more important than these is some sort of rhetorical training or, in Schon's (1987) terms, double-loop learning—where a conscious attempt is made to think about how we think. Although in the frenetic life of most workers in agencies it is hard to envision a training program in critical thinking (Paul 1990:305–49), some attention will have to be given to helping all involved develop a set of skills related to asking and answering questions of clarification and to weighing questions and answers that probe assumptions, reasons, evidence, viewpoints, perspectives, implications and consequences, and questions about the question (Paul 1990:276–78). While related, these are not necessarily the same sort of skills used in everyday clinical practice. A greater degree of self-criticism is required. Theories-in-use have to be contrasted with espoused theories (Schön 1987). Dialectical logic is needed as well as formal logic, curvilinearity as well as linearity. The effect of time as a variable and an understanding of the history of issues and how such history affects thinking are needed.

To achieve all this, most likely there will have to be a reevaluation of the substance of professional education. If critical thinking or at the least theories about how we make judgments and how we persuade are not part and parcel of the curriculum of schools of social work, the long-term possibilities of creating a learning environment in social agencies will certainly be diminished. Hirschman (1991) provides excellent examples for such a curriculum: the drift and slope of such arguments as perversity (things will get worse); futility (the more you try to change, the less happens); synergy illusion (one good thing always helps another), etc.

Yet affirming the importance of debate and rhetoric does not imply disconfirming the real limitations of these as the arbiters of truth. The essential insight of those founders of physical science still holds, that rhetoric alone is full of traps and snares, from sophistry, to obfuscation, to nihilism, and to the devaluation of experience and context as compared with formal logic and rationality.

What is needed in the long run is knowledge garnered from a variety of forms of research and rhetoric that checks the worst in each and brings out the best in both. To paraphrase the old song, it's research and rhetoric, you can't have one without the other.

As a beginning step and part of such a redirection of education and training, agencies could in certain situations conceptualize a new role if not feasible for the administrator to play—that of the "rhetorician" whose job it is to help clarify and question both how we think and how we persuade, to help explicate the dialectic, to suggest ways in which the dialogue or debate shall be judged, as well as to suggest structures and mechanisms that facilitate understanding.

At the least such a role would expose the divergent schemas and implicit theories that individuals bring to their work and at best it would help to clarify and raise the level of learning and practice. In one sense, this can be viewed as broadening the role of the practice researcher.

Developing knowledge is usually thought to be a process that begins with developing ideas, then making them operational, and finally verifying them. At various phases different types of knowledge development processes predominate (Weissman 1990:254–55). Yet in organizational life this type of order can be discerned only through retrospective rationality. The reality is much more discontinuous, the content much more open to debate. It is now time to accept that debating within an agency may be divisive, it may be temporarily demoralizing, but it most certainly is necessary if a culture is to be created that promotes creativity and innovation.

Various authors have sketched out the design of experimental or learning organizations using such terms as the *self-correcting* or *self-designing organization*, emphasizing one or another set of internal structures or processes for creating change (Hedberg, Nystrom, and Starbuck 1976; Korten 1980; Landau 1973; Weick 1977). Notwithstanding all these, a central dilemma remains. If the beginning of wisdom is doubt and uncertainty, how can these thoughts and feelings be harnessed so as not to overwhelm the conviction and motivation to act and act decisively? (Pfeffer and Salancik 1977:23–26). It is perhaps in dealing with this problem that the joining of the ethnographer's understanding of the latent and the administrator's skill with the manifest is most needed.

REFERENCES

Bogdan, Robert. Discussion of paper delivered at a conference on Qualitative Research, School of Social Welfare, Albany, New York, August, 1991.
Brodkin, Evelyn. 1986. *The False Promise of Administrative Reform*. Philadelphia: Temple University Press.
Cheetham, Juliet. Evaluating social work effectiveness. Unpublished paper delivered at a conference, Research and Practice: Bridging the Gap. Center for the Study of Social Work Practice, Columbia University, New York, March 8, 1991.

Feldman, Jack. 1986. On the difficulty of learning from experience. In H. D. Sims and D. Gioia, eds., *The Thinking Organization*. San Francisco: Jossey-Bass.

Gortner, Harold, Julianne Mahler, and Jeanne Nicholson. 1987. *Organization Theory: A Public Perspective*. Chicago: Dorsey Press.

Hedberg, Bo, Paul Nystrom, and William Starbuck. 1976. Camping on seesaws: Prescriptions for a self-designing organization. *Administrative Science Quarterly* 21: 41–65.

Hirschhorn, Larry. 1988. *The Workplace Within*. Boston: MIT Press.

Hirschman, Albert O. 1991. *The Rhetoric of Reaction*. Cambridge, Mass.: Belknap Press.

Korten, David. 1980. Community organization and rural development. *Public Administration Review* 40: 480–511.

Landau, Martin. 1973. On the concept of a self-correcting organization. *Public Administration Review* 33: 533–42.

Majone, Giandomenico. 1989. *Evidence, Argument and Persuasion in the Policy Process*. New Haven, Conn.: Yale University Press.

Martin, Patricia. 1988. Multiple constituencies and performance in social welfare organizations: Action strategies for directors. In R. Patti, J. Poertner, and C. Rapp, eds., *Managing for Service Effectiveness in Social Welfare Organizations*. New York: Haworth Press.

McCall, Morgan and Robert Kaplan. 1985. *Whatever It Takes: Decision Makers at Work*. Englewood Cliffs, N.J.: Prentice Hall.

Mitchell, Terrence, Kenneth Rediker, and Lee Roy Beach. 1986. Image theory and organizational decision making. In H. P. Sims and D. Gioia, eds., *The Thinking Organization*. San Francisco: Jossey-Bass.

Morgan, Garth. 1986. *Images of Organization*. Newbury Park, Calif.: Sage.

Paul, Richard. 1990. *Critical Thinking*. Rohnert Park, Calif.: Center for Critical Thinking and Moral Critique.

Peters, Thomas. 1978. Symbols, patterns and settings: An optimistic case for getting things done. *Organizational Dynamics* 7: 2–23.

Pfeffer, Jeffrey and Gerald Salancik. 1977. The case for a coalitional model of organizations. *Organizational Dynamics* 6:15–29.

Quinn, Robert. 1988. *Beyond Rational Management*. San Francisco: Jossey-Bass.

Schön, Donald. 1987. *Educating the Reflective Practitioner: Toward a New Design for Teaching and Learning in the Professions*. San Francisco: Jossey-Bass.

Weick, Karl. 1977. Organizational design: Organizations as self-designing systems. *Organizational Dynamics* 6: 31–46.

Weick, Karl and Michel Bougan. 1986. Organizations as cognitive maps. In H. P. Sims and D. Gioia, eds., *The Thinking Organization*. San Francisco: Jossey-Bass.

Weissman, Harold H. 1980. Accreditation, credentialing, and accountability. *Administration in Social Work* 4: 4.

Weissman, Harold H. 1990. *Serious Play: Creativity and Innovation in Social Work*. Silver Spring, Md: NASW Press.

SIX

Commentary: Ethnography in Social Work

Anne E. Fortune

Ethnography is the study of other people's cultures, with a goal "to describe the way of life of a particular group from within, that is, by understanding and communicating not only what happens but how the members of the group interpret and understand what happens" (Kornblum 1989:2). Ethnography is conducted by immersing one's self into the culture, primarily through participant observation, augmented by other methods of data gathering such as family interviewing, collecting autobiographies, or taking detailed descriptions of a day's events from all participants (Goodson-Lawes, this volume). Data gathering and analysis may also include spatial and temporal mapping, thick description, grounded theory (as one of many ways of developing categories), and matrix analysis (Berg 1989; Denzin 1989; Glaser and Strauss 1967; Miles and Huberman 1984). The subject matter of ethnography can be an entire culture—the "wholeness of human life," as Goodson-Lawes calls it, or macroethnography (Berg 1989)—or a specific environment such as a clinic waiting room or team meetings—microethnography. Several papers in this volume illustrate these types and their application to social work (the papers by Goodson-Lawes, Sands and McClelland, Goldstein, Lang, and Davis and Srinivasan). These papers raise some issues in the applications of ethnography to social work. I address these by commenting on the utility of ethnographic methods for social work.

ETHNOGRAPHY AND PRACTICE SKILLS

One of the more intriguing ideas proposed by several authors is the parallel between social work practice skills and ethnographic research skills. Goldstein points out some of the shared procedures and assumptions: a goal to understand experience from others' perspective; a sensitivity to context; use of self and one's reactions to generate, gather, and interpret information; suspension of one's own frame of reference or theory to understand the others'; and continual revision of understandings based on new information. One important application of ethnography in social work is using its research skills to enhance or hone the comparable practice skills. For example, most practitioners could improve their skills in observing details such as physical proximity, body carriage, and forms of address as cues to what is important to clients. The suspension of one's own form of knowing, an essential prerequisite for ethnography, is critical in "starting where the client is," in learning to ask "what is going on here?" instead of assuming that one understands the cultural or idiosyncratic experience of clients. The inductive mode of reasoning—moving from observed phenomena to a conceptualization of their meaning—allows a perception of clients' reality that is not possible with deductive reasoning (if the practitioner is able to make sense of the influx of unorganized data). These are, of course, skills that are already part of social work; what ethnography adds to them is a sharpening, a clarity, and a relevance, particularly for cross-cultural practice.

Other skills are not normally a part of social work practice but may be useful for some types of practice. The asking of indirect questions—getting at organization of perceptions obliquely—may help with clients whose cultural norms are offended by the direct and straightforward questioning or topic focus of Western interpersonal approaches. And it may be the only approach with confused or thought-disordered clients. Another typical ethnographic procedure is asking and reasking the same question, perhaps with variations—differences in the answers are critical cues to gaps in the researcher's understanding. Such an approach may be helpful in existential or humanistic practice where the goal is helping a client reconstruct a self— like minimalist music, gradually building an entity through elaboration.

There is a limit to the incorporation of ethnographic skills into social work practice because ethnography and practice do differ in several fundamental ways. First, practice is action focused, while qualitative methods, including ethnography, intend only to describe. Practitioners and ethnographers gather and process data in similar ways up to the point where practitioners must make decisions about practice action. At this point, practitioners match their data with theory to help interpret the data and to decide on action. Thus the demand for action means the practitioner must turn to an outside interpretation while the ethnographer maintains suspension of such an external frame of reference. To do so, the practitioner needs additional skills in deductive and inductive logic, as well as a fine sense of timing about when to stop data gathering and turn to theory and action.

A second difference between social work practice and ethnography lies in why it is done. Ethnography, like all research, attempts to determine underlying principles and concepts about how life and perceptions are organized, a vision of the world that can be communicated to others (Berg 1989). This is generalization: something must be worth studying and communicating, or there is no point to conducting research. By contrast, in social work treatment, the practitioner needs only to understand the client's idiosyncratic reality (and then turn to action); there is no inherent need to communicate that reality to other persons or to generalize beyond the experience of that individual.

In short, these differences in action and purpose between ethnography and practice do require different, additional skills on the part of each. If ethnographic skills are incorporated into social work practice, the line between the two must be clearly drawn and practitioners trained about when to turn from one to the other.

MICROETHNOGRAPHY AND INFORMATION FOR PRACTICE

A second application of ethnography to social work is microethnographic studies, which provide information about settings and situations essential to social work. These can be tailored to social work practice needs and be readily used to generate immediately useful practice information. An example is Sands and McClelland's study of interdisciplinary teams, which highlights the misunderstandings and intraprofessional gaps in team decision making, as well as identifies potential strategies for newcomers to understand the subculture of a group and integrate into it more rapidly. Several studies of the intake process underscore the impact of physical layout, type of greetings offered, and reputation of the agency on client willingness to use service and definition of problems; these include a Catholic family service agency (Maluccio 1979), a British welfare office (Rees 1979), and a public venereal disease clinic (Sheley 1976).

Such setting- or situation-specific studies, if carefully conceptualized, can be circumscribed and hence completed within a reasonable time. Thus, they are feasible for informing practice, a requisite for good social work research, and social workers can define relevant problems of little interest to sociologists or anthropologists. In addition, because most social workers' time and interests are spent in practice and action, microethnographic studies fit well with the resources and energies available. Areas that seem promising for microethnography in social work include closed or semi-closed institutions such as residential facilities or schools; situations in which clients interact intensively with each other and in which interaction is critical to outcome, such as in-patient alcoholism treatment or group homes; and situations in which there are many service providers or other outsiders, because the researcher can be accepted more easily.

BORROWED INFORMATION
FROM MACROETHNOGRAPHY

A final application of ethnography for social work is macroethnographic studies, which increase our understanding of whole cultures, particularly those relevant to social work. Modern macroethnographic studies often deal with subjects relevant to social work and can be especially compelling and vivid in describing client realities. Examples include Williams' (1989) *Cocaine Kids,* about the opportunities drug dealing offers inner-city teenagers; or Sterk's (1989) account of the impact of AIDS on prostitutes; or Kotlowitz's (1991) *There Are No Children Here,* a family study of young boys trying to grow up in gang- and drug-ravaged public housing.

If a group has reason to mistrust social work, macroethnographic studies may be indispensable for the practitioner to gain the understanding necessary for effective practice. Goodson-Lawes's chronicle of limitations of survey research apply equally well as reasons why a social worker may not be able to gain an accurate understanding of a client from another culture: social desirability, fear and mistrust, shame, misunderstanding of joking, a different understanding of what is relevant, etc. Ethnographic studies can give the practitioner information otherwise not available.

The drawback of macroethnography for social work is that doing such research is time consuming and difficult: time in getting accepted in a setting and beginning to understand it from an insider's perspective, creating thick descriptions, making sense of overwhelming amounts of data, and maintaining a direction and purpose (Berg 1989; Jorgensen 1989; Miles and Huberman 1984). Further, the results are only indirectly relevant to social work, through enhanced knowledge of a culture. Certainly social workers, like anthropologists and sociologists, can and should conduct such research when feasible (and should receive professional rewards when they do). But for pragmatic reasons, macroethnographic research is unlikely to be readily incorporated into social work practice or applied research. In Goodson-Lawes's example, a local health clinic sent a culturally illiterate interviewer to find out why residents did not use the clinic. The interviewer failed, not surprisingly. But would a health clinic have the resources to permit a participant observer to live with a family for an extended period, to answer such a specific question, even when the answer would be more valid and more useful to the clinic?

Rather than try to incorporate macroethnography into social work as a research method, it seems more reasonable to learn to borrow knowledge from this source. Social workers can turn more systematically to ethnography to inform practice. Social workers can also seek cooperation from active ethnographers, when available. In Goodson-Lawes's example, the local health clinic clearly missed an opportunity to consult with her, who could (and often did) translate between cultures.

Ethnography is a "natural" fit with social work because of similarity in some basic assumptions about the construction of reality, its ability to provide immediately relevant information to inform practice, and its usefulness for understanding culture. However, it needs to be integrated into social work practice and research selectively, with attention to differences in purpose and resources. Ethnography attempts to describe and understand, while social work goes beyond that to attempt action.

REFERENCES

Berg, B. L. 1989. *Qualitative Research Methods for the Social Sciences.* Boston: Allyn and Bacon.
Denzin, N. K. 1989. *Interpretive Interactionism.* Newbury Park, Calif.: Sage.
Glaser, B. and A. Strauss. 1967. *The Discovery of Grounded Theory: Strategies for Qualitative Research.* Chicago: Aldine.
Jorgensen, D. L. 1989. *Participant Observation: A Methodology for Human Studies.* Newbury Park, Calif.: Sage.
Kornblum, W. 1989. Introduction. In C. D. Smith and W. Kornblum, eds., *In the Field: Readings on the Field Research Experience,* pp. 1–6. New York: Praeger.
Kotlowitz, A. 1991. *There Are No Children Here: The Story of Two Boys Growing Up in the Other America.* New York: Doubleday.
Maluccio, A. N. 1979. The influence of the agency environment on clinical practice. *Journal of Sociology and Social Welfare* 6: 734–55.
Miles, M. B. and A. M. Huberman. 1984. *Qualitative Data Analysis: A Sourcebook of New Methods.* Beverly Hills: Sage.
Rees, S. 1979. *Social Work Face to Face.* New York: Columbia University Press.
Sheley, J. F. 1976. A study in self-defeat: The public health venereal disease clinic. *Journal of Sociology and Social Welfare* 4: 114–24.
Sterk, C. 1989. Prostitution, drug use, and AIDS. In Smith and Kornblum, eds., *In the Field: Readings on the Field Research Experience,* pp. 90–99. New York: Praeger.
Williams, T. 1989. *Cocaine Kids.* Reading, Mass.: Addison-Wesley.

HEURISTIC
METHODS

SEVEN

Science, Not Scientism: The Robustness of Naturalistic Clinical Research

Martha Heineman Pieper

How can we know the dancer from the dance?" —*W. B. Yeats*

Naturalistic clinical research has been denigrated as inferior science by those who espouse scientism, the belief that the experimental group design or its approximation in single-subject research represents the method of choice in the human sciences (Bhaskar 1989). However, in the postpositivist heuristic paradigm of research, which I have described in detail elsewhere (Heineman [Pieper] 1981; [Heineman] Pieper 1985, 1989; following: Bhaskar 1989; Kuhn 1977; Simon 1966; Wimsatt 1980, 1986), there is scientific warrant for harnessing the robust possibilities of naturalistic research to study clinical practice in its full complexity (Adler and Adler 1987; Bronfenbrenner 1979; Ruckdeschel 1985). The heuristic paradigm conceptualizes science broadly as a systematic inquiry into some aspect of reality that is communicated in a way that will allow an interested person to make an informed evaluation of the process of inquiry and its conclusions (Cronbach and Suppes 1969). The heuristic paradigm recognizes that not all scientists will be able to agree on the precise meaning of words such as *systematic, reality, communicated, informed,* and *evaluation* (Manicas and Secord 1983).

   Although naturalistic research has unique strengths and has as much scientific merit as interventionist research, it has been overlooked and underutilized owing to the scientism that has colored the thinking of social work researchers and practitioners since the 1950s (Blenkner 1950; Fischer

1981; Geismar and Wood 1982; Greenwood 1952, 1955; Hudson 1982; Kogan 1960; Thyer 1987, 1989), when social work embraced positivist assumptions and exalted (and, therefore, overused and misapplied) the experimental method. The experimental method entails prospective rather than retrospective studies, control groups, operational definitions, randomized subjects, and data gathering by tape or video recorder, by third-party observers, or by structured instruments (Nelsen 1981, 1985). The experimental method (and the modified form in which it is applied to single-subject studies) is most effective when applied to closed systems and nonhuman subjects; it is often incompatible with the resources and the values of casework, that is, with clinical practice as it occurs naturally. Fortunately, naturalistic research offers an alternative, well-founded approach to the study of clinical process.

Naturalistic research entails the systematic study of clinical practice that is not intentionally altered for research purposes. Naturalistic research is distinguished from Naturalism, which is the philosophical notion that the human sciences can best be studied by the methods of the natural sciences (Bhaskar 1989). The contrast between naturalistic and interventionist research in no way implies the naive view that the participant/subject can be studied apart from interactional researcher effects (LeCompte and Goetz 1982). Rather, the categories of naturalistic and interventionist research refer only to the intentions and practices of the researcher. The interventionist researcher intentionally alters clinical practice for research purposes. In contrast, the naturalistic researcher is a practitioner who aims to minimize research intrusiveness into practice. The focus here is on research into clinical practice, which is why the researcher is referred to as a practitioner. In naturalistic research on an organization, a culture, or a subculture, the naturalistic researcher would be a member of the group under study—not an outsider. Research done by outsiders, no matter how skilled in minimizing research intrusiveness, is always interventionist. Naturalistic research on treatment excludes methodologies that for research purposes dictate, for example, that the client take personality inventories or fill out questionnaires before and during the treatment process, that the treatment process be artificially shortened or lengthened, or that the therapeutic relationship be recorded by third-party observers or electronic recording devices. Data gathering in naturalistic research takes the form of anamnestic process recording.

The unwarranted and largely categorical dismissal of naturalistic research by proponents of scientism is fueled in part by a pervasive category mistake whereby issues of qualitative vs. quantitative data and group vs. single-organism designs are conflated with the more fundamental distinction between naturalistic and interventionist research, with the result that this distinction has been obscured and neglected (Allen-Meares and Lane 1990; Cook and Reichardt 1979; Lincoln and Guba 1985). Qualitative research is frequently equated erroneously with new (postpositivist) research paradigms, while quantitative research is used mistakenly as a synonym for the standard (positivist) research paradigm (Allen-Meares and Lane 1990; Taylor and Bogdan 1984). This conceptual error occurs when issues that pertain to data analysis are confused with issues that relate to data gathering. To illustrate, just as interventionist methods can produce qualitative data (an example is the videotape of a family therapy session), naturalistic designs can generate quantified data (for example, anamnestic process can be coded for the purpose of executing a chi-square test). Moreover, many single-case designs, such as experimental designs and most change process designs, are deemed naturalistic, when they should be categorized as interventionist because they involve manipulations of the treatment process (Berlin, Mann, and Grossman 1991; Bloom and Fisher 1982; Davis and Reid 1988). Research-motivated manipulations of treatment can range from setting uniform limits on client service to using tape recorders or third-party observers (Dean and Reinherz 1986; Nelsen 1985).

I would emphasize that most authors mistakenly define naturalistic research to include interventionist strategies, such as research-driven data gathering by self-report instruments, personality inventories, electronic recording devices, and/or third-party observers (Lincoln and Guba 1985). This mislabeling rests on the unrealistic notion that participants/subjects forget or adjust to research-determined interventions and behave as if they were not there. The fact that subjects do not complain or comment should not be taken to indicate that they are behaving exactly the way they would in the absence of research-determined instruments of observation or inquiry (Bronfenbrenner 1979).

One consequence of the failure to consider the interventionist nature of electronic recording devices, third-party observers, questionnaires, research-motivated adjustments to the therapeutic process, etc., is that the ethical questions raised by research-motivated interventions are rarely if ever considered. By definition, research-motivated interventions introduce nontherapeutic motives and experiences into the treatment relationship and, therefore, always reduce the quality of the service being offered. An example is when limits are placed on client visits for the sole purpose of standardizing the treatment for research purposes. Sometimes authors confuse therapeutic and research aims and argue that research-motivated interventions are helpful to clients, but this argument is irrelevant to the ethical questions raised by the use of interventions that are introduced purely for research purposes (Ivanoff, Blythe, and Briar 1987:418–19). When a given practice theory prescribes ongoing testing or mechanical recording for diagnostic or therapeutic purposes (such as allowing clients to see themselves on videotape), then naturalistic research would obviously encompass use of the data produced by these therapeutically motivated instruments and recording devices. However, because some social work treatment modalities have been developed precisely because they were "researchable," and these models consider interventions therapeutic because they are research driven (Reid 1983; Reid and Epstein 1972). For this reason, I would argue that research on these practice modalities is interventionist rather than naturalistic, even though the research imposes no additional data collection measures.

Treatment quality to serve research purposes should be lowered only after a careful consideration of ethical issues and a weighing of competing values, especially because clients whose treatments are adversely affected are usually both desperate and disadvantaged and lack the means to avoid research protocols by choosing among private service providers.

Ethical issues are also raised by so-called unobtrusive measures, such as hidden cameras, which depend on deception and conflict with both humanistic and social work values. In contrast to interventionist research, naturalistic research raises neither ethical nor privacy issues, because the quality of service is not affected and deception is not an issue.

The position that the only incontrovertibly scientific way to study clinical process is by manipulating that process not only raises ethical questions but also is conceptually flawed because of its unwarranted claim of privilege for its positivist ontology (theory of reality) and its positivist epistemology (theory of how to know that reality).

I have written a number of articles critiquing the scientism that colors the literature on social work research (Heineman [Pieper] 1981; [Heineman] Pieper 1985, 1989) and proposing that social work adopt a more contemporary, sound, inclusive, and promising paradigm of scientific research, which I have termed the heuristic paradigm (Simon 1966; Wimsatt 1980, 1986). The heuristic paradigm is a metatheory—a set of principles that regulate the significance attached to any specific ontology and epistemology. This metatheory recognizes both that researchers' judgments are inherently no more objective or trustworthy than practitioners' trained judgments, and, more importantly, it allows social work research to incorporate social work values. It is important to remember that social work values had never been in conflict with social work research until an erroneous definition of science misled our profession into thinking that its fundamental values represented an unscientific, undesirable, and eradicable type of bias and subjectivity (Tyson, in press).

A heuristic is a problem-solving strategy whose goal is reasonable utility rather than (unattainable) certainty. Nobel laureate Herbert Simon observes that heuristics are inseparable from and indispensable to scientific activity. He emphasizes that science is a problem-solving process and not a neat, uncomplicated process of theory confirmation by means of deducing a predicted event from specified initial conditions (Hanfling 1981). Simon employs the notion of a heuristic to designate the shortcuts that all of us use all the time to solve one of the important problems of living, namely, that we encounter more information than we can possibly assimilate or employ. To illustrate, sensory input, which positivism takes as a direct, uncontaminated recording of external reality, in fact acquires meaning only through strategies that can be termed functional heuristics. These strategies allow us unconsciously to categorize and to edit the wealth of information registered by our senses. The regulatory role that these heuristics play in our perception of reality can perhaps be most clearly recognized when the process fails. For example, in optical illusions our visual strategies, or heuristics, cause us to draw erroneous conclusions about what we are seeing (Segall, Campbell, and Herskovits 1966). If participants/subjects in a dark room observe a light in motion, they will all assume that the light is moving, even when an experimenter has arranged things so that the light actually remains stationary and the subjects and the floor are in motion. Clearly, we would be paralyzed and unable to function if every time we saw motion we stopped to ask if some unseen hand were holding external reality still and moving us. The point is that what we take for direct, unmediated perceptions actually represent interpretations, e.g., conclusions, which are shaped by our experiences and expectations as well as by sensory input.

Every research methodology represents a heuristic by virtue of the fact that it selectively and arbitrarily organizes experience. As a result, every methodology, including the experimental group method and the change process single-case design, comes packaged in its own peculiar bias. In the heuristic approach, bias ceases to be a pejorative word, but, rather, becomes an accepted, inevitable component of all knowing (Wimsatt 1980, 1986). The goal becomes, not the elimination of bias, but the recognition of it (Gadlin and Ingle 1975; Mishler 1979; Orne 1964; Rosenthal 1980; Rosnow and Davis 1977; Wachtel 1980). For example, rather than view the researcher sitting behind a one-way mirror as an unbiased observer, we will want to look at the nature of the biases this intervention introduces, such as the effect on what thoughts and feelings the client willingly shares or unknowingly reveals.

Let me reiterate that I am not replacing one prescriptive paradigm with another by arguing that naturalistic research is inherently superior to interventionist research. The heuristic paradigm emphasizes both that there is no cookbook approach to science and also that there is no intrinsically superior methodology for getting at truth. Rather, any number of equally valid scientific methods are available, any one of which may be especially appropriate for researching a given problem in a specific setting (Hartman 1990). One of the exciting aspects of the heuristic paradigm of research is that it makes the researcher an active decisionmaker and thinker rather than an unreflective follower of obsolete rules (Saleeby 1979; Siporin 1989).

On the other hand, in adopting the position that no single methodology is inherently superior to any other at producing useful, scientific knowledge, the heuristic paradigm is not endorsing relativism, which is a type of epistemological skepticism. Relativists argue that the untenability of the claim of superiority for any one methodology results from the impossibility of a well-founded conviction that a mind-independent reality exists. Consequently, relativists abandon the pursuit of knowledge that reflects or corresponds to reality and instead aim at explanatory coherence. An example is the increasingly popular use of narrative coherence as a therapeutic tool. Advocates of a focus on narrative structures believe that the client lacks and needs a coherent self-narrative and that the curative element is the coherence of the narrative, not the knowledge of the primary causes of the client's psychological dynamics, which they believe to be unattainable. Both relativism and realism (the view that sound reasons exist to posit a mind-independent reality, which is amenable to study) are heuristic choices and, as such, are encompassed within the heuristic paradigm, although they neither define nor exhaust it.

Although the heuristic paradigm does make room for any ontology whose adherents are engaged in doing science, as I have made clear elsewhere, my own preferred ontology is a qualified realism (Pieper and Pieper 1990). That is, my personal preference is the position that external reality exists and can be known, even though this knowledge will always be partial, imperfect, and colored to some extent by the researcher's heuristics (Bhaskar 1989).

The positivists' type of realism is much less qualified. They believe that if we look through the lens of their preferred type of data gathering, reality can be known with a high degree of certainty. The positivist view is that researchers (or their electronic surrogates) but not practitioners can make unbiased observations of events (facts), which reflect the closest possible experience of a direct, empirical, unmediated contact with reality and, therefore, that these observations can confirm or disconfirm theories (Ivanoff, Robinson, and Blythe 1987). The positivist researcher argues that theories confirmed by these "immaculate perceptions" (Hanson 1969:74) can be considered to be "grounded" in this unproblematic reality. Beginning about 1950, the social work research literature repeatedly advocates empirical, atheoretical, and grounded research and condemns naturalistic research, which is deemed old-fashioned, anecdotal, soft, and unscientific

(Austin 1978; Epstein 1986; Siegel 1985). A representative positivist assessment of the scientific status of social work is that although social work "has long claimed to be one of the scientifically based professions, it has not produced more than a handful of clinical scientists" (Briar 1979:132). This erroneous judgment rests on the belief that when data are gathered by the researcher or the researcher's electronic agent—the tape recorder or video camera—they are empirical and unbiased because the data gatherer is neutral and objective. This view reflects the misuse of the word *empirical* by social work authors (Blythe and Briar 1985; Gleeson 1990; Siegel 1985) and explains why positivist authors have mislabeled my position "antiempiricist" (Glisson and Fischer 1987:51). The terms *empirical* and *empiricism* traditionally refer to any experience that originates extracranially. Positivist authors fallaciously apply these terms only to data collected in a manner compatible with the positivist paradigm. In fact, a comparison of theories, an anamnestic process recording, and a client's self-report of the impact of a program or treatment are just as empirical as the data brought to us by a video camera.

Contributing to the confusion is the conflation of a misleading definition of accuracy with the term *empirical*. Certain methods of data gathering, such as the electronic or third-party recording of a participant/subject's words and gestures, are considered to mirror reality accurately and, therefore, to be free from subjectivity. Data that fit this definition of accuracy are assumed to exhaust the category of empirical. The problem is, of course, that accuracy is a construct that reflects a heuristic choice of data rather than an unalterable, one-to-one, uncontaminated correspondence with reality. Therefore, not only are there many viable types of accuracy, but also the choice and pursuit of one kind of accuracy makes other kinds of accuracy more difficult or impossible to attain. For example, to obtain an accurate recording of the exact sequence and details of a client's speech and behavior, one sacrifices an accurate knowledge of what the client would say or do without the research intervention that introduces an electronic recording device.

There is an ostrich-like quality to the definition of "unobtrusive" measures as data gathering that requires "observers to be inconspicuous in their observing role and to guard against disclosing to subjects the specific nature of the data collected" (Allen-Meares and Lane 1990). Those who argue that clients soon "forget" about electronic devices or observers depreciate the intelligence of their clients and mistake compliance for habituation. Even after he spent an entire school year in a California classroom, Jackson (1990) noted that he remained enough of an outsider that when he happened to sneeze, members of the class turned around, whereas the sneezes of teacher and students went unremarked.

In addition, the focus on a single type of accuracy blinds researchers to the biases introduced by their preferred methodologies. For example, references to taping or the presence of third-party observers are made only in passing and the effects on clients of being subjected to numerous rating scales and to repeated evaluations of their treatments are dismissed or never mentioned (Cooper 1990; Davis and Reid 1988; Dean and Reinherz 1986; Nelsen 1985). When clients do express concern about research intrusiveness into their treatment, positivist researchers do not take these concerns seriously. In one instance, a client's anxiety about having her symptoms tape recorded is dismissed as a psychopathological "dysfunctional assumption" that needs correcting (Berlin, Mann, and Grossman 1991:10).

Similarly, since positivist researchers are unaware that many different but equally useful types of accuracy exist, they dismiss other methodologies, such as anamnestic process recordings, as less accurate and, therefore, less desirable than their preferred methods of data gathering. The authors of the influential *Nonreactive Measures in the Social Sciences* deprecate human beings as "low-fidelity observational instruments" (Webb et al. 1981:241). Kazdin (1981) reflects the positivist disapproval of anamnestic process, which he deprecatingly refers to as anecdotal: "scientific inferences are difficult if not impossible to draw from anecdotal information. Indeed, it is the anecdotal information that is the problem rather than the fact that an individual case is studied" (185). However, since in actuality each method of data gathering has its own strengths and limitations, a tape recorder or third-party observer is inherently no more accurate than the trained clinician. Clearly, tape recorders introduce bias. Imagine interviewing a frightened pregnant teenager who is hiding the unwelcome news from her parents, with and without a tape recorder present in the room. In the presence of the tape recorder, the teenager's remarks may be accurately recorded, but the nature of her remarks undoubtedly will differ from, and represent her state of mind less accurately than, the statements she would make in a naturalistic data-gathering process—i.e., in the absence of the tape recorder and in the presence of a practitioner she knows and trusts. Put differently, third-party observers and tape recorders, no less than practitioners, are participant observers, because each one affects, and therefore causes reactions in, the participant/subject (Bronfenbrenner 1979).

Akin to the positivists' misunderstanding of accuracy is their overvaluation of reliability, which is the precept that a practitioner–researcher's perceptions about a client or treatment process lack scientific value unless they are correlated with another qualified person's perceptions about the same or a similar client or process (McVicker Hunt 1959). I suggest that it is more meaningful to focus on credibility than on reliability. Reliable observations are not necessarily credible; no matter how many people tell us they saw the same flying saucer, we are unlikely to find them credible. Clinical credibility—our conviction of the scientific value, i.e., fundamental correctness, of the practitioner-researcher's interventions and theoretical understanding—can rest on the comprehensive, detailed, well-conceptualized presentation by a single practitioner of her/his conduct and understanding of a specific treatment process.

Researchers who confuse reliability and credibility tend to adopt the absurd position that it is acceptable to trust clients' lives and well-being to trained practitioners but that the judgments of these same practitioners about their clients lack scientific merit. Since it has been amply demonstrated that no truly neutral measures exist—that all methods of gathering data introduce their own biases—we are free once again to accord scientific status to (to rely on) the practitioner's informed judgment. In the early days of social work research, social work knowledge often advanced by means of the case study reported by the experienced practitioner. No one who has read Towle's brilliant, humanistic studies (Towle 1940) can doubt that social work's knowledge base was well served by this method (Tyson 1992). In fact, experienced clinicians' understanding of their treatment process will contribute meanings that will be absent from the observations and conclusions of a researcher who has no prior knowledge of the client and who has a professional identity that is antithetical to the development of therapeutic involvement with the client. If experience and involvement count for something in real-life clinical situations, they should also be worthwhile in research situations.

Another impediment the positivist research paradigm places in the path of the naturalistic study of clinical process is the requirement that valid scientific investigation must always be prospective (this is known as the rule against ex post facto research). Scientism has exalted the experimental method, and the experimental method requires that clinical practice must be altered for research purposes before it is undertaken. This insistence on the inherent superiority of interventionist, prospective research designs has seriously damaged the cause of naturalistic research. For example, an agency with limited resources may institute a program that it deems extraordinarily successful. Positivist standards for science dictate that if an agency wants its innovation to be taken seriously, it cannot simply report on its new approach but rather must institute a prospective study in which clients are randomly chosen and assigned into experimental and control groups. This stricture rests on the erroneous belief that to predict an event correctly confirms the power of one's theory to explain it. However, prediction and explanation are entirely different activities and serve unrelated functions (Kim 1981; Salmon 1971). For example, while we can confidently predict that if the sun disappears below the horizon in the evening it will appear at the opposite horizon the next morning, when our investigation assures us that the predicted event has occurred, we are no closer to a causal understanding of planetary motion than we were before. In fact, in addition to the human sciences, many natural sciences, such as Darwinian evolution and seismography, are in principle unable to make specific predictions; yet they yield useful explanations of important events. If the mystique of the prospective study is dispelled, an agency or practitioner can publish the description of a treatment approach that seems to have merit without senselessly expending scarce resources to repeat the treatment for the sole purpose of avoiding the positivist censure of naturalistic research. Agencies and practitioners can make scientific evaluations of ongoing programs or clients and need only to expend monies to reinstitute a program or treatment when this will serve a substantive, clinical purpose, such as the extension of promising services to other client groups.

Another reason that social work's embrace of the positivist paradigm resulted in the disparagement of naturalistic vis-à-vis interventionist research is that the positivists sought universally applicable truths. As a result, they regarded situational or contextual factors as, at best, irrelevant and, at worst, as annoying distraction. However, the search for context-free knowledge has been abandoned as quixotic and unproductive by prestigious researchers in other fields (e.g., Campbell [1975] and Mishler [1986] in psychology; Blalock [1979] and Coser [1975] in sociology). The problem focus is always arbitrary because no level of reality is inherently more important or informative than any other. The decision to call one aspect of what we are studying the problem and to define all other aspects as context is always a heuristic strategy (Wimsatt 1980). As such, it should be determined by consideration of what factors are deemed most important to the question being asked, what resources are available to study the problem, and what the most promising means of studying the problem seem to be. In contrast, positivist researchers prescribe a problem focus that is predetermined by their assumptions about reality; that is, they prescribe small, simple, easily measured units, which they mistakenly believe they can divorce from contextual factors. Conversely, the researcher who uses the heuristic approach realizes that no fixed rules exist for separating the problem under study, or system, from the environment, or context (Witkin 1989; Witmer and Gottschalk 1988). For this reason, the problem environment is best defined as that part of the problem one does not study.

The awareness of the arbitrary nature of problem boundaries leads heuristic researchers to reject quixotic attempts to generate universal truths and to focus instead on the nature and effects of their assumptions and the relevance of their problem definitions to real-life practice. Consequently, researchers gain a new awareness that the determination of the system boundary of what they are studying has sweeping consequences and implications and, concomitantly, that smaller is not necessarily better when it comes to choosing a problem focus. To illustrate, the approach to tuberculosis in which the relevant system was the tuberculosis bacillus made it possible to ignore the poverty and poor health care that allow tuberculosis to discriminate among classes of people (Levins and Lewontin 1985). A similar problem is highlighted in the aphorism, "when the rich get a cold, the poor get pneumonia." In other words, illness can be seen as a social, economic, and class problem, as well as a medical problem, and this redefined focus has far-reaching consequences for our intervention strategies.

Unwanted teenage pregnancy presents an analogous complexity. Whether we see the system, or problem focus, as the teenager, the teenager and her boyfriend, the teenager and her parents, the teenager and her peers, the teenager in the context of her socioeconomic class, the teenager and the opportunities available to her for a satisfying career, or the teenager and the racial and class prejudices of the society in which she lives, will determine not just how we study unwanted teen pregnancy but also the kinds of information our research provides and the interventions we are likely to attempt. In other words, if we study only the teenager and her knowledge of contraception, social inequality will not be part of the equation and cannot appear as a cause of teenage pregnancy that needs to be addressed.

The assertion that value judgments should have no place in scientific activity is a corollary of the positivist argument that optimal science should admit only a narrow range of data, which positivists (mistakenly) believe to be perceptible in unmediated form and, therefore, to appear the same to every observer not brain damaged. From the 1950s until and including the present, in the literature on social work research we see repeated demands that social work research be both atheoretical and value free. We also see constant criticisms of research in which the researcher's values are manifest. Sadly, social work has a rich heritage of meaningful values on which it has turned its back in the pursuit of the unattainable and already outdated belief in the possibility of an objective science based on unmediated facts (Tyson, in press).

Scriven characterizes the positivist researcher as one who has a severe case of "valuephobia," the fear of including value judgments in scientific research (Scriven 1983). In a typical instance from the social work literature, one author insists that "Evaluators must avoid the role of advocate . . ." (Gibbs 1983:90). Actually, positivist researchers evaluate service by goals chosen to conform to their own research values, rather than because they reflect clients' needs or socially useful or prudent solutions. This tacit value system often means that positivist researchers design program evaluations that uncritically accept the goal definitions set by program managers. Scriven argues that researchers instead should incorporate social values and match the effects of programs to "the needs of those whom they affect" (Scriven 1983:235).

It is apparent that the belief in the possibility of value-free science both shackles science and also makes it a handmaiden of the status quo. Today it is neither radical nor socially disruptive to study the extent of teenagers' knowledge about contraception; it is much more radical to research the degree to which the epidemic of unwanted teenage pregnancies is a function of broad social, gender, and racial inequalities that give some teenagers a sense of hopelessness at an age that is usually characterized by boundless optimism. In addition to being a chimera, the goal of scientific objectivity is itself a value, that is, a preference, and the value of objectivity has been exalted over social work's more traditional values, such as the precept of respecting the client's rights and needs.

In addition to the conceptual difficulties with portraying the researcher as a passive recorder of unproblematic data, there is the practical consequence that this depiction of the researcher is antithetical to the erstwhile role of the researcher as the handmaiden of social change, and it is largely responsible for the split in social work between advocate and researcher. Positivist researchers belittle the advocates for being too involved with their clients and, thereby, for falling prey to an unscientific subjectivity. Once they recognize that the ideal of the value-free, atheoretical, neutral researcher is an impossible fiction and also exalts only one of many competing values, the researchers are free to ally themselves with the advocates and to gather facts unapologetically with the aim of supporting and furthering social work's traditional humanistic concerns.

One traditional social work value that has been subverted by the quixotic attempt to eliminate values from social work research is respect for clients' right to self-determination, that is, the right to participate fully in their own treatment process. Researchers routinely bypass clients' judgments and observe them as though they were as unthinking and unfeeling as a bacterium under a microscope. When treatment is driven by the value of satisfying the requirements of the positivist researcher, the value of making treatment client centered is abrogated. An example is the single-case design (Berlin, Mann, and Grossman 1991; Davis and Reid 1988; Thyer 1987). When positivist research principles took hold of social work, it seemed that the traditional case study, as reported by social workers like Richmond or Towle, would never lend itself to the experimental method and, accordingly, could not be a part of good science. For example, in applying an experimental treatment to one client, there are, by definition, no control groups for comparison with the experimental intervention. The presupposition that, to be scientific, case studies had to conform to experimental methodology led researchers to design an experimental version of the single-case study in which the client would serve both as experimental group and also as control group (Hersen and Barlow 1976). In one common variant of the single-subject experimental method, the therapeutic intervention being studied (for example, giving a young bed wetter a toy every morning he slept through the night without wetting his bed) might be withdrawn, or reversed, to see whether the symptoms returned. In this example, if the child's bed wetting recurred after the reward was withdrawn, the researcher would conclude that the reward caused the symptom to improve.

Because positivist researchers assume that science can and should be value free, few question the practice of putting the value of attempting to control for extraneous variables over the value of doing no harm to the client (Hersen and Barlow 1976:92–100; Kazdin 1981, 116–219; Nelsen 1985). Ironically, putting research values over treatment values lowers the quality of the treatment and, therefore, of the research (Lucente 1987). When we include the researcher in the system under investigation, it is clear that the researcher's arbitrary refusal to reward the child for successfully remaining dry all night would confuse the child and disrupt his budding self-confidence in his capacity to regulate his own body. If the bed wetting returns, it is as likely to suggest that the child's bed-wetting behavior is vulnerable to the researcher's cruelty as it is to indicate that material rewards cure bed wetting.

Positivist researchers choose and develop the social work treatment modalities they believe to be the most researchable. The treatment methods that fit most easily into the positivist criteria for research are brief, easily standardized, and focus on readily measured overt behavior rather than on the client's subjective experience. On the other hand, treatment modalities that are long term, focus on helping the client to feel better, and take into account the client's unconscious motives as well as the client's manifest behavior are ridiculed as products of a primitive past, which cannot be studied scientifically. The unfortunate consequence is that our profession's preoccupation with achieving (a spurious type of) scientific respectability dovetails with the government's aim to cut spending and reduce services. Even though we now realize the therapeutic limitations of brief, behavior-oriented treatment, it has become nearly impossible to get funding for long-term, open-ended treatments that focus on the client's subjective experience.

I have argued that social work is committing professional suicide by endorsing the outmoded philosophy that service quality should be narrowly defined by adherence to one value—fiscal accountability measured quantitatively and behaviorally and determined only on the basis of the study of atomistic, simplified interactions ([Heineman] Pieper 1985, 1989). The corollary is that our clients increasingly receive only atomistic, simplified, rigid, short-term interventions. For years we have undermined our standing to propose creative, open-ended, flexible service. Increasing numbers of outpatient clinics that receive public funds are eliminating relationship-oriented, psychodynamic treatment approaches and providing their clients only drugs and behavioral or cognitive therapies. The rationale is not that these modalities have been shown to have superior therapeutic value or that clients do not want a more involved, open-ended therapeutic relationship or help with nonspecific but troubling psychic pain, but rather that the mandated treatments fit better with a value system that defines accountability solely in terms of the value of spending the smallest amount of time and money with any given client. Sadly, social work researchers who espouse scientism intentionally or unintentionally support this limitation of services. And once again the poorest clients, who are dependent on public funding, get the cheapest and most meager services.

In summary, if social work adopts the heuristic paradigm, researchers will cease the single-minded pursuit of the chimerical goal of neutral, value-free science and will be able to integrate the more attainable values of the recognition and regulation of bias with social work's traditional values (such as respect for the client's self-experience, sensitivity to gender and racial discrimination, and concern with social injustice) into their scientific activities (Goldstein 1983).

Further, both the effort of critiquing the positivist claim for the superiority of interventionist research and the concomitant argument for the scientific standing of naturalistic social work research are matters of great concern, because for so many years unwarranted positivist strictures have limited the range of data that are considered legitimate, which in turn restricts social work's ability to study clinical practice in all its complexity. To illustrate, one researcher makes the frightening assertion that "If you cannot measure the client's problem, it does not exist" (Hudson 1982).

Naturalistic research is just as scientifically respectable and able to produce legitimate, helpful, relevant, generalizable knowledge as interventionist research is. If social work were to embrace the heuristic paradigm, one significant consequence would be that research-motivated interventions in casework services, such as the introduction of third-party observers, electronic recording devices, and client instruments, would no longer be misperceived as nonreactive and unobtrusive. These service manipulations would cease to be implemented unthinkingly but would have to be justified both in relation to their potential to contribute significantly to the research being undertaken and in terms of the negative effects they may have on a particular service modality and the degree of their compatibility with the broad spectrum of social work values.

Some of the advantages of naturalistic clinical research are that the values of putting the client's interest first and of doing no harm are respected, that treatment is studied in an undisturbed form from an experience-near perspective, and that the practitioner's trained understanding and assessment of the treatment process are highlighted. The resurrection of naturalistic research will encourage practitioners to leave the sidelines and to participate comfortably in relevant, significant, helpful, humanistic, science (Sherman 1987). Practitioners who for the last forty years have unjustly been made to feel that their experienced and educated judgments are unscientific and, therefore, unimportant can join the effort to devise creative and productive ways to study and shed light on the complex, multifactorial, overdetermined problems that plague us all.

REFERENCES

Adler, P. and P. Adler. 1987. The past and the future of ethnography. *Journal of Contemporary Ethnography* 16, no. 1 (April): 4–24.

Allen-Meares, P. and B. Lane. 1990. Social work practice: Integrating qualitative and quantitative data collection techniques. *Social Work* 35, no. 5 (September): 452–58.

Austin, D. 1978. Research and social work: Educational paradoxes and possibilities. *Journal of social service research* 2: 159–69.

Berlin, S., K. Mann, and S. Grossman. 1991. Task analysis of cognitive therapy for depression. *Social Work Research and Abstracts* 27, no. 2 (June): 3–12.

Bhaskar, R. 1989. *Reclaiming Reality: A Critical Introduction to Contemporary Philosophy.* London: Verso.

Blalock, H. M. 1979. Presidential address: Measurement and conceptualization problems. *American Sociological Review* 44: 881–94.

Blenkner, M. 1950. Obstacles to evaluative research in casework: Part I. *Social Casework* 31: 54–60.

Bloom, M. and J. Fischer. 1982. *Evaluating Practice: Guidelines for the Accountable Professional.* Englewood Cliffs, N.J.: Prentice Hall.

Blythe, B. J. and S. Briar. 1985. Developing empirically based models of practice. *Social Work* 30 (November/December): 483–8.

Briar, S. 1979. Incorporating research into education for clinical practice in social work: Toward a clinical science in social work. In A. Rubin and A. Rosenblatt, eds., *Sourcebook of Research Utilization,* pp. 132–40. New York: Council on Social Work Education.

Bronfenbrenner, U. 1979. The laboratory as an ecological context. In *The Ecology of Human Development: Experiments by Nature and Design,* Ch. 6, pp. 109–31. Cambridge, Mass.: Harvard University Press.

Campbell, D. 1975. 'Degrees of freedom' and the case study. *Comparative Political Studies* 8: 178–93.

Cook, T. and C. Reichardt. 1979. *Qualitative and Quantitative Methods in Evaluation Research.* Beverly Hills: Sage.

Cooper, M. 1990. Treatment of a client with obsessive-compulsive disorder. *Social Work Research and Abstracts* 6 (June): 26–35.

Coser, L. 1975. Presidential address: Two methods in search of a substance. *American Sociological Review* 40: 691–700.

Cronbach, L. and P. Suppes, 1969. *Research for Tomorrow's Schools: Disciplined Inquiry for Education.* London: Macmillan.

Davis, I. P. and W. J. Reid. 1988. Event analysis in clinical practice and process research. *Social Casework* 69, no. 4 (April): 298–306.

Dean, R. G. and H. Reinherz. 1986. Psychodynamic practice and single system design: The odd couple. *Journal of Social Work Education* 22 no. 2 (Spring/Summer): 71–81.

Epstein, W. 1986. Science and social work. *Social Service Review* 60: 145–60.

Fischer, J. 1981. The social work revolution. *Social Work* 26: 199–207.

Gadlin, H. and G. Ingle. 1975. Through the one-way mirror [the limits of experimental self-reflection]. *American Psychologist* 30: (1003–9).

Geismar, L. and K. Wood. 1982. Evaluating practice: Science as faith. *Social Casework* 63: 266–72.

Gibbs, L. 1983. Evaluation research: Scientist or advocate? *Journal of Social Service Research* 7, no. 1 (Fall): 81–92.

Gleeson, J. P. 1990. Engaging students in practice evaluation: Defining and monitoring critical initial interview components. *Journal of Social Work Education* 26, no. 3 (Fall): 295–309.

Glisson, C. and J. Fischer. 1987. Statistical training for social workers. *Journal of Social Work Education* 23: 50–58.

Goldstein, H. 1983. Starting where the client is. *Social Casework* 64, no. 2 (May): 267–75.

Greenwood, E. 1952. Social work research: A decade of reappraisal. *Social Service Review* 31: 311–20.

Greenwood, E. 1955. Social science and social work: A theory of their relationship. *Social Service Review* 29: 20–33.

Hanfling, O. 1981. *Logical Positivism.* New York: Columbia University Press.

Hanson, N. 1969. Logical positivism and the interpretation of scientific theories. In P.A.B. Achinstein, ed., *The Legacy of Logical Positivism.* Baltimore, Md: The Johns Hopkins University Press.

Hartman, A. 1990. Many ways of knowing [Editorial]. *Social Work* 35: 3–4.

Heineman [Pieper], M. B. 1981. The obsolete scientific imperative in social work research. *Social Service Review* 55 (September): 371–97.

Hersen, M. and D. Barlow. 1976. *Single-Case Experimental Designs: Strategies for Studying Behavior Change.* New York: Pergamon.

Hudson, W. 1982. Scientific imperatives in social work research and practice. *Social Service Review* 56: 246–58.

Ivanoff, A., B. Blythe, and S. Briar. 1987. The empirical clinical practice debate. *Social Casework* 68, no. 5: 290–8.

Ivanoff, A., E. Robinson, and B. Blythe. 1987. Empirical clinical practice from a feminist perspective. *Social Work* 32, no. 5: 417–23.

Jackson, P. 1990. *Life in Classrooms.* New York: Teacher's College Press.

Kazdin, A. 1981. Drawing valid inferences from case studies. *Journal of Consulting and Clinical Psychology* 49, no. 2: 183–92.

Kim, J. 1981. Causes as explanations: A critique. *Theory and Decision* 13: 293–309.

Kogan, L. 1975. Principles of measurement. In N. Polansky, ed., *Social Work Research,* pp. 68–92. Chicago: University of Chicago Press.

Kuhn, T. S. 1977. *Foundations of the Unity of Science.* Vol. 2, no. 2. *The Structure of Scientific Revolutions.* 2d ed. International Encyclopedia of Unified Science. Chicago: University of Chicago Press.

LeCompte, M. and J. Goetz. 1982. Problems of reliability and validity in ethnographic research. *Review of Educational Research* 52, no. 1 (Spring): 31–60.

Levins, R. and R. Lewontin. 1985. *The Dialectical Biologist.* Cambridge, Mass.: Harvard University Press.

Lincoln, Y. S. and E. G. Guba. 1985. *Naturalistic Inquiry.* Newbury Park, Calif.: Sage.

Lucente, R. 1987. N = 1:Intensive case study methodology reconsidered. *Journal of Teaching in Social Work* 1, no. 2 (Fall/Winter): 49–64.

McVicker Hunt, J. 1959. On the judgment of social workers as a source of information in social work research. In A. Shyne, ed., *Use of Judgments as Data in Social Work Research,* pp. 38–54. New York: NASW Press.

Manicas, P. T. and P. F. Secord. 1983. Implications for psychology of the new philosophy of science. *American Psychologist* 38, no. 4 (April): 399–413.

Mishler, E. G. 1979. Meaning in context: Is there any other kind? *Harvard Educational Review* 49: 1–19.

Mishler, E. G. 1986. *Research Interviewing: Context and Narrative.* Cambridge, Mass.: Harvard University Press.

Nelsen, J. 1981. Issues in single-subject research for nonbehaviorists. *Social Work Research and Abstracts* 17: 31–37.

Nelsen, J. C. 1985. Verifying the independent variable in single-subject research. *Social Work Research and Abstracts* 21, no. 2: 3–8.

Orne, M. 1964. Demand characteristics and the concept of quasi-controls. In R. Rosenthal and R. Rosnow, eds., *Artifact in Behavioral Research,* pp. 143–79. New York: Academic Press.

Pieper, M. H. 1985. The future of social work research. *Social Work Research and Abstracts* 21: 3–11.

Pieper, M. H. 1989. The heuristic paradigm: A unifying and comprehensive approach to social work research. *Smith College Studies in Social Work* 60: 8–34.

Pieper, M. H. and W. J. Pieper. 1990. *Intrapsychic Humanism: An Introduction to a Comprehensive Psychology and Philosophy of Mind.* Chicago: Falcon II Press.

Reid, W. J. 1983. Developing intervention methods through experimental designs. In A. Rosenblatt and D. Waldfogel, eds., *Handbook of Clinical Social Work.* San Francisco: Jossey-Bass.

Reid, W. and L. Epstein. 1972. *Task-Centered Casework.* New York: Columbia University Press.

Rosenthal, R. 1980. *Experimenter Effects in Behavioral Research.* New York: Oxford University Press.

Rosnow, R. and D. Davis. 1977. Demand characteristics and the psychological experiment. *Etc.* 34: 301–13.

Ruckdeschel, R. 1985. Qualitative research as a perspective. *Social Work Research and Abstracts* 21: 17–22.

Saleeby, D. 1979. The tension between research and practice: Assumptions of the experimental paradigm. *Clinical Social Work Journal* 7: 267–75.

Salmon, W. 1971. Statistical explanation. In W. Salmon, ed., *Statistical Explanation and Statistical Relevance*, pp. 29–88. Pittsburgh: University of Pittsburgh Press.

Scriven, M. 1983. Evaluation ideologies. In *Evaluation Models: Viewpoint on Educational and Human Services Evaluation*. Boston: Kluwer-Nijhoff.

Segall, M., D. Campbell, and M. Herskovits. 1966. *The Influence of Culture on Visual Perception*. New York: Bobbs-Merrill.

Sherman, E. 1987. Hermeneutics, human science, and social work. *Social Thought* 13: 34–41.

Siegel, D. 1985. Effective teaching of empirically based practice. *Social Work Research and Abstracts* 21, no. 1: 40–48.

Simon, H. 1966. Scientific discovery and the psychology of problem solving. In Colodny, ed., *Mind and Cosmos*. Pittsburgh: University of Pittsburgh Press.

Siporin, M. 1989. Metamodels, models, and basics: An essay review. *Social Service Review* 63: 474–80.

Thyer, B. 1987. Progress in behavioral social work: An introduction. *Journal of Social Service Research* 11: 1–5.

Thyer, B. 1989. Response to R. G. Dean and B. L. Fenby. Exploring epistemologies: Social work action as a reflection of philosophical assumptions. *Journal of Social Work Education* 25, no. 1: 174–6.

Towle, C. 1940. A social case record from a psychiatric clinic with teaching notes. *Social Service Review* 14: 83–118.

Tyson, K. In press. *New Foundations for Social Research: The Heuristic Paradigm.* Beverly Hills: Sage.

Tyson, K. 1992. A new approach to relevant scientific research for practitioners: The heuristic paradigm. *Social Work* 37: 541–56.

Wachtel, P. 1980. Investigation and its discontents. *American Psychologist* 35: 399–408.

Webb, E., D. Campbell, R. Schwartz, L. Sechrest, and J. Grove. 1981 (1966). *Nonreactive Measures in the Social Sciences*. 2d ed. Boston: Houghton Mifflin.

Wimsatt, W. 1980. Reductionistic research strategies and their biases in the units of selection controversy. In T. Nickles, ed., *Scientific Discovery: Case Studies*. Boston: Reidel.

Wimsatt, W. 1986. Heuristics and the study of human behavior. In D. W. Fiske and R. A. Schweder, eds. *Metatheory in the Social Sciences*, pp. 293–314. Chicago: University of Chicago Press.

Witkin, S. 1989. Towards a scientific social work. *Journal of Social Service Research* 12: 83–98.

Witmer, S. and S. Gottschalk. 1988. Alternative criteria for theory evaluation. *Social Service Review* 62: 211–24.

EIGHT

Heuristic Guidelines for Naturalistic Qualitative Evaluations of Child Treatment

Katherine Tyson

Since the inception of the social work profession, social workers have devoted themselves to improving the services they provide by evaluating their practice in diverse ways (Tyson, in press). Yet, in the 1970s, some social work researchers who had adopted a positivist philosophy of research claimed that social casework is ineffective (Fischer 1973; Mullen and Dumpson 1976) and that social workers do not evaluate their practice (Briar 1979; Weber and Polansky 1975), and they advanced methods for evaluation of practice that most practitioners have not chosen to implement (Welch 1983). The approaches to single-case evaluation that were developed to conform to positivist standards for legitimate research have many disadvantages for practitioners, such as: (1) time-consuming data collection procedures that in most practice models have no therapeutic rationale, (2) distortion of the client's definition of the problem to fit the operational requirement, (3) a simplified view of the change process that does not reflect the complexities of practice, and (4) the frequent use of ethically questionable procedures that aim to cause client regression by withholding treatment for the sake of experimental "control" (Heineman Pieper 1981, 1985, 1989, and in this volume; Lucente 1987; Ruckdeschel and Farris 1981; Witkin 1991). The positivist approach to research advanced a hierarchy of research designs, according to which naturalistic approaches to evaluating practice were ranked as inherently inferior to those research methods that used procedures such as experimental manipulation, random-ization, and control groups (Reid and Smith 1989; Tripodi 1981). One consequence of social work's adoption of the positivist philosophy of re-search has been that naturalistic qualitative approaches to evaluating social work practice have been largely overlooked (see Heineman Pieper's chapter in this volume). Now, in the humanistic and increasingly accepted postposi-tivist philosophy of scientific research first imported into social work by Heineman Pieper and termed by her the heuristic paradigm, social workers have new conceptual foundations for research (Heineman Pieper 1981, 1985, 1989). This paper uses the new conceptual foundations of the heuris-tic paradigm to respond to the pressing need for systematic and relevant guidelines for naturalistic single-case evaluation.

In the recent debates about social work's philosophy of research, the choice between the positivist and heuristic research paradigms has often been erroneously reduced to a choice between quantitative and qualitative methods (Glisson and Fischer 1987; Mullen 1985; Orcutt 1990; Reid and Smith 1989). In fact, the heuristic paradigm is a comprehensive philosophy of research that encourages researchers to explicate the choices they make when designing the research, including, for example, choices about how to gather and analyze data. When deciding how to collect and analyze data, researchers who adopt the heuristic paradigm are free of the restrictive, unwarranted positivist belief that some methods are inherently better than others for testing social work theories. In planning research the researchers using the heuristic paradigm select, from among all the approaches to data collection and data analysis available to social workers, the approaches that they believe will yield the most relevant, useful information about the problem they want to study:

> The heuristic paradigm is distinguished by its anti-restrictive stance. If the heuristics represented by the experimental method and quantified data are appropriate to the question being studied and the theory used to study it, the heuristic researcher would include and welcome them. The heuristic re-searcher only rejects the attempt to apply the experimental method and quantified data to all research questions and to exalt them above all other research strategies.   (Heineman Pieper 1989:28)

This paper draws from the conceptual foundations of the heuristic para-digm, focuses on how qualitative data can be gathered and analyzed qualita-tively, and formulates guidelines for systematic, naturalistic single-case evaluations that practitioners and researchers can implement with a mini-mum of distortion of the treatment process. Social work treatment of young children is used as an illustration.

Before discussing approaches to evaluations of practice, it is important to briefly conceptualize evaluation. Evaluation entails a comparison between the object of the evaluation and a standard or precept. The standards that social work adopts to evaluate professional practice regulate the quality of social work's contributions to its knowledge base and to social reform and individual services, because those standards define the ideals towards which social workers strive. Social science researchers use diverse standards for evaluation, which include, for example, responsiveness to community needs (Whitaker 1974), cost-effectiveness, expectations for employee competence, the feasibility of the program in relation to the resources allocated, and participant satisfaction (Rossi and Freeman 1985; Scriven 1986). Any evaluation of social work practice uses two types of standards: (1) standards for scientific research, articulated in the assumptions of a research paradigm; and (2) standards for the practice of a particular casework model. After 1950, social work imported standards for the evaluation of practice from the positivist philosophy of research, despite those standards' incompatibility with many social work practice precepts (Heineman Pieper 1981, 1985, 1989; Tyson, in press). One consequence of the incompatibility between the standards of the positivist approach to single-case evaluation of practice and the precepts of practitioners' clinical theories is that most practitioners have rejected or ignored positivist approaches to evaluation of practice (Rabin 1981; Robinson, Bronson, and Blythe 1988; Saleebey 1979, 1989). A history of social work's approaches to research indicates that the contemporary split between social work researchers and practitioners, which often centers around evaluating practice, is a time-bound problem that stems directly from social work researchers' decisions to adopt positivist beliefs about research, starting most notably in 1949 with the Social Work Research Group. With Heineman Pieper's formulation of the heuristic paradigm, this gap is beginning to close (Heineman Pieper 1981, 1985, 1989; Tyson 1992).

USING THE HEURISTIC PARADIGM TO DESIGN NATURALISTIC CASE EVALUATIONS

The word *heuristic* comes from the Greek word *heuriskein,* which means, to discover or find. Heineman Pieper (1981, 1985, 1989) took the name of the heuristic paradigm from Simon's explication of problem-solving methods that guide scientific research (Simon 1966a, b; Wimsatt 1986). Simon described how people necessarily use sets of assumptions, which he called heuristics, to selectively guide problem-solving activity (Simon 1966b). For example, every model of casework practice—such as task-centered casework or psychosocial casework—is a heuristic. Every procedure for gathering and analyzing data—including experimental design, inferential statistics, and the naturalistic single case study—is also a heuristic. Researchers who adopt the heuristic paradigm hold "that no particular methodology is epistemologically privileged" (Heineman Pieper 1985:6). Instead of relying on methodological criteria for scientific meaningfulness, postpositivist researchers recognize the need for "uncovering the underlying background assumptions supporting the research process in the first place" (Mitroff and Bonoma 1978:247).

Problem Formulation

A problem formulation is a heuristic. Postpositivist philosophers of science such as Simon (1966a, b), Nickles (1987, 1988), Laudan (1978), and Wimsatt (1986) view scientific inquiry as a problem-solving process. In keeping with that view, the heuristic approach to social work research does not advance methodological criteria for scientific problem formulation; rather, it construes problem formulation as a heuristic choice that affects all aspects of the research, and it gives priority to recognizing the biases set up by the problem formulation (Heineman Pieper 1989; Nickles 1988). Any problem formulation necessarily sets up biases because it focuses the researcher on particular variables, to the exclusion of other variables, and it guides the researcher toward some solutions and sets up constraints against arriving at other solutions (Heineman Pieper 1989; Nickles 1988, Wimsatt 1980, 1986). Postpositivist researchers such as Dunn and Mitroff (1981) emphasize that "the enterprise of evaluation is a messy, squishy, or ill-structured problem—that is, a problem whose complexity demands that the researcher take an active part in defining the problem" (as cited in Heineman Pieper 1985:8). Evaluation entails "multiple methodologies, multiple functions, multiple impacts, multiple reporting formats—evaluation is a multiplicity of multiples" (Scriven 1983:257), and the researcher using the heuristic paradigm examines how a possible problem formulation guides the evaluator through the multiple alternatives and toward particular theories, decisions about data collection and data analysis, and then problem solutions.

To the researcher who adopts the heuristic paradigm, the diversity of potential problem formulations represents an advantage in that one way to recognize the biases engendered by any one problem formulation is to consider various ways of formulating the evaluation problem and to examine how the different problem formulations lead to the generation of different data and different solutions to the problem. Drawing from Wimsatt's description of the properties of heuristics, Heineman Pieper describes how "heuristics transform the problem to which they are applied to a different, but related problem. Thus, we must always evaluate the appropriateness of our answers to the original problem'' (1989:11). One way to assess a potential problem formulation is to examine whether the problem as formulated will lead to useful information (Heineman Pieper 1989).

Any evaluation problem contains assumptions about the causal factors that effect change in human systems. Postpositivist researchers construe causation, not as linear, but instead as complex, multifactorial, and interactive (Cronbach 1975; Heineman Pieper 1989; Levins and Lewontin 1985). Child therapists have long recognized that the assessment of the impact of interventions with children is extremely complex because so many variables affect the child, including, for example, the child's natural maturational process, changes within the child's family, and the child's experiences at school (Freud 1965). Complex practice problems and broad treatment goals necessitate an inclusive construal of the change process and concomitantly an unrestrictive approach to formulating evaluation problems. Rather than artificially exclude from study diverse influences on the change process in the belief that they have been controlled for, the heuristic paradigm welcomes complex problems without sacrificing conceptual rigor, because the researcher can address the biases introduced when using a heuristic to make the problem manageable (Heineman Pieper 1989).

The following illustrations of evaluation of practice draw from the treatment of a six-year-old boy, Bobby, whose Italian-American family was well educated and from an upper-middle-class income bracket. (To protect the confidentiality of the patients and families in conformity with statute and the social work code of ethics, I have disguised both identifying information and the specifics of the case processes.) He came for help with a protracted and relentless experience of self-hatred, which was so severe that he had on several occasions expressed a desire to die. His parents and teacher reported that he had fought violently with peers in several contexts including a preschool classroom, an afterschool puppet-making workshop, and a children's soccer league. Bobby's other symptoms included enuresis, and his teacher reported that he was disorganized, easily frustrated, and did not follow directions. The treatment plan for Bobby consisted of individual child psychotherapy and parental counseling for his parents, which included helping Bobby's parents to collaborate with his school in setting up a more supportive classroom environment. To evaluate Bobby's treatment, the researcher using the heuristic paradigm could formulate the evaluation research problem in many ways, such as whether there was improvement in Bobby's symptoms of self-directed rage or whether the practitioner's interventions with Bobby were consistent with the precepts of the practitioner's chosen casework model. Each problem formulation causes the researcher to focus on different aspects of the case and will generate very different information.

Delineating the system to study. Every problem formulation focuses the researcher's attention on a system of variables and their interactions. The researcher, of necessity, simplifies the context—or environment—of that system (Heineman Pieper 1989). Hence, an "asymmetry in simplifications" results from how the researcher draws the environment-system boundary (Wimsatt 1986:300). When formulating problems, the researcher adopting the heuristic paradigm considers "a number of possible environment-system boundaries before carefully selecting one, because this choice will have important consequences" (Heineman Pieper 1989:23). The researcher using the heuristic paradigm considers how drawing the environment-system boundaries confers priority on some information and excludes other information (Heineman Pieper 1981, 1985, 1989; Wimsatt 1980, 1986).

An illustration of the impact of where the environment-system boundary is drawn in evaluating practice is that in most contemporary evaluations of treatment of children, the children have been drawn out of the system used to evaluate the treatments administered to them, and instead evaluators have sought the opinions of adults about the child's progress in treatment (Tyson 1991). In addition to setting up an ethically questionable bias against children, drawing the children out of the system used to evaluate the treatment has resulted in a loss of important information. For example, in a metaanalysis that was unusual in that children's self-report measures were included in some evaluation studies, Casey and Berman (1985) found that children's self-report measures of treatment efficacy showed smaller effect sizes than observer ratings of changes in child behaviors did.

By varying the environment–system boundaries, the researcher who adopts the heuristic paradigm can examine how each delineation of the environment–system boundary rotates the perspective on the problem under investigation and generates different biases (Heineman Pieper 1989; Wimsatt 1980, 1986). Two important initial considerations in drawing the environment-system boundary concern whether the researcher and the practitioner are the same person and how the evaluator will handle the impact of the practitioner on the casework process. Practitioner variables such as competence, experience, and theory preference, as well as unique qualities of the therapist-client relationship, have very powerful influences on the outcome of any treatment (Marziali and Alexander 1991). Although researchers may choose not to focus on those variables, they can recognize that by putting them in the environment, the nature of their effects on the outcome cannot be known. Two types of systems are delineated by the problem formulation in any evaluation of practice: (1) the practitioner chooses the client system to be treated, and (2) the evaluator (who may be the practitioner) chooses the system to use to evaluate the treatment.

The system to be treated. In addition to defining the evaluation research problem (for example, was there improvement in Bobby's symptoms?) an evaluator of practice always defines the client's problem. In this example, the practitioner/evaluator defined Bobby's primary problem as motives for pain that were often expressed in self-directed rage. Heineman Pieper emphasized that positivist evaluation research, in its "preoccupation with simplicity and control," has required that the complex, "ill-structured" problems experienced by clients be distorted so that they fit into the positivists' "misguided definition of scientific rigor" (Heineman Pieper 1985:7). Rather than impose methodological restrictions on how client problems can be formulated, the researcher who uses the heuristic paradigm recognizes that several different ways of formulating a client's problem are possible. To illustrate, when parents ask for help for their child, family therapists commonly "reframe" the problem by defining the problem in terms of the family relationships (Hartman and Laird 1983) and treat the family. On the other hand, child psychoanalysts commonly view the child's behavior as symptomatic of the child's intersystemic conflict and focus on treating the individual child (Glenn 1978). Each delineation of the environment–system boundary results in a very different casework process. For example, a sexually abused young child who has been intimidated into silence by her father will be more likely to disclose the abuse in the context of individual play therapy than if she is asked to discuss her difficulties in her father's presence.

The system used to evaluate the treatment. The evaluator's environment–system boundary delineates the sources of data that the evaluator will use, which can range from therapist and client interactions, to information derived from family members, to other collaterals such as school staff or the caseworker's supervisor. Postpositivist evaluation researchers such as Scriven emphasize that the evaluation researcher has a moral responsibility to take the perspective of all involved in the change process into account, even if all those individuals are not sources of data for a particular evaluation problem (1983:249; see also Parlett 1981). Another consideration in delineating the system used to evaluate the treatment is that therapeutic precepts such as preserving the confidentiality of the treatment may preclude going outside the treatment relationship to obtain evaluative data. In such a case, the naturalistic evaluator would use only data derived from therapeutic interactions with the client to evaluate the treatment, because naturalistic research always preserves the integrity of the treatment.

The practitioner's informed judgment. Whereas the positivist approach to social work research assumed that the practitioner's involvement with clients impaired the practitioner's judgment about treatment efficacy, the heuristic paradigm regards the practitioner's informed judgment as a valuable resource for evaluating practice:

> in contrast to the logical positivist, the heuristic researcher values the informed opinions of those in the trenches, including clients, administrators, and clinicians, as much as he or she values the opinions of researchers. It is supremely irrational to trust social workers with the lives and well-being of clients and then to reason that their conclusions about the service they provide are inherently more biased than the reports of researcher-observers. (Heineman Pieper 1989:25)

The worker's informed judgment is a helpful resource in an evaluation of practice because the worker knows the entire context of the treatment, knows the individual client, can interpret the client's feedback about the accuracy of the worker's communications, and can distinguish what changes are occurring.

Clients as informants in evaluating child treatment. Client opinions can be a rich source of evaluative data, and children often communicate their evaluations of the treatment. The significance of client evaluations of practice cannot be understood apart from the context of the ongoing casework relationship. For example, a three-and-a-half-year-old Afro-American child named Sheila originally came for therapy because her parents were engaged in a protracted custody battle, and she wanted help with her intense, self-directed angry feelings about her parents' conflicts. After four months of therapy, Sheila drew a "fire," told the therapist that her father had recently been very angry, and that his angry feelings felt to her like she had been set on fire. She then showed how a fire engine came quickly and put the fire out. When the social worker asked her "what is the fire engine?" she commented that "the house is me, the fire engine is us." Such a statement could indicate that she feels the therapist is stifling her expressions of anger or, alternatively, that she feels the therapy helps her to protect herself from her angry feelings about her parents' conflicts and treatment of her. Several factors can be taken into consideration in evaluating the significance of Sheila's statements: Sheila was increasingly able to share her deep feelings of anger with the therapist; both the therapist and the therapist's supervisor thought that the therapist had not discouraged

Sheila from sharing her anger; and there were other indicators that Sheila felt the treatment was helpful. All these factors led the therapist to conclude that Sheila's statement meant that Sheila felt the therapy was helping her with the anger generated by the custody battles. This example also illustrates the importance of the therapist's informed judgment in evaluations of practice.

Values and problem formulation. Postpostivist researchers recognize that all research is value laden and that researchers cannot be value free (Bixenstine 1976; Sheinfeld 1978). Scriven describes how the positivist belief that evaluation research could be value free, "often and misleadingly called 'empiricism,' '' has "constricted the growth of evaluation severely" (1983:232). One crucial step in heuristic research is examining how the researcher's values regulate the research (Heineman Pieper 1981, 1985, 1989). Social workers' values influence their role in relation to clients and determine, for example, whether workers are advocates, mediators, or resource providers.

Evaluation approaches that focus only on outcome measures have overlooked the utility of evaluations in which the evaluator compares the intervention with social work values. Drawing from the empowerment model of practice with children (Hegar 1989), a value-based problem an evaluator might address is: did the intervention enact the social work value of child protection? For example, a social worker who interviews an abused child may report the abuse to the Department of Children and Family Services, assiduously gather supporting data, and aggressively try to protect the child. However, despite the worker's best efforts, the child may be returned home to an abusive family that refuses services. In such cases, although social workers may not always accomplish the outcomes they desire, they may be gratified if their evaluation indicates that their actions have upheld social work's values.

Choice of Theory

One of the most important advances in understanding scientific inquiry is the recognition that the positivist belief in theory-free observation is untenable and that "there can be no direct or untainted perceptions because all observation is shaped by theory" (Heineman Pieper 1981:378; see also Hanson 1958; Kuhn 1970; Suppe 1977). Theories invariably include ontological assumptions or assumptions about what is real (Wimsatt 1980, 1986). Theories also include epistemological assumptions about how to know that real. An evaluator of practice necessarily makes at least three choices that set up the evaluator's ontological and epistemological assumptions: (1) the choice of a paradigm or metatheory of research, (2) the choice of a practice theory, and (3) choices about how to collect and analyze data.

The choice of practice theory.   The evaluator's choice of practice theory governs the meanings the evaluator ascribes to the casework data. The precepts of social work practice theories are often so different as to be fundamentally incompatible, and even the so-called "eclectic," "research-based" practice models (O'Hare 1991) represent a theoretical approach that is incompatible with many social work practice models. Every practice theory's ontological assumptions define and regulate what the social worker observes (Heineman Pieper 1981, 1985, 1989; Wimsatt 1986). For example, in understanding the behavioral symptoms of childhood hyperactivity, the social worker oriented toward biological explanations for human behavior makes the ontological assumption that central nervous system tissue is the object of study (Johnson 1988). The social worker who adopts behavioral theories assumes neuromuscular behavior is the object of study and defines hyperactivity as a behavior in response to environmental contingencies (Pinkston et al. 1982). The social worker using intrapsychic humanism, a new psychology and philosophy of mind developed by Martha Heineman Pieper and William Joseph Pieper (1990), focuses on the subjective experience of purposiveness, or motive, as the object of study. According to intrapsychic humanism, hyperactive behaviors are motivated (though not necessarily chosen) by the child in the pursuit of an inner esteem based on a sense of effective purposiveness. The experiences that signify this esteem have been distorted in a dysfunctional way owing to the child's early experiences (Pieper and Pieper 1990; Tyson 1991). Each theory also makes very different assumptions about epistemology (Dean and Fenby 1989), or how to know the ontology under study, and so leads to very different ways of generating data. The behaviorist social worker counts behavioral fluctuations in reaction to the reinforcement schedule (Pinkston et al. 1982). A biologically oriented social worker may draw from the many neurological and neuropsychological tests available (Johnson 1988). A social worker using intrapsychic humanism uses the practitioner's understanding of the client's subjective experience of the therapeutic relationship in order to apprehend the client's intrapsychic motives (Pieper and Pieper 1990).

Different practice theories formulate therapeutic goals differently. The goal of psychodynamic treatment according to Basch is a capacity for self-scrutiny (1980:178). By contrast, the goal of a behavioral treatment is a reduction or increase in targeted behaviors (Schwartz 1983). The goal of structure-building treatment using intrapsychic humanism is the autonomous self-regulation of inner well-being, and that of intrapsychic supportive treatment is the ability for an increasingly stable capacity to forgo self-destructive or self-defeating motives (Pieper and Pieper 1990).

In short, given the same client, proponents of different practice models observe radically different variables, formulate client problems differently, generate different data, define change differently, set different goals, and evaluate their practice according to different standards. When the incompatibility between social work practice models has not been recognized, and the distinction between the assumptions of the research approach and practice precepts has not been made, researchers have conflated the precepts of the practice model with assumptions about the research approach, prescribed the precepts of the practice model as the basis for evaluation research, and criticized practitioners who do not adhere to that practice model for not evaluating their practice (Briar 1979; Fischer 1981; Thyer 1989).

The compatibility between the evaluator's and the practitioner's theories.   One of the most important decisions an evaluator makes is whether or not to use the same social work practice model as the practitioner used, and the researcher who uses the heuristic paradigm addresses the implications of that decision. To illustrate, the practitioner and the evaluator may or may not agree on how to define the client's problem, and the researcher addresses the implications of those different definitions. During the first session Bobby defined his problem by drawing a picture of a dot, saying, "sometimes I feel like a dot," and he stabbed the dot with his pencil. When asked if part of him caused him to feel badly about himself, he said "a lot," and when asked if he wanted help with those feelings, he nodded and said, "yes." In that example, the practitioner targeted Bobby's problem as his feelings of pain caused by his self-directed rage and also focused on Bobby's wish for help with that pain. By contrast, an evaluator using behavioral theory might focus on the frequency of the problem behavior, such as the incidence of Bobby's self-harming gestures. The evaluator and the practitioner who target different aspects of Bobby's problem then view the entire treatment in totally different terms.

If the evaluator uses a practice model that differs from the practitioner's, one consequence is that the evaluator will then explain events in the treatment differently than the practitioner does. To illustrate, Bobby came to a therapy session and described as fact an incident that was obviously greatly exaggerated—in other words, he told the therapist a "whopper." According to some behavioral theories, the practitioner should modify Bobby's whopper-telling behavior to make the therapeutic situation as close to the environment outside the treatment relationship as possible (Kendall and Braswell 1985). From the standpoint of ego psychology, the practitioner should interpret and so confront Bobby's "whopper" in the interest of strengthening his reality-testing ego functions (Lieberman 1979). However, from the standpoint of intrapsychic humanism, the theory used for Bobby's treatment, Bobby's "whopper" could be understood as a reaction to two possible experiences: a loss that he is trying to restitute by making up the "whopper" or an aversive reaction to the pleasure Bobby experienced in wanting to share his experiences. According to intrapsychic humanism, an aversive reaction occurs because in psychopathology, people develop motives to seek unpleasure, of which they may or may not be aware, which compel them to withdraw from or sabotage pleasure (Pieper and Pieper 1990:218–20). A pleasurable experience that gratifies the part of the self that has conscious motives for pleasure simultaneously signifies a loss to the part of the self that has unconscious motives for pain, which then rebounds with increased intensity, manifested in the aversive reaction. The intrapsychic therapist decides whether or not to address Bobby's whopper-telling reaction on the basis of whether or not at that moment the therapist thinks an interpretation will help him to identify his motives for pain and so enhance his motivation for conflict-free self-caretaking. Since the therapist may perceive that Bobby is not ready, at that time, to discern the motives for pain that cause the whopper-telling reaction, although the practitioner using intrapsychic humanism would recognize the "whopper" and its implications, the therapist would not necessarily bring it to his attention. Each practice model prescribes different precepts for how the social worker should respond to Bobby's "whopper" and so will lead to a different evaluation of the intervention conducted.

In addition to examining the compatibility between the evaluator's and the practitioner's practice theories, the researcher who uses the heuristic paradigm examines the compatibility between the evaluator's approach to research and the practice theory. One reason why social work practitioners have found the positivist approaches to evaluation of practice to be largely irrelevant is that the positivists' restrictive epistemology proscribed the study of aspects of reality that are the focus of many practice theories, such as subjective experience or unconscious motives (Heineman Pieper 1981, 1985, 1989). The heuristic paradigm does not restrict the researcher's ontological or epistemological assumptions. For example, the researcher adopting the heuristic paradigm can choose practice theories that focus on variables as diverse as the flickers of communication in the initial phase of the treatment of a severely autistic child, to patterns of relationships among children in a therapy group, to changes in the weight of an obese child. One reason why the heuristic paradigm is a "unifying and comprehensive approach to research" (Heineman Pieper 1989:8) is that it does not proscribe the ontological or epistemological assumptions of any social work practice model.

Choices About Data Collection and Data Analysis

As was emphasized above, the heuristic paradigm is a metatheory of research, not a research method. Two steps in designing heuristic research are choosing from among the many ways of gathering and analyzing data that are currently available, including experimental design and inferential statistics (Heineman Pieper 1981, 1985, 1989). The researcher who uses the heuristic paradigm chooses how to collect and analyze data so as to be consistent with the researcher's ontology and epistemology and to yield useful information for solving the problem. In that way, problems dictate methods, "rather than methods dictating problems" (Parlett 1981: 222; see also Nickles 1987). Heineman Pieper emphasized that

> No specific methods of research can ever correctly claim to produce truth or even to produce the best approximation of truth. The requirement of consistency simply means that the choice of the problem and the method of investigating it should be compatible and consonant with your theory, assumptions, and aims which, concomitantly, should be reasonable in terms of the phenomena you have chosen to study.   (1989:24).

Researchers who adopt the heuristic paradigm explicate the thought processes that guide them in their decisions about data collection and data analysis to help the reader enter into the researcher's frame of reference, look at the data with the benefit of the researcher's informed judgment, and give the reader sufficient information to reflectively agree or disagree (Heineman Pieper 1989).

Data collection.   With regard to naturalistic evaluations of clinical social work practice with children, gathering qualitative data has important advantages. Whereas behaviorist single-case designs structure the client's evaluations of the treatment by using predefined instruments or by counting client behaviors (Berlin 1983; Bloom and Fischer 1982; Hudson 1982), qualitative researchers have traditionally valued helping clients communicate their experiences in the way they prefer (Patton 1980; Ruckdeschel 1985; Sherman 1987), and qualitative data are suited to the diverse ways clients want to communicate their experiences (Ruckdeschel and Farris 1981).

Although some beliefs about gathering and analyzing qualitative data draw from positivist standards for research (Kidder 1981; Strauss and Corbin 1990), some postpositivist researchers have conceptualized alternative standards such as dependability, credibility, and trustworthiness (Lincoln and Guba 1985; Mishler 1986; Reason 1981; Ruckdeschel 1985). Those standards entail making the assumptions that guide the research, the data collected, and the analysis of the data as explicit and available to the reader as possible (Campbell 1975). One of the most important advantages of gathering qualitative data and analyzing it qualitatively that has often been overlooked is that, by definition, qualitative researchers present the reader with "thick descriptions" of the research contexts, the data-gathering techniques, and the data that undergird the researcher's findings (Geertz 1973, citing Ryle, pp. 6ff; LeCompte and Goetz 1982).

Drawing from the positivist tenet that it is possible to gather bias-free data, some approaches to single-case design recommend that practitioners ask clients to record their problem behaviors (Berlin 1983; Bloom and Block 1977; Campbell 1990) and that they use audio tapes or videotapes of the treatment (Nelson 1981, 1985). However, research on experimenter effects has demonstrated that no basis exists for the assumption that such procedures produce distortion-free data (Orne 1964; Webb et al. 1981). As Heineman Pieper has pointed out (1981, 1985, 1989; the paper in this volume), audio tapes and videotapes produce data that are biased in a different way, because they introduce a variable into the treatment situation to which the client invariably reacts, and which thereby alters the treatment process. All data collection strategies are heuristics that give priority to one form of accuracy but sacrifice another, and the researcher using the heuristic paradigm considers which form of accuracy is most important in order to address the problem (see Heineman Pieper's paper in this volume).

An alternative and often overlooked data collection strategy for naturalistic case evaluation is anamnestic process recordings. Although biased by the practitioner's selective recollection of the events, these recordings avoid the biases introduced by audiotape or videotape recordings or other instruments (Heineman Pieper 1985), because they do not introduce any nontherapeutic instruments into the treatment relationship. Further, they have the advantage of providing the reader with an experience-near description of the practitioner's view of the client and the therapeutic process. The process recording should give sufficient detail about the interactions between client and therapist to inform the reader about the client, the nature of the interventions conducted, and the impact of the interventions on the client (Ruckdeschel and Farris 1981, 1982).

Data analysis.   One of the single greatest challenges facing the researcher is the organization and interpretation of data. A naturalistic single-case study may draw from many long and detailed process recordings, and so a great deal of data needs to be interpreted and reduced. One way the evaluator organizes the data is by drawing an environment-system boundary around the time frame from which the data will be selected (Wimsatt 1986). The evaluator can select from time frames that range from within-session interactions, as Hollis did when she conducted her classic qualitative analysis of caseworker communications (Woods and Hollis 1990), to the process over several sessions, or the entire length of the treatment. An illustration of how a temporal environment-system boundary influences evaluation of practice with children is that a child whose prior relationships had caused her to feel very fearful was in treatment for six months before she tasted the snacks the social worker had available for her. The significance of the child's tentative trial of the snacks will not be adequately understood unless the environment-system boundary includes the time span of the full six months in which the child did not even touch the snacks.

An environment-system boundary is drawn also when the evaluator decides the level at which to analyze the data. Positivist approaches to single-case design have assumed that "ideal explanations will always be about smaller and smaller units" (Heineman Pieper 1985:5). By contrast, the scientific realist recognizes that reality is stratified (Bhaskar 1989; Manicas and Secord 1983) and can be conceptualized by using higher and lower levels of organization (Wimsatt 1976, 1980). Accordingly, the heuristic evaluator determines the level (or levels) of analysis to use in approaching the data. Each level of data analysis produces different types of evidence and documentation for the evaluator's conclusions (Scriven 1983:257). For example, the evaluator may want to focus on very specific statements made by the client, or alternatively, to look at larger patterns in the therapeutic relationship, or both. One way to address the biases set up by any one level of analysis is to evaluate the practice by using multiple levels of data analysis (LeVine 1981; Scriven 1983). To illustrate, a researcher may choose to analyze the specific communications of the therapist of a children's group (Costantino, Malgady, and Rogler 1986). Yet, very potent effects of the intervention may be connected to factors at a higher level of organization, such as the therapist's ethnicity and social role in relation to the participants (LeCompte and Goetz 1982). For example, in a group treatment program for minority children, group therapists who are themselves members of minority groups, and who have succeeded despite the obstacles of discrimination, may exert very powerful influences on the children because the children find it easier to identify with members of their own minority group and such leaders help the children to believe they can fulfill their aspirations (Lum 1986).

A Change Index

Rather than assume that they can examine theory-free data, researchers who use the heuristic paradigm can select the theoretical assumptions to incorporate into data analysis by using a change index. The concept of the change index is derived from the "sufficient parameter," first advanced by Levins (1966) and then applied to the social sciences by Wimsatt (1981). The change index is a heuristic defined on a given level of analysis that the researcher generates to index and organize data that is, by definition, at a lower level of abstraction (Wimsatt 1981). The evaluator's change index can be context sensitive and embrace complex, interactive properties of systems. For example, the evaluator can develop the change index based on aspects of the client's problem and treatment goals that signify the problem is being resolved. To illustrate, an intrapsychic practitioner may recognize that a child's chronic fighting with peers represents a core conflict and accordingly formulate one goal of the treatment as helping the child to forgo motives for relationship unpleasure and to pursue motives for pleasurable relationships. Accordingly, that problem formulation and goal can inform one change index used to evaluate treatment progress. To organize some lower level information, a change index generates systematic bias because it is selective and necessarily leaves out other lower level information. As Levins (1966) notes, the researcher who recognizes those biases can then generate multiple change indices with different biases. In naturalistic evaluations of practice, the researcher can generate one or more change indices to focus on aspects of the client's problem, treatment goals, and theoretical assumptions that are particularly relevant to how the evaluator wants to study the change process.

Illustration of generating a change index. As was described above, Bobby's therapist, in concert with Bobby, identified Bobby's self-destructive motives as the top priority problem to be treated. As evaluator of the practice, the practitioner also wanted to ascertain whether that problem improved and so formulated the evaluation problem as whether the goal of helping Bobby control his self-destructive motives was being reached. Soon after the therapy began, the therapist saw that Bobby's most acute episodes of self-destructive self-rage (Pieper and Pieper 1990:212–16) occurred in reaction to losses Bobby experienced, such as getting a below-average grade on a test, having to go out of town to visit relatives when he preferred to stay home, or being bullied by an older child. According to intrapsychic humanism, in intrapsychic treatment, the client will become increasingly able to respond to loss by turning to the therapeutic relationship for help with feelings about the loss, rather than pursue motives for pain in the form of isolated rage against self or conflict with others (Pieper and Pieper 1990). Building on one aspect of the problem formulation, one goal of the treatment, and a tenet of the practice theory, the clinician defined Bobby's response to loss as one change index. Accordingly, the evaluator selected for analysis process recordings of the treatment sessions that occurred following a loss, such as when the bus Bobby took with his parents was delayed and caused them to arrive late for the session. That change index helped the evaluator focus on 35 of the 100 process recordings, and even within those 35, to analyze those interactions that represented the child's responses to loss. The evaluator could then see that Bobby's motives for isolated, self-destructive self-rage in response to loss were gradually accompanied by, and then often subordinated to, motives to experience the support of the caregiving relationship for help with the loss.

For example, in the second month of treatment, when Bobby's bus was delayed and he was late to a session, Bobby reacted with acute self-depreciation and shame. He suggested that he and the therapist play hide and seek, and he tried to hide in the garbage can. The therapist interpreted both that one part of Bobby wondered whether the therapist missed him and had been looking for him, and also that another part of him made him feel like garbage that should be thrown out. In response to that interpretation, Bobby said, "yeah," and he came out from behind the garbage can and asked the therapist if he could have one of the popsicles that he had asked the therapist to have for him as a snack. Eight months later, Bobby responded to a similar loss by initiating the hide-and-seek game, but he hid under the chair where, at his request, the therapist was counting with her eyes closed. The therapist suggested that perhaps he was experiencing both a motive to be close to help himself with the loss but also a feeling that he should hide his feelings about the loss. As Bobby grew increasingly able to respond to loss by sharing the painful, self-raging reactions, he also became more able to pursue his motives for caregetting pleasure in the therapeutic relationship. For example, after eighteen months of treatment when he again missed some treatment time because his family was stuck in traffic, he came in and exclaimed, "I was really looking forward to coming today, too!" Bobby's growing ability to handle loss by turning to the pleasure of the therapeutic relationship, rather than to the soothing provided by his self-rage (Pieper and Pieper 1990), coincided with Bobby's describing, in other moments, more pleasurable relationships with peers and also pursuing motives for pleasurable closeness with the therapist, such as asking for her collaboration in painting a brightly colored picture of a very happy bear and his bear friend at the beach.

Although it would not be necessary to obtain another perspective on Bobby's responses to loss, and it might even be countertherapeutic to do so, the treatment plan for Bobby included the therapist's availability to confer with his parents at their request. After the first year of treatment, Bobby's mother reported that there had been only one incident of suicidal ideation. During the therapist's vacation, the family had to cancel a trip to an amusement park that Bobby had been looking forward to for some time; at the same time, an argument had arisen between Bobby's grandparents that provoked Bobby to tearful remonstrations and a statement that he felt like dying. By the end of the second year of treatment, Bobby's mother spontaneously reported that she was "amazed" when she realized a year had gone by and Bobby had never talked about wanting to die. She said that Bobby's new teacher had been very surprised to learn that in the past Bobby had been combative with peers, because he was one of the top students in the class, related very positively with peers, and some other students had enlisted his help in teaching them spelling.

Like all heuristics, every change index focuses on some information but leaves out other important information. The researcher addresses that bias, most importantly, by recognizing it and its effects on the kinds of conclusions that can be drawn based on the data. More than one change index may be used to round out an evaluation of practice. For example, the therapist noticed in the initial phase of treatment that Bobby experienced intense self-criticism and frustration when he was not able to perform a new activity (such as doing a simple crossword puzzle) up to his expectations. During the initial phase of treatment, at those moments he often became so frustrated that he relinquished his motives to pursue the new activity; for example, he would crumple up the crossword and throw it out in exasperation. Therefore, Bobby's reactions to the experience of learning were used as another change index. As the treatment progressed, Bobby became more able to share his feelings of frustration and worry about his ability when he was learning something new, and he became more able to stably pursue his motives to learn. For example, after one year of treatment, he came in to the session and said, "we're learning cursive," and he practiced the new handwriting with the clinician, clearly feeling he could tolerate his mistakes more comfortably in her presence.

Summary of Guidelines

Are the practitioner and the researcher the same person?
   Problem formulation:

1. delineate the system to be treated and the biases introduced by where the environment-system boundary is drawn
2. delineate the system to be used for evaluation of the treatment and the biases introduced by where the environment-system boundary is drawn

3. consider the assumptions about the therapeutic change process

4. consider the values enacted in the treatment and the evaluation

Choice of practice theory:

1. consider the ontological and epistemological assumptions of the practice model chosen by both the practitioner and the evaluator (who may be the same person); assess the biases introduced by those assumptions

2. consider the compatibility between the evaluator's and the practitioner's practice theories

3. consider the compatibility between the assumptions of the approach to research and the practice theories

Choices about data collection and data analysis:

1. evaluate the bias set up by decisions about data collection and data analysis

2. evaluate the environment-system boundaries drawn around the time frame used in the evaluation and the levels of analysis used to analyze the data

3. develop change indices to analyze the data and evaluate the biases set up by each one

For the last forty years, social work's positivist philosophy of research has unjustifiably depreciated one of the profession's most valuable resources: social workers' naturalistic qualitative evaluations of their practice. The new philosophy of scientific social work research imported into social work by Heineman Pieper, and termed by her the heuristic paradigm, recognizes that the positivist hierarchy of research designs is unwarranted. Heineman Pieper's paper in this volume emphasizes that the potential scientific value of naturalistic qualitative single-case evaluations has been underestimated. The heuristic paradigm encourages social workers to explicate the assumptions that guide their research and to tailor their studies to be relevant to the complex, interactive, and multilayered problems that practitioners face daily. The heuristic paradigm does not restrict the practitioner's or evaluator's choice of practice theories but welcomes the diversity of social work practice models currently available. This paper has used the conceptual foundations of the heuristic paradigm to formulate guidelines for single-case evaluation that can be implemented by researchers and practitioners without introducing any intrusive procedures into the treatment process. The approach described here prizes both the informed judgment of the practitioner and clients' evaluations of the practice, and it helps practitioners to systematically and dependably communicate the scope and richness of their work. Naturalistic case studies based on the heuristic paradigm offer social work a promising way to benefit from each social worker's contributions to developing practice models that are responsive, efficacious, and humane.

REFERENCES

Basch, M. 1980. *Doing Psychotherapy*. New York: Basic Books.

Berlin, S. 1983. Single case evaluation: Another version. *Social Work Research and Abstracts* 19: 3–11.

Bhaskar, R. 1989. *Reclaiming Reality: A Critical Introduction to Contemporary Philosophy*. London: Verso.

Bixenstine, E. 1976. The value-fact antithesis in behavioral science. *Journal of Humanistic Psychology* 16: 35–57.

Bloom, M. and S. Block. 1977. Evaluating one's own effectiveness and efficiency. *Social Work* 22: 130–36.

Bloom, M. and J. Fischer. 1982. *Evaluating Practice: Guidelines for the Accountable Professional*. Englewood Cliffs, N.J.: Prentice Hall.

Briar, S. 1979. Incorporating research into education for clinical practice in social work: Toward a clinical science in social work. In A. Rubin and A. Rosenblatt, eds., *Sourcebook of Research Utilization*. New York: Council on Social Work Education.

Campbell, D. 1975. Degrees of freedom and the case study. *Comparative Political Studies* 8: 178–93.

Campbell, J. 1990. Ability of practitioners to estimate client acceptance of single-subject evaluation procedures. *Social Work* 35: 9–17.

Casey, R. and J. Berman. 1985. The outcome of psychotherapy with children. *Psychological Bulletin* 98: 388–400.

Costantino, G., R. Malgady, and L. Rogler, 1986. Cuento therapy: A culturally sensitive modality for Puerto Rican children. *Journal of Consulting and Clinical Psychology* 54: 639–45.

Cronbach, L. 1975. Beyond the two disciplines of scientific psychology. *American Psychologist* 30: 116–27.

Dean, R. and B. Fenby. 1989. Exploring epistemologies: Social work action as a reflection of philosophical assumptions. *Journal of Social Work Education* 25: 46–54.

Dunn, W. and I. Mitroff. 1981. The obsolescence of evaluation research. *Evaluation and Program Planning* 4: 207–18.

Fischer, J. 1973. Is casework effective? A review. *Social Work* 18: 5–20.

Fischer, J. 1981. The social work revolution. *Social Work* 26: 199–207.

Freud, A. 1965. *Normality and Pathology in Childhood*. New York: International Universities Press.

Geertz, C. 1973. *The Interpretation of Cultures: Selected Essays*. New York: Basic Books.

Glenn, J. 1978. General principles of child analysis. In J. Glenn, ed., *Child Analysis and Therapy*. New York: Jason Aronson.

Glisson, C. and J. Fischer. 1987. Statistical training for social workers. *Journal of Social Work Education* 23: 50–58.

Hanson, N. 1958. *Patterns of Discovery: An Inquiry into the Conceptual Foundations of Science*. Cambridge, England: Cambridge University Press.

Hartman, A. and J. Laird. 1983. *Family-Centered Social Work Practice*. New York: Free Press.

Hegar, R. 1989. Empowerment-based practice with children. *Social Service Review* 63: 372–83.

Heineman (Pieper), M. 1981. The obsolete scientific imperative in social work research. *Social Service Review* 55: 371–96.

Hudson, W. 1982. *The Clinical Measurement Package: A Field Manual*. Homewood, Ill.: Dorsey Press.

Johnson, H. 1988. Drugs, dialogue, or diet: Diagnosing and treating the hyperactive child. *Social Work* 33: 349–55.

Kendall, P. C. and L. Braswell. 1985. *Cognitive-Behavioral Therapy for Impulsive Children*. New York: Guilford Press.

Kidder, L. 1981. Qualitative research and quasi-experimental frameworks. In M. Brewer and B. Collins, eds., *Scientific Inquiry and the Social Sciences: Essays in Honor of Donald Campbell*. San Francisco: Jossey-Bass.

Kuhn, T. S. 1970. *The Structure of Scientific Revolutions 2d ed*. Chicago: University of Chicago Press.

Laudan, L. 1978. *Progress and Its Problems: Towards a Theory of Scientific Growth*. Berkeley: University of California Press.

LeCompte, M. D. and J. P. Goetz. 1982. Problems of reliability and validity in ethnographic research. *Review of Educational Research* 52: 31–60.

LeVine, R. D. 1981. Knowledge and fallibility in anthropological field research. In Brewer and Collins, eds., *Scientific Inquiry and the Social Sciences*. San Francisco: Jossey-Bass.

Levins, R. 1966. The strategy of model-building in population biology. *American Scientist 54:* 421–31.

Levins, R. and R. Lewontin. 1985. *The Dialectical Biologist*. Cambridge, Mass.: Harvard University Press.

Lieberman, F. 1979. *Social Work with Children*. New York: Human Sciences Press.

Lincoln, Y. S. and E. G. Guba. 1985. *Naturalistic Inquiry*. Newbury Park, Calif.: Sage.

Lucente, R. 1987. N = 1: Intensive case study methodology reconsidered. *Journal of Teaching in Social Work* 1: 49–64.

Lum, D. 1986. *Social Work Practice and People of Color*. Monterey, Calif.: Brooks/Cole.

Manicas, P. T. and P. F. Secord. 1983. Implications for psychology of the new philosophy of science. *American Psychologist* 38: 399–413.

Marziali, E. and L. Alexander. 1991. The power of the therapeutic relationship. *American Journal of Orthopsychiatry* 61: 383–91.

Mishler, E. 1986. *Research Interviewing: Context and Narrative*. Cambridge, Mass.: Harvard University Press.

Mitroff, I. and T. Bonoma. 1978. Psychological assumptions, experimentation and real world problems: A critique and an alternate approach to evaluation. *Evaluation Quarterly 2:* 235–60.

Mullen, E. 1985. Methodological dilemmas in social work research. *Social Work Research and Abstracts* 21: 12–20.

Mullen, E. and J. Dumpson. 1976. Concluding note. In E. Mullen and J. Dumpson, eds., *Evaluation of Social Intervention*. San Francisco: Jossey-Bass.

Nelson, J. 1981. Issues in single-subject research for nonbehaviorists. *Social Work Research and Abstracts* 17: 31–37.

Nelson, J. 1985. Verifying the independent variable in single-subject research. *Social Work Research and Abstracts* 21: 3–8.

Nickles, T. 1987. 'Twixt method and madness. In N. J. Nersessian, ed., *The Process of Science*. Dordrecht, Netherlands: Kluwer Academic Publishers.

Nickles, T. 1988. Questioning and problems in philosophy of science: Problem-solving versus directly truth-seeking epistemologies. In M. Meyer, ed., *Questions and Questioning*. New York: Walter de Gruyter.

O'Hare, T. 1991. Integrating research and practice: A framework for implementation. *Social Work* 36: 220–23.

Orcutt, B. 1990. *Science and Inquiry in Social Work Practice*. New York: Columbia University Press.

Orne, M. 1964. Demand characteristics and the concept of quasi-controls. In R. Rosenthal and R. Rosnow, eds, *Artifact in Behavioral Research*. New York: Academic Press.

Parlett, M. 1981. Illuminative evaluation. In P. Reason and J. Rowan, eds., *Human Inquiry: A Source-book of New Paradigm Research*. New York: Wiley.

Patton, M. 1980. *Qualitative Evaluation Methods*. Beverly Hills: Sage.

Pieper, M. Heineman (see also Heineman). 1985. The future of social work research. *Social Work Research and Abstracts* 21: 3–11.

Pieper, M. Heineman. 1989. The heuristic paradigm: A unifying and comprehensive approach to social work research. *Smith College Studies in Social Work* 60: 8–34.

Pieper, M. Heineman and W. J. Pieper. 1990. *Intrapsychic Humanism: An Introduction to a Comprehensive Psychology and Philosophy of Mind*. Chicago: Falcon II Press.

Pinkston, E. M., J. L. Levitt, G. R. Green, N. L. Linsk, and T. L. Rzepnicki. 1982. *Effective Social Work Practice: Advanced Techniques for Behavioral Intervention with Individuals, Families, and Institutional Staff*. San Francisco: Jossey-Bass.

Rabin, C. 1981. The single-case design in family therapy evaluation research. *Family Process* 20: 351–66.

Reason, P. 1981. Issues of validity in new paradigm research. In Reason and Rowan, eds., *Human Inquiry: A Sourcebook for New Paradigm Research*. New York: Wiley.

Reid, W. and A. Smith. 1989 (1981). *Research in Social Work*. New York: Columbia University Press.

Robinson, E. A. R., D. E. Bronson, and B. J. Blythe. 1988. An analysis of the implementation of single-case evaluation by practitioners. *Social Service Review* 62: 285–301.

Rossi, P. and H. Freeman. 1985. *Evaluation: A Systematic Approach*. Beverly Hills: Sage.

Ruckdeschel, R. 1985. Qualitative research as a perspective. *Social Work Research and Abstracts* 21: 17–22.

Ruckdeschel, R. and B. Farris. 1981. Assessing practice: A critical look at the single case design. *Social Casework* 62: 413–19.

Ruckdeschel, R. and B. Farris. 1982. Science: Critical faith or dogmatic ritual? *Social Casework* 63: 272–75.

Saleebey, D. 1979. The tension between research and practice: Assumptions of the experimental paradigm. *Clinical Social Work Journal* 7: 267–84.

Saleebey, D. 1989. The estrangement of knowing and doing: Professions in crisis. *Social Casework* 70: 556–63.

Schwartz, A. 1983. Behavioral principles and approaches. In D. Waldfogel and A. Rosenblatt, eds., *Handbook of Clinical Social Work*. San Francisco: Jossey-Bass.

Scriven, M. 1983. Evaluation ideologies. In G. Madaus, M. Scriven, and D. Stufflebeam, eds., *Evaluation Models: Viewpoint on Educational and Human Services Evaluation*. Boston: Kluwer-Nijhoff.

Scriven, M. 1986. New frontiers of evaluation. *Evaluation Practice* 7: 7–44.

Sheinfeld, S. 1978. The evaluation profession in pursuit of value. *Evaluation and Program Planning* 1: 113–15.

Sherman, E. 1987. Hermeneutics, human science, and social work. *Social Thought* 13: 34–41.

Simon, H. 1966a. Scientific discovery and the psychology of problem solving. In R. Colodny, ed., *Mind and Cosmos*. Pittsburgh: University of Pittsburgh Press.

Simon, H. 1966b. Thinking by computers. In Colodny, ed., *Mind and Cosmos*. Pittsburgh: University of Pittsburgh Press.

Strauss, A. and J. Corbin. 1990. *Basics of Qualitative Research: Grounded Theory Procedures and Techniques*. Newbury Park, Calif.: Sage.

Suppe, F. 1977. Introduction: The search for philosophic understanding of scientific theories. In F. Suppe, ed., *The Structure of Scientific Theories*. Urbana: University of Illinois Press.

Thyer, B. 1989. Response to R. G. Dean and B. L. Fenby. 1989. 'Exploring epistemologies: Social work action as a reflection of philosophical assumptions.' *Journal of Social Work Education* 25: 174–76.

Tripodi, T. 1981. The logic of research design. In R. Grinnell, ed., *Social Work Research and Evaluation*. Itasca, Ill.: Peacock Press.

Tyson, K. 1991. The understanding and treatment of childhood hyperactivity: Old problems and new approaches. *Smith College Studies in Social Work* 61: 133–66.

Tyson, K. 1992. A new approach to relevant and scientific research for practitioners: The heuristic paradigm. *Social Work* 37: 541–56.

Tyson, K. (in press). *New Foundations for Scientific Social and Behavioral Research: The Heuristic Paradigm*. Newbury Park, Calif.: Sage.

Weber, R. and N. Polansky. 1975. Evaluation. In N. Polansky, ed., *Social Work Research*. Chicago: University of Chicago Press. (Original work published 1960.)

Welch, G. J. 1983. Will graduates use single-subject designs to evaluate their casework practice? *Journal of Education for Social Work* 19: 42–47.

Whitaker, G. P. 1974. Who puts the value in evaluation? *Social Science Quarterly* 54: 759–61.

Wimsatt, W. 1976. Reductionism, levels of organization, and the mind-body problem. In G. G. Globus, G. Maxwell, and I. Savodnik, eds., *Consciousness and the Brain: Scientific and Philosophical Strategies*. New York: Plenum.

Wimsatt, W. 1980. Reductionistic research strategies and their biases in the units of selection controversy. In T. Nickles, Ed., *Scientific Discovery: Case Studies*. Dordrecht: Reidel.

Wimsatt, W. 1981. Robustness, reliability, and overdetermination. In Brewer and Collins, eds., *Scientific Inquiry and the Social Sciences*. San Francisco: Jossey-Bass.

Wimsatt, W. 1986. Heuristics and the study of human behavior. In D. W. Fiske and R. A. Schweder, eds., *Metatheory in the Social Sciences*. Chicago: University of Chicago Press.

Witkin, S. 1991. Empirical clinical practice: A critical analysis. *Social Work* 36: 158–63.

Woods, M. and F. Hollis. 1990. *Casework: A psychosocial therapy. 4th ed.* New York: Random House.

GROUNDED THEORY
METHODS

NINE

Hand into Glove: The Grounded Theory Approach and Social Work Practice Research

Jane F. Gilgun

The processes of grounded theory, first articulated by Glaser and Strauss (1967), can be used in the development of knowledge in the three main areas of social work direct practice: assessment, intervention, and evaluation. The theory is also useful for studies of policy and program formulation and implementation. The findings of grounded theory research fit the realities of practice because they are steeped in the natural world, the world of multiple variables and multiple meanings. This is the world of practitioners: complicated, untidy, sometimes confusing, and often intrusive and sometimes assaultive of the consciousness and cognitive and emotional space of those who practice social work. In addition, the processes of doing grounded theory research are similar to the processes of practice. Learning how to do this type of research and the use of findings may feel natural to social work practitioners, like sliding a hand into a well-made glove.

The purpose of this paper is to demonstrate the relevance of grounded theory procedures to the development of practice knowledge. It begins with a discussion of the processes of doing grounded theory research and then shows parallels between processes of grounded theory research and the process of direct practice.

DOING GROUNDED THEORY RESEARCH

Researchers use a grounded theory approach when they want to take a fresh look at phenomena. Their purpose is discovery: of ways to define concepts, of relationships among concepts, and of processes (Bogdan and Biklen 1982; Charmaz 1990; Gilgun, in press, a in press, b; Gilgun, Daly, and Handel 1992; Strauss and Corbin 1990; Taylor and Bogdan 1984). Grounded theorists often say they are looking for patterns.

They usually do a thorough literature review before beginning their research, although some do not. Those who do a prior literature review do so for the same reason any other researcher does a review: to survey the field, develop an understanding of what is known, and identity gaps in knowledge, which may give direction to the research. Reasons not to do a prior review include the concerns that the (1) findings of the research may not relate to the literature reviewed—the process is one of discovery, after all—and that (2) previous work may compromise openness to discovery.

Whether or not researchers do prior reviews, they enter the field with minds as open as possible, attempting to be aware of their own biases and preconceptions. As the research proceeds, they begin to define concepts, see relationships among concepts, and discover patterns. They continually pit their emerging empirical findings against new data. They modify their findings to fit the data. They are therefore continually defining and redefining concepts and relationships among concepts. Data collection and analysis involve a series of comparisons, a process Glaser and Strauss (1967) called *constant comparison,* a term that connotes the continual comparisons done within and across cases. The concepts and hypotheses developed through these processes are inextricably linked to the empirical world, hence the name *grounded theory.* These links are clear in the presentation of findings, where the more abstract concepts and hypotheses are presented in concert with the concrete data that support them. Hence, a typical presentation of findings is the following, taken from a research report on how perpetrators of child sexual abuse see their victims

> Three men denied they saw their victims as objects only. Their words, however, suggest that they did. One man said he looked at his stepdaughter as "other than just an object, but as a pretty girl. I had it in my head that she's not just a girl, but she's mine and always will be mine." Thus he perceived the child both as an object and as property.   (Gilgun and Connor 1989:250)

Another form of qualitative research, analytic induction, presents findings in a similar fashion. This approach also shares many procedures with grounded theory. Analytic induction is, however, a hypothesis-testing method whose goal is to generalize to a population. Researchers using analytic induction enter the field with hypotheses to test, and they modify the hypotheses to fit the cases they encounter. Seeking to disconfirm their hypotheses, they test them on as wide a variety of cases as possible. The variety of cases on which the hypothesis is based becomes an argument for the generality of the findings. As is discussed later, grounded theorists argue, not for this type of generalizability, but for an analytic or pattern-matching type of generalization.

Induction and Deduction

Many grounded theorists, but not all, also seek to link findings to previous research and theory. They begin doing this during the process of defining and refining. Their findings may be totally unexpected, and if they did a literature review before entering the field, the review may become marginal, as mentioned earlier. They link their empirical findings to the conceptual material of the existing literature. This linking not only can help researchers to construct definitions and formulate hypotheses but also is a form of cross-validation. Testing these constructs against new data becomes part of the research process.

Cross-validation through related research and theory strengthens the empirical findings. Linking empirical findings to the literature also raises the level of abstraction of findings. The products of this research are conceptualizations based solidly on empirical data. In grounded theory research, then, the openness of induction is often combined with the more deductive processes of hypotheses testing and cross-validation of empirical findings with existing literature.

Grounded theorists who do not do literature reviews at any point are probably motivated by wanting to do descriptions only. They believe that the findings will speak for themselves. Such a stance is challenged today, based on the criticism that such research does not develop higher order concepts and therefore leaves other researchers with little on which to build. Bulmer (1984) criticized the Chicago School of Sociology for this stance, and Adler and Adler (1987) critiqued some contemporary ethnographies for the same reasons. Ethnographies are detailed descriptions of persons in their social worlds, usually including the points of views of informants.

Theoretical Sampling

Theoretical sampling is the type of sampling Glaser and Strauss (1967) recommended for the development of grounded theory. In theoretical sampling, successive cases are chosen on the basis of the likelihood that they will advance the development of findings. The type of case with which to begin the research depends on the research question. Once the first case study is completed, researchers continue to choose cases similar to the first, until they are finding no new information. The point at which the researcher is not discovering new information is called theoretical saturation. Researchers may stop at this point or may chose a case that differs from the others on one or a few variables. The next case chosen is similar to the previous case. This process continues until the researcher is finding no new information. Again, the research can stop at this point, or a third type of case can be chosen, and the process can continue.

In actuality, researchers may never reach an absolute theoretical saturation. The findings of grounded theory research are forever open ended, open to the possibility that the next case will challenge the existing constructs. Researchers can, however, reach a point where they are reasonably confident that they know enough to warrant selection of new types of cases.

This method of choosing cases might not fit in specific research questions and situations. For example, in a study I did of the decision-making processes of an incest treatment team (Gilgun 1988), I did total sampling; that is, I observed the entire team and interviewed all the professional members of that team. In the process of analyzing the data, the constant comparison within and across cases, the modification of findings, and the other processes described earlier continued to be relevant. In other research situations, some form of stratification, with a random start for each stratum, and then theoretical sampling within strata, could be a feasible design for sampling. This sampling design could be helpful in studies with a potentially large number of cases whose population is known, such as children in foster care. As in any other type of research, whatever sampling strategy is used, it must be consistent with the research question.

Data Collection Methods

Data collection methods are open-ended interviewing, participant observation, and document analysis, both personal documents such as diaries and letters and more impersonal documents such as social service and corrections case records. Many grounded theorists use a combination of methods. Open-ended interviewing is particularly amenable to soliciting the points of view of informants (subjects). Since most grounded theory projects involve open-ended interviewing, the products of grounded theory research are usually characterized by an emphasis on the experience and point of view of informants. Observation and interviewing often bring researchers into the social world of informants. For this reason, grounded theory research is commonly naturalistic, that is, taking place in natural settings where people live their lives. Note taking either during or immediately after interviewing or observing and mechanical recording through audiotapes or videotapes are common methods of capturing data. In some instances, informants themselves provide written data, as, for example, when they write out their own life histories (Bulmer 1984; Taylor and Bogdan 1984).

Data Analysis

Data are almost always words, in the form of field notes, audiotapes, and documents. Some researchers use videotapes and their data also include visual images. Data management is challenging and is done through content analysis. Three major procedures aid content analysis: coding, the use of observer comments and memos, and previous research and theory. Codes are names, and they are developed through familiarity with the data. When concepts and hypotheses begin to emerge, researchers give them names. These names are the codes.

Memos and observer comments are observations researchers make either in field notes or through mechanical recording. Observer comments are interspersed throughout the text and usually contain researchers' subjective comments and brief insights into the situation being researched. Memos are more analytical and appear at the end of a day's field notes. In the memos, researchers reflect upon what they are learning and begin the process of developing concepts and hypotheses out of their data. Previous research and theory also provide concepts and hypotheses that can be used to organize data as well as to add to the content of memos. Bogdan and Biklen (1982) and Gilgun (in press, a) provide extended discussions of data analysis.

Involvement with Informants

The three forms of data collection used in grounded theory can bring the researcher into close contact with informants. Especially in open-ended interviewing, relationships of trust can develop between researchers and informants. This can result in a great deal of rich, detailed information that will enhance findings and advance the development of knowledge.

There are, however, at least two potential pitfalls to the closeness of contact with safeguards for both. One pitfall is the risk of a loss of an analytic stance. The researcher needs to stay in tune with informants while at the same time maintaining a focus on concepts and hypotheses that need to be explored and tested. Sometimes the material informants provide is compelling to the point where researchers are drawn so far into the worlds of informants that they do not explore other aspects of informants' experience. The result is a limited description of phenomena. Researchers can lose the balance between being in tune and furthering comparison and testing.

Informants in subsequent cases do not, however, usually focus on precisely what informants from previous cases have focused on. Therefore, over the course of conducting several case studies, multiple aspects of phenomena can be discovered, and the possible narrowness of findings in one case is corrected by findings in subsequent cases. Some grounded theorists reinterview informants to check out whether newer findings also fit previous cases.

A second possible pitfall related to closeness to data in grounded theory approaches is emotional reactions to research findings. Many researchers investigate sensitive issues, such as treatment of persons in institutions, wife battering, rape, and child abuse. Researchers often have strong personal reactions to such content. This, too, can lead to a loss of analytic stance. Grounded theorists, therefore, in order to maintain an analytic stance, can benefit from working in teams. Discussion with other team members not only can help researchers deal with personal reactions but also can help researchers process their findings, leading to further insight into the world of informants.

Contextualized Findings

The "grounded" nature of grounded theory extends in several directions. Sampling strategies and comparison within and across cases lead to findings that encompass multiple aspects of phenomena. Rarely are concepts defined unidimensionally. The goal of describing multiple aspects of phenomena almost automatically leads to embedding phenomena in their context. Findings become inextricably linked to context. The "thick description" (Geertz 1973) characteristic of grounded theory means that findings are presented multidimensionally and in ways that show the phenomena as part of a context (Gilgun 1992).

Findings as Patterns

The use of theoretical sampling leads to the discovery not only of carefully defined concepts but also of patterns of interactions among concepts. Any particular grounded theory study is likely to yield several patterns related to the same phenomenon. For example, if a researcher were to use grounded theory approaches to study the gender role development of preadolescent daughters and sons of parents where fathers batter mothers, this researcher would probably find several patterns related to gender role development. Many patterns are possible, such as daughters identifying with mothers and viewing themselves and other females as potential victims of men, daughters denying identification with mothers and other females and taking on aggressive qualities they see as part of the male role, and sons identifying with mothers and denying their identification with what they perceive as male roles. If one child in this sample displayed a particular pattern, this would be a finding. If most children in the sample shared a particular pattern, this would not prove the dominance of the pattern. All that can be said is that a certain number of children had one pattern, and a certain number of other children had another pattern. Additional patterns are possible, but they were not discovered in the sample.

The theory produced by grounded theory is, therefore, pattern theory, which Kaplan (1964) described as hypotheses arranged in horizontal relationships to each other. Pattern theory is often context specific and therefore can be at a fairly low level of abstraction. Yet, pattern theory attempts to account for dominant and not so prevalent patterns. Many of the research reports in Gilgun et al, such as Murphy (1992), Daly (1992), and Snyder (1992), exemplify pattern theory. An example of pattern theory is in Snyder, who, in discussing her findings on young adults' construction of love, wrote:

> Individual couples also channel energy in particular directions, resulting in the development of a *love theme:* a public enactment of what the couple "stands for." Love themes are best conceived as central tendencies in couples' interactions and are illustrative of some of the significant ways in which persons have negotiated fit in their relationships. Some of the couples in the current study embodied a particular theme more than others; not every couple could be readily described in terms of a theme.   (59)

Snyder then discusses the love themes she identified:

> *The Caretakers, the Entrepreneurs, the Individualists, and the Rebels. Caretakers, for example, saw "Love as Nuturant, Protective. Love was the solution to partners' complementary needs to parent, be parented." Entrepreneurs, on the other hand, were "Pragmatic, Opportunistic. Love was the solution to partners' mutual desires to get ahead, be successful."*   (59)

Pattern theory is quite different from hierarchical theory, characteristic of much logicodeductive research.

Hierarchical theory is composed of a relatively small number of highly abstract principles from which hypotheses are deduced. These hypotheses are then tested, usually by using highly complex mathematical formulas on a relatively small number of variables that are abstracted from context.

Hierarchical theory, especially when combined with probability theory, seeks to account only for findings thought to be dominant and relegates less dominant patterns to the status of error term or outlier. An example of hierarchical theory is that "the most consistent findings from studies of family structure and socialization are that single parents exert weaker controls and make fewer demands on children than married parents, while stepparents provide less warmth than do original parents" (Thompson, McLanahan, and Curtin 1992:368). Such a statement does not account for parents who do not follow these patterns and does not describe contexts, and the statement implies that one pattern fits all cases. It also invites stereotyping. Contextual variables and individual experiences and perceptions are also not taken into account. Evidence for such a statement is based, not on in-depth studies of parents' experience, but usually on one-time telephone or in-person structured interviews. When such thinking is applied to social work direct practice, individualization is lost and information important to specific contexts may be discounted.

In many senses, therefore, the findings of grounded theory are more idiographic than nomothetic. They are focused on understanding individual situations and testing to see whether findings in one or several situations can illuminate and be relevant to other situations. The process of testing to see if previous findings are relevant to a new situation is called pattern matching, where the findings of one case are tested for their fit on succeeding cases. The findings make no claim to be generalizable to all members of a class. Even the findings of nomothetic research cannot claim that their findings will fit a particular situation. Rubin and Babbie (1989) call this the ecological fallacy. What might be true in general of a group may not be true of individual members of that group (Runyan 1982). Cronbach (1975) pointed out that findings in any type of research situation must be treated as hypotheses when applied to local conditions. The processes of pattern matching results in a type of generalizability called analytic, which is much different from probabilistic generalizations, which are most commonly taught in research and statistics courses.

Logicodeductive research, associated with hierarchical theory, is more nomothetic, meaning the search is for general laws, abstracted from time, place, and specific person. Social work practice benefits from both types of research findings—idiographic and nomothetic. Pattern theory may, however, be more useful to social work practice for three reasons: (1) it matches the specificity of the contexts in which social workers practice, (2) it encourages pattern matching rather than generalizing to situations that have not yet been investigated, and (3) it accounts for as many patterns as can be discovered, encouraging individualizing case situations.

Arguments can be made for the generality of findings as the number of types of cases on which findings are based mount up. Even if findings were based on every known type of instance of a phenomenon, however, the grounded theorist is trained to test that finding on each new situation. That new situation could differ significantly from all other instances on which the findings are based. Because findings of grounded theory research are open ended, they are continually open to modification.

PARALLELS TO THE PROCESSES OF DIRECT PRACTICE

The parallels between processes of conducting grounded theory research and direct practice are multiple. This is important because, as Zimbalist (1983) noted in his history of the single-case evaluation, methods of social work research should fit social work practice, and not the other way around. Practitioner utilization of research findings may be enhanced when research methods match practice contexts (Gilgun 1989). The following are some of these parallels.

- The focus on the perspectives of informants is congruent with the social work injunction to start where the client is.

- The emphasis on viewing informants as inextricably part of a wider context fits with the social work perspective of focus on the client-environment interface.

- The detailed descriptions of individual cases fit with the social work injunction to individualize assessment, treatment, and evaluation to fit specific client situations.

- The combination of induction and deduction in grounded theory approaches parallels how a social worker thinks about cases. Social workers use previous research and theory and practice wisdom while attempting to avoid imposing preconceptions on clients.

- Social workers, like grounded theorists, come to conclusions about situations, after interacting with them and after gathering as much data as possible. The conclusions are tentative, open to modification as new information becomes available.

- Social workers bring hypotheses with them into new situations, but for the purposes of seeing whether they are helpful in the conduct of practice. They are fully ready to modify these hypotheses to fit the situation. This pattern matching parallels pattern matching in grounded theory. This is also a form of constant comparison.

- The data collection methods of interviewing, observation, and document analysis are used by social workers as well as by grounded theorists.

- The use of field notes, observer comments, and memos is similar to process recording and problem-oriented case record keeping.
- Social work direct practice by definition involves direct engagement with clients. Social workers, like grounded theory researchers, strive for empathy, characterized by a balance between being in tune with clients and maintaining an analytic stance. Both the practice of social work and the practice of grounded theory benefit from a team approach.
- Grounded theory research, like social work, often takes place in natural settings; for social workers, in the homes and communities of clients.

The processes of grounded theory approaches and of social work practice, therefore, are complementary. This complementarity bodes well for the future of grounded theory approaches in social work research.

REFERENCES

Adler, P. A. and P. Adler. 1987. The past and future of ethnography. *Journal of Contemporary Ethnography* 16: 4–24.
Bogdan, R. and S. K. Biklen. 1982. *Qualitative Research for Education.* Boston: Allyn and Bacon.
Bulmer, M. 1984. *The Chicago School of Sociology.* Chicago: University of Chicago Press.
Charmaz, K. 1990. "Discovering" chronic illness: Using grounded theory. *Social Science in Medicine* 30: 1161–72.
Cronbach, L. 1975. Beyond the two disciplines of scientific psychology. *American Psychologist* 30: 116–27.
Daly, K. 1992. Parenthood as problematic: Insider interviews with couples seeking to adopt. In J. F. Gilgun, G. Daly, and G. Handel, eds., *Qualitative Methods in Family Research,* pp. 103–25. Newbury Park, Calif.: Sage.
Geertz, C. 1973. *The Interpretation of Culture.* New York: Basic Books.
Gilgun, J. F. 1988. Decision-making in interdisciplinary treatment teams. *Child Abuse and Neglect* 12: 231–39.
Gilgun, J. F. 1989. Starting where the practitioner is: Toward a conceptual framework for social work research. Paper presented at the Symposium on Philosophical Methods at the Annual Program Meeting of the Council on Social Work Education, March 4–7, 1989, Chicago, Ill.
Gilgun, J. F. 1992. Definitions, methods, and methodologies in qualitative family research. In Gilgun, Daly, and Handel, eds., *Qualitative Methods in Family Research,* pp. 22–39. Newbury Park, Calif.: Sage.
Gilgun, J. F. In press, a. Discovery-oriented qualitative research relevant to longitudinal studies of child abuse and neglect. To appear in R. Starr and D. Wolfe, eds., *The Effects of Child Abuse and Neglect: Research Issues.* New York: Plenum.
Gilgun, J. F. In press, b. Hypothesis-generation in social work research. *Journal of Social Service Research.*

Gilgun, J. F. and T. M. Connor. 1989. How perpetrators view child sexual abuse. *Social Work* 34: 249–51.

Gilgun, J. F., G. Daly, and G. Handel, eds. 1992. *Qualitative Methods in Family Research*. Newbury Park, Calif.: Sage.

Glaser, B. and A. L. Strauss. 1967. *The Discovery of Grounded Theory*. New York: Aldine.

Kaplan, A. 1964. *The Conduct of Inquiry*. San Francisco: Chandler.

Murphy, S. O. 1992. Using multiple forms of family data: Identifying patterns and meanings in sibling-infant relationships. In Gilgun, Daly, and Handel, eds., *Qualitative Methods in Family Research*, pp. 146–71. Newbury Park, Calif.: Sage.

Rubin, A. and E. Babbie. 1989. *Research Methods for Social Workers*. Belmont, Calif.: Wadsworth.

Runyan, W. M. 1982. *Life Histories and Psychobiography: Explorations in Theory and Method*. New York: Oxford University Press.

Snyder, S. U. 1992. Interviewing college students about their construction of love. In Gilgun, Daly, and Handel, eds., *Qualitative Methods in Family Research*, pp. 43–65. Newbury Park, Calif.: Sage.

Strauss, A. and J. Corbin. 1990. *Basics of Qualitative Research*. Newbury Park, Calif.: Sage.

Taylor, S. J. and R. Bogdan. 1984. *Introduction to Qualitative Research Methods*. 2d ed. New York: Wiley.

Thomson, E., S. S. McLanahan, and R. B. Curtin. 1992. Family structure, gender, and parental socialization. *Journal of Marriage and the Family* 54: 368–78.

Zimbalist, S. E. 1983. The single-case clinical research design in developmental perspective. *Journal of Education for Social Work* 19: 56–61.

TEN

Understanding the Process of Social Drift Among the Homeless: A Qualitative Analysis

John R. Belcher

Professionals attempting to intervene with the homeless often find that many of them have apparent problems with their psychiatric and functioning status (Belcher and DiBlasio 1990a; Linn, Gelberg, and Leake 1990; Solarz and Bogat 1990). Psychiatric and functioning status are determined by several variables including level of food intake, level of environmental stressors, a person's history of health and mental health problems, and social drift. The pathway people travel as they became homeless also influences psychiatric and functioning status; however, it is seldom considered by more traditional researchers.

Despite the wealth of literature on the homeless (First, Roth, and Arewa 1988; Koegel and Burnam 1988; Rossi and Wright 1987), few studies have examined the process of homelessness, particularly the potential for social drift both as people are becoming homeless and after they have become homeless. The focus of much of the homeless literature has been on singular pathways to homelessness, such as mental illness (Perr 1985), and alcohol abuse (Karno et al. 1987). Traditionally, researchers interview homeless people at a point in time and use the psychosocial behavioral symptoms present as indicative of their pathway into homelessness (Kroll 1986). This approach to research can lead to overestimating the contribution of one variable, such as depression, to the process of homelessness (Belcher and DiBlasio 1990a). In addition, the effects of other variables, such as the environment, are minimized.

METHOD

The present study was conducted over a three-month period in the summer of 1989. The author, along with two colleagues, immersed themselves in the homeless community of Baltimore, Maryland, by familiarizing themselves with homeless providers and in particular a health care facility that served the homeless (Belcher, Scholler-Jaquish, and Drummond 1991). As opposed to a predetermined and selected sample, the respondents gradually emerged from homeless provider facilities. Previous researchers, such as Lincoln and Guba (1985), note that small samples can yield valuable information. Marshall and Rossman (1989) further note that an important contribution of qualitative studies is to appreciate the richness that individual respondents bring to bear on the study.

The researchers did not pose as homeless people. Instead, they presented themselves as a combination of university researchers, volunteers, and concerned participants within the homeless community. Many of the scholars who study the homeless tend to observe the homeless from afar in an effort to remain objective and disinterested scientists (Ryan 1971; Shinn and Weitzman 1990).

To guard against viewing the homeless as simply objects for study, a process of interviewing was developed that fostered open communication with the respondents. Belcher (1988) noted that "the process of observation, negotiation with the respondents, and continuing evaluation of discovered information gradually develops into a research instrument producing consistent data" (225). Flexibility on the part of the researchers was the key to gaining the respondents' trust as well as creating an atmosphere where they would openly discuss their fears and frustrations. Attempts to impose structure, such as arranging specific times for interviews, carrying paper and pencil, and carrying notes from previous interviews, can foster an environment that creates anxiety for many of the respondents. Therefore, the researchers incorporated a reflexive approach into the interview process so that they created an interview environment that was sensitive to the needs of the respondents (Bogdan and Taylor 1984). A reflexive approach demanded that the researchers be able to adapt their styles of interviewing to the needs of the respondent. If the respondent was somewhat disoriented and took a great deal of time in answering questions, the interviewers would invest the additional time as well as phrase their questions more carefully and expand on the content of the question.

The researchers used an eight-step process to interview the respondents. First, open-ended orienting questions, compiled by reviewing the literature, were asked. Second, responses from these questions were recorded after each interview into a case file for each respondent. Third, the files were reviewed by using the constant comparative method developed by Glaser and Strauss (1967). This method involves comparing files on respondents over and over again until the researcher becomes satisfied that all possible themes have emerged from the data. Glaser and Strauss (1967) describe a point when the researcher becomes saturated.

Fourth, themes from this review were noted and a second set of orienting questions was developed based on the common experiences and themes found during the first set of interviews. Fifth, the respondents were found again and interviewed with the second set of orienting questions as a guide. Sixth, responses were recorded in the individual case files and were analyzed by the constant comparative method. Seventh, a set of working hypotheses was developed based on the responses from the first and second set of interviews. Eighth, the working hypotheses were negotiated with the respondents to determine whether the researchers had accurately captured the meanings of the respondents. Finally, a set of working hypotheses was developed based on the negotiations that took place in the eighth step.

The process of interviewing led to a "subtle developing interdependence" (Heron 1981:27), which added structure to the researchers' journey. It was particularly important that the researchers capture a gestalt of the environment and not settle for a single view, which can limit construct validity by overemphasizing the bounding of the domain within prespecified parameters.

Establishing Trustworthiness

A common misconception among traditional researchers is that qualitative research is less rigorous than quantitative methods. However, qualitative researchers attempt to establish trustworthiness or credibility, which is analogous to establishing validity and reliability.

Three major strategies are used for establishing the trustworthiness of the data: prolonged engagement, persistent observation, and triangulation. Prolonged engagement is defined by Lincoln and Guba (1985) as "investment of sufficient time to achieve certain purposes; learning the culture, testing for misinformation introduced by distortions either of the self or of the respondents, and building truths" (301). A system of reference points and community informants was established that helped the researchers keep track of the respondents. This process also helped the researchers determine when information provided by the respondents was distorted by the respondent's own feeling of disconnectedness and lack of orientation.

Prolonged engagement led to the researchers' realization that many of the homeless respondents saw themselves as victims and were often discards from plant closings and company restructurings or were discards because they suffered from chronic health problems. The respondents talked about once being actively involved in mainstream society, but an event or their health usually precipitated their losing their place in mainstream society. The majority of the homeless respondents had work histories; however, they also had marginal educations and an extensive history of substance abuse. In fact, the majority of the homeless respondents were in need of rehabilitation that amounted to more than a couple days of detoxification. Particularly noteworthy was that the treatment facilities appeared to have ignored the need for employment training. The realization that many of the homeless respondents were victims led to a dilemma best described by Thorne (1979): "Naturalistic researchers must often struggle with personally painful questions of whether to throw in the towel on doing research and give themselves entirely to helping, or to remain in the field as a chronicler of difficulties" (74). In spite of the daily tragedy of the respondents, the researchers made the painful decision to continue the research.

Over time the researchers found themselves becoming overwhelmed by the plight of their respondents; however, persistent observation helped to provide a framework for the journey and forced the researchers to continue to focus on documenting discoveries. The eight steps already outlined were used to develop the working hypotheses, which relied on the use of persistent observation. This process acted as a reminder to the qualitative researcher that it was important to record a daily observation that yielded a holistic view of the respondents.

The most important part of establishing trustworthiness is the strategy of triangulation. Belcher (1988b) notes "this activity entailed the development of multiple sources of data collection, which were used to verify information received from the respondents" (227). The process of triangulation helps to ensure that all the information fits together by ensuring that any inconsistencies in the data were cross-checked. For example, if respondents maintained that they were thrown out of a shelter, the researchers would verify this information with the shelter operators.

Together the activities of prolonged engagement, persistent observation, and triangulation helped to ensure that the data were credible and that the working hypotheses accurately described the process of homelessness in Baltimore.

FINDINGS

Three phases of homelessness emerged and are described as follows:

Phase 1: This phase consists of individuals who live below the poverty line. Their connection to a home is tenuous and may be episodic as they move in and out of intense poverty. When they do lose their homes, they often

TABLE 10.1

Phases of Homelessness by Sample Characteristics

	Phases of Homelessness					
	First (n = 18)		Second (n = 10)		Third (N = 12)	
	Women	*Men*	*Women*	*Men*	*Women*	*Men*
Gender	7	11	1	9		12
Race						
Black	6	8	1	4		5
White	1	3		5		7
Education						
Less than high school	7	7	1	4		9
High school graduate		4		5		3
Work history						
Never worked	7	7	1	2		7
Worked full or part time		4		7		5
Currently employed (day labor)		2				
Alcohol/drug abuse						
Currently abusing	3	2	1	9		12
Not currently abusing	4	9				
House status						
Live with family of origin	2	2				
Sleep in shelters or missions		2		9		12
Live with a variety of people		7				
Live in AFDC-supported housing	5		1	9		
Income						
AFDC	7		1			
Disability income				2		2
Food stamps only				5		3
Day labor income				2		4
No income				2		12
Mental illness history						
None	2	9	1	6		8
Some treatment	5	2		3		4
Social network						
Multiple relationship	7	6				
Limited relationships		5	1	9		
No relationships						12
Mean ages						
First phase = 26.4						
Second phase = 34.9						
Third phase = 43.2						

move in with friends or family. They do not usually consider themselves homeless. They tend to have connections to service providers and have a social network that helps them to negotiate the complex systems designed to aid the homeless. Anxiety and fear are common, and while substance abuse may be present it is generally not disabling.

Phase 2: This phase consists of individuals who have usually been homeless for nine months or less. They still identify themselves with the mainstream of their communities rather than with other homeless individuals. Substance abuse was more common in the second group and their social relationships were beginning to deteriorate.

Phase 3: This phase consists of individuals who have been homeless for longer periods of time (usually over a year and sometimes for many years). They accept their life experiences as normative, are easily and clearly identifiable as homeless, are extremely suspicious of interacting with members of the mainstream society, and are generally distanced from social networks and mainstream society.

Table 10.1 provides further information about the respondents in these three phases.

First Phase

The mean age of this group was 26.4, and there were eleven men and seven women with fourteen blacks and four whites. Respondents in the first phase were reasonably healthy, thirteen of the eighteen respondents not currently abusing substances and eleven of the eighteen respondents reporting no history of treatment for mental illness. Interestingly, the majority of the respondents (fourteen) had less than a high school education and fourteen had never worked. All these respondents had an active social network, which was defined as more than three relationships.

One of the more important characteristics of this group was that the men were all marginally housed. They were unable to afford a place of their own to live, and the use of shared housing made it more likely they would be evicted. Five of seven of the women did rent their own apartment. In spite of the fact that many of the respondents in the first phase were marginally housed they still identified themselves with the mainstream of their communities. In fact, several respondents noted that it was "normal" to live with others as opposed to renting one's own place. This interpretation of reality apparently resulted from the fact that intense poverty was defined differently by the respondents, who viewed it as normal, than by the researchers, who defined it as representing "marginal homelessness."

Second Phase

The mean age of these respondents was 34.9 with nine men and one woman and five blacks and five whites. Nine of the respondents lived in shelters or missions and only one respondent was a renter. The social networks of the second-phase respondents were deteriorated more than those of the first-phase respondents, the majority (nine) of the second-phase respondents having only limited relationships. Most interesting was that all ten of the respondents abused alcohol or drugs, whereas in the first phase fewer than half of the respondents abused substances.

Respondents in the second phase noted that they were different than the norm and that they were in fact homeless. They also noted that their interactions with family and friends became more strained as they entered the shelters. Particularly noteworthy was that all ten respondents referred to a process of drift. They pointed out that they began to lose things: a relationship, their health, or a living arrangement.

Third Phase

As compared with the respondents in the first two phases, respondents in the third phase talked about losing hope. One respondent noted: "There is a line you cross and when you cross that line, its all over. The streets swallow you up and you lose your identity." This concept was checked out with the other respondents in the third phase. They all talked about becoming so tired and so focused on surviving on the street that the rest of the world became meaningless.

This phase contained all men, probably because those women with children could obtain Aid for Dependent Children (AFDC) and avoid phase three; moreover, some single women apparently found ways of avoiding phase three, such as exchanging sexual favors for housing. All the respondents abused alcohol or drugs, lived in shelters, had no relationships, and had no income.

Respondents in this phase talked about once trying to stay "on top" (apparently meaning an avoidance of homelessness and the streets); however, it became apparent to the researchers that all the respondents in this phase were far more socially and psychiatrically decompensated than the respondents in the first two phases.

The second and third phases of homelessness are far different than the norms of intense poverty in which the respondents lived their lives. The first phase of homelessness probably falls within the norm of poverty prevalent in the city of Baltimore. Perhaps the researchers, who were middle class, viewed the first phase as a phase of homelessness because living with family or friends is not a norm for the middle class. If a type of homelessness or pervasive disconnectedness is in fact a norm for many in poverty, then the gap between the poor and nonpoor is wider than many researchers suspect or are to willing to admit. Interestingly, the federal government has chosen to assume that homelessness is a temporary phenomenon that may not merit serious consideration by policymakers (Belcher and DiBlasio 1990b). The finding that at least the first phase of homelessness is normal for some people in poverty should prompt the federal government to reconsider the widening gap between the rich and the poor.

Drift from phase to phase was accompanied by an increase in substance abuse, loss of relationships, loss of income, and loss of hope. Separating out whether substance abuse led to drift and accompanying losses is difficult because substance abuse may also be influenced by social drift.

The phase concept of homelessness supports increased efforts to prevent homelessness. Once people enter phases two and three it would appear that, because of their increased distance from normative society, interventions designed to help them escape homelessness and return to normative society will be difficult. Future research needs to explore the higher rate of apparent social drift among men as compared with women. It would appear that the lack of consistent welfare benefits available to men is a factor that should be explored (Hopper 1990). While significant social change is necessary to prevent homelessness on a permanent basis (Belcher and DiBlasio 1990b), there may be strategies to temporarily prevent homelessness, such as expanding welfare entitlements to include able-bodied men.

References

Belcher, J. R. 1988. Exploring the struggles of homeless mentally ill persons: A holistic approach to research. *Case Analysis* 2: 221–39.

Belcher, J. R., A. Scholler-Jaquish, and M. Drummond. 1991. Stages of homelessness: A conceptual model of social workers in health care. *Health and Social Work* 16: 87–93.

Belcher, J. R. and F. A. DiBlasio. 1990. The needs of depressed homeless persons: Designing appropriate services. *Community Mental Health Journal* 26: 255–66.

Bogdan, R. S. and S. J. Taylor. 1984 *Introduction to Qualitative Research Methods: The Search for Meanings*. New York: Wiley.

First, R. J., D. Roth, and D. D. Arewa. 1988. Homelessness: Understanding the dimensions of the problem of minorities. *Social Work* 33: 120–24.

Glaser, B. and A. Strauss. 1967. *The Discovery of Grounded Theory*. Chicago: Aldine.

Heron, J. 1981. Philosophical basis for a new paradigm. In R. Reason and J. Rowan, eds., *Human Inquiry: A Sourcebook of New Paradigm Research*. New York: Wiley.

Hopper, K. 1990. Public shelter as a "hybrid institution": Homeless men in historical perspective. *Journal of Social Issues* 46: 13–31.

Karno, M., R. L. Brunam, A. Melonie, J. I. Escobar, D. Timbers, F. Santana, and J. Boyd. 1987. Lifetime prevalence of specific psychiatric disorders among Mexican–Americans and non-Hispanic whites in Los Angeles. *Archives of General Psychiatry* 44: 695–709.

Koegel, P. and A. Burnam. 1988. Alcoholism among homeless adults in the inner city of Los Angeles. *Archives of General Psychiatry* 45: 1011–18.

Kroll, J. 1986. A survey of homeless adults in urban emergency shelters. *Hospital and Community Psychiatry* 37: 283–86.

Lincoln, Y. S. and E. G. Guba. 1985. *Naturalistic Inquiry*. Newbury Park, Calif.: Sage.

Linn, L. S., L. Gelberg, and B. Leake. 1990. Substance abuse and mental health status of homeless and domiciled low-income users of a medical clinic. *Hospital and Community Psychiatry* 41: 306–10.

Marshall, C. and G. B. Rossman. 1989. *Designing Qualitative Research*. Newbury Park, Calif.: Sage.

Peer, I. N. 1985. The malignant neglect of the mentally ill street people. *American Journal of Psychiatry* 142: 883–86.

Rossi, P. H. and J. D. Wright. 1987. The determinants of homelessness. *Health Affairs* 19–32.

Ryan, W. 1971. *Blaming the Victims*. New York: Vintage.

Shinn, M. and B. C. Weitzman. 1990. Research on homelessness: An introduction. *Journal of Social Issues* 46: 1–11.

Solarz, A. and G. A. Bogat. 1990. When social support fails: The homeless. *Journal of Community Psychology* 8: 79–96.

Thorne, B. 1979. Political activist as participant observer: Conflicts and commitment in a study of the draft resistance movement of the 1960s. *Symbolic Interaction* 2: 73.

ELEVEN

Collaboration Between Social Workers and Physicians: An Emerging Typology

Terry Mizrahi
Julie S. Abramson

The current health care scene is characterized by changing demographics and by major efforts to contain costs, most recently through shifts to managed care and by significant modifications to the reimbursement structure (diagnosis-related groups—DRGs) for hospital and physician care. Government regulation has influenced the practice of physicians and curtailed physician autonomy to an extent previously unknown. While social workers traditionally have functioned as agency based rather than as autonomous practitioners, they, too, have been affected by increased regulatory scrutiny of their practice, particularly in hospitals.

Currently in hospitals, social work discharge planners perform an increasingly valued function that can affect hospital and physician revenues. As a result, physicians are more dependent on social work discharge planners to arrange timely discharges for increasing numbers of elderly and chronically ill patients with complicated social needs (Caputi and Heiss 1984; Jansson and Simmons 1985/86; Mizrahi 1988). As the care of these patients becomes more complex, effective and well-coordinated collaboration among their caregivers is critical. Current regulatory, demographic, and disease factors are likely affecting physician/social worker collaboration. However, the nature and meaning of these changing relationships for both disciplines remain largely unexplored.

Our qualitative study in progress examines the process and outcome of actual collaboration between physicians and social workers. Its overall objectives are to:

1. discover patterns of collaborative practice between social workers and physicians

2. identify the structural and interactional factors that contribute to positive and negative collaborative experiences

3. compare generalized perspectives on collaboration with specific (self-reported) collaborative behavior

4. ascertain social worker and physician perceptions of the social work role and function

5. develop a set of research-based practice principles and models for use in social work and medical education

In this paper, we discuss the process used to develop a typology that characterizes physicians and social workers in relation to their collaborative perspectives. Using grounded theory methodology, we developed the typology as part of a process of "discovering theory" through identifying underlying uniformities in our original set of categories and properties (Charmaz 1990; Glaser and Strauss 1967; Strauss and Corbin 1990). A brief overview of the whole typology is provided with illustrations of traditional, transitional, and transformational physician and social work perspectives. The intellectual underpinnings of the typology are explored as are those points in the process of the study that were critical to the development of the typology. Finally, we discuss the complexities and limitations of the still-evolving typology and identify its potential use in future data analysis.

THE SETTINGS AND THE SUBJECTS

We attempted to achieve a balance of breadth and depth in the sample. It was large enough to provide comparisons within and across groups of subjects (M.D.s and social workers), make some limited generalizations, and suggest typical patterns within the settings studied. At the same time, the sample was small enough to allow us to probe deeply and begin to understand the context and meaning of the respondents' reported perceptions and experiences.

Interviews were conducted on a nonrandom sample of fifty-one physicians and fifty-four social workers in twelve hospitals—four in the New York City area, five in the Albany, N.Y., area and three in Western Massachusetts. The hospitals were selected for diverse size and locations.

They were in urban, suburban, and small-town settings and were divided among medical-school-affiliated teaching hospitals, community-based teaching hospitals, and nonteaching hospitals. Three were considered large (600+ beds), four were medium (350–600 beds), and five were small (fewer than 350 beds).

The sample comprised social workers and physicians in internal medicine and surgery and related subspecialties, so as to study collaboration with the largest and most influential branches of medicine. Social workers were selected first from those with in-patient caseloads drawn from internal medicine, surgery, and related subspecialties. Where social work departments had only a few members on relevant services, all participated in the study while significant percentages participated in the larger departments. The sample included fifty-four social workers, the great majority of whom had an M.S.W.; nine were B.A. or B.S.W. social workers from Albany area or Western Massachusetts hospitals.

The physician sample was obtained by having social workers select an in-patient case where they had intensive and extensive collaboration with a physician; we then asked the physician they identified in that case to participate in the study. Of a possible sample of fifty-four physicians, three refused to participate. Therefore, the sample consisted of fifty-one pairs of social worker/physician collaborators.

To achieve a mix of physicians, social workers with more than one appropriate case were guided to select cases of underrepresented physician groups such as house staff (interns and resident physicians), surgeons, or subspecialties where structured teams are common (e.g., oncology, nephrology, rehabilitation medicine). The physicians were divided by specialty as follows: two in rehabilitation medicine, two family practitioners, ten surgeons, and thirty-one internists; six house staff participated (five in internal medicine and one in surgery).

The question of bias in the physician sample and the "truthfulness" of responses—especially of the physicians—can be raised. Because the social workers selected the physicians in the sample through selecting the case, it is possible that a selection bias existed toward those with whom collaboration was positive. In discussion with the social workers regarding selection of cases, we both concluded that case complexity rather than quality of collaboration was the major factor in selecting cases and thus the physicians. The cases were so memorable that neither busy social workers nor physicians had any difficulty recalling details without benefit of the medical record. Conscious bias or distortion on the part of physicians may have been mitigated by the fact that they knew we had already received information about them, their relationship, and performance from the social worker. Moreover, several cases where the collaboration was characterized as negative by one or both respondents were in fact presented, and both groups discussed negative collaborative experiences.

Nevertheless, we must assume that since all subjects knew we were social work professors, this may have distorted their responses to us. Some may have omitted or minimized negative feelings or interactions, as evidenced by the large number of physicians who expressed their view that social workers be treated as equals. The physicians may not have wanted to offend us, and the social workers may have wanted to impress us.

We personally interviewed sixty-eight of the one hundred and four subjects. The other interviews were conducted by four interviewers we hired and trained. Training included reviewing and discussing taped interviews and accompanying one of us to observe an interview where possible. The interviewers' comments on the substance and quality of the interview as well as on the process of interviewing became an integral part of data collection and date analysis.

THE INTERVIEW SCHEDULE

In developing the interview schedule, we drew on many sources: (1) our already developed conceptual framework (e.g., questions on team and other structured opportunities for interaction, those about personal relationships with the other discipline); (2) our own experiences (e.g., questions about the discussion of psychosocial issues); (3) the literature (e.g., social work role); (4) an integration of the literature and our experiences (e.g., the structure of medical and social work hierarchies, the status of social work in the hospital, responsibility and authority for patient management decision making); and finally, (5) a combination of all the above (e.g., the presumed factors contributing to positive and negative collaboration).

The interview took from one to one and one-half hours and was divided into four sections; all were taped and transcribed. The first section of the questionnaire provided demographic and historic information about: the subject's background, current and past experiences with collaboration, current and past professional and personal experiences with the other profession. These variables provided a context for understanding the patterns of collaboration that emerged. In particular, past experiences with the other profession in other settings or on other services are crucial in shaping current perspectives on collaboration; therefore, respondents were asked to make comparisons of the current setting with past settings on several items.

Collaboration was examined in the second section by using an actual case shared by a physician and a social worker. By using the case as a control, comparisons between the collaborative views of the respondents were based in a common reality. Perceptions were sought with respect to the psychosocial aspects of the case and related interventions by the social worker. Data about case outcome were also obtained. Finally, information about satisfaction with the outcome and with the collaborator, as well as comparisons with other cases and collaborators, was collected.

Respondents were asked in the third section to discuss their most positive and negative collaborative experience with the other profession. These data provided information about approximately 200 additional collaborators and cases. We first asked respondents to briefly describe the case and the reasons for its choice as most positive or negative. We then asked them to select those items from a checklist of collaborative behaviors that best reflected the reasons why the collaborative experience had been so positive or negative. The checklist consisted of preset categories that we had developed to identify factors that contribute to positive and negative collaborative interaction.

In both the shared case and in the positive and negative case descriptions, we deliberately skewed case selection toward atypical cases to obtain richer data regarding collaboration. These cases were not expected to reflect normative collaborative experiences. Rather, we assumed that cases involving extensive interaction, complex decision making, or strong feelings regarding the case or collaborator are highly influential in shaping interprofessional perspectives. By using extreme examples, we felt we would be better able to tease out the most salient features and dynamics of collaboration.

The final section of the interview schedule asked the subjects to discuss their general collaborative strategies and to provide hypothetical advice to both social workers and physicians about the ingredients for successful collaboration. They were asked to compare their current and past points of view and experiences and compared themselves with others in their profession. In this section, we explored their conception of collaboration and gained an understanding of how they would teach it.

THE PROCESS OF DISCOVERY: THE EVOLUTION OF A TYPOLOGY

Application of Grounded Theory

The methodology of grounded theory assumes that data collection and analysis will be tightly interwoven processes and must occur alternatively because preliminary analysis directs the amount and type of further sampling (Strauss and Corbin 1990). Our study selected a modified version of this approach in the construction of our interview schedule, in the use of informants and comparative settings, and in the data collection and analysis of preliminary interviews. As a result of initial coding efforts, we: (1) added and modified questions, (2) directed our additional sampling to less represented groups, (3) began to record impressions and themes, and (4) improved our own and the other interviewers' techniques.

The first step in data analysis was to devise a strategy to convert the mass of qualitative data into a systematic schema for examining its meaning, discovering themes and patterns, and making connections among concepts. Given the limited relevant theory from other research to guide the development of categories for coding, we used the constant comparative method proposed by Glaser and Strauss (1967) both to develop codes for specific variables and to gain understanding of broader conceptual issues and themes. The constant comparative method is a process of developing categories, concepts, and broader themes or theory inductively from the data and testing them out at each step by returning to the data to evaluate their fit and appropriateness. Our use of this methodology (elaborated on in Abramson and Mizrahi, in press) was augmented by other approaches suggested by Glaser and Strauss as well as by other qualitative researchers (Lofland 1971; Miles and Huberman 1984; Strauss 1987; Strauss and Corbin 1990; Waitzkin 1990).

Initially, we reviewed a sample of ten transcripts, scrutinizing the responses for each series of related questions to produce provisional concepts that fitted the data. In the mode of open coding suggested by grounded theory (Strauss 1987), the essential meaning of each response and related responses was compared with those already reviewed until the properties or characteristics of the concept became apparent and saturation was reached and no new ideas were emerging.

We then tried to put the data derived through open coding back together in new ways by making connections between and among categories; this process is identified in grounded theory as axial coding (Strauss and Corbin 1990). Through this approach, we identified certain concepts such as the focus of case collaboration or the levels of complexity of a particular case; these were then incorporated into codes for use in analysis. None of these questions was directly posed; rather they were derived and extracted from the data as a way of capturing the essence of, as well as indexing, the collaboration. We continued to test the utility and relevance of these and other codes by applying them to additional transcripts. In the process of developing our codebook, we reviewed approximately one third of the transcripts.

The Emerging Typology

Our process of "discovering" theory or developing a smaller set of higher level concepts (Glaser and Strauss 1967) has led us to identify a typology of physician/social work collaborators and collaboration. Through immersion in the data, it became clear that physicians could be typed along a continuum that reflected their collaborative stance; we labeled their position on the continuum as traditional, transitional, or transformational. We primarily based these characterizations on physicians' attitudes toward control over patient care decision making and the breadth of their definition of the social work role in conjunction with their degree of emphasis on psychosocial issues. Other dimensions of the typology were developed subsequently.

Traditional, Transitional, and Transformational Physicians

Traditional physician collaborators were those who maintained physician dominance over contacts with other professionals, who had little recognition of or interest in psychosocial issues, and who reluctantly accepted social workers as necessary agents for obtaining concrete services required to discharge patients. We found that traditional physicians emphasized their control over care of patients and were resentful of regulatory intrusions into their autonomy. They were willing, at times, to grant autonomy to social workers in those areas where they had less interest.

For example, one physician defined the social work role narrowly and devalued its complexity: "the principal interaction I have (with social workers) is usually about placement out of the hospital. I don't see that as complex; it can be challenging in a sense of a limited number of facilities to choose from, but I don't necessarily think it takes the kind of training that I perceive an M.S.W. to have." Another indicated unhappiness with the independence of the social worker in making discharge plans for his patients. "It may mean that a social worker suggests something to a patient that ends up becoming a problem or inappropriate. . . . I know the patient and I have some history and *I* would know if it is inappropriate."

One physician expressed lack of interest in psychosocial issues. "If somebody comes in with a broken leg, whether they're the straightest arrow in the world or a looney tune, I still have to take care of them. So that's why I don't determine my cases by what somebody's psychological makeup is."

Transitional physicians, while seeing themselves as team leaders, recognized the contributions of others and even delegated aspects of decision making. They acknowledged the importance of psychosocial issues for patient care and often appreciated the assistance provided to them by social workers in the management of their patients, particularly in relation to discharge planning. In describing the social worker's importance to him, one physician said "My time is at a premium . . . so when it comes to arranging placement, it is my feeling that the social worker plays the primary role. . . . Legal issues make the social worker's role even more important to the physician." Another noted that "decision making needs collaboration. The arrangements are taken care of by the social worker while I have the medical information imperative for placement decisions." One physician stated that he depends on the assessment of the social worker to "help me out to explore what the possibilities are after the trauma." A physician who valued the team but saw himself clearly as team leader said "the physician runs the team meeting, tries to gather the reports (from other professionals), pull them together and generate a plan of action. . . . I'm the one legally responsible for the patient."

Transformational physicians shared patient care responsibilities, including those related to psychosocial issues, fully with other professionals. They perceived themselves as interdependent in decision making and were egalitarian in collaborative interactions. These physicians used social workers for a broad range of psychosocial tasks, frequently recognizing counseling elements in various social work activities. Occasionally, they identified the social work contribution to patient management as even greater than their own. In the following quotes, note the use of the pronoun *we*.

When identifying the coordinator of the case, a physician said "From the point of view of the family problems, the social worker was the coordinator. . . . At various other points, I was." Regarding the team, another said "We all collaborated together with the same goals, and it worked in such a way that we complemented each other." Still another clearly valued the assessment of the social worker and shared responsibility for patient care with her. "She was very helpful to me in trying to figure out where the parents were at and in figuring out how we could best approach them. . . . I relied a lot on her judgment. . . . We would often sit down or call each other to talk about how we should handle something. . . . We'd come up with a strategy ahead of time. . . . I think she directed that." One physician gave great importance to understanding the psychosocial impact of illness. "You begin to get a good understanding of how the disability affects their (the patients') lives and it becomes much more a real thing. . . . So I think I've matured in my way of perceiving the patient, and, hence, my relationship with the social worker has improved considerably." Another physician described his most positive relationship with a social worker. "In the earlier years here, there was a social worker who would talk about psychosocial issues with me. I miss that now, and I think that our discussions helped both of us take better care of our patients than usual."

Traditional, Transitional, and Transformational Social Workers

Initially, we were unclear about whether this continuum applied equally to social workers, but on returning to the data, we found that collaborative characteristics of social workers could also be classified as traditional, transitional, or transformational. Although dimensions of the typology were defined somewhat differently than for physicians, social workers also could be described developmentally along the continuum in relation to attitudes toward professional control over decision making, the importance of psychosocial issues, and the breadth of their definition of the social work role.

Traditional social workers accepted physician control of patient care and based social work interventions on physician definition of the problem(s). They gave priority to the administrative side of discharge planning rather than to patient or family psychosocial needs. They often recognized but rarely addressed psychosocial issues; for some social workers, this led to frustration and feelings of burnout. Traditional social workers functioned independently in those areas that did not involve the physician.

One traditional social worker commented on her relationship with doctors: "I always try to ask them what they think, what is their plan. I always throw the ball in their court to let them feel they're directing the case." Another said "I tend to listen to these physicians when they're giving me these orders. . . . I'll kind of agree with them. . . . It's hard at times because I haven't really completed my assessment, so I go by what the doctor's telling me." In describing her role, one social worker said "The focus is discharge planning. . . . With the DRGs, it's a real emergency . . . knowing who the patients are right away, what help they're going to need . . . you get in there quick." Similarly, another noted "I think with medical social work, you're forcing people to make decisions in situations where they aren't willing or able or ready to do that so that's not a good clinical situation."

Transitional social workers also accepted the physician's primary responsibility for decision making but provided consultation to the doctor and often attempted to influence the outcome through their assessments of patient/family circumstances. They frequently presented themselves as resources for physicians by arranging a timely discharge or by facilitating the physician's work with patients and families. The transitional social worker addressed the psychosocial needs of patients and families but often did not integrate counseling services with provision of concrete services, at times devaluing the latter. This most often occurred in discharge planning where social workers saw themselves as reluctantly responding to administrative imperatives instead of doing preferred tasks such as counseling. Transitional social workers were similar to traditional social workers in practicing independently in those areas where authority was delegated. However, they gave greater value to professional autonomy; in fact, they sometimes consciously avoided or circumvented the physician in order to "do their jobs."

One transitional social worker clearly separated her counseling and service provision roles in discharge planning: "One frustrating part of the job is that so much of it is discharge planning. . . . A lot of it is not therapy. . . . It's more concrete than clinical, by far." Another commented on how she used her assessment skills in working out a plan with the doctor: "You start putting the picture together. . . . I shared it with the doctor . . . and I think by him understanding what her social situation was, it helped to educate him that the social issues are just as important as the medical ones." Similarly, a social worker said "We are an aid to physicians with their patients. That's how I see my role and I think I convey that to physicians. So they don't run away from me. I think they do see that we are really sharing the burden and the responsibility of taking care of patients. . . . It's important that physicians see social workers as helpmates." In articulating her supportive role with physicians, a social worker commented "I feel doctors have a tough time dealing with what they have to deal with, and a lot of the postures that other people find difficult, I see as defensive. I try to help them because they have tremendous decisions to make, and they have a great deal of difficulty making them."

One experienced social worker took a different tack in working autonomously from physicians: "I deal a lot with just using the charts to find out what the situation is. . . . I don't need to ask a lot of questions. . . . I'm often able to just deal with the nurses." Another saw herself as team leader: "I felt toward the end, I was the coordinator of the case . . . I was working it out, pulling the pieces together. The doctor had done his part, but I was the one who was on the phone, working it out with the family and trying to come up with some kind of plan."

Transformational social workers were similar to the transformational physician in sharing responsibility for patient care and in integrating psychosocial issues into all aspects of their role. Clinical and service provision tasks were linked conceptually in the discharge planning role as well. Teamwork and collaborative skills and activities were given priority. These social workers also demonstrated less concern for autonomy than transitional social workers did, possibly because roles between social workers and physicians (as well as with other professionals) were not as compartmentalized.

In discussing her team, one social worker said "Collaboration . . . is helpful in presenting ideas to patients and families that they might not be willing to look at at this time. They may be very resistant to accepting their diagnosis or the treatment plan, and they need help from all the disciplines together." Another described her significant role in patient care. "I was the only person she could ventilate to, who could give her the time . . . as a counselor but also key in figuring out what the discharge plan would be for her . . . it was a dual role." A social worker demonstrated her respect for her physician colleague's psychosocial assessment. "This particular doctor has been working with this patient for many years, so he really knows this family intimately, knows all the psychosocial problems . . . so he was helpful to me in making an assessment of this family and their dynamics, how this patient could be best cared for." Another described sharing responsibility with a physician in a difficult case. "The doctor had to go in and tell her that she was in fact going to die. . . . I told him he needed to do it in a simple way, and he said to come with him. I said OK so we did it together." One social worker, in giving advice to other social workers, stressed that "I present myself as equal to doctors but certainly respect their knowledge and expertise in an area, but in turn I want them to do that for me."

In summary, we were able to develop a theoretical framework for understanding collaborative characteristics of physicians and social workers by using inductive techniques to build theory. At this stage, we are ready to apply our typology to each respondent.

THE PROCESS OF EVOLVING THE TYPOLOGY

In reflecting on how this typology has evolved, we have come to recognize that we drew on a number of sources, both intellectual and experiential.

The First Stages of Theme Coding

While interviewing the first group of respondents, we began to recognize certain patterns in their overall responses. As a result, we began to systematically record our postinterview summary observations of the subjects with respect to: (1) their degree of involvement in the interview; (2) their general view of the other profession; (3) their attitudes toward collaboration; (4) their definition of the social work role and function as narrow versus broad; and (5) the degree of importance they gave to psychosocial issues. In addition, we characterized physician respondents on a process/outcome continuum: from those who understood the process by which social workers bring about particular outcomes to those whose only concern was the outcome of social work intervention. Following are some notes from interviewer summaries that helped us to identify overall themes and concepts.

A surgeon was characterized by the interviewer as someone who "saw the social work role as placement of patients. . . . He demonstrated a good understanding of patients' psychosocial problems but was not too clear about how the social worker worked in counseling patients. . . . He left the social worker to do her job but felt badly for her in this difficult case—even wished that she could have talked more about her frustrations but felt that she was too reserved for that and that he was too reserved to reach out. . . . He was an interesting mix of rather impoverished responses and limited interest in social work while having an unusually good sense of the patient and the structural obstacles faced by social workers in solving problems. . . . Yet, he was primarily interested in outcome."

A family practitioner was described as viewing "other professionals with respect although he may not understand how they get done what they do. . . . He identified himself as coordinator of the case which he saw as appropriate for a family practitioner. . . . The most important thing to him is what a social worker can do for the patient and what they can help him do with his patient. . . . He values social work, is interested in sharing perceptions about patients and in having mutual goals."

In our initial conception of the typology, we also drew on: the respondents' comparisons of current and past collaborative experiences and of themselves to others in their discipline, their advice to their profession and to the other regarding collaborative strategies, and their characterizations of collaboration and actual collaborative behavior in both the shared case and in the positive and negative case examples they provided. In addition, there were certain specific questions we posed that crystallized our understanding of attitudes toward professional control over decision making such as: Who was central to decision making? Who coordinated the case? Is the team helpful?

From reviewing various sections of transcripts and from interviewer summaries, we began to classify and code certain dimensions of collaboration: the importance of psychosocial issues, narrow versus broad definition of social work role, emphasis on teamwork, emphasis on process versus outcome of social work interventions, attitudes toward emotional support given to and received from collaborators, and preferred communication patterns. Before perceiving that they were, in fact, elements of a typology, we began keeping notes of interesting examples of these dimensions on the back of transcripts for future reference. At a subsequent point, we recognized that the dimensions had coherence as components of a typology to characterize collaborators; namely, that they made up a traditional, transitional, or transformational perspective on collaboration, equally applicable to social workers and physicians.

The Contribution of Our Intellectual Roots

The literature on professional socialization processes was a clear and conscious influence on us throughout the study. We began the empirical phase of our work after having defined the strategies to enhance collaboration as a negotiated resource model (Abramson and Mizrahi 1986). The literature on professionalism supported our experiences collaborating with and studying physicians; namely, that physicians have more power, professional autonomy, and greater authority over patient care than other professionals do, including social workers (Freidson 1970). Our strategies for enhancing social work influence on patient care decision making were based on the premise that an unequal relationship exists between the two professions. We also presumed that physicians, in general, have limited interest in the psychosocial needs of patients and only minimal understanding of the contribution of social workers to patient care.

We postulated that social workers had moved from handmaiden status vis-à-vis physicians to an expanded and increasingly self-defined role that included greater professional autonomy (Abramson and Mizrahi 1986). It was only as the typology began to emerge from our data that we recognized, with hindsight, our assumption that a typical collaborative relationship involved a traditional physician and a transitional social worker. Given this configuration, it then makes sense that strains would be evident between them (Mizrahi and Abramson 1985). Therefore, the development of the typology helped us to locate our prior work on a continuum of social work/physician relationships.

Conceptual Expansion

It became clear from our data that our prior model did not sufficiently capture the range of collaborative perspectives we were uncovering. For example, there were many physicians who either had never been traditional or who had shifted from a traditional collaborative stance to what we now labeled as transitional. We also recognized that there were social workers in our sample who could be classified as traditional, based on the way they defined their role and on their interaction with physicians. These social workers either did not value or did not actively seek professional autonomy.

For another group of social workers, we began to shift our view about the meaning behind their autonomous actions in relation to collaborating with physicians. We found some social workers who avoided or worked around physicians, doing things on their own or with nurses where feasible. They seemed to be claiming certain areas of practice as their own, perhaps in reaction to control by physicians over other areas. Others appeared to work independently as a response to a perceived lack of interest by physicians in the psychosocial aspects of patient care. We began to label this behavior "autonomy by default"—a reaction to the nature of their collaborative relationships rather than a deliberately chosen and preferred style of professional behavior. We expect it to occur primarily in response to more traditional physicians.

We had expected that many social workers would be motivated to achieve autonomy and authority comparable to medicine (Livingston, Davidson, and Marshack 1989), with respect to independent identification of appropriate clients, assessment, and task definition. Leaders in hospital social work have been seeking such autonomy and documenting the impact of independent social work case finding on patient care for many years (Berkman and Rehr 1969, 1970, 1972, 1973). In reviewing the data, it became clear that transitional social workers did emphasize their professional autonomy, often noting the contribution of their assessment of clients and families to better patient care outcomes and collaboration.

Unexpectedly, we also discovered a subset of social workers and physicians for whom autonomy is giving way to another perspective on professional practice: interdependence and mutuality. Hierarchy is unimportant to these practitioners; sharing responsibility and authority is the norm. They seem to have given up or never acquired the norm of self-reliance, so common in medical settings. For these transformational professionals, the whole (of patient care) is greater than the sum of its many parts (isolated professional perspectives).

We have tried to reflect on the evolution of our typology as "self-consciously" and deliberately as possible. However, we acknowledge the ultimate subjectivity of any such process. We recognize that many interactive elements have contributed to the development of the typology and cannot thus be adequately communicated in the linear fashion necessary for a written analysis.

CURRENT STATUS AND POTENTIAL USE OF THE TYPOLOGY

Having identified certain collaborative patterns that we labeled traditional, transitional, and transformational, we are now at a point of considering the utility of these labels for categorizing both the respondents and their collaborative relationships. As we complete coding of all the transcripts, we will be characterizing respondents as traditional, transitional, or transformational in relation to their self-described collaborative perspectives and relationships in the shared, positive, and negative cases. However, we anticipate variation among the respondents in relation to different aspects of the typology. For example, physicians could be traditional on their view of control over decision making but transitional in their emphasis on psychosocial issues in patient care. Given that the world of professional practice is in flux, we feel this is to be expected. Also, as we continue coding, we expect to further refine and articulate the definition of each dimension of the typology, dealing with inconsistencies and subsuming some under others.

Our goal will be to make sense of these inconsistencies or apparent contradictions. We will also look at issues that arise from different combinations of collaborative types. For example, does greater compatibility exist when both collaborators are traditional in orientation? Is there a positive, dynamic tension that characterizes relationships between certain combinations of professionals or are other combinations less compatible? Perhaps a transitional social worker might experience the transformational physician's emphasis on sharing positively while the physician may be frustrated by the social worker's tendency to function independently. Can there even be a transformational social worker without a like physician with whom to collaborate (or vice versa)? These and many other questions await further investigation.

We have begun, however, to recognize that collaborators and collaborative relationships have certain characteristics that can predict whether they will be stable or will vary across different settings and with different individuals. We hope to provide some insights into the nature of the professional self. We propose that the stability of that self will vary depending on the derivation of collaborative perspectives. Are they based on: (1) intrinsic or core qualities and beliefs of the individual, (2) interactions with specific collaborators, or (3) institutional factors? Intrinsic qualities refer to a consistent way of perceiving or defining collaborators. This appears as a core part of a professionally developed self, is expressed as a generalized perspective, and is applied consistently to a variety of different collaborators. For example, "I always treat physicians as if they are deaf and forgetful." The subject behaves and acts similarly in most if not all situations; in short, it is a matter of *who you are*.

When a collaborator or collaborative behavior is characterized as interactional, it is a function of a variable way of responding to a collaborator, depending on the relationship with or attitude toward particular persons. It is a situational perspective, reflecting a reaction to the persons, namely, *who they are*. For example, "I have a better relationship with someone who is a nice person."

When the character of collaboration derives from institutional or structural factors, it can be expected to vary according to a structured set of norms, which vary by roles, functions, or settings; in this case, *where you are* determines the properties of collaborative interactions. For example, "I relate to house staff differently from attendings"; or "I collaborate differently on the renal service than I did when I was on general internal medicine."

We have presented the background, methodology, and some preliminary theoretical findings of our study of social work/physician perspectives on collaboration in hospital settings. We have obtained both the general views of the respondents and exemplars of their actual collaborative practices on shared cases. In this paper, we describe the evolution of a conceptual framework, a tripartite typology that identified patterns of physician/social worker collaboration as traditional, transitional, or transformational. We presented a tentative formulation of the collaborative orientation of the different types of physicians and social workers.

Ultimately, we expect that knowledge acquired about effective social work/physician collaboration will improve the quality of patient care through strengthening team functioning and interdisciplinary decision making.

REFERENCES

Abramson, J. S. and T. Mizrahi. 1986. Strategies for enhancing collaboration between social workers and physicians. *Social Work in Health Care* 12, no. 1: 1–21.
Abramson, J. S. and T. Mizrahi. 1993. Examining social work/physician collaboration: An application of grounded theory methodology. In C. Riessman, ed., *Qualitative Studies in Social Work Research*. Newbury Park, Calif.: Sage.
Berkman, B, and H. Rehr. 1969. Selectivity biases in delivery of hospital social services. *Social Service Review* 43, no. 1: 35–41.
Berkman, B. and H. Rehr. 1970. Unanticipated consequences of the casefinding system in hospital social service. *Social Work* 15, no. 2: 63–68.
Berkman, B. and H. Rehr. 1972. Social needs of hospitalized elderly: A classification. *Social Work* 17: 80–88.
Berkman, B. and H. Rehr. 1973. Early social service case finding and the timing of social work intervention. *Social Service Review* 47: 256–65.
Caputi, M. and W. Heiss. 1984. The DRG revolution. *Health and Social Work* 9, no. 11: 5–12.
Charmaz, K. 1990. Discovering chronic illness: Using grounded theory. *Social Science and Medicine* 30, no. 11: 1161–72.
Freidson, E. 1970. *Professional Dominance: The Structure of Medical Care*. New York: Aldine-Atherton Press.

Glaser, B. and A. Strauss. 1967. *The Discovery of Grounded Theory*. Chicago: Aldine.

Jansson, B. and J. Simmons. 1985/86. The ecology of social work departments: Empirical findings and strategy implications. *Social Work in Health Care* 11, no. 2: 1–16.

Livingstone, D., K. Davidson, and E. Marshack. 1989. Education for autonomous practice: A challenge for field instructors. *Journal of Independent Social Work* 4, no. 1: 69–82.

Lofland, J. 1971. *Analyzing Social Settings*. Belmont, Calif.: Wadsworth.

Miles, M. and A. Huberman. 1984. *Qualitative Data Analysis: A Sourcebook of New Methods*. Newbury Park, Calif.: Sage.

Mizrahi, T. 1988. Prospective payment systems and social work. In J. McNeil and S. Weinstein, eds., *Innovations in Health Care Practice*, pp. 1–15. Silver Springs, Md: NASW Press.

Mizrahi, T. and J. Abramson. 1985. Sources of strain between physicians and social workers: Implications for social workers in health care settings. *Social Work in Health Care* 10, no. 3: 33–51.

Strauss, A. 1987. *Qualitative Analysis for Social Scientists*. Cambridge, England: Cambridge University Press.

Strauss, A. and J. Corbin. 1990. *Basics of Qualitative Research: Grounded Theory Procedures and Techniques*. Newbury Park, Calif.: Sage.

Waitzkin, H. 1990. On studying the discourse of medical encounters: A critique of quantitative and qualitative methods and a proposal for reasonable compromise. *Medical Care* 28, no. 6: 473–87.

TWELVE

Commentary: Grounded Theory Methods—Applications and Speculations

Susan R. Sherman

The grounded theory approach, first developed by Glaser and Strauss (1967), is particularly appropriate to research in social work. Glaser and Strauss have used this approach in many action-oriented settings, and the work relates to a variety of professions. Grounded theory methods are a category of qualitative research and at the same time make use of methods and data sources found in other qualitative and quantitative research. Without theory development, qualitative methods alone do not meet the criteria of grounded theory.

Gilgun begins by describing methods of grounded theory. She then explains how closely these methods and findings fit into social work practice, both process and substance—a theme in several papers in this book. Her paper leads into the second and third essays of this section, which describe explicit applications of the use of grounded theory methods in two critically important and topical substantive areas: Belcher's paper on social drift in homelessness and Mizrahi and Abramson's paper on the social worker and physician collaboration. These two studies richly complement each other, for they study practice from the two perspectives of the client and the professional, respectively.

These three essays are synthesized by using Gilgun's framework of grounded theory methods to organize Belcher's and Mizrahi and Abramson's applications of the methods. Additionally, Gilgun's parallels to practice are indicated within the same framework.

As a further illustration of the strength of grounded theory methods, some of my own research is included. Finally, three critical issues that must be addressed in doing qualitative research, including research using grounded theory methods, are outlined.

A SAMPLE OF GROUNDED THEORY RESEARCH METHODS APPLIED TO SOCIAL WORK RESEARCH AND PRACTICE

Induction and Deduction

Gilgun suggests that the interweaving of induction and deduction is similar to interweaving theory and practice wisdom with new knowledge from the client. Conclusions are drawn after data are gathered from the client and are subject to modification on the basis of new information.

In Belcher's study of social drift in homelessness, open-ended orienting questions based on reviewing the literature were asked. Responses were reviewed by use of the constant comparative method. Themes from that review were noted and a new set of questions was asked in reinterviews. Responses were again analyzed by means of the constant comparative method. Finally, working hypotheses based on the first and second set of interviews were developed, and checked with respondents, leading to a new set of working hypotheses.

Mizrahi and Abramson also used grounded theory approaches of alternating between data collection and analysis. For example, their analysis of preliminary interviews led them to modify questions, redirect sampling, and improve interviewing techniques. Inductively, using three stages of progressively more abstract coding, they reached a tentative typology of the physician's collaborative stance. They then deductively tested this back against their data.

Data Collection Methods

Gilgun reminds us that the same data collection methods of interviewing, observation, and document analysis are used in social work practice. Throughout these essays is an emphasis on the flexibility of the interview. Belcher points out how his research instrument was developed gradually, through continued evaluation of discovered information. Trustworthiness and credibility are established through triangulation, i.e., depending on multiple sources of data collection.

Mizrahi and Abramson emphasize the advantages to be gained through using grounded observations, particularly for studying the process of collaboration. Having the social worker and physician discuss a shared case grounds the research in the realities of practice. Mizrahi and Abramson make serious use of interviewers' comments on substance.

Data Analysis

Mizrahi and Abramson describe several steps they followed, using open, axial, and theoretical coding. Initially their preliminary coding involved comparing each response to the previous series until saturation was reached. When they discovered more overlap between the worlds of the two professions than had been expected, they included more about the physician's role and reciprocity, rather than simply two perspectives of the social work role. During axial coding procedures the authors reviewed large sections of the interview, rather than merely one question. New questions were formulated, at a higher level of integration than the original questions posed to respondents. Finally, the investigators moved to a higher level of concepts approaching theory, illustrated by their typology of the physician's role. Later stages in their research add causality to this model.

Involvement with Informants

Gilgun reminds us that the emphasis on the perspective of the persons being studied parallels the social work principle of starting where the client is. Additionally there is the parallel of balancing involvement with the client and maintaining an analytic stance. This is discussed further below.

Belcher "seeks understanding as it is interpreted by the research participants." His team tried to understand the norms of the community, similar to the stance of the ethnographer. For example, several respondents in the first stage of homelessness considered it "normal" to live with others as opposed to renting one's own place, whereas the middle-class researchers did not share these norms. Belcher reminds us that trustworthiness of the data is established by "prolonged engagement" (Lincoln and Guba 1985) and persistent observation. On the other hand, this closeness caused difficulties for researchers because of the temptation to abandon research and turn to direct services. This is discussed further below. Belcher contends that qualitative research, demanding close interaction between respondent and researcher, provides an effective means of advocating for the client.

Contextualized Findings

Gilgun indicates that the emphasis on context relates well to the person-environment framework of social work practice. Additionally, grounded theory research and practice frequently take place in natural settings to immerse the researchers and practitioners in "the world of [their] subjects." Gilgun suggests that bringing hypotheses into social work practice against which to measure the new situation is similar to pattern matching and constant comparison in grounded theory.

GROUNDED THEORY RESEARCH METHODS APPLIED TO STUDIES OF AGE IDENTITY

Considerable interest has arisen in age identity, both from a role/social structural point of view and from a psychological/life span development perspective. The former perspective has most frequently been used to study questions of identification as old or elderly, while the latter perspective has been used more frequently to study transitions in middle age. In the study reviewed here (Sherman, in press), I treated the issue of age identity in a continuous manner, asking the question of persons over six decades, without artificial demarcations into preset age categories. Although my interests in age identity began in the context of two large survey studies, with 1200 respondents in each (Sherman 1975; Ward, La Gory, and Sherman 1988), I have become increasingly interested in the sort of information that does not seem to be accessible in large surveys. We hear ordinary people in the real world allude to questions of age identity at every turn. We need to evaluate the effect of change from the individual's perspective. The concepts are elusive, though common, as people search for the meaning of their own age and aging.

As part of a larger study, pertaining to timing of aging, role models/peer support with aging, norms/sanctions for aging, and intergenerational expectations, I focused, not on chronological age categories, but on respondents' personal interpretations of their aging process, affording them the opportunity to reflect on changes that led to their feeling older and to note special events or birthdays that held particular significance.

Sixty-seven women and thirty-four men, aged forty-one to ninety-six, ranging from blue-collar workers to professionals, were interviewed. Data were collected in writing and on audiotape. A grounded theory approach was used: interview questions were modified as data analysis proceeded; new age cohorts were added to the sample as well. Content analysis was performed on written transcripts of the taped interviews. This research employs the phenomenological approach of using the respondents' own words, as a way to give meaning to previous survey results. I share the view that people take an active role and interpret the messages on aging in their own way. We show how people are aware of change and of process age markers at every age.

Four categories seemed to describe the ways respondents perceived their own aging. These were the comparative self, the reflected self, the retrospective self, and the mature self. The resulting framework relies heavily on symbolic interactionist theory. Most interestingly, this framework was useful for the entire age range of six decades, despite the fact that age identity is usually studied over attenuated age ranges.

Comparative Self

Social evaluation theory and reference group theory would imply that one draws conclusions about one's own age identity by comparing the self with others on this dimension. In the present context, these comparisons are likely to be with peers and family. A reference group of peers can lead to an older age identity by reflecting one's own aging or by providing positive role models. By contrast, peers can serve as a comparison against which one is "doing better." A few of the respondents mentioned comparisons with peers as influences on their own age identity: "There's a few here [community center] you say if I could be like them. Some in their 90s, their minds are wonderful, they still swim."

The sense of aging was also triggered by the aging of one's family—younger generations, one's own generation, and older generations—as well as by illness and dependence of the oldest generation: "With . . . the grandchildren growing up and getting married and the great-grandchildren. That makes you feel really ancient."

Reflected Self

Our identity depends not only on how we compare ourselves with other persons as described above but also on the views we believe others hold of us. For some respondents, the way they were perceived or treated influenced their age self-definition. This contrasts to the previous category: in the previous category, the respondent compares self with others; in this category, the other is perceived to be judging and defining the respondent: "People always say to me 'you aren't old, you're young.' Well I am as old as some of them, but I guess they don't realize it. So it depends on how you look."

Retrospective Self

In addition to a comparative self and a reflected self, some respondents indicated an aging self defined by comparisons with the former self. These comparisons could refer to changes in appearance or to changes in health and strength: " 'Cause I can't do what I did when I was younger, like get on a ladder and take the curtains down and wash em. And when you have to do something that's a little strenuous and you say 'Oh, I am getting old.' "

Mature Self

This group of respondents did not primarily compare themselves with others or with their former physical selves. Nor did they "interpret" themselves in the perceptions of others. Instead, they looked inside and found an inner maturity. This new self-awareness affected their time perspective and their worldview:

> Late 40s. A certain maturity of thought made me realize that I had 'grown up.' Up to that point I kept thinking that I have to. I'm not thinking or perceiving or reacting to things like I would like to and by the late 40s I had reached that point where I could then look at myself, and say, "yes, I have now grown up and achieved a maturity that has . . . stayed the same," not that I'm stagnating, but I worked toward this and achieved it so I can say now I'm 53 and look back at the late 40s. Yes, I was right in saying that I had achieved a maturity because I can see that it has remained.

The study demonstrated how much richer and more productive the data are when qualitative methods of open-ended interviewing and grounded theory methods are used. Although I had ideas about possible categories from my earlier survey studies and from the literature, as is typical with grounded theory methods, most of the categories emerged from the data themselves. Furthermore, the overall theoretical framework emerged at a later stage of conceptualization. My analysis might be said to have begun somewhat deductively, looking for concepts based on earlier work. It then became more inductive as I rearranged response concepts and developed the overall theoretical framework that seemed most coherent for the data at hand.

DISCUSSION OF CRITICAL ISSUES

The following questions are raised about these papers—questions that pertain to qualitative research, including grounded theory methods, in general and need to be considered in a book such as this.

Classification into Stages or Types When Categories Are Multidimensional

Belcher uses income, connection to service providers, social networks, substance abuse, etc. as dimensions of stages of homelessness. Mizrahi and

Abramson include the dimensions of definition of social work role, control of decision making, communication patterns, orientation to teamwork, etc., as dimensions for the continuum of collaboration. The dimensions (or properties) obviously do not correlate perfectly, so it is crucial to determine how to classify persons who fit into one category, i.e., first stage of homelessness or traditional collaboration on several dimensions, and another category (or categories) on the other dimensions, i.e., second or third stage or transitional or transformational collaboration. It is likely that in the latter study subcategories will emerge, e.g., fitting the transformational end of the continuum on psychosocial and process; transitional on definition of role, teamwork, and active communication; and the traditional end of the continuum on control and attitudes toward support. It is more difficult in a qualitative than in a quantitative study to combine across dimensions and classify a person in only a single category. Particularly because of this difficulty, it is essential to be explicit about how this is done. Can persons be classified in a single category? How much discrepancy is allowed for the person still to be considered of that type? How many subcategories are considered useful? If the cases in a subcategory begin to pile up, should that be considered a new category?

Moving from a Descriptive Category System to a Dynamic Model

Belcher needs to show how a person drifts from stage to stage in homelessness. Mizrahi and Abramson refer to their model as a developmental continuum, and transitional, for example, is a dynamic label, but they need to explain how this transition begins or how the physician is transformed. Is it a transition between cohorts of medical students or truly a transition in individual development? In other words, what do we know about the actual process of moving from one stage to the next? Strauss and Corbin (1990) see the description of process in the development of grounded theory as critical.

When we view process "as stages and phases of a passage" grounded theory studies should include "an explanation of what makes that passage move forward, halt, or take a downward turn." Alternatively process can be conceptualized "as nonprogressive movement . . . flexible, in flux, responsive . . . to changing conditions" (Strauss and Corbin (1990): 157).

> Does everyone move through the steps at the same pace? Is it slower for some, faster for others? Why? Does everyone who starts off . . . move to the top? If not, why not? Where do they stop, slide backwards, and why? What critical factors come into play and when to prevent, hinder, halt their forward

progression? How does a change in context by place and time affect rate and degree of progress? (146) . . . Identifying and specifying change or movement in the form of process is an important part of grounded theory research. Any change must be linked to the conditions that gave rise to it.   (256)

Perhaps because the data in a qualitative research study are so rich at any one point, extending data collection and analysis may seem overwhelming. And yet this is perhaps the only way we can have confidence that the model is indeed dynamic. Belcher tells us retrospectively that the homeless people had had loss or they had lost hope. All in the second stage referred to a *process* (italics added) of drift, including losing a relationship, health, or a living arrangement. Respondents "noted that their interactions with family and friends became more strained as they entered the shelters." Belcher found some fluidity, viz., respondents could go back from stage two to one, but not from three to two. He quotes a respondent in the third stage who refers to the process: "there is a line you cross, and when you cross that line, it's all over. The streets swallow you up and you lose your identity." If the persons could be followed longitudinally, would we observe someone passing from stage one to stage two to three? A longitudinal study would give us a sense of the direction of causality and the process of change over time. For example, in Belcher's study, do substance abuse, poor health, poor social relationships, and decompensation lead to or result from homelessness?

Qualitative methods are useful where linear causality does not apply; they permit us to use a transactional explanation of causality. Whether we are discussing drift in homelessness or changes in physician and social worker relationships, it is likely that development is reciprocal rather than unidirectional. Qualitative research lends itself perhaps more easily than quantitative research to a sensitivity to transactional and reciprocal processes.

According to Mizrahi and Abramson, physicians reported changing over time. As they moved from the internship or residency role, their stake in things changed and their perspective and their ability, or need, to cope with psychosocial issues changed. The authors concluded that some of the change is part of the physicians' own internal development and some of it is in terms of the context, i.e., changing external realities of our health care system, with its increased need for the social work function (e.g., in discharge planning). Given the authors' interest in medical school and social work curricula, as well as their optimism, it is necessary to understand the process of change. If we had the right kind of curriculum, and if we accept the authors' evaluative stance that stage three is optimal, could a student be moved from stage one to two to three?

Role of the Researcher and Relationship to the Respondents

Grounded theory methods, as with other qualitative research, e.g., ethnographic methods, present both the advantages and disadvantages of being close to the data, and hence, to the people we are studying. Gilgun points out two potential problems inherent in closeness to the informants. The first is becoming too involved, such that the researcher loses the analytic stance. This can be overcome, she suggests, by studying other informants. The second potential problem is emotional reactions to research findings. Belcher raised a related question: how does the researcher ethically stand by and observe without intervening? A common question in participant observation research is whether the observer can intervene, and what effect this has on the observation. Gilgun suggests that teams of researchers can help to process and deal with personal reactions. Belcher suggests that the research should encompass action while gathering data. Finally, he finds a role for action in the researcher's frequent consultations for policymaking bodies, e.g., state agencies and legislature.

The methods in this essay were described largely by using Gilgun's exposition and applying it to chapters by Belcher and Mizrahi and Abramson. An additional illustration of the use of these methods was presented, viz., the author's research on age identity. Finally, issues to be addressed for the researcher using grounded theory methods were described. These were multidimensional classification; longitudinal, dynamic, and transactional models; and roles of the researcher and respondent.

REFERENCES

Glaser, B. and A. Strauss. 1967. *The Discovery of Grounded Theory*. Chicago: Aldine.
Lincoln, Y. S. and E. G. Guba. 1985. *Naturalistic Inquiry*. Newbury Park, Calif.: Sage.
Sherman, S. R. 1975. Mutual assistance and support in retirement housing. *Journal of Gerontology* 30: 479–83.
Sherman, S. R. In press. Changes in age identity: Self perception in middle and late life. *Journal of Aging Studies*.
Strauss, A. 1987. *Qualitative Analyses for Social Scientists*. Cambridge, England: Cambridge University Press.
Strauss, A. and J. Corbin. 1990. *Basics of Qualitative Research*. Newbury Park, Calif.: Sage.
Ward, R. A., M. La Gory, and S. R. Sherman. 1988. *The Environment for Aging: Interpersonal, Social, and Spatial Contexts*. Tuscaloosa: University of Alabama Press.

NARRATIVE
METHODS

THIRTEEN

The Human Sciences, the Life Story, and Clinical Research

Bertram J. Cohler

Across the past two decades, interest in the human sciences as a mode of understanding within both the social sciences and the humanities has increased. Reflecting a shift away from the logical–experimental social science, which has become the accepted "normal" method of study, the human science perspective is founded on experience-near study of the presently remembered personal or social past, experienced present, and anticipated future. Human science inquiry highlights study of personal and social life within the context of discourse between teller and listener (including oneself as listener), situated within a particular time and culture. Indeed, from the human science perspective, relationship between teller and listener, together with cultural context of meanings, largely determines both structure and content of the narrative or story that is told.

For example, changes within psychoanalysis have led to a shift from the effort to revise and extend Freud's philosophy of science in the light of advances in cognitive and biological science, to increased focus on the clinical theory emphasizing the significance of wish and sentiment enacted within a relationship between two people (Galatzer-Levy and Cohler 1990; Gill 1976; Klein 1976). Changes within anthropology have led to renewed focus on a reflexive understanding of the relationship with the informant as the most important source of ethnographic evidence (Crapanzano 1980, 1981; Rabinow and Sullivan 1979). Finally, emphasis has shifted within developmental psychology itself from assumption that the course of development is largely the result of a biologically determined epigenetic program to increased awareness of social context itself, including the relationship between caregivers and offspring, in shaping the course of development (Stern 1985, 1989a, b; Vygotsky 1934/1978; Wertsch 1991).

This emerging human science perspective has had important impact on the study of both the expectable course of life and lives in distress, from earliest childhood to oldest age. This impact has been particularly significant in the context of the reevaluation of the very goal of longitudinal study from concern with demonstration of stability over time to focus on determinants of change and discontinuity over the course of life (Bandura 1982; Gergen 1977, 1989; Neugarten 1969). Not only do different methods provide quite different portraits of continuity and change across the life course (Block with Haan 1971; Kagan 1980; Kagan and Moss 1962; McCrae and Costa 1984), but also theoretical perspectives regarding the understanding of the course of development shift over time. The human science perspective recognizes both that subjective experience is critical in understanding the life story and also that the actuality of this narrative of the personal past is a consequence both of point in the course of life and context in which the life story is told.

For example, Vaillant (1977) and Vaillant and McArthur (1972) have shown that the story of adolescence retrospectively recounted by men across the college years is quite different from the story of their adolescence recounted by these same men at midlife. Events may be recalled in different ways at different times across the course of life; the significance of these events for the life history as a narrative may also change with the passage of historical time across successive cohorts or generations. For example, the place of childhood events as presumed determinants of subsequent personality is viewed in a quite different manner since the Enlightenment, particularly Rousseau's *Emile* (1762) than in earlier times (Aries 1962). Present understanding of the role of childhood for adolescent and adult personality development emphasizes the context in which the narrative of development is told, the nature of the relationship between teller and listener, and the reconsideration of the course of development itself within postmodern intellectual culture (Homans 1989; Toulmin 1989).

"NORMAL" PSYCHOLOGICAL SCIENCE AND THE STUDY OF THE LIFE STORY AS NARRATIVE

Emergence of a human studies approach (Cohler 1988; Polkinghorne 1983) has led to marked controversy within the social sciences, psychiatry, and psychoanalysis (Cohler 1988). This controversy reflects the dilemma first noted by Weber (1904–05) and Toulmin (1981) regarding the emphasis on rationality and logic within our own culture as the foundation of knowing. Toulmin (1989) has suggested that the uncertainty evident in the seventeenth century, confronting the challenge of modernity, led to enhanced search for certainty believed to be uniquely possible through logic or rational argument independent of context. As Toulmin (75) observes: "For the first time since Aristotle, logical analysis was separated from, and elevated far above, the study of rhetoric, discourse and argumentation."

The consequence of this shift to logic independent of the source of the analysis was a shift away from concern with narrative and rhetoric to the search for context-independent "facts" reflected in Popperian "normal" science (Popper 1959; Suppe 1977) in natural and social sciences alike. Again, as Toulmin (1989) observes, "the received view of modernity that was second nature to those of us who grew up in the 1930s and '40s was based on the rationalist assumptions that underlay the original program of the 17th century "new philosophers" [Descartes, Newton], whose works the advocates of the received view so warmly admired (1989:81).

Reliance on a received view of "normal" or science based on "brute facts," (Anscombe 1957–58) has the virtue, at least in theory, of being verifiable in terms of external criteria, beyond evaluation of the narrative coherence of the life history or story. However, predictive study may also make assumptions regarding the elements of the purported life history or story as "brute fact" (Anscombe 1957–58). These assumptions are contradicted both by clinical study of lives over time and by focus on determinants of change rather than continuity in developmental psychological study. Concern with external validation or verifiability requires some sacrifice of understanding of wishes and intents, including that induced by the need to maintain a coherent autobiography.

Mishler (1990) has suggested that, in any event, the claims of positive or "experimental" science approaches, such as in the study of lives, may be more an ideal than a reality: experience-based contextual knowledge developed largely through apprenticeship training may be a more accurate portrayal of the manner in which inquiry is conducted than a model stressing abstract rules and so-called "logic of discovery." In fact, normal science more closely reflects the human studies in reliance on tacit understandings and shared practices than any formal model of scientific experimentation (Polanyi 1958; Toulmin 1982).

EMPATHY, INTERSUBJECTIVITY, AND UNDERSTANDING THE LIFE STORY

The human science perspective relies on a reflexive mode of inquiry in which mode of study and observation or evidence are inextricably a part of the shared experience of the participants in this inquiry. Consistent with modes of practice in the mental health disciplines, emphasizing the therapeutic relationship as the foundation of change, the human science approach focuses on the observer's experience of the phenomenon, together with the manner in which the encounter is experienced by each of the participants, as a significant source of information. This human science perspective shifts focus of study from a phenomenon existing outside the field of the observer to reliance on the observer's experience of the phenomenon, or present construction of the phenomenon, as the only evidence that exists.

Kohut (1959, 1971, 1977) maintains that psychoanalysis represents a mode of study that relies on the method of empathy, or vicarious introspection, which may be contrasted with the experience-distant mode of experimental laboratory study. As contrasted with the experience-distant mode of study, characteristic of the logical-experimental method of study within much of the behavioral sciences, the experience-near mode emphasizes the place of the observer, relying on own self-reflexive understanding or vicarious introspection from within the field of observation of self and others, which constitutes evidence and understanding. The logical-experimental or experience-distant mode of study rules out such reflexive observation as unreliable, and "unscientific," and inappropriate.

Addressing this issue of the so-called scientific status of empathic observation in systematic inquiry, Kohut (1975/1978) has suggested that the issue is not whether empathically obtained observations are subsequently transformed into counted data but is rather the perspective of the observer within the study. In support of much human science inquiry (Crapanzano 1980; Rabinow and Sullivan 1979), the issue is the recognition of the intrinsic significance of the observer in determining the very phenomena to be studied (Mishler 1986). It is as impossible to understand the significance of the ethnographic or other research interview as it is to understand the clinical interview apart from the context of the relationship, including not only the relationship between the two participants but also the interviewer's own reflexive understanding of the interview in terms of the empathic response to the informant.

LIVES AS TEXTS: INTERSUBJECTIVITY AND THE STUDY OF THE LIFE STORY

Understood as the systematic study of stories told either to others or to oneself regarding the course of life, including a presently recounted past, experienced present, and anticipated future, the concept of narrative is central both to the systematic study of lives over time and to the effort to intervene in order to reduce the experience of personal distress, leading to enhanced sense of personal integrity. The very telling of the life story fosters an enhanced sense of integrity. At least in part, reminiscence is soothing precisely because it elicits memories of important persons and events across the course of life, including adversity overcome through the passage of time and recall of important persons living on in memory even when physically absent or lost. The concept of the life story or personal narrative is central to both inquiry and intervention and provides a common focus for understanding the role of psychotherapy in personality change and a means for the study of lives over time.

Telling the life story is particularly significant as a means of realizing enhanced personal integrity across the course of life because of the appreciative efforts of the listener to understand the story. At least to some extent, this is true even when oneself is serving as the appreciative listener. An important aspect of psychotherapeutic intervention is devoted to enhancing this capacity to be an appreciative listener, serving the same function for oneself as has been served by the therapist within the context of the therapeutic relationship. At least a part of the successful outcome of psychotherapy may be an enhanced capacity to retell the life story to oneself and to be a good listener, serving as a source of self-soothing in the manner of the therapist.

The ethnographic interview and the clinical interview share in common a relationship between two persons, in the context of which meanings are successively defined in ways understandable to each. It is possible to clarify those communications regarding which some uncertainty exists. Over time, each participant contributes to the joint meanings, albeit recognizing that the respondent or analysand may contribute most extensively in the emergence of this shared meaning. At least part of the process of understanding emerging from this shared exchange is that of the intentions and sentiments that underlie these communications. Within the clinical interview, it is understood that every aspect of the analysand or client's communications is intentional and reflects the enactment of the presently understood life story within the context of the therapeutic relationship. For example, the most salient aspect of a dream may be what it communicates regarding the therapeutic relationship understood within the context of this narrative of the life history. Analysand and analyst work together in an effort to understand the dream in terms of the analysand's experience of the analyst, although not always in a manner that is accessible either to the analysand's awareness or to the analyst's understanding of this enactment.

Just as recounting a dream within the psychoanalytic hour assumes a relationship between analyst and analysand in which the dream serves as a means of portraying aspects of the experience of this relationship, the ethnographic or life history interview serves as a means for the shared meaning of that dream as coconstructed by analyst and analysand. The most significant aspect in either the ethnographic or other interview or the reading of any text, including the interview as transcribed into text beyond the immediate situation of the relationship, is the creative space engendered by the encounter between the reader and what is read.

Subsequently, particularly in the case of transcribed ethnographic, life history, or clinical interviews, as the interview becomes a transcript, it is obviously no longer possible to inquire regarding issues of meaning and intention. What was a relationship between the respondent and the interviewer now becomes a transcript that reflects a relationship between reader and text. At this point the task of interpreting the interview protocol is no different from the task in criticism, more generally, of making "sense" of the text. The relationship between reader (or "coder") of a text and the text is parallel to that other relationship of interviewer and respondent or analysand or client (Crapanzano 1981; Freeman 1985; Ricoeur 1971).

Significant change takes place as relationship is transformed into transcript. As Ricoeur (1971, 1977, 1979, 1983) and Freeman (1985) have noted, it is possible to make inquiry, to seek to clarify areas of confusion, and, in general, to explicate meanings emerging within the clinical or ethnographic interview situation. Once the particular session or interview has ended, relationship becomes transcript. Subsequent effort to understand meanings now takes place between text and interpreter. At least to some extent, the interpreter of the text places oneself in a position similar to that of the analyst in the initial encounter. Interpretation of a texts changes over time, both as a function of the changing perspectives of the interpreter and as a result both of larger sociohistorical changes and changes in the theory itself. For example, Kohut (1979) presents two quite different interpretations of an analysand's dream reflecting emergent understanding of psychopathology and treatment of disorders of the self.

Consistent with this method for collaborative, multidisciplinary study of psychoanalytic history and life history, initially portrayed by Kohut (1981), Pletsch (1985, 1987) attempted a "parallel process," in which meanings jointly constructed in understanding the Nietzsche autobiography provided a means of reflexively understanding Nietzsche's life. Moraitis and Pletsch have provided separate commentary on their collaboration, providing a unique opportunity for understanding this method in terms of joint construction of texts in which meaning is employed through the "intermediate space" of scholarly, humane, collaboration (Green 1978; Winnicott 1951). Consistent with this human studies approach, the narrative emerging from this collaboration was less an effort to reconstruct meanings inherent in the original text being studied than an additional reading of the autobiography founded on this shared reading. Issues such as rebellion and the relationship of father and son, as explicated in the jointly enacted meanings, both of their relationship to each other and with the texts in which they were involved, permitted each of the collaborators increased understanding of Nietzsche's work.

This focus on lives as texts, and texts of lives, has led to caution regarding both decontextualization and substitution of text analysis for first-person encounters through field work (Ewing 1987; Geertz 1988; Kracke and Herdt 1987). Just as more generally in the study of criticism, there is concern with issues of authoritorial or cultural intent. Hirsch (1976) has argued that, regardless of subsequent interpretations, the author does have a purpose in writing, and that purpose must not be subverted by subsequent study. Problems presented by the study of cultures are not unlike that of the author's intent.

Lives must be understood within the complex context of culture, and subsequent study either of the text of ethnographic inquiry or of the psycho-analytic interview must preserve recognition of context, including that of ethnographer and informant or analyst and analysand. Understood as a statement of method regarding life history materials obtained from both the psychoanalytic interview and field work, the interpretive perspective raises important questions regarding methods of study in the human sciences. The interpretive perspective points to the importance of understanding ethnographic inquiry as an open system in which analysis of texts from interviews as diverse as psychoanalytic process, and inquiry with informants in ethnographic study, is continually open to new interpretations based on continuing scholarly study and emerging theoretical perspectives.

Too often, critics of the human science approach fail to appreciate the extent to which any reading of a text inevitably changes over time, with changes in the reader, the context of reading, or subsequent changes in theory. A common experience for clinicians discussing a transcript of a therapeutic hour is to find more than one interpretation of the process reflected in the transcript of this hour. A misunderstood effort may be made to recover the original intent of the participants during this hour, without recognition that success in this effort is in no way possible. No intention exists beyond that presently available in the effort of the reader to make sense of the text in the ways that the reader brings to the text. No authority is greater than that of the reader in the ''here-and-now,'' making sense of the text in particular ways.

The human science approach to the comparative study of life course and experience of personal continuity, including personal distress resulting from adversity and conflict, reflects the awareness emerging in our own time that the task of understanding lives requires appreciation of the interplay of multiple perspectives, which are difficult to encompass within the logi-cal–experimental approach reflected in normal psychological science. In-deed, more than a century of such inquiry has yielded little understanding of the human condition. The human sciences approach stresses the founda-tion of all social inquiry within the context of a relationship, first between participants in a conversation or interview and, subsequently, as interview becomes text, through the dialogue of reader and text. Empathic under-standing founded on the concept of intersubjectivity is equally significant in the interview and the subsequent engagement of reader and text. Indeed, no meanings exist apart from those presently recognized within the text, just as it is impossible to consider the life story apart from the manner in which it is told.

The life story or personal narrative occupies a privileged position within the human sciences. Founded in the telling, even if in the telling to oneself, no life story is possible apart from the telling, and no understanding of the significance of this life story is possible apart from the relationship between teller and listener or, subsequently, the reader and the autobiography, reflected in the written or told biography, which is a present construction of the life history, just as the narrative of the collective past focuses less on event than on meaning of event within the context of a presently understood record of this past.

Telling and listening take place within the context of a relationship between two persons or person and text. While differences are obviously present between the interview and the process of reading a transcript of the interview, they share the common characteristic of not having intrinsic meanings or presenting authorial intent apart from present readings. Clearly, the interviewer has the opportunity that is denied to the reader of making inquiry; indeed, the very participation of the interviewer changes the nature of the story that is told (Mishler 1986). At the same time, the very act of telling a life story, and of listening to this story, provides an enhanced source of coherence and integrity. A universal human characteris-tic appears to be that we like to be understood by others, and the very act of attempting understanding, whether in psychotherapy or in the process of the research interview, promotes enhanced solace.

The human studies approach provides increased understanding of three particular problems related to study of the life course (Tobin 1991). In the first place, the issue of continuity, assumed in much developmental study, emerges as a major problem to be addressed: continuity is a function of the assumptions and methods included within texts or transcripts conveying particular intentions for persons of a particular time; dynamics of developmental processes inhere in the meanings that persons attach to these processes rather than to particular behaviors. In the second place, the human studies approach questions the assumption of scientistic study of lives that information may be collected from another relatively independent of the relationship between them. Meanings are jointly constructed with intersubjectivity fashioned out of that intermediate or transitional space so well portrayed, first by Winnicott (1951) in his discussion of the transitional object, later elaborated by Viderman (1970) and Green (1978), as well as by both Habermas (1968) and Taylor (1971) in discussing the role of intersubjectivity as the basis for creating meaning in the human studies.

The human studies approach focuses renewed attention to the means by which knowledge of intention first becomes possible. Understanding of another is a distinctively human attribute although little is known about how understanding is realized (Kohut 1971, 1977, 1982). Empathic understanding of others sharing a similar culture is requisite for realization of knowledge in the human studies. Psychometric procedures such as interrater reliability beg the question by assuming what is still to be understood. Further study is required regarding processes that foster concordance among raters and facilitating such understanding of lives over times.

The human science perspective is ideally suited for social inquiry concerning the impact of personal and social adversity on morale and mental health. From such natural disasters as the flood at Buffalo Creek (Erikson 1976) to the terrible tragedy of Boston's Coconut Grove nightclub fire (Lindemann 1949), to the study of lives in disorder, such as resulting from the impact of poverty and psychiatric illness, the human science perspective is the most appropriate mode for understanding development and social change as forces impacting on the study of lives over time. The human science perspective is the foundation of inquiry regarding both personal development and such directed intervention as psychotherapy and community intervention. The human science perspective provides an important means of understanding the foundations of the variety of modes of intervention associated with the mental health professions.

References

Anscombe, G. E. M. 1957–58. On brute facts. *Analysis* 18: 69–72.

Aries, P. 1962. *Centuries of Childhood: A Social History of Family Life.* Trans. R. Baldwick. New York: Random House–Vintage Books.

Bandura, A. 1982. The psychology of chance encounters and life paths. *American Psychologist* 37: 747–55.

Block, J. with N. Haan. 1971. *Lives Through Time.* Berkeley, Calif.: Bancroft.

Cohler, B. 1988. The human studies and the life history. *Social Service Review* 37: 552–75.

Crapanzano, V. 1980. *Tuhami: Portrait of a Moroccan.* Chicago: University of Chicago Press.

Crapanzano, V. 1981. Text, transference, and indexicality. *Ethos* 9: 122–48.

Erikson, K. 1976. *Everything in Its Path: Destruction of Community in the Buffalo Creek Flood.* New York: Simon and Schuster.

Ewing, K. 1987. Clinical psychoanalysis as an ethnographic tool. *Ethos* 15: 16–39.

Freeman, M. 1985. Paul Ricoeur on interpretation: The model of the text and the idea of development. *Human Development* 28: 295–312.

Galatzer-Levy, R. and B. Cohler. 1990. The developmental psychology of the self and the changing world-view of psychoanalysis. *The Annual for Psychoanalysis* 17: 1–44.

Geertz, C. 1988. *Works and Lives: The Anthropologist as Author.* Stanford, Calif.: Stanford University Press.

Gergen, K. 1977. Stability, change and chance in understanding human development. In N. Datan and H. Reese, eds., *Life- Span Developmental Psychology: Perspectives on Experimental Research,* pp. 32–65. New York: Academic Press.

Gill, M. 1976. Metapsychology is not psychology. In M. Gill and P. Holzman, eds., *Psychology Versus Metapsychology: Psychoanalytic Essays in Memory of George S. Klein,* pp. 71–105. New York: International Universities Press. Psychological Issues Monograph 36.

Green, A. 1978/1986. Potential space in psychoanalysis: The object in the setting. In A Green. *On Private Madness,* pp. 277–96. London: The Hogarth Press and The Institute for Psychoanalysis.

Habermas, J. 1968/1971. *Knowledge and Human Interests.* Boston: Beacon Press.

Hirsch, E. D. 1976. *The Aims of Interpretation.* Chicago: University of Chicago Press.

Homans, P. 1989. *The Ability to Mourn: Disillusionment and the Social Origins of Psychoanalysis.* Chicago: University of Chicago Press.

Kagan, J. 1980. Perspectives on continuity. In O. G. Brim, Jr. and J. Kagan, eds., *Constancy and Change in Human Development,* pp. 26–74. Cambridge, Mass.: Harvard University Press.

Kagan, J. and H. Moss. 1962. *From Birth to Maturity.* New York: Wiley.

Klein, G. 1976. *Psychoanalytic Theory: An Exploration of Essentials.* New York: International Universities Press.

Kohut, H. 1959/1978. Introspection, empathy, and psychoanalysis: An examination of the relationship between mode of observation and theory. In P. Ornstein, ed., *The Search for the Self: Selected Writings of Heinz Kohut, 1950–1978,* 1: 205–32. New York: International Universities Press.

Kohut, H. 1971. *The Analysis of the Self: A Systematic Approach to the Psychoanalytic*

Treatment of Narcissistic Personality Disorders. New York: International Universities Press. Monograph 1 of the Psychoanalytic Study of the Child Series.

Kohut, H. 1975/1978. The psychoanalyst in the community of scholars. In Ornstein, ed., *The Search for the Self: Selected Writings of Heinz Kohut, 1950–1978,* 2: 685–724. New York: International Universities Press.

Kohut, H. 1977. *The Restoration of the Self.* New York: International Universities Press.

Kohut, H. 1979. The two analyses of Mr. Z. *International Journal of Psychoanalysis* 60: 3–28.

Kohut, H. 1981/1985. On the continuity of the self and cultural self objects. In Strozier, ed., *Self Psychology and the Humanities: Reflections on a New Psychoanalytic Approach by Heinz Kohut,* pp. 232–43. New York: Norton.

Kohut, H. 1982. Introspection, empathy, and the semi-circle of mental health. *International Journal of Psychoanalysis* 63: 395–407.

Kracke, W. and G. Herdt. 1987. Introduction: Interpretation in psychoanalytic anthropology. *Ethos* 15: 3–8.

Lindemann, E. 1949. Symptomatology and the management of acute grief. *American Journal of Psychiatry* 101: 141–49.

McCrae, R. and P. Costa. 1984. *Emerging Lives, Enduring Dispositions: Personality in Adulthood.* Boston: Little-Brown.

Mishler, E. 1986. *Research Interviewing: Context and Narrative.* Cambridge, Mass.: Harvard University Press.

Mishler, E. 1990. Validation: The social construction of knowledge—A brief for inquiry-guided research. *Harvard Educational Review* 60: 415–42.

Neugarten, B. 1969. Continuities and discontinuities of psychological issues into adult life, *Human Development* 12: 121–30.

Pletsch, C. 1985. Returning to Nietzsche. In S. Baron and C. Pletsch, eds., *Introspection in Biography: The Biographer's Quest for Self Awareness,* pp. 107–28. Hillsdale, N.J.: Analytic Press.

Pletsch, C. 1987. On the autobiographical life of Nietzsche. In G. Moraitis and G. Pollock, eds., *Psychoanalytic Studies of Biography,* pp. 405–34. New York: International Universities Press.

Polanyi, M. 1958. *Personal Knowledge: Toward a Post-Critical Philosophy.* Chicago: University of Chicago Press.

Polkinghorne, D. 1983. *Methodology for the Human Sciences: Systems of Inquiry.* Albany: State University of New York Press.

Popper, K. 1959. *The Logic of Scientific Discovery.* London: Hutchinson.

Rabinow, P. and W. Sullivan. 1979. The interpretive turn. In P. Rabinow and W. Sullivan, eds., *Interpretive Social Science: A Reader,* pp. 1–14. Berkeley: University of California Press.

Ricoeur, P. 1971. The model of the text: Meaningful action considered as a text, *Social Research* 38: 569–72.

Ricoeur, P. 1977. The question of proof in Freud's psychoanalytic writings. *Journal of the American Psychoanalytic Association* 25: 835–72.

Ricoeur, P. 1979/1981. The function of narrative. In J. B. Thompson, ed., *Paul Ricoeur: Hermeneutics and the Human Sciences,* pp. 274–96. Cambridge, England: Cambridge University Press.

Ricoeur, P. 1983. Can fictional narratives be true, *Analecta Husserliana* 14: 3–19.

174   *Qualitative Methods: Narrative*

Rousseau, J. J. 1762/1979. *Emile or On Education.* Trans. A. Bloom. New York: Basic Books.

Stern, D. 1985. *The Interpersonal World of the Infant.* New York: Basic Books.

Stern, D. 1989a. The representation of relational patterns: Developmental considerations. In I. A. Sameroff and R. Emde, eds., *Relationship Disturbances in Early Childhood: A Developmental Approach,* pp. 52–68. New York: Basic Books.

Stern, D. 1989b. Developmental prerequisites for the sense of a narrated self. In A. Cooper, O. Kernberg, and E. Person, eds., *Psychoanalysis: Toward the Second Century,* pp. 168–80. New Haven, Conn.: Yale University Press.

Suppe, F. 1977. Afterward—1977. In F. Suppe, ed., *The Search for Philosophic Understanding of Scientific Theories,* pp. 617–730. Urbana: The University of Illinois Press.

Taylor, C. 1971. Interpretation and the sciences of man. *Review of Metaphysics* 25: 3–51.

Tobin, S. 1991. *Personhood in Advanced Old Age.* New York: Springer.

Toulmin, S. 1981. On knowing our own minds. *Annual for Psychoanalysis* 9: 207–21.

Toulmin, S. 1982. The construal of reality: Criticism in modern and postmodern science. *Critical Inquiry* 9: 93–111.

Toulmin, S. 1989. *Cosmopolis: The Hidden Agenda of Modernity.* New York: Free Press.

Vaillant, G. 1977. *Adaptation to Life.* Boston: Little-Brown.

Vaillant, G. and C. McArthur. 1972. Natural history of male mental health. I: The adult life-cycle from 18–50, *Seminars in Psychiatry* 4: 415–27.

Viderman, S. 1970. *La Construction de l'espace analytique.* (The Construction of the Analytic Space.) Paris: Denocel.

Vygotsky, L. 1978. *Mind in Society: The Development of Higher Psychological Processes.* M. Cole, V. John- Steiner, S. Scribner, and E. Souberman, trans. and eds. Cambridge, Mass: Harvard University Press.

Weber, M. 1904–05/1955. *The Protestant Ethic and the Spirit of Capitalism.* Trans. T. Parsons. New York: Scribner.

Wertsch, J. 1991. *Voices of the Mind: A Sociocultural Approach to Mediated Action.* Cambridge, Mass.: Harvard University Press.

Winnicott, D. W. 1951/1953. Transitional objects and transitional phenomena. In D. W. Winnicott. *Collected Papers: Through Pediatrics to Psychoanalysis,* pp. 229–42. New York: Basic Books.

FOURTEEN

"Thick Description" Revisited: Family Therapist as Anthropologist–Constructivist

Joan Laird

Family therapists, in the last few years, have been "discovering" anthropology, dressed in the postmodern garb of constructivism, hermeneutics, and narrative theory. Many have not only been attracted to postmodern theory, a body of thought converging from many directions, including linguistics, anthropology, literary criticism, philosophy, and psychology, but also have taken leadership in interpreting and applying the implications of this complex body of thought for the clinical endeavor. Story, narrative, text, myth, folklore, ritual, the very stuff of ethnography in its older and newer versions, are becoming dominant metaphors in the family therapy field.

At the same time, family therapy researchers, like most researchers in all the mental health disciplines, tend to still have their feet deeply planted in the soil of the scientific method and logical positivism, with its emphasis on linear "outcome" models. Indeed, the familiar gap between research and practice may be even wider in the family field, with its languages of systems, cybernetics, and ecology. The tasks of trying to track or quantify the complex processes of communication, structure, organization, and interaction in families; to "control" for variables; to account for change; and to predict behavior are monumental. While family therapy research generates very useful information, performs the important function of challenging practice folklore, and offers heuristic answers for certain kinds of questions, clinicians and researchers continue to face off over a very large espistemological and practical canyon. Researchers search for orderliness, pattern, and predicitability while clinicians face a radically untidy everyday world in which meanings are constantly shifting and coevolving, a world that seldom stands still for measurement. The researcher continues to try to track an elusive "reality," while the postmodern clinician is more interested in symbolism, rhetoric, narrative, and text—a search for meaning rather than "truth."

In this essay I describe some of the emerging ideas in family therapy that are grounded in postmodern theory and especially in newer ideas from anthropology but at the same time have strong linkages to older forms of ethnography. What emerges, I believe, is new definition and new respect for the "case" method, however we define the boundaries of "case," as well as a potential narrowing of the gap between researcher and practitioner. In ethnography, after all, the goal is holistic, to produce "thick description," to screen in and make sense of what may seem at first glance chaotic or unintelligible; it is not to screen out, to dispose of the messy, to control. In postmodern work grounded in an ethnographic stance, every practitioner is a researcher and every researcher must be close to practice. Just as clinician and client coevolve and change together, each influencing the other, so is the researcher part of the researched.

Furthermore, ethnography is above all else about writing, and what we never fail to write is ourselves, our perceptions, our interpretations, our creations (Clifford and Marcus 1986; Geertz 1988). As writers we are never able to completely bracket our biases or escape from our own metaphors. But those biases and metaphors can at the same time help us to critique the biases and metaphors of others. And so it is with this author. Never able or willing to shed my feminist glasses or political convictions, they color what I see, but at the same time perhaps they allow for another perspective, a critical stance. In this paper I draw upon feminist thinking to express some reservations, to question the politics of the "new epistemology," to urge us to be cautious as we once again passionately embrace a new paradigm.

POSTMODERN THEORY IN FAMILY THERAPY

Family therapists identified with the "new epistemology" have drawn inspiration from a wide range of postmodern and constructionist thinkers from many disciplines. No one has had more influence on contemporary thinking in family therapy than Gregory Bateson (1972, 1979), whose work, termed "second order cybernetics," has now inspired much of the most innovative thinking across at least two generations of family thinkers. Watzlawick (1984), who worked with Bateson in the early Palo Alto project and was also drawn to, among others, the ideas of von Glasersfeld (1984) and von Foerster (1984), challenged our logical positivist notions of truth and reality in his book *The Invented Reality*. More recently, family therapists (e.g., Lax 1991, in press; White 1989), also influenced by Bateson, have been probing the riches to be found in French deconstructionism as expressed in the works of, for example, Derrida (1986) and Foucault (1980). And recently, a number of thinkers have been turning to the potential of narrative and interpretive metaphors for inspiring a new epistemology of practice. Anderson and Goolishian (1988, in press), Hoffman (1985, 1990) White (White 1989; White and Epston 1990) and many others are turning to narrative psychology and to anthropology for new metaphors and new directions for theory and practice. Gergen (1985; Gergen and Davis 1985; Gergen and Gergen 1983), for example, a leader in the narrative field, has consulted with several family thinkers and has become a familiar figure at family therapy conferences.

A few people have worked to apply anthropological ideas to family therapy (e.g., Imber-Black, Roberts, and Whiting 1988; McGoldrick, Pearce, and Giordano 1982; White and Epston 1990). My own work in anthropology in the early 1980s, before the postmodern deluge, led me to believe that families were far more like small societies, like "cultures," than they were like information-processing or mechanistic systems. What were seen as fruitful sources of understanding in small societies, the cultural performances and expressions found in language, folklore, mythology, ritual, drama, art, symbolism, and so on were also fruitful sources for better understanding families (Allen and Laird 1990; Laird 1984, 1988, 1989). These categories of social action are the ways families, like cultures, attempt to articulate their meanings. Constructivist thinking and narrative approaches to understanding of the text allowed for new ways of thinking about history, about story, and about meanings and beliefs, a natural and comfortable way to combine older and new approaches to ethnography.

Difference, Power shifts, and the Reflecting Team

As these ideas were percolating and family therapists in a postmodern era were deciphering their implications for clinical work (e.g., Hoffman 1985, 1990; Tomm 1987) a family therapist from the north of Norway one day did something innovative that gave new meaning to the concepts of reflexivity and circularity that were central in family systems thinking. While family therapists had for years invited various family members to come behind the mirror to watch other family members being interviewed, the power of the "mirror" and the observing team belonged to the therapists.

No one had had the idea to change the basic hierarchy implicit in the therapeutic relationship. Andersen (1987), heading a team watching a young family interviewer "drawn into the pessimism of the family he was interviewing" (415), asked whether the family and interviewer would like to hear the team behind the mirror talk. The lighting and the sound were switched, and the family and young therapist proceeded to listen to the team discuss their observations (or "reflections" as they have become known).

Andersen, like most of mainstream family therapists, had been greatly influenced by the ideas of the anthropologist Gregory Bateson (1972, 1979), as well as those of Humberto Maturana, the Chilean biologist (1978). Both argued that it was the "observer" who generates the distinctions we think of as "reality." Bateson emphasized the notion of "difference," arguing that it was the sharing of different versions of the same world (double or multiple descriptions) that might allow a stuck system to move away from its "standstill" definition of a problem. Andersen refined Bateson's famous statement that information *"is a difference which makes a difference"* by unpacking the notion of difference. For him, a system that is not changing "contains too many repeating samenesses and too few new differences" (417). The helper must both respect the sameness and introduce new ideas, finding "a not too unusual setting in order to talk about not too unusual issues in a not too unusual manner" (417). If the new idea is not different enough, it will not be heard, it will not make a difference. If it is too innovative or unusual, it may threaten the family, stimulating their resistance. "So," says Andersen, "we must let our imagination fly freely, but not too freely, in order to find questions that will be different enough but not too different from those the system usually asks itself" (417).

The notion of "therapeutic conversation" is central to Andersen's approach, as is the notion of reflexivity. Therapy is no longer defined as a matter of some kind of more or less powerful expert "diagnosing" a faulty family according to some prior epistemological map (e.g., family structure or rule system) and designing strategic or systemic "interventions." Further, the usual therapeutic hierarchy is dismantled to reflect a more democratic arrangement in which both therapists and clients are seen as coparticipants in an ongoing dialogue, a notion Hoffman (1990) and Anderson and Goolishian (1988) also endorse. The therapist is seen as a conversational artist, a conferee, a consultant, an ethnographer. As the conversation unfolds, no participant's observations or ideas, including those of the therapist, are privileged over those of any other. Therapists do not proceed from prior theories about family structure or systemic processes, nor do they make working hypotheses about the functions of individual "symptoms" and how they connect to the larger family system. In Andersen's approach, therapists or "conversationalists" have ideas that are presented to the family in the form of reflections. The reflections are connected to the information that has emerged during the conversation and do not concern either unconscious processes or nonverbal exchanges or strong emotions that seem to have been unexpressed.

Similar to anthropologist Victor Turner's (1969) notion of the multivocality of symbols and Bateson's notion of double description in which a both/and rather than an either/or stance is sought, in Andersen's approach, multiple ideas are generated, none privileged, again staying within the range of "difference" it is thought the family can tolerate and within the family's own ways of reflecting in terms of rhythym, speed, and modes of communication. Ideas are always offered tentatively and speculatively and usually positively connote the strengths and positives in family communication.

STORIES AND NARRATIVES

Another voice from across the sea, this time from down under, has had considerable influence in shaping the newest family therapy ideas in this country. White (1989; White and Epston 1990), drawing particularly on the work of Foucault (1980) about the relationship between knowledge and power and anthropologist Edward Bruner's (1986a, b) ideas about the relationships among narrative, history, language, and "reality," adopted the metaphors of "text" and of "story" to conceptualize the ways in which individuals and families develop systems of meaning and belief. White is particularly interested in how individuals and families construct narratives about their problems or "symptoms," how they explain them to themselves and to others. Stories, not underlying pathology or structure, are seen as constitutive, that is, as shaping lives and relationships. People not only give meaning to or interpret but actually organize their experiences through storying and performing those stories. For White, with every such performance, people are reauthoring their lives. Similarly, therapy itself becomes another restorying or reauthoring process. "Problems" or "symptoms" are seen, not as having some existence or essence internal to the person, nor as existing in the interactions between persons. Rather, the problem is the story itself and the person's or family's relationship to that story/problem. Problem stories are stories that do not match or neglect important aspects of one's lived experience. People come to therapy with "problem-saturated stories"; therapy becomes a matter of challenging the dominant story and externalizing the problem, in the process constructing alternative knowledges/stories that have previously been subjugated. White and Epston (1990) make extensive use of various narrative forms, such as letters, documents, and certificates in the therapeutic reauthoring process. A letter, for example, may be used to invite family members to ally against a common oppressor such as a child's symptom, or a certificate used to celebrate a wife's winning fight against depression, or a child's taming of fears. White calls his work "a therapy of literary merit."

In my own work, the metaphor of "culture" became central, as I began to explore the possibility of using the categories that anthropologists used in studying small societies to study families. After all, families, like small societies, had common legacies and transmitted something resembling culture over the generations, usually through family story, myth, folklore, and ritual. These categories, as I said earlier, provide powerful windows into family relationships and cultures. Family therapists, with a few notable exceptions (e.g., Imber-Black, Roberts, and Whiting 1988), had been thinking about categories such as myth, story, and ritual only in their so-called pathological forms, failing to recognize them as universal categories that are rich sources of culture and meaning. The story/narrative metaphor is relevant to both individual and family therapy in several ways. First, story can stand for life history or biography, the ways in which people constructs their own histories (Cohler 1988; Spence 1982). A second way stories provide a window into individual identity and family culture is through the tracking of family folklore, that constellation of fables, legends, myths, and family stories that tends to contain the family's prescriptions and proscriptions, its world view, its paradigm for living. These stories, like our evolving histories, tell us what we should value, whom we should admire, how we should be men and women, and so on, and thus are powerful resources for change. In fact they are changed as they are told (Laird 1989). Third, the problem story and the "why I/we came to therapy" story is central to the therapy endeavor, an idea that appears in one form or another in the work of Allen and Laird (1990), Andersen (1987), Anderson and Goolishian (1988), Lax (1991), and White and Epston (1990). Finally, the new, coevolving narratives/stories in the ongoing therapeutic conversation are, of course, central to the work.

A point to be mentioned here and returned to is that individuals and families find inspirations and guidelines for their stories, as well as rules for storying, in the larger social discourses that surround them. Story genres, that is, the modes of narrative available to various peoples, are shaped by issues of power/knowledge (Foucault 1980), by gender, ethnicity, social privilege, and so on. Whether certain of our narratives will even be heard, recognized, or interpreted or whether they will be subjugated and silenced depends on prevailing power relationships in the constituting of social discourse.

THE LANGUAGE-DETERMINED SYSTEM

At the same time, influencing and being influenced by Andersen, Hoffman, Tomm, and others who locate themselves in a social constructivist/narrative frame, Anderson and Goolishian of the Houston Galveston Family Institute were also incorporating narrative ideas into family therapy. Anderson and Goolishian have reconceptualized the notion of the therapeutic social unit from the individual or family to a linguistic system distinguished by those who are "in language" together about a problem. The therapy system is a "problem-organizing, problem-dis-solving system" (1988: 372). Since, in their view, meaning and understanding are socially and intersubjectively constructed, the therapy system is one that has coalesced around some "problem"; that is, a group of people is engaged in evolving language and meaning specific to itself, specific to its organization and specific to its dissolution around "the problem." Thus the therapy system is distinguished by the assigning of language to a problem rather than by a social structure. The problem dis-solves when it has been storied or languaged in a new way or acquires a new set of meanings.

In a recent paper, Anderson and Goolishian (in press) go a step further in defining the stance of the therapist. In the dialogical therapeutic conversation, the client is seen as the expert, while the therapist assumes a position of "not-knowing." The therapist

> leaves latitude for the client to tell his/her story, unchallenged by the therapist's preconceived notions. The therapist joins in this natural unfolding of the client's narrative through a sincere effort, and with boundless curiosity, to learn about and to understand the client's meanings. The aim of learning in this therapeutic context is not the discovery of knowledge, but rather the creation of a dialogic conversational process in which new meaning and understanding is mutually evolved and always constrained by the locally negotiated rules of meaning.

The therapist is always in a state of "being informed" by the client. In what is analogous to the emic, ethnographic position of anthropologists as described by Geertz (1979), therapists bracket their own ideas or theories, making no assumptions about the intent or meaning of any action. The therapeutic conversational artist, however, in contrast to most of formal anthropology, never takes the etic, more distant position of the ethnologist who has been described as constantly tacking back and forth between experience-near and experience-far (Geertz 1979), since the hermeneutic process is seen as always collaborative, always experience-near, always coevolving.

POWER AND CONTEXT: CRITICAL COMMENTS

Family therapists, as we can see, have adopted (in general without crediting, I might add) the old and familiar role of the ethnographer who comes to the exotic and unfamiliar society as the stranger/explorer. The ethnographers have left their prepackaged theories at home, ready to listen and to try to enter the world of the "other," hovering low over the data and recognizing that both they and the others will be changed in the ensuing conversation (Rabinow 1977). These family therapists are symbolic anthropologists and hermeneuts, interested in the world of semiotics, of meaning rather than etiology or measurement. Family therapists (unlike anthropologists, who usually hoped things would remain the same, uncontaminated by Western technology, in those exotic societies they love to visit) used to believe in change. The postmodern family therapist believes only in keeping the conversation open; change cannot be plotted; the dis-solving of problems is a matter of coevolving a new language, with new punctuations, in the ongoing conversation. The job of the therapist is to keep the conversation going in a way that generates new ideas.

This revised ethnographic/hermeneutic stance fits very comfortably into postmodern theory as it is expressed in constructivist and narrative philosophy. Its beauty is that therapists in this tradition are no longer as blinded by their prior networks of assumptions, conjuring up before their very eyes what it is they were sure they would see, the borderline woman, the enmeshed or disengaged family, the codependent couple. Hence, therapists are freer to listen to the family's own narrative, to allow families to explore their own meanings; they are more respectful, perhaps less pompous, and more democratic. It is a therapy of *glasnost*. In defining the problem as "in language" (Anderson and Goolishian 1988) or as the relationship a person has with a particular story, the problem is externalized (White and Epston 1990), freeing people from the expert-blaming and self-blaming traps sprung and perpetuated by various systems of labeling and diagnosing.

However, some risks and some limitations are also present in the narrative and constructivist stances as they are currently being formulated, or at least some problems are not yet adequately articulated or addressed. These include the problem of power and the problem of context.

The Problem of Power

Postmodern therapists are, according to Hoffman (1985), moving beyond a position of power and control. They are abandoning the position of expert, in which the therapist assumes responsibility for change or solution to the family's troubles, to a spirit of collaboration, in which no one's solutions are privileged. The therapist tries to shed power, assuming the position of neutral conversationalist. Therapy becomes a matter of keeping the conversation going long enough so that new stories, new meanings can emerge. Families are usually not urged to contract for long periods or even short periods of therapy but rather are invited to consult as frequently or infrequently as they wish.

This old–new stance is extremely attractive, in my view. For one thing, the combined constructivist/ethnographic stance frees therapists from more narrow, religious-like devotions to particular theories. No particular ideas or narratives are favored. It offers a potential bridge between the psychological and the systemic, between individual, family, and group modalities, for all are interested in meaning; neither theory nor size of client system becomes a divisional marker in the mental health professions. Constructivism is, says Hoffman (1990), a lens through which to view other lenses. It depathologizes. We are no longer required to fit the narratives we hear into some prior structure or tired script. It allows for many voices to be heard and considered. It is extremely respectful, judging not.

But some caution is in order. At the same time the family therapy constructivist, like the new ethnographer, has become more conscious of the implicit power relations in traditional modes of therapy and in the imposition of privileged texts, of the constant colonialization and subjugation of the "other," this new philosopher–constructivist–family therapist–conversationalist seems to be largely ignoring the power issues relevant to the shaping of all narrative. There seems to be a naive belief that all narratives are equal and that each individual has the power to shape his or her own narrative. Interested in the personal story, this new group seems to have forgotten that personal and social narratives are intricately and intimately connected or, if that is remembered, the assumption is that the social is embedded in the personal in such a way that, if relevant, it will emerge in the therapeutic conversation.

As Foucault (1980) has taught us, knowledge and power are inseparable. We do not have equal access to knowledge, and all stories are not equal; many conversations are not possible because certain voices have been repeatedly silenced, some silenced to the point where the story cannot be told even to the self; one's lived experiences cannot be voiced (Laird, in press). Such has been the case with childhood victims of incest, with African–Americans and American Indians, with men who experience atrocities in wars whose purposes are unclear and who return to contexts in which no one wants to hear their stories. Women's ways of knowing, for example, are often disparaged, their learning and speaking genres often ridiculed (Belenky et al, 1986); they learn they cannot participate in certain social discourses or not to speak at all (Coates 1986). New family therapists claim that no one's story, no one's voice, including their own, is privileged. I would argue that certain voices are privileged in every conversation. Our personal voices are strengthened or weakened by virtue of our abilities to locate ourselves in and shape the larger social discourses that in turn shape and define us and these abilities. Our narratives are privileged or constrained by such things as sex or sexual orientation, income and wealth, education, skin color, or, put another way, by how these various narratives are storied in the larger social discourse. Can we create the conversational spaces in which silenced voices may be heard if we do not understand and if we are not constantly aware of, sensitive to, and committed to fighting the oppressions that create such silences? I think not. If we are not always sensitive to the power contexts in which the personal narrative is shaped, we will by default privilege certain voices in our therapeutic conversations.

A second issue has to do with neutrality, a stance implied in the nonprivileging of any narrative. Can we be neutral when we are working with families in which women are brutalized by their husbands, or women are brutalizing their children, or the entire family is being brutalized by the state and the community? Minuchin (1991) argues against the tendency, in constructivist therapy, to "concentrate overmuch on the idiosyncratic 'story' of the individual family and ignore the social context that may actually dictate much of the 'plot' of their lives" (49). Hoffman (1985) tries to do away with this problem by acknowledging that we must render unto Newton the things that are Newton's. By this she means that nonneutral, linear attitudes and actions are often necessary, appropriate, and what we usually get paid for. Clearly their are times when our first priorities must be to protect some people and control others, for example, but this, she would argue, is not therapy; these kinds of nonneutral actions do not alter the basic recipes in the family. In her view, we must always be clear about whether we are wearing a social control hat or a therapeutic hat. In the former role we do and must make moral judgments; in the latter role we must divest ourselves of power and enter into genuine dialogue.

In contrast, Minuchin (unpublished) maintains that:

> When the constructivists equate expertise with power, and develop a new technology of interventions that avoid control, they are only creating a different use of power. Control does not disappear from family therapy when it is re-named "co-creation." All that happens is that the influence of the therapist on the family is made invisible. Safely underground, it may remain unexamined.

Wife abuse, child sexual and physical abuse, and other ills endemic to the modern family cannot be "languaged" or "storied" away in conversation, however collaborative. I find myself agreeing with Minuchin (unpublished) when he says "If the writing of these stories is made invisible, stories are told as if they were constructed by the families themselves."

The Problem of Context

A second concern, closely related to the problem of power, has to do with context. I wrote above about the relationship between the personal and the social, one level of context, that is about the social and institutional contexts in which personal stories are shaped. In research circles, to date there has been far more interest in structural and other microanalytic approaches to the deconstruction of the personal narrative than there has been in the interaction between personal and social discourse. Here I would like to make two suggestions, one a largely political one and one that will return me to the question of research.

First, I believe the time has come for family therapists to examine themselves in context, an appeal also made by MacKinnon and Miller (1987) in examining the sociopolitical context of the Milan approach. How might we understand the meanings of the infatuation with constructivist/ narrative pursuits in this time and space? Why have we become so entranced with a search for meaning, for language, with its elegant and seductive philosophies? Is it because our social surround is falling apart? Is it because it rescues us from having to think about a world in which more than half of all black men are unemployed, cities in which the conditions are so inhumane people are slaughtering each other, a world rotting with pollution, a world in which governments change hands frequently and in the process starve and murder their own peoples, a world in which women are battling not just for equality but for survival? Constructivism has taken hold in a period when we have watched helplessly while our own government has destroyed the social programs we cared about and rechanneled resources to the already rich. We do not want to call these stories "realities" or "truths." It is too painful. We need to locate ourselves in our sociopolitical context, that is, the context in which our constructivist story has taken shape, and to critically examine what we find. Is there something "escapist" about the story metaphor?

Second, in keeping with social work's historical allegiance to the relationship between person and environment, we need to continue to try to develop models of practice and models of research that are holistic, not reductionistic. I would argue that many of the microanalytic approaches to narrative analysis and even the metaphor of the text tend once again to remove figure from ground, personal narrative from social context. In our haste to run from universals, from superorganic views, are we returning to the notion that culture is located inside mind and in language—an extreme relativist and subjectivist position that Geertz (1973) has called the cognitive fallacy?

IMPLICATIONS FOR PRACTICE-RESEARCH

Nevertheless, caveats in hand, the postmodern clinician has much to offer the burgeoning area of qualititative research. The clinician has unique opportunities to hear how people make meanings in their lives and to offer a context in which new meanings may be collaboratively forged. Clinicians by default are in contexts where they can "hover low over the data," where description can be thickened, each family its own small culture, its own ethnographic study. The disciplined exploration of the client narrative, using ethnographic and narrative strategies encompassing power and contextual issues, can be a valuable research endeavor.

In my view, the ethnographic metaphor as so colorfully and richly deconstructed by Geertz in 1973 still offers rich guidance, an umbrella under which we may subsume narrative and textual interpretation, practice, and research. We can approach interpretation of the conversation, the narrative, only if we understand the nests of context and power relations, the familial and social worlds in which meaning is generated.

For Geertz, culture is a context, something within which signs, symbols, narratives, social events, historic patterns, ritual, folklore, myth, and so on can be understood. We begin with ourselves, with our own interpretations of what our informants are up to, or think they are up to, and we then try to make sense of these interpretations. Coherence, now a favorite concept among narrative analysts, cannot be the only or major test of validity for a cultural description. As Geertz puts it, there is nothing so coherent as a paranoid's delusion or a swindler's story. The force of our interpretations cannot rest on the tightness with which they hold together, or on the more formal structures or patterns into which social actions seem to arrange themselves, at least in our minds. What ethnography consists of is "thick description," the tracing of a curve of social discourse, inscribing it and fixing it into some inspectable form. We cannot understand the said and the unsaid, in my view, without understanding the surrounding forces that make possible the said and mandate the unsaid.

For Geertz, the pursuit is particular. The ethnographic study is akin to the clinical case, a situation in which the "scientist" remains close to the ground, avoiding abstraction. "The whole point of a semiotic approach to culture . . . is to aid us in gaining access to the conceptual world in which our subjects live so that we can, in some extended sense of the term, converse with them" (1973: 24). The point is not to generalize or to codify abstract regularities but to make thick description possible, not to generalize across cases but to generalize within them. To abstract is to decontextualize. But what ethnography can give us, aside from the particular, are ideas, questions, tentative principles that increase our abilities to hear, to search for meanings in the next "culture" we encounter, to bear witness to human experience.

In ethnography, "the office of theory is to provide a vocabulary in which what symbolic action has to say about itself—that is, about the role of culture in human life—can be expressed" (1973: 29). In other words, the ethnographic study stands on its own. It is never reliable, never finished, always incomplete. As Geertz puts it: "It is a strange science whose most telling assertions are its most tremulously based, in which to get somewhere with the matter at hand is to intensify the suspicion, both your own and that of others, that you are not quite getting it right."

RREFERENCES

Allen J. and J. Laird. 1990. Men and story: Constructing new narratives in therapy. *Journal of Feminist Family Therapy* 2, nos. 3 and 4: 75–100.

Andersen, T. 1987. The reflecting team: Dialogue and meta-dialogue in clinical work. *Family Process* 26: 415–28.

Andersen, T., ed. 1991. *The Reflecting Team: Dialogues and Dialogues About the Dialogues*. New York: Norton.

Anderson, H. and H. Goolishian. 1988. Human systems as linguistic systems: Evolving ideas about the implications for theory and practice. *Family Process* 27: 371–93.

Anderson, H. and H. Goolishian. In press. The client is the expert: A not-knowing approach to therapy. In K. Gergen and S. McNamee, eds., *Inquiries in Social Construction*. Newbury Park, Calif.: Sage.

Bass, E. and L. Davis. 1988. *The Courage to Heal: A Guide for Women Survivors of Sexual Abuse*. New York: Harper and Row.

Bateson, G. 1972. *Steps to an Ecology of Mind*. New York: Ballantine.

Bateson, G. 1979. *Mind and Nature: A Necessary Unity*. New York: Bantam.

Belenky, M. F., B. M. Clinchy, N. R. Goldberger, and J. M. Tarule. 1986. *Women's Ways of Knowing: The Development of Self, Voice, and Mind*. New York: Basic Books.

Bettelheim, B. 1977. *The Uses of Enchantment*. New York: Vintage.

Bruner E. 1986a. Ethnography as narrative. In V. Turner and E. Bruer, eds., *The Anthropology of Experience*. Chicago: University of Chicago Press.

Bruner E. 1986b. Experience and its expressions. In Turner and Bruner, eds. *The Anthropology of Experience*. Chicago: University of Chicago Press.

Clifford J. and G. E. Marcus, eds. 1986. *Writing Culture: The Poetics and Politics of Ethnography*. Berkeley: University of California Press.

Coates, J. 1986. *Women, Men, and Language: A Sociolinguistic Account of Sex Differences in Language*. London: Longman.

Cohler, B. 1988. The human studies and the life history. *Social Service Review* 62: 552–75.

Derrida, J. 1986. Differance. In M. C. Taylor, ed., *Deconstruction in Context*. Chicago: University of Chicago Press.

Ferreira, A. 1963. Family myth and homeostasis. *Archives of General Psychiatry* 9: 456–63.

Foucault, M. 1980. *Power/Knowledge: Selected Interviews and Other Writings*. New York: Pantheon.

Geertz, C. 1973. *The Interpretation of Cultures*. New York: Basic Books.

Geertz, C. 1979. From the native's point of view: On the nature of anthropological understanding. In P. Rabinow and W. M. Sullivan, eds., *Interpretive Social Science: A Reader*, pp. 225–41. Berkeley: University of California Press.

Geertz, C. 1980. Blurred genres: The refiguration of social thought. *American Scholar* 49, no. 2: 165–79.

Geertz, C. 1988. *Works and Lives: The Anthropologist as Author*. Stanford: Stanford University Press.

Gergen, K. 1985. The social constructionist movement in modern psychology. *American Psychologist* 40: 266–27.

Gergen, K. J. and K. E. Davis, eds., 1985. *The Social Construction of the Person*. New York: Springer-Verlag.

Gergen, K. and M. Gergen. 1983. Narratives of the self. In T. R. Sarbin and K. E. Scheibe, eds., *Studies in Social Identity*, pp. 254–73. New York: Praeger.

Heilbrun, C. 1988. *Writing a Woman's Life*. New York: Ballantine.

Hoffman, L. 1985. Beyond power and control: Toward a second-order family systems therapy. *Family Systems Medicine* 3: 381–96.

Hoffman, L. 1990. Constructing realities: An art of lenses. *Family Process* 29: 1–12.

Imber-Black, E., J. Roberts, and R. Whiting. 1988. *Rituals in Families and Family Therapy*. New York: Norton.

Laird, J. 1984. Sorcerers, shamans, and social workers: The use of ritual in family-centered practice. *Social Work* 29: 123–29.

Laird, J. 1988. Women and ritual in family therapy. In E. Imber-Black, J. Roberts, and R. Whiting, eds., *Rituals in Families and in Family Therapy*, pp. 331–62. New York: Norton.

Laird, J. 1989. Women and stories: Restorying women's self-constructions. In M. McGoldrick, C. Anderson, and F. Walsh, eds., *Women in Families*, pp. 428–49. New York: Norton.

Laird, J. In press. Women's secrets—women's silences. In E. Imber-Black, ed., *Secrets in Families and Family Therapy*. New York: Norton.

MacKinnon, L. and D. Miller. 1987. The new epistemology and the Milan approach: Feminist and sociopolitical considerations. *Journal of Marital and Family Therapy* 13: 139–55.

Maturana, H. R. 1978. The biology of language: The epistemology of reality. In G. Miller and E. Lenneberg, eds., *Psychology and Biology of Language and Thought*. New York: Academic Press.

McGoldrick, M., J. K. Pearce, and J. Giordano, eds. 1982. *Ethnicity and Family Therapy*. New York: Gulford Press.

Minuchin, S. 1991. The seductions of constructivism. *Family Therapy Networker* 15, no. 5 (September/October): 47–50.

Minuchin, S. Unpublished. The restoried history of family therapy.

Myerhoff, B. 1978. *Number Our Days*. New York: Dutton.

O'Flaherty, W. 1980. Inside and outside the mouth of god: The boundary between myth and reality. *Daedalus* 109: 93–125.

Rabinow, P. 1977. *Reflections on Fieldwork in Morocco*. Berkeley: University of California Press.

Schafer, R. 1981. *Narrative Actions in Psychoanalysis*. Worcester, Mass.: Clark University Press.

Selvini-Palazzoli, M. et al. 1977. Family rituals: A powerful tool in family therapy. *Family Process* 16: 445–63.

Spence, D. 1982. *Narrative Truth and Historical Truth: Meaning and Interpretation in Psychoanalysis*. New York: Norton.

Tomm, K. 1987. Interventive interviewing: Part II. Reflexive questioning as a means to enable self-healing. *Family Process* 26: 167–84.

Turner, V. 1969. *The Ritual Process*. Chicago: Aldine.

von Foerster, H. 1984. On constructing a reality. In P. Watzlawick, ed., *The Invented Reality*. New York: Norton.

von Glasersfeld, E. 1984. An introduction to radical constructivism. In P. Watzlawick, ed., *The Invented Reality*. New York: Norton.

Watzlawick, P. ed. 1984. *The Invented Reality*. New York: Norton.

White, M. 1989. *Selected Papers*. Adelaide, South Australia: Dulwich Centre Publications.

White, M. and D. Epston. 1990. *Narrative Means to Therapeutic Ends*. New York: Norton.

FIFTEEN

Life Forces of African-American Elderly Illustrated Through Oral History Narratives

Ruth R. Martin

This paper has as its purpose the discussion of life forces of African-American elderly revealed through oral history narratives. The paper is divided into four sections. The first section describes and defines life forces. The second section defines oral history, discusses its roots, and provides a rationale for its use. The third gives a brief description of the narrators and the final section is devoted to two types of narratives: narratives that depict oppressive forces and narratives that depict positive life forces, or how the narrators "got over."

LIFE FORCES

Life forces is a term reintroduced by Germain (1990). She draws on Bandler (1963), who describes life forces as being "parental, progressive, developmental, and educational processes."

The oral history research presented in this paper may support Bandler's argument, which holds "that the more we learn about natural life forces, the more able we are to help people to identify and remove obstacles in their paths, and to rediscover their own capacities for achieving satisfying family and community lives" (Germain 1990:138). Our responsibilities should not end here, however, for as we learn more we realize that obstacles often arise such as racism and oppression that people alone cannot be expected to remove. As Harrington (1962) wrote, "if all the discriminatory laws in the United States were immediately repealed, race would still remain as one of the most pressing moral and political problems in the nation" (73). Twenty-nine years later, Harrington's perception of racism and oppression still prevails.

ORAL HISTORY METHOD

Baum (1970) defined oral history as

> a way of taking down reminiscences by means of a tape recorder; not random reminiscences but planned interviews on a subject of historical interest about which the narrator can speak with authority . . . the interviewee can be someone who was in an influential position at the time of the event . . . an observation post . . . or articulate representative of a class of person . . . or old timer who can describe a past way of life.   (1970, transcript)

Roots of Oral History

The methodology of oral history dates back to Asian, Middle Eastern, and African cultures (Haley 1976; Ong 1977). Many African-Americans have learned that Africa was not a "primitive culture" but a highly civilized society that kept oral history long before human beings knew how to write. Oral histories, according to Ong (1977), "encourage a sense of continuity with life—a sense of participation because it is itself participation." Haley (1976) portrayed this sense of continuity when he traced his family's life history to Africa covering seven generations. He discovered, to his amazement, the continued existence of *griots*—men who are walking archives in the older back-country villages of Africa. Like Ong, Haley ruminated on the ancient origins of oral history: "Every living person ancestrally goes back to some time and place when no writing existed . . . when . . . human memories and mouths and ears were the only way those human beings could store and relay information" (Haley 1976:574). Much of what African–Americans have learned of a positive nature regarding their continuity with life, their culture, self-help techniques, and contributions to American society was handed down in a like manner.

Rationale for Using Oral History

Oral history allows individuals, families, and small groups to talk about themselves and tell their life stories or narratives. "Unskilled, uneducated, and even illiterate persons" can use their own words to "relate their observations and experiences," expressing their innermost feelings—and depicting their very existence in "an uninhibited spontaneous and natural manner" (Lewis 1963:xxii).

Subjects selected for oral history research need not have client status or be facing some adversity or unresolved problems. Oral history provides a means of acquiring a knowledge base on well-functioning individuals and families with good social and survival skills. This can serve as teaching resource material for practitioners who can then utilize this knowledge to enhance practice interventions with families in need of help (Martin 1987:5–10). We cannot assume that students' curiosity or hunger for knowledge about minorities will lead them to research racism, oppression, and powerlessness. This lack of information hampers professionals in their attempt to assist their African-American clients with tools of empowerment (Martin 1985:3).

Because the African-American family has often been portrayed as dysfunctional, oral history narratives can serve as a useful tool to help professional educators and students understand the adaptive functional strength of the family. Indeed, a wealth of historical data is available that has not been recorded about African Americans with remarkable survival skills.

Berry and Blassingame (1982) seem to support this thesis. They contend that "the history of the African-American family is a largely uncharted field. The family and the church enabled African-Americans to endure American racism, slavery, segregation, violence and oppression. . . . These institutions provided the foundation for personal identity, communal strength, individual triumphs in the face of overwhelming odds, creative and rewarding lives, and pride" (70). It is, therefore, important that their narratives be recorded and disseminated. Not only can they serve to interpret the past for the present generation, but also they can provide a broader knowledge base for future generations. Our progeny might then be motivated by these historical insights to work to ensure that "racial degradation, exploitation and segregation will not be perpetuated" (Martin 1987: 5–10).

Oral histories can reveal the human diversity in the African-American experience, showing how the experience is different for people within the same subculture. As one conducts the oral histories, the researcher can begin to understand that "African-American families, like African-American individuals, are like all other families in the United States, like some other families, and like no other African-American family all at the same time" (Solomon 1976:181). One also learns how coping techniques have differed.

The oral histories reveal the effects of racism, violence, and oppression on the total African-American experience. Cafferty and Chestang (1976) offers a graphic description of the African-American experience. "The

African-American experience connotes the deferred dreams and frustrated aspirations of a people oppressed by society. It may also convey the ideas of a culture, style and social pattern developed to cope with life situations to which society consigns the African-American" (61).

The African-American experience is best understood if viewed from three conditions that Chestang says are "socially determined" and "institutionally supported": social injustice, societal inconsistencies, and personal impotence.

Oral history helps broaden the awareness of the interdependence between family, community, and political systems and of the psychological forces within the wider society that impinge on the African-American family. Oral history also enhances the awareness of their impact on the quality of family life, including the manner by which families have adapted, coped, floundered, and succeeded (Martin 1987).

THE ORAL HISTORY NARRATORS

The following narratives are taken from oral histories of fifteen African-American families. The participants' ages ranged from sixty to eighty-five years. This was an exploratory and qualitative research study that focused on the adaptation of black families. The oral. history method guided the data collection procedures. The qualitative researcher often deals with smaller numbers than in quantitative research but goes into the subjects' lives in much greater richness and detail. One participant helped to clarify this view in very vivid terms. When I arrived at his home and attempted to explain to him and his wife my interest in conducting qualitative research through the oral history methodology and to learn how African-American families survived political, social, and economic oppression, he responded, "In other words, you want to put some meat on the bones."

As Stern (1985), has observed, reconstructing a developmental past through narrative has therapeutic value. He contends that when one acquires language, the ability to narrate one's own life story and change the perception of oneself is obtained. In his view, "narrative-making may prove to be a universal human phenomenon reflecting the design of the human mind (Stern 1985:174). The oral history narratives in this article focus on the African-American elderly and how various historically routed life forces affected the "paths they have taken over their life course" (Germain 1990:138–39). Some of these life forces have severely limited access to larger portions of the life space as the elderly have proceeded through their life course. Despite the pervasive life forces that permeated nearly all aspects of their lives, the participants in this study have shown "resilience, self-healing, mutual aid, self-help, and other life forces" (Germain

1990:138). They have adapted, survived, prospered, and created opportunities for their young to achieve mastery and competence.

They had to traverse through first- and second-order life issues. First-order life transitions occur very frequently and are expectable. These are "continuing biological- and social-maturational transitions from birth to old age that present family members with new requirements and opportunities for mastery. Second-order life issues consist of severely painful transitions and life events ranging from job loss to natural catastrophes, and are not expectable in the average family's experience" (Germain 1990:144). However, because of pervasive racism and oppression, these life issues for African-American elderly who were born around the turn of the century became expectable life issues. Some of these have affected every facet of African-American life.

The following narratives, then, present a view of what actually happened to these African–American elderly during their life transactions. The narratives were selected to represent oppressive life forces such as: racism, political and economic inequality, segregation, and education. The narratives also reflect the positives that came out of the Freedman's Bureau of 1865, especially the benefit African-Americans derived from the Bureau's work as an educational agency—its encouragement of the founding of African-American schools and its provision of financial aid. The participants would later benefit from attending these all-black institutions.

OBSTACLES: OPPRESSIVE FORCES

Axinn and Levin (1983) and Trattner (1979) have well depicted the plight of African-Americans and their oppression in the colonial period, pre-Civil War era, after the Civil War, the New Deal period, and the Civil Rights movement. However, when viewed through the lens of these participants, oral narratives bring new meaning to their life issues. The oppressive forces discussed in this section include discrimination in employment, poor wages, unequal facilities and education, and inferior housing. For example, in the following narrative the participant tells how discrimination kept African-Americans from working in the trades, a necessary source of survival money.

> I don't know exactly how I was able to adjust to it, but in the meantime, I
> say that I did take industrial arts. I had several trades that I was active in. I
> first took the trade of painting during high school. I did carpentry, and a bit
> of electricity, a bit of plumbing, and a bit of mechanics. And, of course, I
> did have a general knowledge of all of those trades. And when I came out of
> school, well, I was disillusioned. I was disillusioned because I wanted to
> follow some of those trades. And, of course, I was a bit outstanding in the

field of carpentry, and I felt that there was a need for it. And I tried to integrate myself into the school here, into Brewster Vocational School. That was for whites only. And, of course, you couldn't work even with the white people within the community. You could hand them some of their materials or what have you, but you couldn't drive a nail. They wouldn't allow that and of course I wanted to work along with somebody who was doing some work—scab work—among the blacks. They wouldn't accept me. So, I was thinking that I needed to do something too, because the times were so bad during that time, it was in the depths of the Depression. And, of course, I went to Key West. The salaries were $90. And I went to Key West, and I was still in search for something that I needed. And, of course, that something was money to be able to survive.

The following narrative depicts oppressive forces in the fearsome form of the Ku Klux Klan:

I could not survive in another neighborhood. I would have to get used to it, you know. I would get used to it. But I'll always want to be in a black neighborhood. I don't care about integration. Although when we moved here this was a mixed neighborhood. There were very few blacks between 22d and 29th. That was a Ku Klux Klan area during that time (back in the twenties). When we moved in this area, they didn't want blacks in this area. The KKK put signs in the yards. Everybody was very fearful. For instance, across the street was an old house. And the whites were leaving when we bought it. So when they found who had bought it, then they broke the windows, threw a brick through the window. It was already an old raggedy house. And so, now there were this minister and his wife, and they set his house on fire. And he was the only black in these two blocks. And we were the second black family. And so they set his house on fire, but they (the family) were able to put it out before it burned completely. And I remember one residence where they threw these big placards. "First and last there will be no niggers in this area. KKK." And they threw them in your yard at night. And some of the people went downtown. And they say downtown at the courthouse they told them, anybody you catch in the yard, just drop them. And see we were all blacks, two black families in this block. A black family moved into this house over there, the old house. And they ran them out, way late in the night. And they ran over to our house. And my father opened the door and let them stay over. It was a Saturday night. And the next morning they got up and they moved.

How I/We "Got Over": Positive Life Forces

There is an old religious song that African-Americans sing that questions, "How I got over, how I got over. I look back and wonder how I got over?" The participants, in telling their stories, individually and collectively indicated that they were able to get over by believing in God (each participant in this study was a church member and goer), fighting back through political activism, taking family responsibilities seriously, school and community working together, holding to African-American traditional values, having good role models, families working together, self-empowerment, and believing in the future of African-American youth.

Role Models

Parents, teachers, ministers, and people of the African-American community were all positive role models. Some additional strong role models were Booker T. Washington, George Washington Carver, and Benjamin Mays. The participants' discussions of the importance of good role models were voiced again and again, specifically with regard to black youth.

One narrator below had this to say about his parents.

> I think my parents motivated me. My daddy lost his father at a very early age and he was not able to attend school. He could not read nor write. My mother did finish elementary school. And by the mere fact that they lacked an education, they encouraged my sister and I to get an education. And my father worked at Seaboard Railroad Company. And he saw to it that we were able to go to school, go to college, and finish. And I might say that we were, my sister and I, the first two grandchildren of my mother's family, to finish college. And, of course, since that time, there have been others. And I was looking for my "roots" book, because in there it gives a history of just how many have gone on from that family. My mother was one of fourteen children.

Families Working Together

The extended family was one of the strengths that kept the African-American community going in the past. The death of parents did not necessarily exclude a child from a secure future. Grandparents, aunts, uncles, or even a nonrelative from the African-American community would not hesitate to take an orphan into their home and raise this child as their own.

The following narrative paints a vivid picture of family members teaching by example, caring for their children, and taking in the extended family.

> My father was a graduate of Florida A & M normal school. And he was the principal in Apalachicola, Florida. My mother was a dressmaker. And, of course, they both died. My mother died when I was five years old, and my father died when I was nine years old. But I was living over at my grandparents. I was motivated by their activities in the community. And, of course,

they were good church people. We were close, our family was close to the church. They did get me an opportunity to go to Florida A & M after finishing eighth grade in Apalachicola.

This participant describes how each family member had specific roles in maintaining their home.

I cooked dinner, then my husband and I would go to church. They (her children) went to the day nursery just a little while, but not very long. We just taught them all we knew at home before they went to school. Then they got old enough to wash dishes. I made them wash dishes, and make that bed, and help with the work, and help with the yard. My husband had a push mower and they mowed the lawns, but even with the push mower, when they were eleven and twelve years old, they would mow the neighbors yard and make money and so then, when they got in the teens, my husband bought them a power lawn mower. So then they made more money change. I told you about the oldest son, he delivered groceries for this wholesale grocerer company and the youngest boy worked as a bus boy. . . . Yeah, yeah when we lived over there where the Holiday Inh is and those bad children lived in front of us, I told you about how I'd keep them in and that's why we hurried and moved over here to get away from them. They would come over here, wanted to play with our children and I'd say, "They can't play, go back home." I sent them back home fast so they got tired of coming and going back home, so they soon stopped. I made them stay home and studied and made them do everything they could learn how to do. The boys used to make woodwork, they made that little old whatnot stand, one of them made tables and different things and they used to make hot pads in school and all kinds of things. Our daughter can sew too. And they should be taught about the Lord, that's the first thing, and not to run the streets. I would let lots of young boys come here and talk, the porch would be full of boys and an old lady in the neighborhood, she came in and said, "What are you doing with all those boys, why don't you let them get in the streets somewhere?" I said, "For what? There isn't anything in the street but something bad and I said that's why I let them come here, I don't want them to run the streets." Oh they would have the best time. We would buy like ten pounds of white potatoes and all the hot dogs you could eat. They would chip in for popcorn and Kool-Aid, and I would let the oldest pay, make hotdogs and make Kool-Aid and they would sit under the mango tree and play cards.

Perspectives on the Future

The narrators, having given an overview of their lives, were asked to focus and comment on the future of African-American youth in view of teenage pregnancy, education, and so forth.

The next narrator would give the following advice today, in terms of motivation, in terms of school, and in terms of the youths' making something of themselves.

> If I had to give advice, my advice would be to, the thing that's closest to me now, I think, is economics. To develop a monetary base that we can work with. And I have just accepted the idea of speaking and working with the community constituency, this monetary base. And we can't live and prosper as individuals. We must come together with our thoughts and our actions and move in a direction where we would be responsible one to the other. And so those would be the things that I would more or less tell to people, black people, of today. Stay in school. Education is important. And even though I had one child, there are many, many children that I had valued and have helped.

The narrators in these oral histories challenge some of the stereotypes about the elderly. For example, the elderly are often referred to as living in isolation. This researcher did not experience a sense of isolation among the African-American participants in this study. The family was seen as resource for growth, coping, and adaptation. During research visits to the participants' homes, relatives telephoned, and children, grandchildren, great-nieces, and nephews stopped over for a brief visit.

The networking of the elderly was impressive, for they were taking care of grandchildren, grandnieces, nephews, and the like. The family that shared the evening meal at their home with their son and his family, the eighty-year-old who met her grandnephew at the school bus stop around the corner and watched him until his mother got off work, the seventy-six-year-old who actively participated in community activities, all reflect their meaningful social integration and involvement.

One realizes that even though life forces in the early decades were and continue to be oppressive, these families have "overcome"; they have shown resilience, have mastered their environments, and have demonstrated a level of competence second to none. They are weary and disillusioned, but they are also hopeful for the future of African-American youth—this, in spite of the teenage pregnancies, crime, poor school attendance, and the like. As one participant put it, "You hear about one youth who is making it and you believe there is hope."

It is hoped that these narratives demonstrate the value of oral history method as an important tool in social work research. It can also provide valuable teaching materials about human diversity and behavior in the social environments of critical concern for social work students and practitioners alike.

REFERENCES

Axinn, J. and H. Levin. 1982. *Social Welfare: A History of the American Response to Need*. 2d ed. New York: Harper and Row.

Bandler, B. 1963. The concept of ego-supportive psychotherapy. In H. J. Parad and R. B. Miller, eds., *Ego-Oriented Casework: Problems and Perspectives*, pp. 27–44. New York: Family Service Association of America.

Baum, W. K. 1970. Transcript of speech at Oral History Association Seminar. Harrisburg, Pa.

Berry, M. F. and J. W. Blassingame. 1982. *Long Memory: The Black Experience in America*. New York: Oxford University Press.

Cafferty, P. S. J. and L. Chestang. 1976. *The Diverse Society: Implications for Social Policy*. Washington: NASW Press.

Germain, C. B. 1990. Life forces and the anatomy of practice. *Smith College Studies in Social Work* 60, no. 2 (March): 138–52.

Haley, A 1976. *Roots: The Saga of an American Family*. New York: Doubleday.

Harrington, M. 1962. *The Other American: Poverty in the United States*, p. 73. New York: MacMillan.

Lewis, O. 1963. *The Children of Sanchez: Autobiography of a Mexican Family*. New York: Random House.

Martin, R. R. 1985. *Oral History as Pedagogy*, part II focus: *Chronicling the Black Extended Family*, p. 1. Paper presented at the Council on Social Work Education, APM. Washington, D.C., February 17–20.

Martin, R. R. 1987. Oral history in social work education: Chronicling the black experience. *Journal of Social Work Education* 23, no. 3: 5–10.

Ong, S. J. 1977. *Interface of the Word: Studies in the Evolution of Consciousness and Culture*. New York: Cornell University Press.

The Oral History narratives were collected between 1982 and 1986 in the southeastern region of the United States.

Solomon, B. B. 1976. *Black Empowerment: Social Work in Oppressed Communities*. New York: Columbia University Press.

Stern, D. N. 1985. *The Interpersonal World of the Infant*. New York: Basic Books.

Trattner, W. I. 1979. *From Poor Law to Welfare State: A History of Social Welfare in America*. New York: Free Press.

SIXTEEN

Commentary: Narrative in Clinical Research

Sheldon S. Tobin

Martin comments in her paper on the usefulness of personal narratives for practitioners and students. Indeed, the gathering of narratives of elderly African Americans by African-American social work students was perceived to be of special benefit to them. Through narratives they gained an appreciation of their culture, particularly how adversity has been overcome in past decades. Moreover, the face-to-face contact enhances a sense of pride and feelings of belongingness with other African-American students, especially if they are only a small group among a majority of white social work students. In turn, the narratives in the aggregate provide rich data for understanding the collective earlier experiences of elderly African-Americans. Although there may be some retrospective distortion in reconstructing the past, a topic discussed by Cohler in his article, reconstructions of the past provide for understanding the historical context of oppression and how oppression is perceived and confronted.

The importance of personal narratives for the teller and for the listener is echoed throughout these essays. In therapeutic encounters, practitioners must allow clients to tell their life stories without inhibiting their reconstructions of the past. Sometimes expectations cause a premature assessment that is not valid because the full story has not been allowed to be told. In these instances it is likely that theories of human behavior and practice evoke constructs that are imposed on clients instead of using the telling to lead us to greater appreciations of lives that have been lived and lives in progress.

The commonality in Laird's and Cohler's perspectives are evident: the therapeutic encounter can be understood only if it is a shared experience of empathic understanding within the context of the relationship. Only then, through Laird's thick description or Cohler's experience-near mode, can it become possible to know how people make meanings, whether we label the approach human science as Cohler does or constructivist as Laird does. Moreover, whereas storying in itself enhances personal integrity, therapy becomes, as Laird so ably communicates, restorying as the therapist adopts the role of conversationalist artist.

Arriving at premature closure can be harmful in family therapy where conversations of family members can be revealing of meanings of current interaction, of latent conflicts, and of etiologies of family dynamics. By permitting and facilitating conversations, the therapist avoids imposing structure that can limit understanding by family members, as well as by therapist. Systematic study of this, and other phenomena, is warranted if personal narratives and stories are to become useful data for clinical research.

But it is not only ourselves as therapists and our clients that can benefit from greater reconstructions; it is also larger audiences. In much the same way that tapes of autobiographies of African-Americans can be helpful to students, the shared experiences of a variety of disenfranchised and oppressed groups can be helpful to members of these groups. The shared experiences, for example, of gay and lesbian individuals can be invaluable to them.

Yet, we must also value disseminating the yield from the gathering of personal narratives or life histories or stories of targeted groups to those who are not members of these groups. The communication of life experiences is indeed instructive for understanding human diversity and for correcting distorted perceptions. Unfortunately, however, dissemination is lagging far behind reports of narrowly focused empirical studies. Although human science and constructivism are rightly taking their place alongside traditional logical positivism, vehicles for publication are scant. Journal editors are hesitant to fill precious pages with more lengthy thick description and experience-near reports than are warranted and necessary to communicate findings. Editors should consider monographs that permit the dissemination of qualitative studies that can richly illuminate the human experiences.

DISCOURSE
ANALYSIS

SEVENTEEN

The Dialogical Analysis of Case Materials

Adrienne S. Chambon

Verbal exchange in client-worker encounters is a complex performance that combines several activities into one: a narrative activity centered on the exchange and interpretation of a particular sort of stories, the life story or life project; a conversational form of speech activity characterized by the asymmetric distribution of roles; and a transformational process with mutual attempts at influencing or persuasion, participants using a range of repertoires to achieve strategic effects.

The dialogical analysis of the therapeutic dialogue proposed here (and part of a larger research project conducted under the auspices of the Laboratoire de Changement Social at the University of Paris VII) incorporates these three facets of verbal activity. Bakhtin's (1986) concept of "speech genre" as oral and textual discourse provides an anchoring to this comprehensive understanding. Located between the general and the particular, discursive activity is neither a transcription of a language system nor the idiosyncratic product of individual performance. Instead, "speech genres" are associated with specific social exchanges and sociohistorical contexts.

Second, speech is not the additive product of distinct utterances but rather the outcome of a dialogical activity of interpersonal adaptation and intertextuality, the participants activating multiple systems of connotations and stylistic modalities through explicit and implicit means. Third, content is inseparable from form. The semantic dimension of oral and written texts is not established before their stylistics. Semantic, lexical, and grammatical features combine to constitute "speech genres." Last, far from being a ritualized exchange with limited combinations, the therapeutic dialogue as an informal speech genre is an open territory used creatively in its transformational purpose.

The therapeutic encounter places telling and talking as major vehicles of the therapeutic activity, sanctioned by institutional arrangements and competing professions. The interactional stakes are high: making sense of a life project, relieving some of the confused pain, deciphering versions of life happenings, having past and future visions, defining what is possible, separating out multiple voices, and developing one's own. This explains the participants' investment in their performance and the exquisiteness of a "heightened language" (Tambling 1988) developed, not as a poetic function, but to conduct a heightened form of conversation.

The way that people talk in therapeutic conversations seems on the surface a very ordinary way of talking in the service of deconstructing/reconstructing a life project. One often observes a "flowing quality" in the exchange between a client and a worker after a number of sessions. A working experience demystifies this illusion. Talking in therapeutic conversations is not quite "regular talk"; the language used is not that of normal conversations.

A particular language use is developed over time by each client–worker pair with a unique range of narrative modalities, insider vernacular, and syntactic use. The resulting pattern, made of minor alterations from ordinary conversation and storytelling activity, is constituted by dialogical strategies and related effects. The same worker develops a different language use with a different client; similarly, clients not only tell a different story to a different worker, they also tell it in different words. Institutional context and social situation contribute to shaping specific versions of this speech genre.

What is the link between "telling" and "talking"? How are contents and forms of language use articulated? By implication, how are interventions on the narrative and speech planes related? Increasingly, word use is given an independent status in literary texts. Stories are told through words, but words in turn can make stories happen. Similarly, the relative autonomy of the two semiotic planes is a major tenet of recent psychoanalytic discussions (e.g., Milner 1982).

In clinical social work, interventions and interviewing techniques tend to be conceptualized separately. An exception is the linkage made between verbal exchange and phases of the problem-solving process (Epstein 1985). With the growing interest in interpretive understanding in social sciences and social work (Polkinghorne 1988; Ricoeur 1976; Scott 1989), closer attention has been given to life stories, narrative processes (e.g., Bruner 1987; Cohler 1988; Saari 1991; Schafer 1980), and speech analysis (Sands 1988; Sherman and Skinner 1988). The emphasis tends to be on the client's performance, assessment, and movement. Analysis of interactional processes, although encouraged (Gendlin 1986), has mainly focused on the sequential processes of influence in speech acts (Labov and Fanshel 1977), with limited applicability to narrative transformations in complex exchanges.

A dual reading of the imbricated facets of story and conversation follows, identifying verbal interventions available to the practitioner in the narrative and speech planes.

NARRATIVE INTERVENTIONS

In an interpretive perspective, all narrative is discourse. Adopting this stance is to claim that the aim of therapy does not consist of the faithful transcription of a life well remembered and gathered together toward a point of closure; instead it is an open interpretive activity. This assumption is a disturbing one for clients who come to share their story and expect from the worker an interpretation or the concluding episode of a drama. Clients do not usually differentiate between narrative as history (*histoire*) and narrative as discourse (*discours*) to take up Benveniste's (1966) linguistic distinction (adopted by Culler in his theory of narrative).

Emotionally/cognitively/ existentially, the tellers have positioned themselves at a fixed distance from the object, adopting a particular perspective on their life projects. The story is presented as history, the way things happened—confusing as it may be. Adherence to a single perspective is defined as objective. The task of the therapist consists in ungluing the teller from the story told, multiplying the vantage points, encouraging the construction of a complex narrative, and fostering open-ended interpretation and structuring (Barthes 1985). Narrative interventions achieve various degrees of defamiliarization, "making the familiar strange by impeding automatic, habitual ways of perceiving in order to promote awareness"— through a process of transposition as in literature (Prince 1987: 18).

Story-Commentary Distinction

The story–commentary distinction enables clients to step out of the "story" frame into a metastory by multiplying the planes of "reading." Commentaries are often embedded in stories. The worker helps the client identify what is told as "story" and what is told as "commentary." The comment-arial–reflective or metanarrative plane, which expands over the course of therapy (Nye, this volume), is encouraged through such questions as: "What do you think of that? How does this make you feel now?"

Story Components

Narrative interventions include working through narrative components. Stories can be said to consist of three major features: (1) Events (or Episodes, as subjectively defined events; cf. Harré and Secord 1979)—past, present, and future/possible—they are elicited by questions such as: "What happened? What is happening? What do you think could/will happen?"; (2) Themes, which concern the "aboutness" of stories, or "What is this about?"; and (3) Person, the subjective sense of self associated with questions such as "What does it mean for you, for who you have been, for who you want to be?", and representations of significant others and different parts of self as characters and protagonists.

The concept of character or person needs to be distinguished from the notion of voice, the source of statements and the act of authoring, as in: Who is doing the talking? Multiple voices inhabit a person, and a center-stage character may be described by another's voice. Voices are explored by asking: "Is that what you would say, or is that something that somebody else would say?"

Strategies dealing with story components are of two sorts: (1) exploring narratives by eliciting the more meaningful items within each category, i.e., central events, themes, and perception of the self; (2) operating narrative shifts by switching from one type of component to the other. The first strategy differentiates the more central from the less central story elements and explores their significance, clarifying the interconnectedness of events, the interrelations among themes, and the complementary and conflictual perceptions of self and others.

The second strategy is of a different order. It treats components no longer as content but as angles of vision or perspectives. Interventions on story modalities consist in examining how events come together to give shape to a theme (e.g., victim theme), how themes become filters for perceiving events ("This always happens to me"), and how events and themes are closely related to the images of self-in-the world. These shifts foster multiple interpretations and distancing to what is told.

A shorthand illustration can be drawn from possible responses to a phrase such as "it's chaos!" (followed by silence), taken as a narrative unit. In this form, this narrative fragment presents an objective and static vision of experience, timeless and subjectless. A question such as: "What is happening/has happened which is like chaos?", eliciting material from the eventful plane, operates as a close-up focus. "Where does chaos, like that, leave you?" operates another shift to the person plane, with the individual at the center of the narrative. "Chaos" may be part of a thematic category organized around a cognitive principle such as chaos/order, chaos/harmony, chaos/energy, or chaos/new beginning.

Multiplicity of Story Genres

Clients tend to adopt a particular story genre, such as drama or adventure, and subgenres, such as the victim story or the perpetual crisis story, based on familiarity of use, family habits, social background, and expectations of clinical exchanges and institutional context (mental health setting vs. welfare agency).

Story formats are accompanied by sets of characters, story plots, and narrative resolution. Different narrative modes highlight various moods and ways of perceiving; e.g., tragedy is in sharp contrast to the humorous mocking of life narrative, factual stories, to metaphoric fables. One genre does not disclaim the vision of another but tempers it. Interventions around story genres encourage plurality of formats, alternative plots and possibilities.

Client and worker stories stem from their respective social background. The resulting narratives are the negotiated outcome of what each considers "acceptable" stories. Psychological stories tend to be brought to social workers out of general expectations and the diffuse psychologization of our society. The social texture of life stories (class, race, income, life conditions), even if not explicit, needs eliciting. Defining one's self as an alcoholic with interpersonal difficulties without mention of work experience can be taken as a truncated story. Practitioners draw from their own repertoires influenced by professional identity, institutional affiliation, training, and theoretical orientation. Health and illness stories are told in health settings, income stories in welfare assistance settings (Goffman 1974). Narrative interventions aim at expanding these narrow definitions.

SPEECH INTERVENTIONS

It is through word use that stories come to be told, and story genres are associated with particular lexical and syntactical repertoires. Similarly to narrative interventions, speech interventions follow: (1) exploration of patterned usage; (2) attempts at modification through shifts of usage. Three speech mechanisms are outlined below: lexical usage, syntactical usage, and intonation. Their relation to narrative processes is briefly identified.

Lexical Usage

Lexical use involves the identification of key words, pet phrases, or "handle words" (Gendlin 1981) that seem central in client statements and are usually recurrent. They can be words or phrases, nominal terms, such as *cow*, qualifiers, such as *little*, or connecting words, such as *but* or *maybe*. They can be considered condensation/or displacement terms in a psychoanalytic perspective or structural terms in a cognitive perspective. Rich in connotation, they organize the story. Their exploration ("tell me more about that") encourages word association and the unpacking of embedded stories.

Words do not stand alone. Lexical explorations can extend to the semantic field, i.e., the organization of words around central parameters of meaning, identifiable through the clustering of closely related words as used by the client, and contrast terms with opposite values. Event/theme/person characterizations may take on such structural organization. Such lexical intervention corresponds to the cognitive analysis of semantic domains and procedures of categorization.

Alternative vocabularies may be encouraged to expand the possibilities of talking and thus of telling. The practitioner's use of empty terms, the use of "fuzzy" language—such as "this kind of feeling . . . this funny thing," by refusing to ascribe a predetermined attribution to an experience, performs a denomination or unlabeling function that encourages the development of a new wording. The use of multiple labels "so you think it was more of a . . . or maybe . . . or a combination of the two," by offering alternatives, conveys the message that no single category can characterize an experience in absolute terms; it is often a phenomenon of a complex texture. Such techniques encourage the exploration of textual ambiguity and polysemy.

A different sort of lexical intervention consists in expanding the vocabulary by modulating the original usage of words. A word like *upsetting* can be rephrased as *uncomfortable, annoying,* or *frightening*. Each transformation opens up a different avenue.

Terms and phrases, jointly developed by client and worker, become part of the lexicon of future sessions. They serve as a reminder of the work in progress and a bridge to new stories. For instance, a client may refer to earlier work on categorical opposites as "my black and white thing," inviting further exploration.

Syntactical Use

Syntactical use is an important part of the narrative. Syntactical patterns such as the use of verb tense (always/never talks in the past tense), use of personal pronouns (says/seldom says "I") (cf. Sherman, this volume) provide clues about the quality of the client's experience. Syntactical shifts that occur within a sentence or speech unit signal a change in content or viewpoint that needs to be attended to. For instance, a switch from the future tense to the conditional tense, from "I will" to "I could do this" is a significant indicator of a story shift (Halliday 1973), or the presence of embedded stories—the story about what the client will do and the story about what the client could do—and their difference. Syntactical usage can be explored and shifts introduced through rephrasing, replacing "could" by "will," for instance.

Intonation

Intonation and rhythm, how the voice suddenly rises or falls, slows down or accelerates, all contribute to the specific "music" of the words. Phrase intonation signals an act of emphasizing a meaning unit. Pitch and intensity can underline expected units or may add relief to the statement. It is as much the emphasis as the shift in emphasis that serves as significant marker. Intonational emphasis is often associated with a meaningful lexical unit ("handle word") or can mark a transition from one story genre to another and from one story to another.

Manners of speech are part of social repertoires. The referential communities of the teller (client) and listener (worker) contribute to shaping the stylistic performance of their shared speech. Some mutual adaptation is necessary to allow transformations of word use to occur and to maximize the generativeness of language use in the encounters.

A short segment of a therapeutic dialogue will serve as illustration, though it should be borne in mind that not all components are present in a single segment of interview:

w: So tell me, how was your Christmas and your New Year's?
c: (beaming) It was great! I mean it was really good. Kathy and I went to see her folks down in A., and her relatives were really friendly to me, not one of those phony kinds of greetings. . . . They were really glad to see me . . . oh, it was great.
w: Glad to hear it. Tell me more about what you did over there.
c: Well, it was nice just visiting her relatives . . . they all live pretty

> close together . . . and they all were so glad to see me . . . we
> had fun . . . we talked . . . you know . . . that sort of stuff. We
> didn't really do anything except that.
> w: Sure made you feel good to feel accepted and welcome like that.
> c: Yea . . . You know, I'm really glad I visited *her* relatives and not
> *mine* . . . my aunt used to drag me around.
> w: What do you mean, "drag me around"?
> c: (disgustedly) She always would go dragging me around at parties
> and introducing me like "This is little Jimmy" (says contemptu-
> ously) . . . treats me like I was a little kid.
> w: Don't like that at all.

The worker initiates the dialogue by asking the client to describe a situation that took place since their last meeting. In response, the client offers an overall evaluation "it was great," followed by "it was really good," and concluding with "it was great." Word use, the emphasis of intonation transcribed as an exclamation, the use of a close restatement, an actual repetition, all contribute to emphasizing that aspect of the statement and conveying the importance of the situation.

The actual events are deemphasized, briefly described as background, "K and I went." What is foregrounded is the relationship between client/ self and others, in this case family/relatives, not his own. In the expressions "her relatives were really friendly to me" "really glad to see me," the client places the self or person at the center of the narrative.

Further, a relationship theme becomes apparent in the client's first statement. Initially, the word *really,* associated with positive feeling terms *really glad, really friendly,* is a statement about the possibility of genuine positive feelings toward the self, while the second half of the sentence alludes to the opposite, "not one of those phony kinds of greetings." The client has delineated a relationship theme of the person/self and others— specifically family members—with polar opposites, which seems important to explore.

The worker responds by acknowledging the client's enthusiasm. His statement, "glad to hear it," is a weak response that fails to amplify any of the client's words or narrative components. However, in his follow-up sentence, he indicates an interest for the key situation and a readiness to explore it. His suggestion "Tell me more about what you did over there" defines the parameters of the next exchange, defining the critical situation as the central narrative frame. The use of the verb *did* (vs. "what hap- pened" "how it was") suggests an action-oriented or eventful narrative.

The client answers by reiterating what he previously said: "It was nice just visiting her relatives . . . they all were so glad to see me." Such a word-by-word repetition indicates that, as far as the client is concerned, this is a central element, and it has not been dealt with sufficiently. It is therefore reintroduced in the narrative.

In the expression: "they all live pretty close together," the word *close* indicates geographic as well as emotional proximity, the words *together* and *all* further underline the notion as a value term.

In "We had fun . . . we talked . . . we didn't really do anything," having fun is introduced as a new concept that could be explored. In this statement the client indicates that no major event has occurred. The very nature of the interaction is to be taken as the major event.

The worker's third statement: "Sure made you feel good to feel accepted and welcome like that" encapsulates a key dimension of the client's narrative. It is well centered, in that the person component is the core—as in the client's story. While the word *welcome* restates the client's use of *greeting* in a slightly broader way, the introduction of the term *feeling accepted* goes further in eliciting material around the relationship theme. By using this term, the worker performs a modulation of the client's words, from *friendly/close* to *accepted,* which operates a narrative shift. By using such a powerful expression for a person statement, further decontextualized from a specific situation, the worker makes alternative story frames possible. The material can now be expanded through a range of narrative frames.

The client seems comfortable with the worker's statement, signifying his agreement with "yea." The next phrase, "I'm really glad," indicates a syntactic shift on the part of the client, who until then used neutral or collective pronouns (person) as in "it was great," "it was nice," "we had fun." In this sentence, the client expresses a greater ownership of the feeling by the self. He then responds to the worker's invitation by developing the narrative and making an overt link between one narrative frame and another: "I'm really glad I visited her relatives and not mine."

In the statement "My aunt used to drag me around," the client has actually shifted narrative frames and introduced a new set of characters, situation, and narrative time. He is talking about the past ("used to") and his own family. What he was hinting at in his initial statement—"not one of those phony kinds of greetings"—is now clearly into view. The phrase "drag me around" illustrates a negative and dependent interaction of which the person is the object.

The worker, closely following the cue of the client, underscores the phrase "drag me around" by restating it and asking for clarification.

The client pursues the new narrative frame and starts describing new situations and providing the corresponding image of the self "She always would go dragging me around at parties and introducing me like 'this is little Jimmy.' Treats me like I was a little kid." In his use of the present tense, the client acknowledges that the devaluing of the person continues to be a relevant component of the present narrative. "Little Jimmy, little kid" cuts across multiple narrative frames. A new transition is now occurring, which the worker acknowledges by saying "don't like that at all," suggesting a new shift by eliciting reflective and commentarial statements from the client.

This short segment illustrates the negotiated nature of the client–worker exchange. Beyond the specific strategies of amplification and shift on the narrative and speech planes, what stands out is the client's insistence on a particular centering of the narrative before proceeding any further. Until that takes place, the client reintroduces identical statements. The worker's strategies of expansion and transformation are also revealed. Overall, this dialogue shows the complexity of these negotiated features.

The therapeutic dialogue is a multilevel activity in which dialogical interventions are simultaneously performed on the narrative and speech planes. The exploration of the mechanisms involved enables one to conceptualize the articulation between telling and talking activities. A number of tools were identified that can be used to analyze the therapeutic process and possibly its outcome. Adopting this dialogical approach entails implications for social science, and specifically, social work: a reconsideration of the relationship between interventions and techniques and between interventions and theoretical orientations. A definition of "interview skills" closely connected to narrative analysis leads to modifications in social work training to incorporate this dimension. By use of a narrative framework, theoretical orientations to interventions become identified with the mobilization of distinct story genres and narrative types.

REFERENCES

Bakhtin, M. M. 1986. The problem of speech genres. In C. Emerson and M. Holquist, eds., *Speech Genres and Other Late Essays,* 60–102. Austin: University of Texas Press.

Barthes, R. 1985. Textual analysis of a tale of Poe. In M. Blonsky, ed., *On Signs,* 84–97. Baltimore: The Johns Hopkins University Press.

Benveniste, E. 1966. *Problèmes de linguistique générale* [Problems of general linguistics]. Paris: Gallimard.

Bruner, J. 1987. Life as narrative. *Social Research* 54, no. 1: 11–32.

Cohler, B. J. 1988. The human studies and the life history. *Social Service Review* 62: 552–75.

Epstein, L. 1985. *Talking and Listening: A Guide to the Helping Interview.* Columbus, Ohio: Merrill.

Gendlin, E. T. 1981. *Focusing*. 2d ed. New York: Bantam.

Gendlin, E. T. 1986. What comes after traditional psychotherapy research? *American Psychologist* 41, no. 2: 131–36.

Goffman, E. 1974. *Frame Analysis: An Essay on the Organization of Experience*. New York: Harper and Row.

Halliday, M. A. K. 1973. The syntax enunciates the theme. In M. Douglas, ed., *Rules and Meanings*, pp. 279–94. New York: Penguin.

Harré, R. and P. F. Secord. 1979. *The Explanation of Social Behavior*. Towota, N.J.: Littlefield, Adams.

Labov, W. and D. Fanshel. 1977. *Therapeutic Discourse: Psychotherapy as Conversation*. New York: Academic Press.

Milner, J-C. 1982. *Orders et raisons de langue*. Paris: Editions du Seuil.

Polkinghorne, D. E. 1988. *Narrative Knowing and the Human Sciences*. Albany: State University of New York Press.

Prince, G. 1987. *A Dictionary of Narratology*. Lincoln: University of Nebraska Press.

Ricoeur, P. 1976. *Interpretation Theory: Discourse and the Surplus of Meaning*. Fort Worth: Texas Christian University Press.

Saari, C. 1991. *The Creation of Meaning in Clinical Social Work*. New York: Guilford Press.

Sands, R. G. 1988. Sociolinguistic analysis of a mental health interview. *Social Work* 33, no. 2: 149–54.

Schafer, R. 1980. Narration in the psychoanalytic dialogue. *Critical Inquiry* 7: 29–53.

Scott, D. 1989. Meaning construction and social work practice. *Social Service Review* 63: 39–51.

Sherman, E. and K. W. Skinner, 1988. Client language and clinical process: A cognitive–semantic analysis. *Clinical Social Work Journal* 16, no. 4: 391–405.

Tambling, J. 1988. *What Is Literary Language?* Milton Keynes, England: Open University Press.

EIGHTEEN

Discourse Analysis Methods and Clinical Research: A Single Case Study

Catherine Nye

Discourse analysis methods have much to offer social workers interested in clinical research. The term *discourse analysis* is often used broadly to encompass a number of different and sometimes incompatible approaches to talk, including interaction analysis, sociolinguistics, speech act theory, and conversation analysis (Garvey 1986; Levinson 1983). What these approaches share, and what distinguishes them from traditional linguistics, is a focus on units of analysis that go beyond the sentence. These include, for example, query–response pairs, conversation, interactional sequences, and particular types of discourse such as narratives, jokes, or disputes. Discourse analysis is concerned with the function and structure or organization of moves in connected talk. It is interested in how categories of talk function and how they are organized hierarchically. Discourse analysis seeks to identify the structural principles of interpretation, production, and sequencing, which govern the organization of talk, and to generate a grammar of discourse rules.

As clinical social workers we are trained to work with process recordings and to focus on the details of the talk between client and worker in order to understand how that talk functions. We reflect on what we are trying to accomplish with a particular piece of talk and examine the client's response to our interventions. This level of analysis is familiar and comfortable to us as social workers. Discourse analysis also works at this level; it addresses similar issues of function and seeks to understand the structure of verbal interaction. It offers social workers interested in clinical research a developed body of methods that are congruent with a clinical approach, methods that are "experience near" and "user friendly." Discourse analysis potentially provides social workers with tools to address clinically relevant questions and offers a systematic way of working at a familiar and comfortable level of analysis. Though discourse analysis methods have been used in the past to explore process in clinical social work (see, for example, Labov and Fanshel 1977), they have the potential to be more widely used and to make a more extensive contribution to knowledge in the field.

In order to demonstrate the relevance and value of discourse analysis methods to clinical research and to illustrate how these methods can be adapted and used by the individual researcher to address clinical questions, this paper describes their use in one single-case study. The paper focuses on the methods, rather than the findings of the study, describes how particular methods from discourse analysis were adapted to address specific clinical questions, and provides examples of coding from the data.

THE STUDY

Data for the study consisted of audiotapes and typed transcripts of a completed two-and-a-half-year psychoanalysis by a senior training analyst. There were 256 sessions in the analysis; each session comprised more than twenty pages of transcript. I was interested in studying the patient's narratives and the way they changed over the course of the analysis. Psychoanalysis has traditionally recognized the importance of patient narratives and is interested in the way narratives function in treatment. The literature has focused on the patient's construction and reconstruction of a "life history narrative" over the course of treatment and on the narrative versus historical truth of this account (Leavy 1988; Novey 1968; Schafer 1981; Spence 1982). Psychoanalytic discussion remains largely a matter of theory, however. Little is known empirically about how patients tell stories in treatment. I was interested in addressing this question by doing a detailed study of patient stories in one analysis. I was particularly interested in the formulation of narrative meaning, in how the patient understood her narrated experience, and in how her understanding changed over time.

In seeking relevant methods for approaching this task, I discovered that discourse analysis had developed an extensive literature and systematic procedures and tools for studying narrative as one form of discourse. These tools had been developed and used to study narratives in interview settings and ordinary conversation; they had not been applied to a systematic study of narratives in psychotherapy. After some exploration, I decided to adapt discourse analysis methods to perform a microanalysis of patient narratives in the analytic case I was studying.

DATA ANALYSIS

From the 256 sessions of the completed analysis, an evenly distributed sample of ten sessions was selected at random. Each of these sessions was divided into three components: (1) narratives, the stories the patient told about her experience; (2) talk about narratives in which patient and analyst together clarified the facts of the patient's stories and explored their meaning, and (3) nonnarrative talk, those segments of the talk that did not relate directly to the narratives. Nonnarrative material included, but was not limited to, discussion of dreams and fantasies, talk about the immediate interaction between the patient and analyst, and the patient's plans for the future. (Counting the number of lines of transcript was used as a method of quantifying and/comparing the amount of narrative, talk about narrative, and nonnarrative-related talk in the sessions.)

The first step in coding was to identify the narratives by using Labov and Waletsky's (1967) criteria in which narratives match a "verbal sequence" of clauses to the sequence of events that actually occurred. The simplest narrative consists of two events linked by a "temporal juncture," a shift in

FIGURE 18.1 *Discourse Ratings*

Session

I. Narrative	II. Talk about the narrative	III. Non narrative talk
A. Content	A. Individual turns function:	(no further coding)
1. Childhood	Provide or request	
2. Adult past	1. Confirmation/disconfirmation	
3. Present	2. Restatement	
	3. Explication	
	4. Reformulation	
B. Function	B. Complete segment	
1. Referential:	1. Function	
Events, narrative facts	Type 1 provides additional factual	
2. Evaluative:	information about narrative	
Narrative meaning	Type 2 enlarges narrative meaning	
	Type 3 transforms narrative meaning	
	2. Function accomplished by	
	A = the analyst	
	P = the patient	
	AP = patient and analyst working	
	cooperatively	

time. By this definition, the statement "first this happened and then that happened" constitutes the simplest form of a narrative.

The selection and adaptation of discourse analysis methods, which were developed with very different purposes in mind, to address specific questions and meet the particular needs of clinical research were of critical importance in the design of this study. Because discourse analysis methods are complex and labor intensive, coding in an unfocused way can absorb much time and energy. To avoid being overwhelmed by the complexity of coding it is essential to be selective and to make carefully thought through decisions about what is coded and why.

Labov and Waletsky also describe two possible functions of narrative clauses that seemed directly relevant to the questions of the study. They describe narrative clauses as fulfilling either a "referential" or "evaluative" function. Referential narrative clauses answer the question "Then what happened?" They give the facts of the story and describe the basic sequence of temporally ordered events. Evaluative narrative clauses answer the question "So what?" They suspend the action of the story and tell what significance or meaning the events have for the narrator. These distinctions seemed useful in exploring questions about the formulation of narrative meaning and changes in the formulation of meaning over the course of the analysis and were, therefore, included in the coding. After narratives were identified, narrative clauses were coded as fulfilling either a referential or evaluative function (figure 18.1, IB). Narratives were also coded for time of occurrence (childhood, adult past or present) (figure 18.1, IA).

After the narratives had been identified and coded, talk about the narratives was identified. Structurally, this consists of a segment of dialogue between the patient and the analyst. It can follow a narrative or be embedded in it. The patient may, for example, begin a story, the analyst may interrupt it with a question, there may be some discussion back and forth, and then the patient goes on to finish the story. More than one segment of talk can refer to any given narrative. Methods of coding talk about the narrative were adapted from Catherine Garvey's (1977) discourse analysis of what she calls "contingent queries." Garvey defines a contingent query as a request for information that occurs within the domain of another speech act, in our case the narrative.

Once talk about the narrative was identified, by using a modified form of Garvey's model, individual utterances or turns by patient and analyst were coded for function (figure 18.1, IIA) as follows:

1. Confirmation/Disconfirmation (C). The speaker repeated or confirmed what had already been said without restructuring or the addition of information, or the speaker rejected or disagreed with what had been said.

2. Restatement (R). The speaker summarized in different words what had already been said without adding new information. The restructuring of material sometimes resulted in a better organized, more coherent, and precise presentation.

3. Explication (EX). The speaker requested or provided a clearer more detailed understanding of what had already been said; the speaker made explicit what was implicit in a previous statement, enlarged upon, or added to it.

4. Reformulation (RF). The speaker went beyond what had already been said and what was clearly implicit in it, to explore and transform it. The speaker provided new meaning and/or reframed or reformulated. Statements coded reformulation raised questions about the stated causes or meaning of events and/or their relationship to one another. Included in this category were statements traditionally described as interpretations.

Each individual turn or utterance by the patient (P) and analyst (A) was coded as either providing (P) or requesting (R) one of these four functions. For example, a turn in which the analyst (A) provided (P) a reformulation (RF) of narrative meaning would be coded APRF.

After the individual turns were coded, talk about the narrative was coded on a second level, the level of the complete segment, i.e., not the single statement or turn but the whole portion of the talk about the narrative on a given topic (figure 18.1, IIB1). Three basic functions were identified for the segments of talk about the narrative. Type 1 segments of talk about the narrative provide additional factual information about the patient's story and fill in details of place, time, or character. In type 2 segments, the talk enhances or enlarges the stated meaning of the narrative. In type 3 segments, the discussion radically transforms the stated meaning of the narrative. Finally (figure 18.1, IIB2) each complete segment of talk about the narrative was coded for whether the analyst (A) the patient (P) or the dyad working cooperatively (AP) accomplished the function.

Using these methods, adapted from discourse analysis, I coded each of the ten sample sessions. Even with this simplified and clearly focused coding procedure, coding was time consuming; it took two months to code each session. For purposes of reliability selected sessions were coded by a second independent rater. Interrater agreement on the narrative codes ranged from ninety-one to ninety-eight percent. Agreement on the codes for talk about the narrative varied from seventy-seven to eighty-three percent. Disagreements between raters were resolved by consensus.

FINDINGS

Predictions about expected changes in patient narratives and talk about these narratives were based on the analytic literature on the self-analytic function. Schlessinger and Robbins (1983) have described the acquisition of the self-analytic function as the single most important outcome of analytic treatment. According to analytic theory the patient acquires the capacity for self-observing, the ability to reflect on and think about the experience, in the course of prolonged dyadic interaction with the analyst. The study predicted that the acquisition of the self-analytic function would be reflected in changes in the patient's narratives and talk about them; that, for example, the proportion of evaluative to referential content in the patient's narratives would increase over the course of time; and that, in the talk about the narrative, the patient would participate more actively in explicating and

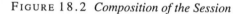

FIGURE 18.2 *Composition of the Session*

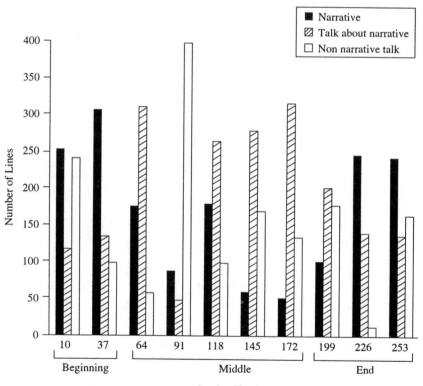

reformulating the meaning of the narrated experience. Such changes were, in fact, documented in the data.

The study identified three phases, a beginning, middle, and end, in the process of telling and talking about narratives over the course of the treatment. These shifts in process are reflected in figure 18.2.

During the beginning phase the patient told many stories. These stories were composed largely of referential material; the patient described events with little reflection on their meaning. There was little talk about these narratives; the talk that did occur was often directed at clarifying facts rather than at enlarging meaning. During the middle phase the patient told fewer narratives, and there was more talk about them. Both the stories themselves and the talk about them focused on understanding and elaborating the meaning of the patient's experience. During the end phase the patient told more stories, and there was less talk about them. In this sense the end phase resembled the beginning phase of the treatment process. However, the content of the narratives and talk about them during this phase was qualitatively different from that of the beginning phase. The patient's stories during the end phase were largely evaluative in content,

FIGURE 18.3 *Reformulation of Meaning in Talk About the Narratives*

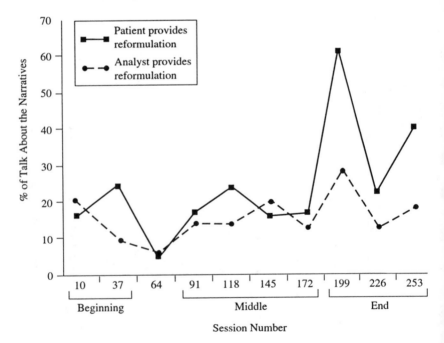

and in the talk about them, she functioned independently to reflect on and reformulate their meaning. This change is illustrated in figure 18.3.

EXAMPLES

Examples from the data are provided to illustrate the usefulness of discourse analysis methods for documenting change in clinical process. The examples given here are of narrative and talk about narrative from the beginning and middle phases of the treatment. Though the differences between material from sessions in the beginning and middle phases of treatment are intuitively obvious to the trained clinician, discourse analysis provides a means of documenting and quantifying change essential for purposes of research.

The first example, a narrative from session thirty-seven, is from the beginning phase of treatment. During this phase the patient told many stories and there was little talk about their meaning. In session thirty-seven the patient tells thirteen stories; ten of these stories are told in succession, with few interruptions by the analyst, and relate the patient's sexual history from childhood to the present. She tells the analyst these stories in the hope that he will be able to connect them with the phobic symptoms that brought her into treatment. The first story in this series of ten, about playing "doctor" as a child, is representative. Evaluative narrative clauses are underlined.

Pt: *I don't know which came first in-in two incidents,* uh—I know the one time, we were at my grandmother's house and, uh, there's like 21 grandchildren and I'm the second oldest and my cousin, J——, is the oldest and there's a bunch of kids below us and, uh—there's a lot of cousins—there's me and my cousin. M——, my cousin, R——*I don't know if J——was there or not. She was littler,* but we were all in the back bedroom and I guess we were monkeying around. *I can't remember any specific things, but,* I guess— I just kinda remember like we were playing doctor or something, you know, and I guess some of us had our clothes off and some of us didn't, you know, and I just remember—*I don't even remember who it was*—but I remember a couple of aunts coming in, you know, and kinda scolding us—this is a no-no, you don't play like this, you know, *but I can't remember, you know, exactly what we were doing or who hollered at us or anything like that.*

Like most of the narratives in the beginning phase, this narrative is primarily factual in content. Sixty-eight percent of the narrative clauses (11.5 lines) describe the events of the story; only thirty-two percent of the narrative clauses (5.5 lines) are evaluative. What evaluative content there is reflects on the patient's inability to remember the particulars of her story; there is little exploration of her feelings about this experience or of the meaning the events had for her. In contrast, a narrative told in session 145, during the middle phase, has a very different feel. During the middle phase the patient told fewer narratives and there was more talk about them. The focus of the narratives themselves and of the talk about them during this phase was on the meaning of the patient's experience. In session 145 the patient tells only two narratives, and talk about them continues throughout the session. In this narrative the patient describes her disappointment that her husband, who is on a vacation trip with friends, has not returned as scheduled.

> Pt. 8: (Husband didn't come home yet and *he was suppose to be home last night* (sighs). His Aunt M called me yesterday morning and start giving me some feeble excuse that the bus had mechanical difficulties so they weren't gonna come in, you know, and I said, "What kind?" Just the fact that they want to stay another day 'cause they were having a good time . . . uh, *I was—first. I was kinda mad because the time I wanted to stay at Chula Vista one extra day*—they were having Peter Nero—*and, uh, we didn't stay. It was just like another typical example of when I want to do something, he just doesn't help to go along with it, but yet, when somebody else want to, he's just right there. He jumps right in. It probably was his idea too and it kinda hurts and then, what really made me mad was that he couldn't call himself and tell me, he had to go through Aunt M and then he put her in a position of lying to me about that the bus broke down rather than him telling me personally, "Look, I want to stay another day 'cause I'm having a good time." Now it's like—uh, you know, that hurt my feelings too. Jesus, you know, what am I gonna say, what am I gonna do, what can I say. I'm not his mother. I'm not gonna yell and scream (sighs) That-that-that bothered me. Made me think that he was like a little kid, he can't even stand on his own two feet and tell me (sighs)* (2, 3).

Factual content in this narrative is less detailed; only thirty-one percent of the narrative clauses (7.5 lines) relate the events of the patient's story. The meaning of the events, the patient's response to and reflections on them are, however, more thoroughly developed. Fully sixty-nine percent of the narrative clauses (16.5 lines) elaborate the meaning of the narrated events. On the basis this and similar additional data, we can conclude that a quantifiable difference exists between narratives told in the beginning and middle phases of this analysis.

Talk about the narrative, like the narratives themselves, changes over the course of treatment in measurable ways. In session thirty-seven the patient tells the ten narratives about her sexual history in succession, with few interruptions from the analyst. When the analyst does interrupt with a question it is to clarify the facts of the patient's stories, to determine details of place and time. At the end of her series of stories the patient says:

Pt. 8: That' sex (laughs) I don't know (sighs) (pause). Is that a lot or is that nothing or is that something? Now is there something we should look into and talk about? Is this gonna change my, uh, going out? I don't know (sigh) (patient provides reformulation).

Dr. 8: The one thing about it that struck me is that you said several times, uh that you think it's normal as if you're afraid that I might think there's something abnormal about what you had to tell (analyst provides reformulation).

Pt. 9: Well, I-I use to think it was very grotesque and wrong (patient provides explication).

Dr. 9: Which part? (Analyst requests explication.)

Pt. 10: Well, just doing anything like that with another girl (patient provides restatement).

Dr. 10: Oh, it's the—it's the business with another girl (analyst provides restatement).

Pt. 11: Yeah (patient provides confirmation).

Dr. 11: . . . that you think might be abnormal (analyst provides restatement).

Pt. 12: Yeah (patient provides confirmation).

Dr. 12: Like maybe you're a homosexual or something or what? (Analyst provides explication).

Pt. 13: Well, don't they call them lesbians or something? (Patient provides explication).

Dr. 13: Lesbians. Yes (analyst provides confirmation).

The patient begins the talk about the narrative by asking the analyst to tell her what her experience means in relation to her phobic symptoms, her difficulty "going out" (Pt. 8). Her request is coded patient requests reformulation. (Codes for individual turns are in parentheses.) The analyst responds by providing a reformulation (Dr. 8); though she has repeatedly described her experiences as "normal" he wonders if she may be concerned that he will think they are abnormal. The patient (Pt. 9) corroborates this reformulation and elaborates on it (patient provides explication). In the talk that follows, patient and analyst enlarge on this newly formulated narrative meaning. This segment of talk about the narrative is coded type 4A; in it narrative meaning is reformulated by the analyst. In this example, as is typical in the beginning phase, the patient's role is restricted to validating and enlarging the analyst's reformulation.

In contrast, in talk about narrative from the middle phase of treatment, the patient is more actively engaged in reflecting on and transforming her understanding of her experience. In session 145 the patient's two narratives are interrupted repeatedly by talk about them. Following the narratives there is a lengthy discussion of their multiple meanings. The narrative quoted above, for example, was told on pages two and three of the transcript. The following discussion of it occurs on page nine, and references back to this story continue over twenty pages of transcript. In this example the patient is questioning her anger at her husband for failing to return from his trip as planned. She says:

> Pt. 34: (crying) I don't know. I don't think it's—I think I'm all wrong. I don't know how to have fun. I don't know how to enjoy myself and maybe I'm jealous of people who do. I don't know how to have fun—that's what I'm thinking the whole thing is too and if I just take my time and I work on it, then I'll be just like the rest of you (patient provides reformulation).
>
> Dr. 35: The rest of you? (Analyst requests explication).
>
> Pt. 35: Oh, all the kids and (husband) and you (patient provides explication).
>
> Dr. 36: People who have fun (analyst provides restatement).
>
> Pt. 36: (pause) Maybe I'm wrong. I don't have any justification at all. That's what's so confusing. I can't make up my mind if I should feel like I felt or if I should feel differently (crying). I don't know. I can never have fun like he has fun. I can never let loose like that (p. 9) (patient provides explication).

In this segment of talk about the narrative from the middle phase of treatment the patient begins by providing a reformulation of the meaning of her story (Pt. 34); she wonders whether her anger is "justified," whether she is entitled to be angry at her husband, or whether she is just jealous of his ability to have fun. In the talk that follows she expands on this idea (patient provides explication). The analyst's interventions are restricted to clarifying her statements (analyst requests explication, analyst provides restatement). It is the patient who is responsible for the reformulation of narrative meaning, she who is dissatisfied with accepting her responses at face value, and she who is instrumental in questioning and exploring them. This segment of talk about the narrative from the middle phase of treatment is, therefore, coded type 4P; in it the patient takes primary responsibility for reformulating the meaning of her narrative.

The purpose of this paper has been to demonstrate, by using examples from one single-case study, the usefulness of discourse analysis methods for research in clinical social work. Discourse analysis provides a conceptual approach, structural functional categories, and methodological tools to study the complex verbal interactions that are central to the therapeutic process; to document intuitively evident change in clinical process over the course of treatment; to code, quantify, and measure it; and to make comparisons over time.

Discourse analysis methods have the additional benefit of being "user friendly" for social workers trained to think about the function of therapeutic interventions and to work with process in a hands on, line-by-line fashion. Discourse analysis provides methods of studying talk and the function of talk in interaction. These methods are consistent with social work's understanding of the importance of interactive talk—dialogue—in the treatment process. As this one analytic case study makes clear, discourse analysis potentially offers researchers in clinical social work a rich and appropriate conceptual frame and methodology that can potentially deepen and enrich our understanding of clinical process and treatment interactions, and make an important contribution to the knowledge base of clinical social work.

References

Garvey, C. 1977. The contingent query: A dependent act in conversation. In M. Lewes and L. Rosenbloom, eds., *Interaction, Conversation, and the Development of Language*. Wiley.

Garvey, C. 1986. Discourse analysis. Paper presented at the colloquium: Psychology Department, Wayne State University, April 16.

Labov, W. and D. Fanshel. 1977. *Therapeutic Discourse: Psychotherapy as Conversation*. New York: Academic Press.

Labov W. and J. Waletsky. 1967. Narrative analysis: Oral versions of personal experience. In J. Helm, ed., *Essays on the Verbal and Visual Arts*, pp. 12–44. Seattle: University of Washington Press. American Ethnological Society.

Leavy, S. A. 1988. *The Psychoanalytic Dialogue*. New Haven, Conn.: Yale University Press.

Levinson, S. C. 1983. *Pragmatics*. Cambridge, England: Cambridge University Press.

Novey, S. 1968. *The Second Look: The Reconstruction of Personal History in Psychiatry and Psychoanalysis*. The Johns Hopkins University Press.

Schafer, R. 1981. *Narrative Action in Psychoanalysis*. Worcester, Mass.: Clark University Press.

Schlessinger, N and F. Robbins. 1983. *A Developmental View of the Psychoanalytic Process*. New York: International University Press.

Spence, D. P. 1982. *Narrative Truth and Historical Truth: Meaning and Interpretation in Psychoanalysis*. Norton.

NINETEEN

Discourse Analysis in the Framework of Change Process Research

Edmund Sherman

Several years ago a colleague and I attempted to analyze client language as a means of assessing process and change in a sample of ninety-five verbatim transcripts of audiotaped clinical sessions (Sherman and Skinner 1988). The schema we used for the analysis was derived from cognitive therapy and linguistics, notably semantics, so we referred to it as a cognitive–semantic method. Although the study did show some evidence of corollary changes in client language and case movement, it left much to be desired.

The major problem was the inability of the cognitive–semantic method to capture the conditions and changes in the larger context of practice, both within and across treatment sessions. What was needed was a framework in which to capture this larger context and to provide more information about the worker's role in both the dialogical and external change processes. I suspect this is a problem for discourse analysis in general. So I would like to propose a framework designed to capture much of the varied and complex elements of this larger context. This framework comes from the change process research literature in psychotherapy (Greenberg 1986; Greenberg and Pinsof 1986; Rice and Greenberg 1984).

CHANGE PROCESS RESEARCH

Change process research has shifted the focus from outcome at termination of treatment to a focus on the interrelationship of treatment events and client change during the treatment. This focus on change during the treatment is the centerpiece of change process research (Reid 1990). Until fairly recently, research in clinical social work as well as psychotherapy and counseling in general has focused almost exclusively on pre–post and, sometimes, follow-up measures of change, with rather gross measures or descriptions of treatment input and processes, and with little if any articulation of their interrelationship. In short, the emphasis is almost entirely on evaluation of outcome, not process. The tendency has been to classify and aggregate treatment events (particularly worker intervention activities and techniques) and relate these to global outcome measures. In this respect, change process research also represents a shift in focus from the clinician as the almost exclusive agent of change to the client as agent and subject of change. "It is the client who changes, and we are trying to find out how that change comes about" (Rice and Greenberg 1984:21).

Change process research is concerned with outcomes but always in relationship to what is going on in treatment. Greenberg (1986) claims that to study the process of change it is possible to measure three types of client outcomes or changes over the course of treatment: immediate outcomes, intermediate outcomes, and ultimate (or final) outcomes. He describes these as follows:

> An immediate outcome or impact is that change that is evident in the session. It is important to be able to specify and measure important in-session changes that result from specific intervention or from the overall interaction. These in-session changes then need to be related to extrasessional, intermediate changes such as those measured by session outcome measures designed to evaluate changes in target attitudes and behaviors. Changes in these targets then need to be tracked over time to establish the robustness of the intermediate changes and to shed light on the process of outcome, that is, to see how these intermediate changes vary over time and how they relate to final outcomes. Final outcomes are taken at the end of treatment and at follow-up and represent ultimate change. To provide a complete picture of the change process, outcomes at all three points need to be simultaneously related to each other.   (4)

Three levels of process need to be studied in relationship to the outcomes, and these are speech act, episode, and therapeutic relationship. The level of speech act is the discourse element of the research model, and it refers to the pragmatics of discourse or how people get what they want by using language (Austin 1962; Searles 1969). Labov (1982) has referred to this performative use of languages as "verbal action." He and other linguists note that speech acts can inform, advise, direct, promise, threaten, insult, and so on. The episode is the next larger unit or level of process analysis that should be coded. Van Dijk (1982) refers to the episode as a semantic unit of analysis that consists of an important sequence of sentences that have thematic unity, and it can be distinguished by clearly recognizable opening and closing sentences or phrases. Finally, the level of relationship describes the particular qualities that the parties attribute to the ongoing relationship that go beyond any specific content, act, or episode. Implicit understandings are usually present among the parties that make up the "we" sense of the attributes of the relationship.

Greenberg (1986) proposed this hierarchical model as a heuristic device for understanding communication in psychotherapy in terms of units of analysis and levels of meaning. The three levels provide a context for each other, and this in turn helps to define the meaning of any communication. Thus, the same act in a different context will have a different meaning. As an example, Greenberg (1986:5) notes that the statement, "I feel like a small child," would count as a speech act of disclosure in the context of an episodic event of resolving a conflict in the context of a good working relationship. But in the relationship context of a poor working alliance (one in which there is no sense of working together and in which goals and tasks are not agreed upon) and in the episodic context of discussing problems in the therapeutic relationship, the same statement could count as a complaint or accusation.

The procedures and tools of change process analysis are very detailed and time consuming, so they are not an unmixed blessing. For example, Berlin (1990) has reported on her efforts to use the change process model to study cognitive behavioral treatment of depression and has found that the time required to perform all the procedures at all the hierarchical levels of outcome and process analysis is prohibitive. However, she finds certain of its methods to be highly valuable in the development and testing of practice theory and the education of clinical social work students, particularly the method of task analysis. (Berlin, Mann, and Grossman 1991).

Much of the language used in describing change process research (e.g., tasks, goals, targets) has a rather mechanical or instrumental flavor. However, these are only labels that can be used to cut across different theoretical approaches. Thus, in psychodynamic practice the overall client task of gaining insight into the developmental origins and ongoing dynamics of current psychosocial problems would be made operational in terms of a number of subtasks related to self-reflection and insight.

What I am proposing here is that as both practitioners and researchers we look at all this more flexibly and qualitatively as a framework rather than an exhaustive model. Berlin (1990) has noted that when applied to a single case, change process methods offer a feasible way to gain much information that is of immediate practical value to practitioners, even if they do not carry out complete change process studies every time. In this spirit the following case is presented and the framework for its subsequent analysis is applied.

CASE ILLUSTRATION

The following case example is necessarily a rather abbreviated and truncated one that cannot depict all the complexity and specificity necessary for a full change process analysis, but it is hoped enough is here to show how the process hierarchy of speech act, episode, and relationship can provide a meaningful context for discourse analysis.

The client in this case is a forty-two-year-old married man with two teenaged children. He applied for individual counseling to the same family service agency in which his wife had received counseling in the recent past. He applied at the urging of his wife who indicated that she would seriously consider divorce if he did not get some help for his own "personal problem." Her prior worker at the agency indicated that the wife was willing to consider couple's therapy at a later point, but she could no longer handle his moody and explosive (but nonviolent) behavior. He had promised to change many times, tried, and failed on his own. At the time of the intake interview he had a discouraged air about him and he spoke in an unexpressive monotone throughout most of the session. In the following verbatim segment from the intake interview "C" stands for client and "W" stands for worker:

1. w: Would you like to tell me what brought you here?
2. c: Well, it's my wife. She says she's at her wit's end with me and that I better get help if the marriage is to survive . . . so here I am.
3. w: That's how your wife feels about it. How about you?
4. c: Well, there's no question things have gotten much worse in the marriage, and they can't keep going the way they are.
5. w: Well, you're talking about the marriage, which involves two people. How is it that you have come here for individual counseling rather than marital, as a couple?
6. c: Uhm . . . ah . . . What's happening in the marriage is really my fault. She claims I'm really not able to communicate with her and that she feels shut out . . . and when I do communicate with her it's not good communication . . . too aggressive and loud.
7. w: So, this is how she sees it. How do you?
8. c: She's right. Normal family communication is not something

that comes naturally to me.. . . It has to do with the fact that I
was an only child raised by older parents.

9. w: Older parents?
10. c: Yes. My father was in his fifties when he married my mother
who was in her late thirties. They didn't talk much to one another . . . or to me. They both had to work to make ends meet,
so I spent a lot of time by myself. Now it's showing up in my
marriage . . . at least on my side. My wife's good at communicating. She grew up in a nice normal family. She was . . . and is
. . . very close to her parents and her brothers and sisters. She
expected to have that in the marriage from me, and it hasn't happened . . . and she's very upset.
11. w: Is it the *lack* of communication from you that's upsetting her?
12. c: Mostly . . . but it's also that I'm not good at it when I do.
She asks me how I *feel* about things . . . likes to talk about feelings and says I never share mine . . . that's upsetting to her.
13. w: What is it that you do . . . or don't do . . . that's most upsetting to her? Can you give me some concrete examples . . . situations?
14. c: Uhm . . . Let's see . . . at dinner, for example. It is not easy
for me to get into the small talk of my wife and children . . .
used to read the paper at dinner table until my wife called a halt
to it. I really tune them out. It really takes a major effort on my
part . . . cause I seem to be into my head all the time, thinking,
usually about work . . . but even when I watch T.V. or read the
newspaper I get so engrossed I tune out everybody . . . and every thing. I even lose track of time. I don't know what can be
done about it. I've tried, but that's me. I don't see what can be
done.
15. w: Sounds like you have some doubts . . . maybe reservations
. . . about getting counseling for this.
16. c: Right. You know, I almost didn't come here today, even
though I set up the appointment. It's a good thing you're not a
woman.
17. w: Not a woman?
18. c: Yeah. You know, my wife was seeing Mrs.—— here almost
all of last year . . . and my wife raves about her, about how
much she helped her, but . . .
19. w: But . . .?
20. c: But my wife's been a lot more critical of me and the marriage
ever since, and . . .
21. w: And Mrs. —— is a woman.

22. c: Yeah. It's not a sexist thing, but it worried me.
23. w: Worried that you might not be understood, or maybe even teamed-up on?
24. c: Yeah. Right. I couldn't take that. As it is, I'm not sure if I can take this.
25. w: It's not easy, I know. It took a lot for you to come here, but you did and that means a lot. It's a good sign.
26. c: I hope so. We'll see.
27. w: Right. We'll see. That's a start. Now let's find out a little more about what needs to be done about what.

At the end of the intake interview the worker gave the client the Beck Depression Inventory since the client acknowledged feeling somewhat discouraged and "down" over the past several weeks. The inventory indicated a score of seventeen, which represented a borderline clinical depression. The items he checked on the inventory that had the highest depression ratings were "I blame myself all the time for my faults," and "I don't get any real satisfaction out of anything anymore." The former item reflected his basic feeling that he was indeed to blame for all the problems in the marriage. This was an area that was targeted for attention by the worker and one that the client expressed willingness to explore.

The latter item indicated how anhedonic the client was at the time of intake. He acknowledged that he had not felt any real pleasure in anything for quite a while and that he would like to change this. He claimed to be a "workaholic." He not only had a regular civil service job in the state department of taxation but also had recently started a private tax business on the side, mostly preparing real estate tax statements. He was spending a lot of time entering and analyzing property tax data on his computer. He was also preoccupied and worried about the business but knew that this was "silly" because he had a secure regular job and did not have to depend on the new business.

The contracted treatment plan called for twenty sessions based largely on the model of cognitive therapy of depression (Beck, Shaw, and Emery 1979). The beginning work focused primarily on pleasure therapy in which a number of pleasurable activities, particularly with his wife and family, were planned and carried out. He kept a weekly activity schedule and rated the activities on a pleasure scale of zero to five. This homework seemed to reassure him that he could do something about his situation and he worked diligently at it.

The following segment of discourse occurred in the fifth session. In addition to keeping the daily record of activities, he was beginning to monitor distressing events, emotions, and thoughts on a daily record of dysfunctional thoughts. He had gone out with his wife to movies and dinner several times at his initiation and had taken his family skiing twice since his treatment started. He claimed to be enjoying this and feeling more relaxed, although he still worried about his new business. However, he forced himself to spend less time at the computer and more time with his family. He was also having some difficulty identifying feelings and differentiating his emotions on the daily record of dysfunctional thoughts, so the worker raised this issue in the fifth session.

28. w: So, you say that you've always had trouble knowing and expressing how you feel?
29. c: Yeah. My wife says I never tell her what I'm feeling unless I get angry at her.
30. w: When does that happen?
31. c: When does what happen?
32. w: That you get angry at your wife.
33. c: Ah . . . let me see. It seems to happen a lot about the right way to handle the kids. We have disagreements about that.
34. w: What kind of disagreements?
35. c: Well, we have different ways of handling them. I tend to be more direct, maybe demanding, about what they should be doing about school work and chores at home. She tries to reason with them, to show them why it's best to work at those things and then gets agreements from them.
36. w: And what do you do?
37. c: I tell them that they *should* do these things, that I had to work hard at outside labor when I was their age (thinks a moment). . . . I guess I lecture them. That's what my wife tells me all the time . . . and that it doesn't work.
38. w: And, does it?
39. c: Not always. Sometimes it seems like their eyes glaze over and they tune me out . . . and that gets to me, especially if they don't follow up right away and do what I tell them to. Then I start yelling at them, and that's when my wife gets after me. It happened just yesterday.
40. w: Tell me about it.
41. c: Well, my daughter had been out to several parties over the past week and she had an English exam coming up today. Then I heard her talking on the phone yesterday with a girlfriend, and they were talking about getting together in the evening. So, I guess I really lost it and began yelling at her while she was still on the phone with her friend—telling her she damn well better stay home and study. That did it.

42. w: Did what?
43. c: She really got upset. Told me I had embarrassed her something awful—"'mortified'' her—while her girlfriend was still on the phone and could hear everything. Then she started crying, stomped up to her bedroom, and slammed the door. That's when my wife got after me. Told me I was insensitive and too aggressive. So we get into this argument about the right way to handle the kids, and I guess I'm getting defensive so I start attacking and telling her she's too easy on them, like a pal instead of a mother. I'm getting really angry and louder and louder. It's that infuriating way she has of looking at me in these arguments.
44. w: How does she look?
45. c: Kind of *down* at me. Like I don't know what I'm talking about and that I'm just yelling to cover up that I'm wrong . . . and that she's right. She acts so goddam sure of herself . . . so smug . . . and she's always right.
46. w: Always?
47. w: It sure seems that way, and it really makes me feel awful.
48. w: Tell me how that feels.
49. c: It makes me feel like a little kid . . . ashamed . . . but still defiant.
50. w: Sort of like you felt with your mother when you were a kid?
51. c: Huh? Well, I can't say. It was different. My mother yelled a lot . . . domineered me.
52. w: Domineered?
53. c: No! Wait a minute here! I don't mean domineered. She was a very hard working woman and quite sickly . . . was totally blind in one eye . . . and she worked in the needle trade. It was hard on her. She'd come home tired. (Then, in an irritated tone) Anyway, I thought we were talking about my relationship with my wife.
54. w: You're right, we were. So, let's get back to what was actually said between you and your wife . . . after the phone episode with your daughter.

After this fifth session work both in and out of sessions focused on communication problems with his wife and children. It began with the distinction between assertive and aggressive communications, the use of "I" statements, and the expression of wishes and wants rather than demands and threats. The worker and client role played a number of scenarios that were recurrently problematic, and there were a number of subtasks involving in vivo uses of these newly learned communication skills. These helped in his relationship with his wife and his children but more so with his children. He thought the reason for this was that a number of the marital issues were of a different order and that the assertiveness skills worked more consistently with the children.

He was still dissatisfied with his inability to get at, to differentiate, and to express his feelings in his interactions with his wife. Many times he could not articulate appropriately assertive statements because he did not know what the feeling was that needed to be articulated assertively. At this point (twelfth) session the worker introduced Gendlin's (1981) experiential focusing technique to help the client identify, describe, and "shift" feelings. It requires the client to focus on the bodily felt sense or referent of a problem or situation rather than engage in an intellectual analysis of it. This was intended not only to get at his feelings but also to enhance his experiencing in a number of areas of his life, particularly in experiencing pleasure. The following segment from the seventeenth session deals with the client's experience in using the focusing technique up to that point.

55. c: It has really been helpful to me in more ways than one. The focusing on my body has made me aware of my body in a different way. You know, I'm an avid jogger—have been for a long time. It always helped me keep in shape physically, but I would drive myself at that, too, like everything else. Now I'm more aware of how my body feels and I'm letting go of the tension—I can actually feel the tension flowing out—as I jog at more of a natural pace.

56. w: You're looking more relaxed.

57. c: Yeah. It also helped me to know better what I was feeling, so that I can tell my wife now what I'm feeling. It isn't all there yet but I'm getting there. It still happens now and then that she will give me that smug look and I get that awful feeling. . . . I can feel it right now as I think of it.

58. w: Can you stay with that feeling, in your body, and get a sense of it right now?

59. c: Yeah. I think so (long silence). It's a blocked-off feeling . . . like a block of ice or something in here (pointing to his lower neck area just above the chest). It's like part of me is frozen and it's keeping things down. . . . It needs to thaw and there's something that needs to get out (looking tense). It's not clear. I can't really get at what it is . . . right now.

60. w: Make a space for that unclear thing, since it's not clear what it is yet. It seems to be making you tense.

61. c: Yeah. I really feel the tension.

62. w: Right. Take a break now. Just step back a little from that unclear thing. You'll get back to it again soon, when the time's
right.

63. c: Yeah. I will (relaxes and shifts in his chair). I know I will
(smiles). You know lately it feels good right here (pointing to
the upper part of his stomach). When I feel good there that's
when I know I'm feeling good about other things—that I'm enjoying them. I used to be up in my head all the time, but I can really get with that basic sense of things—for me—now.

Treatment of this client ended after twenty-one sessions over a period of
five months. His score on the Beck Depression Inventory at termination
was 4, which was well down in the normal, nondepressed range.

APPLICATION OF THE FRAMEWORK

Discourse analysis within the change process framework focuses on speech
acts, and these have been reported in various ways by different investigators. Client and therapist response modes have been studied relative to the
function or effect of these speech acts on the change process (Hill 1986).
Another approach has been to study the speech act in terms of the depth of
experience reflected in the language (Klein et al. 1969). This latter approach
is the primary method of analyzing the discourse in the case discussed
above.

The Experiencing Scale is a seven-point scale that has been used in
numerous process research studies (Mathieu-Couglan and Klein 1984;
Klein, Mathieu-Couglan, and Kiesler 1986). The Experiencing (EXP) Scale
was designed for use with tape recordings and transcripts of individual
therapy sessions. The seven scale "stages" define the progression of client
involvement in inner referents or feelings from impersonal (1) or superficial
(2) through externalized or limited references to feelings (3), to direct inner
referents (4), to exploring an unclear inner referent (5), to focusing with a
step of resolution (6), and then to the point where focusing provides the
connections of inner discourse (7). There are expressive stylistic indicators
of remoteness versus immediacy of feeling relevant throughout the scale
with evidence of direct sensing and changing of experience at the top end
in stages 6 and 7. In short, stages 1–3 define the progressive ownership of
affective reactions. Stage 4 represents a critical transition that marks a shift
from self-as-object to self-as-subject. It also represents the fulcrum of
change in most psychotherapies in that it is the point where content and
focus shift from outside to inside (Mathieu-Coughlan and Klein 1984).

Stages 5–7 define the progressive expansion and integration of this perspective.

Applying the scale to the first segment in the case above, the client's discourse begins (2 and 4.C) at a rather impersonal level (EXP 1) with no ownership in that it is his wife and his marriage that bring him to the agency for help. It then moves to EXP 2 when he discusses his parents (10.C), which is a bit more personal and provides a behavioral self-description relative to largely external (parental) circumstances. It does not really move to EXP 3, although he gives some limited behavioral self-description in describing the family dinner scenario (14.C) He sustains this level and at one point somewhat owns the feeling (22.C) of being worried about possibly getting a female worker. To fully own the feeling he would have had to say "I am worried" rather than "it worried me." Process researchers who have used the EXP Scale have found that the absence of an "I" is the basic linguistic indicator of the lowest level of experiencing (Klein et al. 1986).

In addition to the analysis of discourse by the Experiencing Scale, there are other linguistic or speech act indicators of importance. There was, for example, much more frequent use of "me" than "I" in the client's early discourse. "Me" is usually used as the object of a verb and indicates passivity in that the person is depicted as the recipient rather than the initiator of an action. This is abundantly clear in the client's response (2 and 4.C) to the worker's query about what brought him to the agency. This frequent use of "me" has been found to be characteristic of depressed speech and to be reflective of the passivity in depression (Weintraub 1989). In this regard it is informative, and reflective of change, to see the increased ratio of "I's" to "me's" in the later segments of the case.

Now, to take a look at the episode and relationship elements of the framework in the analysis of this discourse a key event or marker occurred when the client (14.C) indicated doubts that anything could be done about his situation. The worker picked up on this (15.W) and the ensuing discourse (16.C through 27.W) involved an exploration of the client's fears and doubts. Its culmination represents the beginning of a working alliance as indicated in the client's statement, "I hope so. We'll see (26.C). Within this is the beginning sense of "we," which represents the bonding aspect of the working alliance (Greenberg 1986). In their Working Alliance Inventory Horvath and Greenberg (1986) identify client–worker convergence in treatment goals and tasks as the second and third aspects of alliance after bonding.

By the fifth session (segment 2) the client was heavily involved in subtasks related to evident goals. The EXP levels of segment 2 are consistently above those of segment 1, largely because the worker has focused the discourse on the client's difficulty in knowing and expressing what he is feeling (28.W). The client is more consistently at EXP level 2 rather than 1 and 2. It then gets up to EXP 3 when he describes himself as "getting defensive" and "really angry" (44.C) in response to his wife's criticism of him over his handling of the interchange with his daughter.

The relationship component in segment 2 begins with an apparent congruence with respect to goal and task. The worker is trying to get the client in touch with his feelings and the client appears to be engaging in some self-exploration around this. In fact, the client gets to EXP level 4 when he acknowledges that at times his wife's behavior toward him makes him feel "like a little kid . . . ashamed." This is the first time we get a sense of what it is like to be he, because he has moved from self-as-object to self-as subject.

This fruitful exploration of feelings could have continued and deepened, if the worker had not opted for a different approach when he focused on the client's statement that his mother "domineered" him (52.C). The worker apparently chose the route of interpretation, of making a psychodynamic connection between the developmental origins and current manifestation of a behavioral pattern. However, he lost the client in the process and the relationship was set back. The client made it evident that such psychogenic explorations were not part of his understanding of treatment goal or task. His irritation suggested some negative, if only transient, effect on the bonding component in the working alliance. The worker's quick validation of the correctness of the client's understanding was an attempt to restore the prior level of alliance.

The third segment begins with a good deal of self-description at EXP level 3 with the client's positive description of enhanced body awareness by using the focusing technique (56.C). It then goes to EXP 4 when he talks about the "awful feeling" he gets when his wife gives him "that smug look" and the fact that he can feel it "right now," in the present. He is at EXP 5 when he silently focuses on his "blocked-off feeling." This marks a sharp shift inward toward a bodily felt sense or meaning for that feeling (60.C). However, he does not get beyond EXP 5 at that point because he was beginning to feel tense and unclear about it. Frequently, when clients reach EXP 5 in therapy, their discourse becomes halting and dysfluent, because they are focusing inwardly to find the right words or images to capture what they are feeling.

Although this was a short segment, it illustrates several things about the relationship and working alliance at that stage of treatment. First, the client willingly engages in focusing on his feelings at the worker's request (59.W), which suggests a congruence with respect to goal, task, and bonding at that stage of treatment.

This illustration of the application of the change process framework was intended to look at its actual and potential value for qualitative research. The three levels of process (speech act, episode, and relationship) appear to have more immediate relevance for discourse analysis than the three levels of outcome do (immediate, intermediate, and ultimate). Much of the change process research refers to "measurement" of both process and outcome variables, which means quantification. Qualitative research methods have been referred to as "procedures for counting to one," or the process of determining what is to count as a unit of analysis (Van Maanen 1986). Accordingly, speech acts, episodes, and relationships would count as meaningful units of analysis for the purposes of qualitative research.

The EXP Scale has been used quantitatively as a "variable," but one could argue that each of the seven levels in the scale actually represents a *qualitatively* different category of experiencing. However, even if it is used as a variable rather than a set of categories it can fit readily into the change process framework. Episode and relationship were used categorically in the case illustration even though the Working Alliance Inventory is a quantified measure of relationship. What was done was to view each of the components of bonding, goal, and task in a unitary qualitative sense. On the other hand, the Beck Depression Inventory (pre and post) was used as a quantified measure of outcome. This is consistent with the point made earlier that the change process framework allows for the combining of qualitative and quantitative methods. Most important, however, the framework enables the researcher to more meaningfully analyze the discourse (speech acts) within the larger treatment context.

REFERENCES

Austin, J. I. 1962. *How to Do Things in Words*. New York: Oxford University Press.
Beck, A., A. J. Rush, G. F. Shaw, and G. Emery. 1979. *Cognitive Therapy of Depression*. New York: Guilford Press.
Berlin, S. B. 1990. The utility of change-process research for the education of practitioners and single-case evaluation. In L. Videka-Sherman and W. J. Reid, eds., *Advances in Clinical Social Work Research*, (pp. 159–62). Silver Spring, Md.: NASW Press, 1990.
Berlin, S. B., K. B. Mann, and S. F. Grossman. 1991. Task analysis of cognitive therapy for depression. *Social Work Research and Abstracts* 27: 3–41.
Gendlin, E. T. 1981. *Focusing*. New York: Bantam.
Greenberg, L. 1986. Change process research. *Journal of Consulting and Clinical Psychology* 54: 4–9.
Greenberg, L. and W. M. Pinsof. 1986. *The Psychotherapeutic Process: A Research Book*. New York: Guilford Press.

Hill, C. E. 1986. An overview of the Hill counselor and client verbal response modes and category systems. In Greenberg and Pinsof, eds., *The Psychotherapeutic Process: A Research Handbook,* pp. 131–59. New York: Guilford Press.

Horvath, A. O. and L. Greenberg. 1986. The development of the working alliance inventory. In Greenberg and Pinsof, eds., *The Psychotherapeutic Process: A Research Handbook,* pp. 529–56. New York: Guilford Press.

Klein, M., P. Mathieu, E. Gendlin, and D. Kiesler. 1969. *The Experiencing Scale.* Madison: Wisconsin Psychiatric Institute.

Klein, M., P. Mathieu-Couglan, and D. Kiesler. 1986. The experiencing scales. In L. Greenberg and W. M. Pinsof, eds., *The Psychotherapeutic Process: A Research Handbook,* pp. 21–71. New York: Guilford Press.

Labov, W. 1982. Speech actions and reactions in personal narrative. In D. Tannen, ed., *Analyzing Discourse: Text and Talk,* pp. 219–47. Washington, D.C.: Georgetown University Press.

Mathieu-Coughlan, P. and M. H. Klein. 1984. Experiential psychotherapy: Key events in client-therapist interaction. In L. Rice and L. Greenberg, eds., *Patterns of Change: Intensive Analysis of Psychotherapy Process.* New York: Guilford Press.

Rice, L. and J. Greenberg. 1984. *Patterns of Change: Intensive Analysis of Psychotherapy Process.* New York: Guilford Press.

Reid, W. J. 1990. Change-process research: A new paradigm? In Videka-Sherman and Reid, eds., *Advances in Clinical Social Work Research,* pp. 130–58. Silver Spring, Md.: NASW Press.

Searles, J. 1969. *Speech Acts: An Essay on the Philosophy of Language.* New York: Oxford University Press.

Sherman, E. and K. Skinner. 1988. Client language and clinical process. *Clinical Social Work Journal* 16:391–405.

van Dijk, T. A. 1982. Episodes as units of discourse analysis. In D. Tannen, ed., *Analyzing Discourse: Text and Talk,* pp. 177–95. Washington, D.C.: Georgetown University Press.

Van Maanen, J. 1986. Series introduction. In J. Kirk and M. L. Miller, eds., *Reliability and Validity in Qualitative Research,* pp. 5–6. Newbury Park, Calif.: Sage.

Weintraub, W. 1989. *Verbal Behavior in Everyday Life.* New York: Springer.

Zimring, F. 1990. Cognitive processes as a cause of psychotherapeutic change: Self-initiated processes. In G. Lietaer, J. Rombarts, and R. Van Balen, eds., *Client Centered and Experiential Psychotherapy in the Nineties,* pp. 361–80. Leuven, Belgium: Leuven University Press.

TWENTY

Commentary: Discourse Theory and Analysis

Max Siporin

A sign of a new era in social work education and practice is that we now give attention to discourse theory and analysis. This represents a major shift in our thinking about therapeutic processes, to what we have called "communication theory." In this section three papers dealt with qualitative research on discourse analysis.

COMMUNICATION THEORY

For many years, beginning largely during the 1960s and the onset of the new family therapy movement, communication was an extremely popular subject for attention and discussion in the helping professions, including social work. Satir's (1967) teaching about communication difficulties between family members was particularly influential for theory and practice. Much helpful work was done in identifying communication difficulties between social worker and client (i.e., Baldock and Prior 1981; Bloom 1980; Cormican 1976, 1978; Hammond, Hepworth, and Smith 1977; Seabury 1980). So striking and popular were the notions about dysfunctional communication, metacommunication and disjunctions, communication blocks, and inadequate sending and receiving of messages that these ideas pervaded the popular culture. Many problems in social living were defined as "communication problems," and clients frequently gave as a presenting complaint, "We just can't communicate."

The limitations of the communication perspective have often been noted, particularly its inadequate regard for the complex dynamics of interpersonal relationships and for the inner life of thinking and feeling between people engaged in dialogue. Although Satir (1967:98) declared that communication referred to "all interactional behavior" between people, the concern has been with overt behavior. Discourse theory and analysis represent a current effort to clarify and understand the construction and meanings of life narratives and stories, which people overtly and intersubjectively exchange in conversation with each other. This content about the inner worlds and experiences of human beings is what we seek to apprehend through this form of inquiry.

THE DISCOURSE PERSPECTIVE

The discourse perspective is a relatively new approach to understanding the helping process. It is a response to the increasingly observed discrepancy between the concepts and language used to describe practice activities and their actual reality. Rojeck, Peacock, and Collins (1988) emphasize this observation in stating that the "cultural crisis of social work" consists of the gap between the "received ideas" in the language used for practice and the actual actions of practice. They contend that this language is dehumanizing, forces clients to fit classifications, confuses relationships, "places a shield between worker and client, (and) creates problems and imposes solutions" (137,143). They endorse discourse analysis as a critical corrective:

> Discourse analysis produces a linguistically grounded model of social work,
> . . . says that language is used to construct reality rather than reflect it, . . .
> (and) encourages the social worker to regard relations of social work as
> relations of power, i.e., relations which are both enabling and constraining,
> liberating and repressive.   (137, 144)

Nye's paper in this section of the book defines discourse analysis as seeking "to identify the structural principles of interpretation, production and sequencing, which govern the organization of talk, and to generate a grammar of discourse rules."

Currently, a major aspect of discourse theory is its emphasis on language and semantics. Because language is power that acts to define, shape, and control reality, it is an appropriate focus for understanding the discourse transactions between practitioners and clients in helping situations. For this, we need to develop appropriate concepts, theory, principles, methods, and instruments, particularly through research efforts. Because of the complex dynamics and the highly subjective and intersubjective nature of discourse between practitioner and client, research on the helping process and qualitative methods of research are particularly suitable. It is fortunate that the preceding three papers deal with qualitative research on discourse analysis.

Chambon, Nye, and Sherman share a common interest in the narratives or life histories of clients, as related to their self-identity, locus of control, and sense of responsibility for one's own behavior. Each believes that the language, interpretations, and meanings of narratives, are an important basis of individual self-identity and social functioning. Apprehending these experiential meanings requires viewing the language used in the context of situational relationships and events, and as expressing the characteristic social work person-in-situation perspective.

Narratives thus are accorded central importance in understanding the therapeutic process. Chambon, Nye, and Sherman seek to understand the change process of treatment as it is influenced by the language the clients use in presenting their personal narratives and their meanings. The treatment process is understood in terms of how the narratives are told and discussed and of how the language of their telling and meanings changes.

The three papers presented in this section are fine examples of qualitative research on therapeutic discourse, using new techniques and procedures of discourse analysis.

The focus on the therapeutic dialogue means a concern with data that are subjective and intersubjective. These types of data require a qualitative method of research that can apprehend their dynamic, complex character. The tools of discourse analysis are very suitable for such a qualitative research methodology. With attention to contextual factors, they can well identify experiential meanings of client narratives. This approach is broader and more meaningful than research in the technical linguistic features of the helping process.

The studies by Nye and Sherman made use of both qualitative and quantitative methods of analysis. Some of the data, obtained and categorized according to the coding schemes used, were made accessible for quantitative measurement and comparison. Thus, as Sherman emphasized, use can be made of linguistic research without restricting it to an exclusive use of qualitative methods.

This research confirms the practice wisdom that has informed and guided social work helping efforts. Our practice wisdom has given much significance to helping people with their life stories, now referred to as narratives, and with the language used to communicate these life stories to others.

A major influence in social work practice was the work of Satir and her emphasis on helping clients to use "I" statements. Satir (1967) taught that mature and well-functioning communicators are direct, delineated, and clear; are responsible for what they say and do, and use the first person "I" followed by an active verb and ending with a direct object. According to Ragg (1977), a central function of casework treatment is to help clients reformulate their life stories and their meanings.

Still another bit of practice wisdom is the importance of stimulating self-reflective statements and activity by clients; this was emphasized by Hollis (1964) and was part of her casework treatment typology. The confirmation of such social work practice wisdom in the research reported here is gratifying.

A needed direction of further research is to understand the rhetorical uses and functions of speech about life stories. Richan (1972:17) contended that "the central activity of social workers is persuasion," that clinicians "try to influence the attitudes and behavior of their clients," and that this requires a "system of rhetoric, or persuasive language." Glaser (1980) similarly suggested that psychotherapy is essentially a rhetorical and therefore an artistic enterprise, in that the therapist uses style as a basic rhetorical element to influence clients, to resolve tension, and to alter beliefs, feelings, and behavior. Rhetorical language is a basic means of involving clients and convincing them of the importance and truth of interpretations and directives. The use of rhetorical language is consistent with social work values and ethical practice principles, in that the worker's persuasive activity respects the client's self-determination in making informed choices.

These papers by Chambon, Nye, and Sherman are significant contributions to our understanding of the therapeutic discourse between client and social worker and of how qualitative research can advance effective practice.

REFERENCES

Baldock, J. and D. Prior. 1981. Social workers talking to clients. *British Journal of Social Work* 11: 19–38.
Bloom, A. A. 1980. Social work and the English language. *Social Casework* 61: 332–38.
Cormican, J. D. 1976. Linguistic subcultures and social work practice. *Social Casework* 57: 589–92.
Cormican, J. D. 1978. Linguistic issues in interviewing. *Social Casework* 59: 145–51.
Glaser, S. Rhetoric and psychotherapy. 1980. In M. J. Mahoney, ed., *Psychotherapy Process*, pp. 313–33. New York: Plenum.

Hammond, D. C., D. H. Hepworth, and V. G. Smith. 1977. *Improving Therapeutic Communication*. San Francisco: Jossey-Bass.

Hollis, F. 1964. *Casework*. New York: Random House.

Ragg, N. M. 1977. *People, Not Cases*. Boston: Routledge and Kegan Paul.

Richan, W. C. 1972. A common language for social work. *Social Work* 17: 14–22.

Rojeck, C., G. Peacock, and S. Collins. 1988. *Social Work and Received Ideas*. London: Routledge and Kegan Paul.

Satir, V. 1967. *Conjoint Family Therapy*. Palo Alto, Calif.: Science and Behavior.

Seabury, B. A. 1980. Communication problems in social work. *Social Work* 25: 40–44.

II

Qualitative Approaches to Evaluation

CLINICAL CASE
EVALUATION

TWENTY-ONE

The Qualitative Case Study and Evaluation: Issues, Methods, and Examples

Roy Ruckdeschel, Pat Earnshaw, and Andrea Firrek

This article undertakes the tasks of arguing for the utility of the qualitative case study in evaluation and of demonstrating its relevance for student researchers. The case study is an in-depth form of research that may focus on a person, a group, a program, an organization, a time period, a cultural incident, or a community (Patton 1990:54). Although the case study may be quantitative, qualitative, or some combination of the two, the focus here is on qualitative applications. The instructor/author's point of view about the utility of the case study is in large part informed by his fifteen years of teaching qualitative methods to MSW students in a school of social work. The student/authors' point of view is informed by their experience in that class. The case study is one of the major models around which the course is organized and is the major learning experience for both the students and the instructor. This course has forced the authors to struggle with a number of basic issues relative to evaluation in general and the case study in particular. Specifically, the paper addresses three central issues in the conduct of the case study; the student co-authors turn show how these were dealt with in their own projects. Although the paper is part of a symposium on outcomes, issues of outcome and evaluation design are treated as matters of discourse rather than as matters of instrumentation. Accordingly, the starting point is the issue of meaning.

Evaluation: Finding the Value, Finding the Meaning

Social work has struggled for a considerable period of time with the fundamental questions of evaluation. The author/instructor as an educator has had to confront these questions both on a personal level and in the classroom. The educational task is made all the more imperative by the current policy statement of the Council on Social Work Education (CSWE), which requires that students be taught skills to systematically evaluate their own practice and that such instruction be emphasized throughout the curriculum (CSWE 1988:127).

The social work literature on evaluation provides only modest insight on how this task is to be engaged but is instructive on the current state of affairs. The abstract for a recent article in a social work journal is both informative and typical in this regard: "The social work profession has strived for nearly a century to implement scientific methods to evaluate practice. Evidence indicates, however, that social workers currently do not evaluate their own practice" (Gleeson 1990:295).

The article documents the alleged failure and proposes a remedy; interested readers are encouraged to read this article for the specifics. For the purposes of our article, what is of central interest is twofold. First, the profession has apparently not done a very effective job of persuading either practitioners or students that evaluation is an important part of practice. Second, this article essentially poses the issue of evaluation as one primarily of the implementation of scientific methods.

One might wonder if the two are linked and whether in fact the linkage contributes to the problem. Social work research texts primarily approach evaluation in instrumental terms and as part of what has been termed scientific social work (Bloom and Fischer 1982; Rubin and Babbie 1989; Tripodi 1983; Wodarski 1981). The emphasis is placed on issues of measurement and outcomes, although a variety of process-oriented evaluation approaches may also be presented.

Numerous difficulties arise with the formulation of evaluation as the implementation of scientific methods. Certainly, one of these is the failure to engage the interest of either practitioners or students. Perhaps this is because the field of social work itself has not really engaged the meaning of evaluation. Neither in social work education nor in the field have we made it our issue.

The instructor/author has found it useful both in his qualitative class and for himself to engage in a kind of deconstruction of evaluation as a concept. Deconstructionism is a rigorous methodology with roots in literary criticism (for an example in social work, see Cutler 1991). Its value is a matter of much current debate in the academic community. However, the intent here is simply one of stressing the process implied in deconstruction rather than to treat it as a formal method. The task then is to treat evaluation as a kind of text that must be interpreted by each reader/researcher.

Evaluation is a term that admits of many possible meanings and agendas. When evaluation is presented in the context of scientific social work, the discussion will most probably reflect what Gouldner (1970) terms the domain assumptions of the writer. That is, it becomes embedded in a given author's broader understanding of the nature of science and of scientific method. These domain assumptions may be part of the discussion but are more likely to be treated implicitly.

The meaning of evaluation is also embedded in a political context. Scriven (1967) has reminded us that evaluation is normative. All programs and all forms of intervention have implicit notions about what constitutes the "good." To objectify the process is potentially to miss the centrality of the issue. This is particularly the case when notions of the "good" are intertwined with the realities of power. Unfortunately, the rhetoric of research always has the potential to disguise power relationships. Rein and White (1981) note that social workers already have a tendency to deemphasize the importance of power and to fall back on what they term the myth of skills as the defining characteristic of the profession.

All this represents only a fraction of the many meanings and issues related to evaluation. The more significant point is that the researcher, the practitioner, the student must engage the issue of what evaluation means to them. Deconstruction is simply an analogy to emphasize the need to engage this process.

The author/instructor's own attempt to deconstruct the term eventually led to an old dictionary. The first definition of *evaluate* in that dictionary was "to find the value" (Webster's 1961). This seems a strikingly simple and useful way to think about evaluation and the one that is employed by the authors in this paper. Evaluation as the process of finding the value is the first and perhaps most important phase of the research whether it be in the classroom or in the field. It is also an ongoing process that ought to involve the full range of potential actors. Thus, finding the value almost inexorably leads us into the life world of decision makers, of practitioners, and of those with whom we practice. It suggests the importance of interactive research approaches and active participation in those social worlds. The qualitative case study represents an approach to finding the value through interaction.

FINDING THE VALUE THROUGH INTERACTION

The qualitative case study has its own set of mandates and requirements. "Regardless of the unit of analysis, the qualitative case study seeks to describe that unit in depth and detail, in context and holistically" (Patton 1990:54).

The case study is inherently interactive and participative. Many of its conceptual roots lie in symbolic interactionist theory. Symbolic Interactionists such as Blumer (1978) have long maintained that meanings are social and emerge in human interaction. The instructor/author has elsewhere argued for interactionism as a cornerstone of a qualitative research perspective in social work (Ruckdeschel 1985).

Whether one approaches interactions from a rigorous theoretical stance or from a more pragmatic interactional point of view, an understanding of two different kinds of interactions can inform the case study approach to finding the value. These interactions concern the research process and the study of the life world of the client. Some researchers even maintain that the case study is the best and perhaps only way to study human interaction (Sjöberg et al. 1991).

While less obvious and more taken for granted than other forms of interactions, the research process itself can be understood in interactional terms. Denzin (1989), for example, uses the expression "the research act" to emphasize the social and interpretative aspects of research. One consequence of viewing research as a social act is to focus as much attention on process as on the product.

Part of that task is to examine how research problems come to be defined and who participates in the decisions. Kirk and Miller (1986) maintain that the reporting out of the decision-making process is the essence of reliability in qualitative research. This reporting out makes the process accessible to others by establishing the context of the research.

Thus the entire process of evaluation as information seeking, finding, and reporting can be usefully viewed as interactional. Correspondingly, the same is true of the relationship between the information seeker, the information sought, and the information user. In fact, the persuasive power of the research may be more closely linked to this process than to the effects of the findings. Of this relationship, House says: "In the fullest sense, then, an evaluation is dependent both on the person who makes the evaluative statement and on the person who receives it" quoted in Patton 1990:469).

In a similar sense, Patton (1980:273) notes that one of the tasks of evaluation is to "provide relevant and useful information to decision makers, the criteria for usefulness and relevance being negotiated with decision makers and information users during the conceptual phase of the evaluation.''

Clearly in this interactive view of evaluation and the case study, instrumentation is secondary. Qualitative methods and procedures such as the use of observation, documents, and various forms of interviews are generally employed, and knowledge of their use is important. However, researchers must come to see themselves as "instruments," a point illustrated later in this paper.

Ultimately, perhaps the most important form of interaction to consider is that involving what Hollenshead (1982:5) terms the "life world" of the client. While clients have been the focus of much research in social work, relatively little of that research has been directed to describing and attempting to understand the worlds of clients as worlds of meaning. Surely an implication of the case study approach is that the life world of the client is vastly different from that of most practitioners and is neither easily entered nor easily grasped.

The attempt to describe life worlds in both detail and in a fashion that allows the reader to enter them is what Geertz (1979) refers to as thick description. Denzin has extended and incorporated this concept into what he terms *behavioral specimens*. Behavioral specimens as nearly complete descriptions of interactions between individuals within particular time frames are the stuff of the case study.

The task confronting the would-be researcher of client worlds is difficult. This is particularly true when the life world is that of the poor and the disenfranchised. Whatever the difficulty, the case study approach offers the most promise. In fact, Sjöberg et al. (1991:34) forcefully argue that the two ends of the spectrum, the truly powerful and the truly disadvantaged, can be effectively studied only with the in-depth case study approach. The task of research, particularly the case study, is to give the poor a voice:

> If the truly disadvantaged are to be given a voice—if they are to be heard—it must be through the collection of careful case material by social scientists who take the world view of the economically disadvantaged and set the latter's voices (and their pain) in relationship to the powerful organizational structures that impact their lives and over which they have so little control. (49)

The student/author case studies demonstrate the importance of interactively entering the life world of the client and of the poor and illustrate an interactive approach to the research process.

FINDING THE MEANING
THROUGH TRANSFORMATION

The reader may well wonder about the product of all this effort. Part of the intent of the redefinition of evaluation was to shift the focus away from measurement and instrumentation and instead to concentrate on the more emergent and interactive issues. The notion of outcomes and the supposed importance of outcomes for evaluative research also require some reconsideration. The term *outcome* has come to have such a generalized meaning that even qualitative researchers will occasionally employ its use. This is appropriate as long as case study outcomes are not wrapped in the gloss of positivist terminology. However, the author/instructor finds it more useful to consider at least some of the products of the case study as instances of transformations.

Linda Barbara-Stein (1979) has discussed transformations as a normal part of the qualitative research experience. Transformations constitute ways in which the researcher chooses to report the experience of the research to others. The specific transformations in Barbara-Stein's research involved the ways in which negotiations to gain access into the field were on the one hand experienced and on the other hand reported. The logic of transformations has particular application to the qualitative case study. The task of the qualitative researcher is to meaningfully transform the richly textured data of the case study into useful information for the reader and consumer of the research. It is no doubt the hope and belief of most researchers that information may lead to change. Extensive and rich "thick description" facilitates this possibility.

The task of transforming the data of the field into information for use approximates the reporting of outcomes in conventional evaluations. It is, as implied above, a difficult but vital task. It is also correct to note that transformations must be plausible if they are to be believed and if they are to have the potential to produce change. That is, they must engage the consumers and the decision makers. House notes that "evaluation cannot produce necessary propositions. But if it cannot produce the necessary, it can provide the credible, the plausible, and the probable. Its results are less than certain but still may be useful" (quoted in Patton 1980:273).

Persuasion as transformation involves some of the issues already discussed such as reporting in detail the processes and the decisions of the research. It also involves struggling with conceptualization as an important part of the transformation process. The attempt to empirically ground the concepts or themes that emerge from the research is an issue of validity. Kirk and Miller (1986:23) term this dialectical and interactive approach to validity "calling things by the right names."

Data are not the only phenomena affected by transformations. If the conduct of research and the carrying out of the case study are seen as a social act, the researcher as actor influences the nature of the phenomenon being studied and is in turn influenced. The latter involves transformations of a different order than those discussed thus far. These are in essence transformations of self. Transformations of self actually occur throughout all phases of the research. Wax (1971:14) regards these changes as a necessary precondition for fieldwork. In her view, researchers must undergo a secondary socialization or resocialization if they are to grasp the meanings of the setting. In a related fashion, qualitative textbooks generally recommend that fieldworkers record their own feelings, thoughts, and impressions throughout the research. The author/instructor, for example, suggests that students in his qualitative methods course use a separate category, the "OS" or observations on self, for this purpose.

However, if transformations are seen as kinds of products or outcomes, the transformation of self that occurs by the conclusion of the research is of most interest. It is also potentially one of the most profound aspects of the well-done case study. The phrase "well done" is deliberately used to emphasize that nothing is automatic about this process nor are all transformations "wondrous." The student/authors discuss various types of transformations in the following material derived from their original research papers (Earnshaw 1991; Firrek 1991).

Case 1—Hemodialysis Unit by Pat Earnshaw

Studying the perception of patients with end-stage renal disease (ESRD) became my qualitative research focus based on three factors. As a former chief radioimmunoassay technologist, I had acquired particular interest in renal physiology. Additionally, a recent MSW practicum experience at a hospital in-patient hemodialysis unit had exposed the other side of the needle, the gruesome reality of people faced with renal failure. Third, access to the research setting, a free-standing outpatient hemodialysis center, was facilitated through knowing a hospital nephrologist who provided medical services to that center. Putting aside medical jargon and left-brain perceptions, I took the first step into the qualitative labyrinth.

While I had driven this way countless times before, today, in the early morning silence, I notice the cinema marquee guarding the entrance to the economically depressed shopping plaza. The top three titles, *Home Alone, Silence of the Lambs,* and *The Neverending Story,* beckon me with metaphorical urgency. Scribbling my first field notes, I enter the outpatient dialysis center and am immediately overwhelmed by the swishing, humming noises of medical technology. As the machinery alarm erupts,

"BEEP! BEEP! BEEP!," my pen jumps across the paper. "Whaaaat you doin' over here? Actin' up on me?" A nurse responds but there is no answer. She studies the fifty-two-gadget front of the dialysis machine and carefully examines two blood-filled tubes coming from the patient's arm. "Oh, God!" exclaims the bearded man across from my wallside post. A nurse lowers the head of his dialysis chair and supplies him with a green emesis basin.

A ceiling full of fluorescent lighting illuminates the white thermal blankets that envelop the mummy-like sleeping figures. While I note minimal and survivalistic interaction between staff and patients, one dialysizing woman observes me. I feel uncomfortable in my student role without a well-worn label; I am neither injecting patients with radionuclides nor am I composing social histories. In this situation and in the absence of interaction, I have defined myself as unimportant, lacking in purpose. As I survey my captive audience, my thoughts succumb to familiar terminology, "compliance" and "noncompliance." Like Theseus about to journey into the labyrinth, I am at the mercy of Ariadne. Who will offer me a thread?

During coffee break with the nurses I sense common ground, a familiar paradigm. Following a banter of medical terminology, the head nurse asks who I have decided to interview and I explain that I have not. She offers a name and provides a brief medical history. Having completed ten hours of unobtrusive observation, I take this thread for next week's journey and eagerly approach Walter, an apple-cheeked sixty-five-year-old man. After the introductory litany of my role and purpose, I request basic medical background, which includes how long he has been having dialysis, why dialysis is necessary, and what dialysis means.

> Being on the machine is the only way I can survive. Just have to accept the fact. Look at it as your best friend, realize you wouldn't be here if this happened twenty-five years ago.

I remarked that he has accepted dialysis and Walter explains that nurses have him talk to new "hemo patients." Comfortable with his role as mentor, Walter imparts a wealth of data drawing from his seven-year dialysis history and experiences in eighteen different dialysis centers. Now retired, Walter reflects on the pain of ultrafast dialysis machines, the pleasure of munching a cup of ice during treatments, the contentment he feels at this dialysis center, and the love he has for his successful grown children, his wife, garden, pets, hobbies, and travels. I never regret conversing with Walter, though, for his story provided a template for a self-constructed interview guide. I realize Walter socializes the fledgling dialysis patients because he is compliant, an example of failed renal physiology turned hemodialysis success.

The next week, again on break, I inquire about the man across from my observation point. "Oh, Vince?" Martha exclaims, appearing shocked that I mention him. "He pretty much does what he wants." Another nurse reveals, "I can't prove that he drinks before dialysis but I have smelled beer on his breath, usually on a Monday." Heeding the nurses' warning, I move to Vince and hold onto a certain professional reserve as I expect a less than credible exchange of information. But well into the interview I am mesmerized by Vince's story.

Forty-one-year-old Vince, whose face is bronzed by years of circulating toxins, has had both hips replaced owing to bone deterioration caused by medication used to prevent donor kidney rejection. When I remark on the difficult issue of mobility, Vince explains that "I do anything I want. Just takes me longer than most." In spite of using a walker Vince wants to work but loses his disability if he does. This is Vince, the man who dresses as Santa Claus to cheer the kids at the hospital. "Sounds like you give a lot of yourself," I remark and Vince says, "It goes both ways. . . . There's always somebody worse off than me." By the time Vince and I finish the conversation I know he understands, well enough, the diet, drugs, procedure, and the consequences of cheating.

> That's like the gal that would sit by me and brag about cheating on her diet . . . sick 99% of the time . . . doin' a number while she was on the machine. Boy! if you're gonna' cheat, just do it the night before the machine. Don't do it on a Friday night so the toxins stay for two days in your system.

How does an unmarried Vince see himself when he's ninety? "I tell you what. I don't know . . . I am gonna fight it all the way."

From a population of forty-two outpatients I had taped eight in-depth interviews over a period of fifteen weeks. Using a cognitive map and later memorizing questions from my interview guide yielded 107 pages of fieldnotes that emerged into workable themes. I also uncovered sensitivities and struggles of seven dedicated professionals who imparted another dimension to the research process and who provided one source of triangulation for my data. Through interaction I understood the voices of those silenced by medical technology and how we as professionals, comfortable in our labels and categories, reduce people to static objects because they are easily managed and measurable.

Case 2—Hot Lunch Program by Andrea Firrek

For our qualitative case study, our team of three researchers studied a hot lunch program for the poor offered each Sunday by a small inner-city church that two of us attend. Despite its fifteen years in existence, this

program had remarkably little documentation available either on programmatic aspects or on the client population being served, other than that it
attracted predominantly single black men. For all intents and purposes, this
program remained an unknown entity and therefore seemed an appropriate
focus for our research efforts. We were also intrigued by the cultural and
symbolic meanings inherent in the act of preparing and serving a meal on
the one hand and of sharing a meal on the other. A qualitative case study of
this program held the prospect of fresh insights into the worlds of meaning
of the participants on both sides of the serving window.

Despite my own connection with this church and my familiarity with the
church hall where the lunch was being served, nothing could have prepared
me for the feeling of strangeness upon entering the research setting that first
Sunday. It was as if I were seeing the hall for the first time that day as the
presence of these new "tenants" assigned not only a new function but also
a new meaning to this setting for me.

We soon came to understand that we would only learn about "the
hungry poor" one man at a time, as interaction by interaction we began to
accumulate not only generalized impressions but also concrete, individual-
ized personal data from all the men we interviewed. We also realized in
short order that we did not unilaterally control this research process. Research became a two-way street with active and reactive roles constantly
shifting between us, as "researchers" traded places with the "researched."
This became readily apparent as one of the men took the lead, initiating our
very first interaction by asking if we were reporters: "What are you writin'
down? 'People gettin' high'?" This man, with his characteristic blend of
pride, humor, and defiance, was Bo, who became one of my key informants
as the project unfolded. Bo asserted his right to actively engage us in
conversation rather than let us direct the nature of our relationship. His
stance seemed to defy us to dare to label him, stereotype him, or otherwise
reduce him to the status of "research subject." In my first attempt to get a
sense of his circumstances, I asked him, innocently if ineptly, what he
would do if programs like this one were not available, to which he responded half-seriously, half in jest, "I guess I'd be robbin' and stealin'. I'd
be robbin' and stealin' from white folks." Noting the rebuke in his tone, I
responded in kind: "Well, don't look at *me!*" Bo laughed, breaking the
tension, and we both lightened up. Over the course of our interactions
together we both adopted a teasing stance whereby he would challenge me
to buy into some definition of himself as "outlaw" or "desperado." I
understood this to be his way of testing me: would I accept him as a unique
individual with his own set of personal circumstances, or would I buy
into stereotypes about "the hungry poor," "the disadvantaged," "the
underclass?" Whether it was merely my perseverance paying off or his

readiness finally to confide in me, on our last day in the field Bo dropped his fronting pose and shared some of his secrets with me after one last test. It had been four weeks since he had shown up at the church hall when he suddenly appeared, explaining his absence as follows:

A.: (Exclaiming) Hey! Where you been? I've missed you!
BO: I been shoppin'.
A.: Shoppin'?
BO: Yeah. Shopliftin'.
A.: (Pretending to be shocked) No! Really?
BO: (Laughing) No, I've been workin'. I got me a job. That's why you haven't seen me around here. It'll be four weeks tomorrow.

In the course of my ten Sundays in the field I interviewed a dozen men, each with his own story. My initial conservation with Bo and his two "running buddies" yielded information on their networking of various legal and extralegal resources that helped me to conceptualize the direction of the rest of my interviews. It also helped me crystallize my interviewing strategy throughout the remainder of the project. From the beginning we understood that it would be impossible to interview the men at the tables where there was no privacy and where their main order of business and survival was eating as fast as they could so that they could cycle through the line again for seconds or thirds. Through a process of trial and error, I also learned the folly of approaching men as they waited in line: the lack of privacy and the public nature of our interaction led to either "canned" or evasive responses or no response at all.

I would arrive at the church about an hour and a half before the lunch was scheduled to begin and would sit on the low retaining wall along the sidewalk leading into the church hall. Sometimes I would approach individual men as they would begin to appear; on other occasions I would intercept them after they had eaten lunch as they were leaving the hall. The warm spring weather and the flowering crabapple trees provided a relaxed atmosphere within which the men and I felt comfortable talking about their lives and their concerns.

I soon abandoned the structured interview guide when it seemed to produce pat responses. The most important thing I experienced interviewing was the realization that it was not any specific set of questions that was the instrument or measuring device but that I myself was the instrument. I brought everything I had to this experience: my history and familiarity with poverty programs and my experience and friendships with people of color; my attention to detail; my "ear" for language; my sense of humor; my sense of self. I had to calibrate this instrument with every person I interviewed, keying off each person's mood and affect, body language, and off the sensitivity of the information each one revealed. For Bo, with his fronting, "in-your-face" attitude, I mirrored that attitude and got right up in his face, too. For Jesse, despondent over his "trials and tribulations," I murmured my questions in a subdued tone, as he confessed his despair at not being able to support his family: "When a man gets to that point he's subject to lose his mind."

My interviews yielded intriguing information about the men's view of why they were at the hot lunch program compared with their perception of why the other men were also there at the same meal. Their responses revealed varying degrees of alienation from or solidarity with the others sitting next to them at this meal. These views seemed to correlate with divergent opinions of what was ultimately responsible for their presence at this program, ranging from self-blame to governmental indifference to the plight of the poor.

My final report was submitted in its entirety to the rector of the church sponsoring this hot lunch program; there was no attempt to censor the men's remarks to conform to a more standardized, formal level of discourse. To his credit, the rector expressed his genuine appreciation for these insights into their lives. I like to think that these research outcomes provided valuable information to the rector who later that year became very active as an advocate protesting the escalating murder rate in the black community in our city.

I can attest to my own transformation as a result of my experience with the men I interviewed. For many years now I have been a frontline supervisor in the local welfare office, where I am charged with instructing and monitoring the work of caseworkers assessing the eligibility of their clients for income maintenance grants and food stamps. Working within this bureaucratic system, it is all too easy to adopt a reductionistic perspective wherein the clients become nothing more than the sum total of their eligibility factors. My experience with the men coming to the hot lunch program renewed in me a profound respect for each person's dignity and resilience in the face of economic hardship. This respect for each individual's innate human dignity is what I struggle to preserve in myself and in those I supervise.

This paper demonstrates that the qualitative case study can contribute much to the understanding of social work practice and of the context of that practice. While potentially a powerful research perspective, it is most clearly not for everyone nor is it suited for all purposes. The case study has, however, been presented as a way to find the value and thereby to find the meaning of practice. In this sense it is evaluative. It is also in this interactive search for meaning that the transformational process has the opportunity to work.

REFERENCES

Barbara-Stein, L. 1979. Access negotiations: Comments on the sociology of the sociologist's knowledge. Paper presented at the annual meeting of the American Sociological Association. Boston, Mass.

Bloom, M. and J. Fischer. 1982. *Evaluating Practice: Guidelines for the Accountable Professional.* Englewood Cliffs, N.J.: Prentice Hall.

Blumer, H. 1978. Society as symbolic interaction. In J. G. Mannis and B. N. Meltzer, eds., *Symbolic Interaction: A Reader in Social Psychology,* pp. 51–70. Boston: Allyn and Bacon.

Council on Social Work Education. 1988. *Handbook of Accreditation Standards and Procedures.* Washington, D.C.

Cutler, C. 1991. Deconstructing the DSM-III. *Social Work* 36: 154–57.

Denzin, N. 1989. *The Research Act.* 3d ed. Englewood Cliffs, N.J.: Prentice Hall.

Earnshaw, P. 1991. *The Neverending Story: A Qualitative Study of Dialysis Out-patients.* Saint Louis, Mo.: School of Social Service, Saint Louis University.

Firrek, A. 1991. *Martha's in the Kitchen/Mary's "on the Line": Talking with the Guys in the Hot Lunch Line.* Saint Louis, Mo.: School of Social Service, Saint Louis University.

Gleeson, J. 1990. Engaging students in practice evaluation: Defining and monitoring critical initial interview components. *Journal of Social Work Education* 26: 295–307.

Geertz, C. 1979. From the native's point of view: On the nature of anthropological understanding. In P. Robinson and W. Sullivan, eds., *Interpretative Social Service: A Reader,* pp. 225–41. Berkeley: University of California Press.

Gouldner, A. 1970. *The Coming Crisis of Western Sociology.* New York: Basic Books.

Hollenshead, C. 1982. The human science research paradigm: Underlying assumptions. Paper presented at the annual meeting of the Gerontological Society of America. Boston, Mass.

Kirk, J. and M. Miller. 1986. *Reliability and Validity in Qualitative Research.* Beverly Hills: Sage.

Patton, M. 1980. *Qualitative Evaluation Methods.* Beverly Hills: Sage.

Patton, M. 1990. *Qualitative Evaluation and Research Methods.* Newbury Park, Calif.: Sage.

Rein, M. and S. White. 1981. Knowledge for practice. *Social Service Review* 55, no. 1: 1–41.

Rubin, A. and E. Babbie. 1989. *Research Methods for Social Work.* Belmont, Mass.: Wadsworth.

Ruckdeschel, R. 1985. Qualitative research as a perspective. *Social Work Research and Abstracts* 21: 17–21.

Scriven, M. 1967. The methodology of evaluation. In R. W. Tyler, R. M. Gagne, and M. Scriven, Eds., *Perspectives of Curriculum Evaluation.* AERA monograph series on curriculum evaluation, no. 1. Chicago: Rand McNally.

Sjöberg, G, N. Williams, T. Vaughan, and A. Sjöberg. 1991. *A Case for the Case Study*. Chapel Hill: University of North Carolina Press.

Tripodi, T. 1983. *Evaluative Research for Social Workers*. Englewood Cliffs, N.J.: Prentice Hall.

Wax, R. 1971. *Doing Field Work: Warnings and Advice*. Chicago: University of Chicago Press.

Webster's New School and Office Dictionary. 1961. Greenwich, Conn.: Fawcett.

Wodarski, J. 1981. *The Role of Research in Clinical Practice: A Practical Approach for the Human Services*. Baltimore: University Park Press.

TWENTY-TWO

Integrating the Data Processing of Qualitative Research and Social Work Practice to Advance the Practitioner as Knowledge Builder: Tools for Knowing and Doing

Norma C. Lang

This essay is concerned with differences in the data-processing strategies of social work practice and qualitative research and with how the two might be integrated. An integrated methodology would enable the practitioner to handle practice data both for intervention requirements of the specific practice and for generating knowledge from observation of practice. This dual approach to the practice data may be the means of advancing the knowledge-building function of the profession on a large scale.

A COMPARISON OF THE DATA-PROCESSING METHODOLOGIES OF SOCIAL WORK PRACTICE AND QUALITATIVE RESEARCH

Although social workers and qualitative researchers use some of the same competencies in working to form abstractions from concrete, observational data, their paths diverge from the beginning of the data-processing cycle on a number of dimensions. In this section, the steps in data reduction, data processing, and data analysis, as these are employed by social work practitioners and qualitative researchers, are compared. The writer uses the simple methodological activities of observing, describing, abstracting, generalizing, categorizing, classifying, organizing, conceptualizing, and contextualizing to demonstrate the correspondences and disjunctures between the activities of the qualitative researcher and the social work practitioner.

At the bottom levels, the strategies of data processing contain strong commonalities and probably began together in the early development of the profession, when social work and sociology were closely intertwined during the early period of qualitative naturalistic inquiry.

DATA-GATHERING STRATEGIES

Observing

Both methodologies begin with first-hand observing and describing in full detailed process recordings. The observer may be in a participant or nonparticipant role in qualitative research studies; in social work, the practitioner is presumably always in a participant-observer role.

The purposes of observation differ, the social work practitioner's purpose being more complex than that of the qualitative researcher. Although the discovery of "what is" and "how it happens"—inquiry for its own sake—may occupy observers in both methodologies, the focus on "what needs to be done" and how I can contribute" is an additional concern of the social work practitioner. The need to determine the action to be derived from observations differentiates the social work practitioner from the qualitative researcher, who stops short of "doing" and is content with "knowing."

The role of the social work practitioner is more complex than that of the qualitative researcher. The practitioner carries a participatory actor or intervener role not present for the qualitative researcher. Professional discipline may enable the practitioner to maintain objectivity comparable to that of the qualitative researcher, even while participating in the interaction as an internal constituent.

An observational focus on "knowing" is present in social work in particular circumstances. These include such instances as the following: when practitioners enter a practice sphere new to them through a change of employment or assignment; when practitioners address a new social problem or population and pioneer a new practice; when some variation in the "knowns" of a practice presents itself, stimulating inquiry; when a practitioner's accumulating experience situations leads to some abstracting and generalizing about a particular type of practice (Garbarino 1980); and perhaps most continuously, when the practitioner seeks to comprehend the specific meaning of events, situations, and relationships to each client or clients.

When practice is more habituated, however, inquiry may be less prominent, and the purpose of "knowing" may be less focused than the purposes of "acting and doing," which are central to the practice role. Thus we may use observation mainly to develop practice directives for immediate use. The here-and-now moment then propels us to function in the "developing present."

For practitioners who have incorporated the task of "knowing," habituated practice may contain sustained ongoing inquiry, along with a focus on "doing."

Patterns of data gathering.   While "intimate familiarity" with data (Lofland 1976) characterizes both methodologies, the pattern for the accumulation of observations occurs differently for each. The researcher observes in a focused, time-limited, pervasive, concentrated immersion; the practitioner observes over an extended time frame, in a cyclical, intermittent, or staggered time sequence, as ending clients are terminated and new clients begun, and work with clients may be at various stages of progression. A focus must be evolved to direct and maintain the practitioner's inquiry in such scattered or distributed observational processes.

Specific instances of practice contain the possibilities both for comparison with other observational data previously experienced and recalled and for comparison arising from progressions occurring within the practice, and each instance of practice can become a small ethnographic study in itself.

In both methodologies successive entries into the observational field will yield expanding portraits. The depth of observation achieved by the social work practitioner may be much greater than that of the qualitative researcher because of the nature of the practitioner's engagement with people and their problems, because of the repeated entry into the practice sphere, and because of the development of shared meanings. Indeed, the practitioner can be said to experience the data as a participating actor in the practice situation on a level much deeper than the researcher in a participant-observer role can achieve. The practitioner is an internal constituent in the practice, the researcher, an external constituent.

The demands of practice in a heavy workload may constrict opportunities to observe, reflect, and generate a line of inquiry. The practitioner may be only dimly aware of phenomena in practice to be explored but may be too busy to pause and observe them actively, with conscious intent to see where they may lead.

Describing

The second step in data gathering is to describe what has been observed, in full, rich detail. Full-process recording of observations is a strategy employed by both the social work practitioner and the qualitative researcher.

For the qualitative researcher, the process recording of observations generates the data out of which the research flows and from which abstraction, generalization, classification, and conceptualization can proceed. It is the means of capturing observations before their significance is known and is the method by which potentially important and rich details of phenomena are documented.

In social work practice, the process of describing is also central to the capturing of significant observations and constitutes the data from which analysis of the practice can occur and from which directions for the practice can be derived. Ultimately it is the means of self-supervision for the autonomous practitioner who has learned to scrutinize the practice through use of the records of practice. For some practitioners, it is also the set of source materials from which knowledge development can proceed.

Thus, here, as in the observational step, a double purpose can be detected for the social work practitioner, who may employ the recording chiefly in relation to the professional demands of practice or, as well, in pursuit of the knowledge development potential inherent in the process recording.

The process of describing the selected particulars of what has been observed is a means of accessing knowledge that is not yet conceptualized. It can make visible practice phenomena otherwise overlooked and unrecognized, advance one's competence as a practitioner by highlighting the details of one's practice, and advance practice knowledge. Without such documentation of practice, uniquely processed through the experiential and perceptual lens of the participating practitioner, this avenue to theory building is lost to the profession.

The promotion of and provision for large-scale process recording by numerous practitioners as a professional requirement would enable the profession to enter an era in which qualitative research methods could become widely used for theory-building purposes. Through recordings, comparable individual practices can be linked to generate more extended studies of practice such as the landmark study by Garland, Jones, and Kolodny (1965), which yielded a grounded theory of group developmental phases.

DATA PROCESSING AND DATA TRANSFORMATION

The tasks of data processing are intended to reduce and transform the concrete data in ways that make possible concept formation and the construction of conceptualizations in various forms. This is an inductive theory-building process grounded in and arising from observational data.

Its yield is a small typology, or classification of phenomena; an overarching summary conception; a descriptive profile; a model of how things work; a case study; a portrait of a culture or sub-culture; a small piece of grounded theory; a new concept; a new organization of materials; a new paradigm.   (Lang 1990:6)

At the first levels, processes of abstracting, generalizing, and categorizing are derived from the philosophy of knowledge (Alexander 1967; Lofland 1976).

Abstracting

The first step in data processing is that of abstracting features and characteristics that seem prominent in the concrete, recorded data. This step has the effect of data reduction as well as the transformation of data from its original concrete state into an abstracted, generalized form, separated from the specific concrete particulars of time, place, situation, and persons. This step gives mobility to the data and readies these for comparison with other data. Low-level abstraction moves the data from the specific, particular, and concrete to the "generic" (Lofland 1976).

Generalizing

Closely linked to abstracting is the step of generalizing. Generalizing is a process in which abstracted features and characteristics that are similar are identified and linked or recognized tentatively as having connections. Alexander (1967: 230) defines this as a process of "grouping together to form a class, or of adding more members to a class."

"This is like this" is the step taken. It is the step that begins to create tentative categories of data. The process of generalizing has the effect of characterizing and ordering the nature of the data, connecting the pieces in new ways.

Together, these two steps separate the data from the concrete, move the data into a form capable of being processed further, highlight the features of the data, and begin to sort and organize the data into categories.

Abstracting and generalizing constitute a first level of data processing, employed by both social work practitioners and qualitative researchers, but in differing ways with different purposes.

Qualitative researchers employ these steps to prepare the data for further, higher level processing.

Two patterns of data processing are visible in social work practice at the first level of abstracting and generalizing. The predominant pattern is action focused, the secondary pattern, knowledge focused.

The action-focused pattern is employed by the social work practitioner who seeks to derive appropriate interventions for immediate implementation in practice. The pattern involves (1) abstracting from the concrete data of practice, (2) generalizing the abstracted features, (3) matching these features of data to an appropriate part of existing practice theory in order to derive an intervention, and (4) returning to the concrete to implement it.

The demand for action in the immediate situation thus propels the practitioner into a different process, in a direction different from that of the qualitative researcher, in data processing.

Bloom (1975) identifies as a "paradox of helping" the fact that social workers must be able to move between the concrete and the abstract, in order to take direction from practice theory in the abstract and give help in the concrete. A second paradox is identified here in that the practitioner, in so doing, sidesteps into a different pathway in this move, leaving the process of qualitative inquiry behind.

The immediacy of a specific practice moment may prompt the connecting of data to theory, in order to derive direction for action or intervention; practitioners reflect, in this move, the ways in which they have been taught to think about practice, and the place awarded to existing practice theory rather than to inquiry, by the profession.

Following the steps of abstracting and generalizing, the action-focused social work practitioner, matching data to theory, uses theory to interpret the data and to derive appropriate action. To interpret is to deduce, give explanation, construe; this process interferes with the inductive abstraction of knowledge from data. It involves fitting data to existing classification rather than evolving classification from data.

Thus the practitioner in the action-focused pattern may run on a short cycle of inductive data processing limited to the first level of abstraction and generalization, followed by a deductive process involving interpretation of data in the light of theory, derivation of action, and a return to the concrete.

It is necessary to distinguish the practitioner who is located in a specific moment of practice and seeks direction for immediate action from the practitioner who is working reflectively and in a more summary way, gathering up observations across instances of practice with a knowledge-building intention.

The second pattern of data processing in social work, which is knowledge focused, closely approximates the steps in the qualitative research methodology but may occur over an extended time frame and be diffused across multiple practice experiences. Inquiry itself may arise out of a developing awareness of features repeatedly emerging in practice.

The social worker may follow a processing pattern like that of the qualitative researcher, but more intuitively and perhaps less completely, unless a research strategy is deliberately employed.

The social work practitioner may also link current data to previous data, in efforts to derive actions that were serviceable in prior instances of comparable practice (Lewis, 1982). The matching of data may stimulate inquiry and promote an abstracting and generalizing process, which puts the practitioner into a knowledge-building mode. Practice anomalies may propel the practitioner into a deliberate knowledge-developing cycle, and in the summary gathering up of practice experience the practitioner may evolve classifications and conceptualizations.

The action-focused social work practitioner tends to link data to theory, while the qualitative researcher links data to other, similar data. The researcher purposely avoids the influence of existing theory at this level of processing in order to generate new theory from the data; the practitioner turns to theory quickly. The practitioner "names" the data through reference to theory; the researcher "names" the data through a conceptualizing process that derives from the features of the data.

It is here that social work may lose the possibility of practitioner-generated theory arising from practice data. The press to know what to do, what action to take, may close the avenue of knowledge development from practice for many practitioners.

The competency for generalizing is the same for both constituencies— the capacity to recognize and identify "like" phenomena. If a dual purpose can be established for practitioners, giving "knowing" equal importance with "doing," and if a pattern for managing both activities concurrently can be established, then the social work practitioner will be able to incorporate a knowledge-developing dimension into the processing of practice data.

The major abstracting and conceptualizing work of the profession may be conducted principally by academicians who have been practitioners in the past or who may maintain a small ongoing practice along with the tasks of academia and whose teaching responsibilities stimulate theory-building efforts. In this circumstance, the cycle of data processing and analysis may be distributed and truncated, such that the practitioner carries the bottom levels of observing, recording, and first-level abstracting, while the academician works in the upper levels of abstraction, generalization, classification, and conceptualization.

From the tasks of abstracting and generalizing, the qualitative researcher proceeds to a second and third level of data processing.

Categorizing

Developing categories is a process of linking, sorting comparable items, and naming them as a class, possibly in a unique new way. It is a connecting and organizing step that begins to focus and elaborate inquiry and to advance the processing of the abstracted data. The process of naming emergent categories has the effect of generating a higher level of abstraction and a new precision in descriptors and creates the beginnings of a classification scheme or typology or some ordering of the phenomena under study. The categorizing process may develop into a larger classification process.

Classifying

All data processing seems to undergo a step where separated pieces of data are brought together in a new form. This may be an organizational step in which the data are assembled into a whole capable of portraying its features in new, transformed, and elaborated ways. The organizing may take provisional forms until its best ordering evolves and becomes visible.

Conceptualizing

Although conceptualizations may emerge at the categorizing and classifying steps, it is frequently possible to rise one step further to a summarizing or characterizing conceptualization that encapsulates the study, perhaps in a catchphrase or in profile, model, or paradigm form. This may represent the theory-building yield of the study.

Contextualizing

The qualitative researcher does not turn to existing theory until the end of the process of abstracting/generalizing/categorizing/conceptualizing. Upon completion of the study, the researcher looks at what related prior conceptualizations exist in literature, how they differ from the new one generated by the current study, and how the new piece fits with relevant previous theoretical materials. In holding the connection to prior knowledge until the completion of the study, qualitative researchers deliberately insulate themselves against the contamination of their view of data by other theoretical perspectives, attempting to keep as free of these as possible in order to develop strands of new theory from the data. Thus researchers places the evolved new piece of theory in the context of relevant theoretical materials in the final contextualizing step.

FIGURE 22.1   *Cycles of Data Processing in Research and Practice*

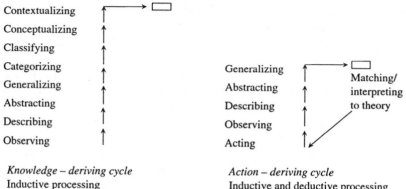

Contextualizing

Conceptualizing

Classifying

Categorizing

Generalizing

Abstracting

Describing

Observing

Knowledge – deriving cycle
Inductive processing

Generalizing

Abstracting

Describing

Observing

Acting

Matching/
interpreting
to theory

Action – deriving cycle
Inductive and deductive processing

↑   = Sequencial steps in data – processing
▭   = Existing theory

A comparison of the cycles followed by the two constituencies shows that the social work practitioner is likely to run on a short cycle, sidestepping from first-level abstracting/generalizing to connect deductively with theory for actional directives and returning to the concrete to make relevant action operational. The qualitative researcher runs on a long cycle with multiple levels of inductive processing, visiting other relevant theory at the end of the inquiry.

Pictorially, these differences are portrayed in figure 22.1.

It may be true that the principal data-processing strategy of social work practice is action focused and uses a methodology that exits from knowledge-building processes at bottom levels of abstraction. If so, then the profession can be said to have limited access to potential knowledge development on the part of practitioners who are closest to the data of practice and who are the largest professional constituency.

The profession appears to have an imbalance between strategies that produce knowledge and those that direct action. The deficit in knowledge development strategies makes the profession exceptionally vulnerable to borrowing and importing rather than developing its own special knowledge, and potential knowledge is continuously being unarticulated and lost. It is desirable that this imbalance be corrected. Qualitative research methods of data processing, a methodology close to and congenial with our own methods of processing practice data, offer the means of doing so.

REQUIREMENTS FOR INTEGRATING THE DATA-PROCESSING METHODOLOGIES OF QUALITATIVE RESEARCH AND SOCIAL WORK PRACTICE

This section gives consideration to what the requirements might be for incorporating the data-processing cycle of qualitative research into the cycle employed by social work practitioners, to permit both knowing and doing to be derived from the same data.

The first requirement might be a professional declaration of intent to address both knowledge-developing and action-deriving purposes in the processing of practice data, to open a new era of theory building by practitioners.

This requirement directs the profession to employ the qualitative research methodology, with its powerful knowledge-building capability, for data processing. In so doing, it calls for (1) a suspension of the early sidestep to existing theory; (2) the abandonment of the use of deductive, interpretive matching of data to theory; (3) a redefinition of the place of existing theory in data processing from its current position of primacy to the last step in the cycle; and (4) a comparative use of existing theory with newly derived contributions conceptualized from data.

In effect, the adoption of the qualitative research methodology for data processing opens the possibility that knowledge and action can emerge together, the knowledge component informing the action component. This is in contrast to the short cycle identified in this paper, which tends to limit practice by reference to existing theory rather than generate and extend new theory.

The move to employ the qualitative research methodology should open an exploration to determine what actions can be derived from the process of abstracting and conceptualizing from the features of the data, whether both knowledge and action can be derived from the same data-processing cycle, and what the nature of each will be. A logic of practice might become visible from this alternate route of data processing on the long cycle of qualitative research; that is, the nature of the data itself might direct the action taken by the practitioner.

Adoption of such a strategy would expand the research methodology to carry responsibility for generating an action component not addressed by the qualitative researcher. One can expect this expansion of the research methodology to be effective because of that deeper, experiential level of observation achieved by social work practitioners.

Action derived from the abstracted, conceptualized features of the data gives promise of developing a grounded theory of practice at a near-operational level. "What do I know" from this processing, and "therefore, what should I do" seem to represent the guiding questions of such data processing.

The immediacy of the demand for action may limit the social work practitioner to the lower levels of data processing—abstracting and generalizing—before taking action in salient moments of practice. The abstracting/generalizing steps may be performed intuitively and instantaneously. However, the practitioner may be able to remain in the inductive pattern of data processing, making the upper levels of processing still accessible, by pulling action out of the features of the data rather than out of existing theory.

The long cycle of data processing employed by qualitative researchers in knowledge development might then play out in a two-stage process. The first stage would include abstracting, generalizing, deriving action from the abstracted/generalized data and taking action. The second stage in the cycle is still possible, because the data have been treated inductively; the practitioner would carry the data through additional levels of abstraction and conceptualization subsequently, after the moment of demand for an immediate intervention in the practice situation.

There is also the possibility that, upon observing the effects of an action, the practitioner might return to the first abstracting/generalizing steps with these additional data, process these further, and then move to the higher levels of processing in stage II, to evolve and consolidate the knowledge generated.

This would create a kind of double cycle of processing at stage I and incorporate the action taking into the portrait of the data before rising to higher levels of abstraction.

Thus the practitioner can be involved in deriving knowledge both at the micro level of specific moments in a particular practice and in the processing of numbers of incidents of "like" data processed in a form that makes them available for larger knowledge-developing enterprises; this may give action directions on a larger scale, at the top of the cycle.

Recording

Because data may accumulate slowly and in a less focused inquiry, there must be provision for recording them so that their features can be retained and highlighted.

The capturing of practice data in a form that lends itself to knowledge development is a necessity in the shift to a dual-function practitioner. The process recording must become a major tool in the knowledge-building process and be seen as both a research and a practice-advancing document. Perhaps it will be employed selectively, where inquiry is focused. So much potential is being lost currently by practitioners who do not document their practice in forms from which conceptualization can be developed that the profession continually loses much of its derivable knowledge.

Inductive Thinking and Place of Theory

In the process of incorporating an altered methodology, social workers must learn to think inductively and to replace the process of interpreting data in the light of theory with the process of generating theory from data. The ad hoc and improvisational nature of practice methodology must be allowed to become even more so, in order for the practitioner to be free to abstract knowledge. Existing theory must have a more provisional status, a less central locus in our practice teaching, in order to open the possibility of theory building. It must be examined in terms of its relevance, scope, potency, adequacy, and completeness.

Finally, the earliest experiences in class and field for the beginning student practitioner should include inquiry about "what is" and "how does it happen," so that upon entry into the profession, the social work practitioner is habituated to asking questions, thinking about practice, and exploring "what the practice tells". Inquiry should become as important as intervention.

There must be a period of experimentation, to discover whether intervention can be derived along with knowledge from a knowledge-building cycle and whether it is different from intervention derived from an action-deriving cycle; whether it begins to specify practice theory in new ways at more operational levels; and whether it specifies forms of intervention that, because they are derived from the practice data, are any more appropriate or powerful than those derived from existing theory.

There is a need for a socialization process so that the integrated data-processing methodology is known to practitioners and made accessible through the acquisition of competencies for using it. Practitioners need to be aware of the possibility of pursuing inquiries in their practice and to know how to go about it.

The first requirement is to learn to process the data through higher levels of abstraction, toward the possibility of generating knowledge as well as deriving intervention. This suggests that in the curricula of education for social work, content on qualitative research should be incorporated into the teaching of practice. Practitioners must learn to think about the data of practice in a new way, which blends both knowledge-advancing and intervention-deriving functions, through use of an altered cycle of data processing. There is a strong argument for integrating the teaching of practice and research so that the methodologies can be synthesized.

This paper calls for the mobilization of the neglected side of our practice methodology—the knowledge-building side—so that every practitioner can assume a dual task of intervening in practice and abstracting important knowledge from that practice. We have not thought of the practitioner as knowledge builder, yet no social worker is in practice very long before accumulating expert knowledge from practice experience. We recover only a fraction of this knowledge because it may not be articulated or formulated into a transmittable, shareable state and because our emphasis in practice is on doing.

Can the two methodologies of data processing be integrated? When I consider the eagerness of student researchers to inquire; the astute lines of inquiry they develop in their practice; the power of their tiny ministudies to inform, alter, and redirect agency practice; their excitement in discovery from practice data; the sophistication and inventiveness of their conceptualizations; their sense of owning this methodology and wanting to use it again; the fluidity with which they incorporate a knowledge-building function along with their interventive function; and ways the knowledge they derive directs their action, my answer has to be ''yes.''

This paper recommends the adoption of the qualitative research methodology of data processing for knowledge-building purposes but also conceives of the methodology as having the capability of being used for action-deriving purposes through the derivation of action from the abstracted features of the data. In effect, this expands the qualitative research methodology and integrates it with social work practice methodology by defining a new route from which intervention can be derived. The new route holds promise for the development of theory in social work practice out of the data of practice.

REFERENCES

Alexander, Hubert G. 1967. *The Language and Logic of Philosophy*. Albuquerque: University of New Mexico Press.
Bloom, Martin. 1975. *The Paradox of Helping: Introduction to the Philosophy of Scientific Practice*. Toronto: Wiley.
Garbarino, James. 1980. *Understanding Abusive Families*. Lexington, Mass.: Lexington Books.
Garland, James, Hubert Jones, and Ralph Kolodny. 1965. A model for stages of development in social work groups. In S. Bernstein, ed., *Explorations in Group Work*. Boston: Boston University.

Jacobs, Joseph D. 1964. Social action as therapy in a mental hospital. *Social Work* 9: 1.
Lang, Norma C. 1990. An accessible research strategy for the study of social work groups: The use of qualitative research methods. Invitational paper presented at 12th Symposium for the Advancement of Social Work with Groups, Miami.
Lewis, Harold. 1982. *The Intellectual Base of Social Work Practice: Tools for Thought in a Helping Profession.* New York: The Lois and Samuel Silberman Fund, Haworth.
Lofland, John. 1976. *Doing Social Life: The Qualitative Study of Human Interaction in Natural Settings.* Toronto: Wiley.

TWENTY-THREE

Commentary: A Practitioner's Perspective on Qualitative Case Evaluation Methods

Ruth G. Dean

In responding to some of the ideas in the three very fine essays by Ruck-deschel, Tyson, and Lang I would like first to describe contemporary concerns arising from the practice context in which qualitative research is taking place. What I hope to do is extend the meaning of some of the concepts in these papers in relation to some current practice issues. I also discuss contemporary ways of thinking about clinical practice that could be more fully integrated with qualitative case evaluation models. I believe these research methods are very compatible with the newer practice paradigms.

I approach this subject as a teacher of clinical practice and, more importantly, as a practitioner in a community clinic in one of the poorest towns in Massachusetts and in private practice. While I can discuss practice only in a small part of Massachusetts, my hope is that these concerns are fairly representative of practice across the country.

DO SOCIAL WORKERS EVALUATE THEIR PRACTICE?

As a teacher, supervisor, and clinician I see social workers evaluating and reflecting on their practice all the time. These evaluations are not systematic nor are they written. Sometimes they occur in discussions between colleagues or in supervisory sessions and sometimes they simply occur in the clinician's mind. But a form of evaluation goes on continuously. The challenge is to find the bridge between qualitative methods and the kinds of questions that social workers do ask when they evaluate their practices. If we could pay more attention to these questions and start where the practitioner is, then I think we could integrate qualitative forms of research with practitioner's needs.

As a way of stimulating this integration let us consider some of the questions practitioners are asking. They can be organized into two categories—the first clinical and the second clinical/administrative. In the clinical category, several questions are frequently raised:

1. Did I do the right thing in this particular case or clinical encounter? (This is a question about method.)

2. Is the client making progress? (This is a question about outcome.)

3. What is or are the appropriate goals for this client? (This is a question about fit between method and client.)

Researchers could help clinicians answer these questions through teaching them systematic ways of studying cases. Workers would learn how to evaluate what is happening right in the action of the clinical encounter through a refined form of "reflection in action" (Schön 1983, 1987) and to conduct studies after the action described by Fleck-Henderson (1989) as "reflection on action" in an extension of Schön's idea.

Practitioners are raising another set of questions more and more frequently, related to clinical and administrative matters, as a result of the current political climate. They are questions related to goals and time constraints imposed by third-party payers commonly referred to as "managed care." These questions include the following.

1. Is there a piece of work that can be effectively done within the time limit imposed by the funding source? This question relates to ethical concerns such as whether brief treatment will be helpful or impractical and even harmful.

2. How do we manage practice so as to make it cost-effective and yet responsive to client needs? A related question is: How do workers meet agency productivity requirements and maintain a sense of integrity about their work?

3. How do we separate those clients who need long-term work from clients who can be helped in brief episodes of treatment?

4. How do we engage clients who are not accustomed to regular weekly appointments but tend to come only in times of crisis without appointments?

5. How do we monitor the effects of these constraints on practice, on clients, and on workers?

6. How do we make note of which clients get seen and which drop through the safety net as a result of the pressures on current agency practice?

These are urgent questions that both individual agencies, workers and students are asking. It would be very helpful if clinicians learned ways to keep track of successes and failures and of the results of specific actions in their practice with different clients. Qualitative case study methods can help them do so.

Unfortunately, as Ruckdeschel suggests, it has been hard for practitioners to relate the "scientific methods" of evaluation that have been taught to the everyday questions they are asking. The qualitative case study method and the heuristic paradigm have much to offer as approaches that could more readily be responsive to current, pressing clinical concerns.

FINDING THE VALUE

In order to consider Ruckdeschel's appropriate definition of evaluation, "finding the value," in a way that is relevant, we need again to look at the context of current practice. I believe that practice is moving in two divergent directions. The first is monitored (or "managed") practice—practice for which the limit and scope have been set by funding sources. The second is practice that is not monitored by funding sources, for which the client pays the fee. While both private practice and agency practice are being monitored, in agencies, these regulations are more frequently applied to disturbed clients, dysfunctional families, those who are marginal in terms of their abilities to cope, and those who have been seen in long-term treatment for years. In many community centers in poor neighborhoods, clients have been followed up intermittently for years with different family members seen at different times and different generations of a family known to the same worker or agency. This form of service could be called "general, family practice." Many families have been helped to remain stable or even improve their situations and reach their goals with this kind of care. While the work is often designated as long term, it more often than not occurs in a series of short-term episodes of treatment. Until recently, the rhythm has been determined by the client. Current restrictions imposed by funding sources have interfered with this natural rhythm for treatment.

How do we find ways to work with clients who benefit from this form of general family practice under the present constraints? How do we make the "value" of this form of practice evident and obvious to funding sources? Finding answers to these and similar questions through the use of the case study method would require the kind of interactional process that Ruckdeschel described. The interaction would take place between client and worker and also between worker and agency administrator. Together they could study and evaluate current work.

We need to find ways of knowing when short-term, crisis-driven work is valuable. We also need to document the times when a short-term approach to clinical practice is more destructive and expensive than long-term work. And as we learn something about the value or lack of value in these time constraints we will need to be able to report or "transform" our findings so that they are meaningful to others.

The other form of contemporary practice, long-term work that is not monitored by funding sources, is confined to those clients who can afford to pay private fees and are not dependent on insurance. It occurs in both agencies and private practice. We need to find ways of evaluating or "finding the value" in this type of practice as well. Too often, social workers tend to overvalue this work (perhaps because of the limiting conditions of agency practice) and to see it as best in all situations. It is not, and students need to learn this. The case study method offers the possibility of helping us "find the value" in both monitored and unmonitored forms of practice. By studying both, there is an opportunity for "crossover learning," i.e., letting what we learn about the value of time-limited work affect long-term practice and letting what we learn about the value of long-term practice inform our approach to time-limited work.

HEURISTIC PARADIGM

As a practitioner, I find the heuristic paradigm interesting because it allows for the complexity and richness that are characteristic of practice and because it makes use of the practitioner's judgment and expertise. It is a flexible model that is open to a diversity of practice approaches and practice theories. For these reasons, I would like to see some of the newer ways of conceptualizing practice incorporated into the current description of this research model. In discussing these newer models I draw on several sources: writings about professional practice by Argyris and Schön (1974), and later, Schön (1983, 1987) and the writings by Anderson and Goolishian (1988); Efran, Lukens, and Lukens (1990); Hoffman (1988); Scott (1989); White and Epston (1990); and others regarding constructivist approaches to practice.

In discussions concerning the evaluation of practice, the tendency is to describe a clinician's theory base as if it were exclusively based on one theory and never changed. The further suggestion is made that only theory or mainly theory informs a clinician's way of practicing. I prefer the descriptions of professional practice developed by Argyris and Schön (1974) and Schön (1983, 1987). They state that theories, as we use them, consist of fragments rather than monolithic models (1974). These fragments are combined with the clinician's personal and professional experiences. This total gestalt forms the backdrop for a clinician's work. Argyris and Schön refer to the professional's "theories in use," indicating that a difference exists between theories we read, study, and "espouse" and theories as we use them in actual practice. Discussions of research need to incorporate more realistic ways of thinking about the clinician's theory base.

Also important is that research models use descriptions of practice that incorporate its evolving nature. All too often, practice is described in static terms. Not only does a clinician's practice model evolve over time, but also, in particular cases, problem definitions change throughout the course of clinical work (Anderson and Goolishian 1988). Therapeutic methods may shift during the clinical process, the client or client group may change over time, and clinicians' thoughts about cases are also in a continuous process of evolution. Clinicians' reflections on clinical work would be different in the middle of a clinical encounter, if we could stop the action, from reflections occurring days, months, and years later, because ideas about practice shift according to clinicians' interests, studies, readings, experiences, and contexts. Research paradigms and future discussions of case study methods need to more closely reflect the continuously evolving process of practice and reflections on practice. Qualitative methods of analysis, because of their more detailed and individually oriented focus, can incorporate a more accurate sense of practice.

BUILDING KNOWLEDGE FOR THEORIES AND KNOWLEDGE FOR CLINICAL ACTION

Finally, I address Lang's interesting ideas about the possibility of combining the processes of knowledge development and action derivation in clinical practice. I wonder whether the practitioner can address both knowledge-developing and action-deriving needs simultaneously. My impression is that a tension exists between these two goals and two different kinds of consciousness and reflexivity are involved.

When a clinician responds to a client's comment, the reaction is both emotional and intellectual. The response may be intuitive based on "tacit knowledge" (Polanyi 1962) and uttered with little or no premeditation. Or it may be a more conscious response based on a more systematic and explicit way of knowing. In some, but not all instances, the clinician may think about the ways she understand the client's comment and how she wishes to respond to it before responding. "Ways of knowing" in clinical practice are many and varied (Dean 1989).

Another kind of reflexivity is involved in clinical work when the clinician begins to think about the clinical action in terms of building knowledge about practice or knowledge about the particular client. As clinicians become involved in knowledge building, they move further and further away from connections with clients. It is possible that a focus on knowledge building in the action could distort the clinical process.

Those who design research strategies need to be careful not to burden clinicians by asking them to attend to too much in the clinical encounter. Encouraging reflection on clinical practice after the clinical encounter might work better than trying to combine clinical action and knowledge-building activities.

In summary, the papers by Ruckdeschel, Tyson, and Lang provide creative and stimulating qualitative approaches for the study of clinical practice. Qualitative case study strategies offer considerable hope for the integration of research and practice if they incorporate ways of being more responsive to the questions clinicians ask, the evolving nature of theories in use and practice, and the tension between clinical action and knowledge-building activities.

REFERENCES

Anderson, H. and H. A. Goolishian. 1988. Human systems as linguistic systems: Preliminary and evolving ideas about the implications for clinical theory. *Family Process* 27, no. 4: 371–93.

Argyris, C. and D. A. Schön. 1974. *Theory in Practice: Increasing Professional Effectiveness*. San Francisco: Jossey-Bass.

Dean, R. G. 1989. Ways of knowing in clinical practice. *Clinical Social Work Journal* 17, no. 2: 116–27.

Efran, J. S., M. D. Lukens, and R. J. Lukens. 1990. *Language, Structure and Change*. New York: Norton.

Fleck-Henderson, A. 1989. Personality theory and clinical social work practice. *Clinical Social Work Journal* 2: 128–37.

Hoffman, L. 1988. A constructivist position for family therapy. *The Irish Journal of Psychology* 9, no. 1: 110–29.

Polanyi, M. 1962. *Personal Knowledge: Towards a Post-critical Philosophy*. Chicago: University of Chicago Press.

Schön, D. A. 1983. *The Reflective Practitioner*. New York: Basic Books.

Schön, D. A. 1987. *Educating the Reflective Practitioner*. San Francisco: Jossey-Bass.

Scott, D. 1989. Meaning construction and social work practice. *Social Service Review* 63: 39–41.

White, M. and D. Epston. 1990. *Narrative Means to Therapeutic Ends*. New York: Norton.

TWENTY-FOUR

Commentary: Wanted! Social Work Practice Evaluation and Research—All Methods Considered

Susan B. Stern

Various explanations have been advanced concerning why more social workers do not evaluate their practice or use research findings. Typically, academic researchers have tackled the problem by trying to identify strategies for increasing the systematic evaluation of practice and encouraging practitioners to base their practice on empirical knowledge. In turn, the concern with the interface between practice and research in social work has contributed to the debate about what kinds of knowledge and research methods the profession needs. The notion that practitioners do not evaluate their practice has been challenged as researchers consider that there may be many different ways to evaluate practice and that we actually know surprisingly little about how practitioners naturally evaluate their cases or about what knowledge is useful to practitioners (Kirk 1991; Stern 1991).

Ruckdeschel, Lang, and Dean advance our understanding of how qualitative methods can help bridge the practice–research gap. They believe these methods capture the richness of clinical practice and can be responsive to the realities of practitioners' worlds. Although these three articles focus on different aspects of qualitative case evaluation, a common theme is the possibility of congruence between research methods and practitioners' ways of thinking and doing.

In a qualitative case study, according to Ruckdeschel, the social work practitioner or student finds meaning through two different kinds of interaction. The first form of interaction involves immersing oneself in the clinical encounter and entering the life world of the client. The second type of interaction concerns the research process itself. For example, the process of transforming data into useful information for knowledge building and decision making involves finding meaning through interaction with the life world of consumers of research, practitioners, and policymakers. As a result of interaction, a transformation occurs, whereby the practitioner actually becomes a participant in a change process. Ruckdeschel considers transformation for the practitioner as one of the most important outcomes of qualitative research. The value of qualitative methods for understanding client worlds, as well as the process of practitioner transformation through interaction with these worlds, is richly illustrated in the case descriptions by Ruckdeschel's collaborators, Earnshaw and Firrek.

Taking a different tack to qualitative case evaluation, Lang examines the differences in the way practitioners and qualitative researchers process data and suggests how qualitative research strategies can be adopted by the practitioner to both inform pressing practice realities and generate future knowledge. She proposes that social work clinicians need to fulfill dual roles as practitioners and knowledge builders so that the profession does not lose the contributions of those closest to the data of practice.

In her thoughtful response to these previous papers, Dean brings an important practitioner and practical perspective to the integration of practice and qualitative research by articulating questions clinicians are asking regarding the evaluation of their cases and, additionally, questions about how to be effective in the political context in which practice occurs today.

In my commentary, I focus on three related issues that have emerged as I reflected on these papers: the meaning of evaluation and its relevance to outcome; the distinction between evaluation and research; and the need for qualitative and quantitative methods for both case evaluation and practice research.

EVALUATION: FINDING THE MEANING

Empirically oriented social work practitioners define evaluation in relation to case progress or achievement of a desired outcome. Whereas Ruckdeschel and his students succeed in conveying the potential of qualitative case evaluation for enhancing our understanding of client worlds, they do not (admittedly) address methodology or outcome in qualitative case evaluation. Because social work is a practicing profession (Kirk 1991), if we are to be responsive to those questions that are asked by practitioners, we must apply qualitative methods to issues of treatment process and outcome (i.e., to the "doing" as well as the "knowing").

Only Dean, from her perspective as a practitioner, explicitly speaks to issues of treatment decisions, outcome, and treatment efficacy as an integral part of evaluation. Relevance for the practitioner addresses questions of what to do. Is it the right thing? Is it working? Is my client getting better? I agree with Dean that practitioners do evaluate their practice, although perhaps not in systematic ways. Practitioners assess client progress, and when their interventions do not appear to be working, they are likely to modify the intervention. In their appraisal, case progress is evaluated, whether formally or informally, in diverse ways: in relation to specific goals, previous level of client functioning, or some previously established norms when they exist (social validity).

What contributions can qualitative methods make to case evaluation that focuses on treatment process and outcome? First, qualitative methodology has a distinctive contribution to make to assessment because a full understanding of our clients' worlds is critical to assessment, whether of an individual (family, group) client or a social problem. Put another way, as applied to assessment, good qualitative inquiry is good social work practice, and finding the meaning is evaluative. I also think we have often failed to adequately capture both process and outcome for our clients and that qualitative methods have a contribution to make in studying the complexities of practice.

Unfortunately, much of the discussion of qualitative case evaluation in the social work literature focuses on the comparative worth of qualitative and quantitative methodologies and debate about the epistemologies underlying each of these paradigms. I think it is essential to move beyond debate to matters of instrumentation and to a discussion of how we best capture the treatment process and client outcomes in case evaluation. In this regard, social work would benefit from more actual examples of good qualitative case evaluation.

EVALUATION OR RESEARCH?

Both Ruckdeschel and Lang focus on knowledge building through qualitative case evaluation. In so doing, both the terms *evaluation* and *research* are used, often interchangeably. Unfortunately, failing to make the distinction in meaning of these terms confuses the issue of social worker as reflective, self-evaluating practitioner with social work practitioner as researcher. As noted, evaluation asks whether progress is being made on a case; that is, is the client getting better? Although we would hope that our interventions have something to do with clients' improvements, establishing this connection goes beyond evaluation and requires an understanding and application of rigorous research methods, whether they be qualitative or quantitative.

Dean rightly questions whether we are unrealistic when we expect practitioners to fulfill research knowledge-building roles at the same time as they practice, a question raised about quantitative single-case evaluation as well. Clearly it is time to rethink case evaluation, whether it be qualitative or quantitative, and not only recognize but also appreciate and validate the priority for practitioners of providing the best possible service they can. Academic researchers must work with practitioners to understand how they naturally evaluate their cases. In an analogy to "start where the client is," Kirk (1991) suggests that qualitative studies involving the observation of and in-depth interviews with clinical practitioners may be the way to begin; in this way, researchers can enter and more thoroughly know the world of practitioners. Then in a true collaboration, researchers and practitioners can develop user friendly and practice-relevant measurement strategies to systematize evaluation.

Lang is right on the mark in her concern for the data lost to the profession by not effectively tapping into practitioners' knowledge. If practitioners are no longer expected to participate in knowledge building as part of their routine activities, we, as researchers, must still find ways to capture their wealth of knowledge accumulated from experience. For example, in-depth interviews with practitioners can involve them in knowledge-building activities without burdening them with the requirements of research methods. As a result of being closer to the worlds of clients and practice, clinicians have a special contribution to make to our understanding of those worlds. Clinical researchers need to recognize the expertise and unique insights practitioners can bring to the study of treatment process and outcome. Furthermore, if practitioner expertise is sought in planning and implementing research, researchers can be kept cognizant of practice realities, and questions about clinical relevance can be raised before a study is undertaken.

WHAT KINDS OF METHODS DO WE NEED?

We need all kinds of methods! To this end, I briefly address both the need for practice-relevant evaluation and research regardless of methodology choice and the integration of qualitative and quantitative methods.

Practice Evaluation

Evaluation of treatment outcome is an integral part of social work practice and needs to be integrated into practice courses in schools of social work. Students should be exposed to both qualitative and quantitative evaluation strategies, for both may be relevant in the course of a clinical career. Some practitioners will find existing single-system methods (e.g., specifying problems and goals) and measurement tools (e.g., standardized questionnaires, rating scales, self-monitoring, direct observation) useful for evaluation, especially once the expectation no longer exists for also using research designs considered unnatural to practice. Others may resonate to Lang's recommendation for detailed process recording as a way to evaluate and modify ongoing practice. It is unrealistic, however, to think that the profession will heed Lang's call for required process recording. In the same way that the push for the use of rigorous single-system designs probably impeded adoption of empirical evaluation methods, Lang's call for rigorous widespread process recording is, again, an unrealistic requirement for many hard-pressed practitioners that may impede the adoption of qualitative case evaluation. Limiting process recording to critical incidents may allow practitioners to still use this form of qualitative analysis to look for patterns in their data. The clinical relevance of any evaluation strategy will ultimately be tested by the extent of its use by practitioners.

Practice Research

Lang makes an argument for the value of using the inductive strategies of qualitative research to advance practice knowledge. She is in good company in her appreciation of moving from the data to theory building. Sherlock Holmes admonished Watson: "Data, data, my dear Watson. It is a capital mistake to theorize before one has data. Insensibly one begins to twist facts to suit theories, instead of theories to suit facts."

In the process of building knowledge inductively and discovering new practice theory, it is important to recognize existing research knowledge on practice effectiveness and previously validated practice theory so that knowledge building in social work is cumulative. In qualitative research, this typically occurs at the end of the data-processing cycle as part of the contextualizing step where new findings are integrated with previous conceptualizations. The potential value of inductive qualitative methods in knowledge building may also be maximized at times by connecting this approach to the knowledge derived from alternative research methods prior to the end of the data-processing cycle; in this instance, there would be more of an interaction between inductive and deductive data processing. If we value the existence of diverse research methodologies and "ways of knowing," perhaps we can strike a better balance between building on "what we know" and finding the best ways to learn "what we need to know."

Both qualitative and quantitative methods have a contribution to make in the continued development of a social work practice research base. In my opinion, their integration offers the best hope for understanding the context and process of treatment and linking these to outcome in the important study of treatment efficacy. Thus, quantitative methods play a critical role in treatment outcome research by allowing us to establish relationships between intervention and client outcomes and generalize findings to inform the social work practice knowledge base. And qualitative methods complement quantitative ones in treatment outcome research by facilitating the measurement of interactional and relationship variables, tapping multiple dimensions and perspectives on change, balancing insider and outsider perspectives, and better capturing contextual and process variables (Moon, Dillon, and Sprenkle 1990). Incorporating attention to these kinds of variables in knowledge-building activities will, one hopes, increase practitioner use of research findings because of their increased relevance for practice.

REFERENCES

Kirk, S. A. 1991. Research utilization: The substructure of belief. In L. Videka-Sherman and W. J. Reid, eds., *Advances in Clinical Social Work Research,* (pp. 233–50.) Silver Spring, Md.: NASW Press.

Moon, S. M., D. R. Dillon, and D. H. Sprenkle. 1990. Family therapy and qualitative research. *Journal of Marital and Family Therapy* 16: 357–73.

Stern, S. B. 1991. Single-system designs in family-centered social work practice. In Videka-Sherman and Reid eds., *Advances in Clinical Social Work Research,* 48–53. Silver Spring, Md.: NASW Press.

PROGRAM AND
POLICY EVALUATION

A Positive Approach to Qualitative Evaluation and Policy Research in Social Work

Robert Bogdan and Steven J. Taylor

Social work practice and applied qualitative research have had a precarious relationship. Often qualitative researchers disappoint social work practitioners. One reason for this is the basic difference in the way the two approach their world. Human service professionals believe in the efficacy of what they do—they are optimistic about their profession's contribution. They are trained to see their organizations as rational instruments for goal attainment. This optimistic view gives meaning and spirit to human service work, a necessary element in the enterprise. On the other hand qualitative researchers by training are skeptics, people who turn a critical eye on unsubstantiated pronouncements. Words such as *goals, success, clients,* and *rehabilitation* and diagnostic categories like "mentally ill," "alcoholic," "mentally retarded," and "disabled" are examined critically as social constructions. Qualitative research reports of professional practice are often harsh on practitioners and are interpreted by the subjects as being critical rather than objective and destructive rather than helpful. Qualitative researchers defend themselves by appealing to their position of being an objective outsider whose job is to tell the truth. In this paper we a describe an approach to research that can partially reconcile the conflict.

As researchers trained in qualitative methods we have been conducting evaluation and policy research in the field of special education and disability since the early 1970s (Bogdan and Taylor 1975; Taylor and Bogdan 1984).

Our early work described the conditions that were destructive to human life inside institutions for people labeled mentally retarded and mentally ill (Bogdan and Taylor 1982; Bogdan et al. 1974; Taylor 1977, 1987; Taylor and Bogdan 1980).

Our own work studying institutions and the lives of people confined to them, as well as the works of Goffman (1961) and others, led us to question the policy of institutionalizing and segregating people with mental retardation and other disabilities. As a consequence, we became strong advocates for deinstitutionalization, although we were not quite clear about what integration into the community might entail.

With the exposés of the 1960s and 1970s, federal court cases challenging institutional conditions, and changes in federal and state policy, the populations of public institutions for people labeled mentally ill (Scull 1981) and mentally retarded (Braddock, Hemp, and Fujiura 1987) have declined at a steady pace. Yet the trend toward deinstitutionalization has spawned its own set of abuses. In many cases, it has resulted in transinstitutionalization, the transfer of people from large public institutions to somewhat smaller ones in the community or dumping, leaving people to fend for themselves on the streets. Recent qualitative studies have documented that many people labeled mentally retarded and mentally ill have been transferred to board and care facilities that are as segregated from the larger community as the public institutions from which they came (Bercovici 1983; Emerson, Rochford, and Shaw 1981). Some critics go so far as to claim that deinstitutionalization is a myth and a sham, a thinly veiled effort to absolve government of responsibility and to put money in the hands of greedy profiteers (Scull 1981; Warren 1981).

The exposés of both public institutions and private facilities leave policymakers, and especially practitioners, in an untenable position. If life in the community is just as miserable as life in institutions, then there can be no hope that practitioners can bring about change and make a difference in the lives of people who are served by the human service system and who have housing needs.

This pessimistic view of deinstitutionalization reflects in part the reality in many places and in part the muckraking perspective within the social and policy sciences. Dark shadows always fall between policy and practice, between intentions and reality. We all have illusions about what we do, whether we are human service professionals or academic researchers.

While we have observed abuse, neglect, and dehumanization in the community, we have also seen another side of integration. Over the last decade, the focus of our research has shifted from documenting the dark side to looking at the bright side, that is, to identifying positive examples of integration with a view toward creating change. For example, we have studied how regular public schools can accommodate children with severe disabilities (Bogdan 1983; Taylor 1982).

We are not neutral on the issue of integration. No amount of evidence of dehumanizing conditions in the community could convince us that people with service needs are better off being dehumanized in total institutions. As a value position, we would like to see integration be the rule, even for people with the most severe disabilities. Knowing that some schools and human service agencies have found ways to integrate people with disabilities with at least partial success, the question we ask ourselves is: how can these positive examples be held up to create a standard for how others should treat people with disabilities?

We want our research to help conscientious practitioners—people who are leading the reforms in the direction of integration—and advance their efforts at social change. We call such research, the kind that is positive about practice and helpful to practitioners, "optimistic research." We are also traditionally trained field workers. We believe in systematic and rigorous data collection and analysis and in the importance of critical inquiry and the analytic power of bracketing assumptions. We have evolved an approach to research that has helped us bridge the gap between the activists, on the one hand, and empirically grounded skeptical researchers, on the other. The approach has implications for researchers who have strong opinions about the issues they study and who want to contribute to social change and remain researchers as well.

We have been successful in selling our qualitative research approach to various federal funding agencies. Not only have our proposals been funded but also practitioners have followed our findings. Our work is widely read by those trying to be effective in integrating children and adults with disabilities into schools and communities.

The paper begins with an overview of a study we are conducting that illustrates "optimistic" research. We then discuss the dimensions of the design. We conclude with a discussion of how our findings and our approach can contribute both to practice and to basic knowledge.

COMMUNITY LIVING FOR PEOPLE WITH SEVERE DISABILITIES

For the past five years we have been engaged in a qualitative research study that looks at agencies across the country that have as their stated goal to help children and adults labeled severely developmentally disabled (people with severe mental retardation and multiple disabilities) to live in the community. The thrust of the research is to produce information and understanding that would be helpful to practitioners who are attempting to integrate people with severe and profound disabilities into the community. We are looking at programs such as small group homes as well as more innovative approaches to community integration such as supporting people in their own families and homes.

As part of this project, we are funded to study eight programs per year. One observer goes to each site and spends two to four days on location. In total we will have data on forty programs. The field workers have had experience in qualitative research, and all but one have been formally trained in the qualitative approach. Three of the observers have taught this approach at the university level. While two to four days is not enough time to do a thorough traditional participant observation study, observers take extensive field notes, conduct tape-recorded interviews, and collect official documents and other material from agency files. In addition to turning in field notes and transcripts each researcher writes a twenty- to sixty-page case study describing the program visited and highlighting agency practices and dilemmas. We are also interested in identifying themes that cut across different sites (Bogdan and Taylor 1987).

ASKING THE RIGHT QUESTION

Many evaluation and policy studies fail to provide useful and positive information to practitioners because they ask the wrong questions. The "Does it work?" approach to research exemplifies this. For example, in early childhood programs, like Head Start, evaluation and policy researchers typically collect data to compare the achievement of children who are in the program with those who are not, or they look at changes in IQ among children in the program before and after. They collect such data in pursuit of the question "Does Head Start work?" New programs or practices that involve a change in the way things are done are almost always approached this way. They need to prove their worth. Programs that are well established such as kindergarten, suburban nursery schools, and even undergraduate education are rarely looked at in terms of their efficacy. They are an accepted part of our culture. The question "Does it work?" functions as an exclusionary gatekeeper rather than as an encouraging teacher.

The "Does it work?" approach has been the mainstay of the research on the integration of people with disabilities. Researchers have approached the topic asking: "Does integration work?" or, put a slightly different way, "Is integration efficacious for people with disabilities?" Numerous studies have been made of the efficacy of community programs and deinstitutionalization (Conroy, Efthimiou, and Lemanowicz 1982; Landesman-Dwyer 1981). Some studies show that integration helps disabled people, and others show that it does not. Yet these studies are plagued by a host of problems: a narrow definition of what constitutes success (typically measurable behavioral or psychological outcomes), a failure to make distinctions in the quality of programs they study, and a lack of consideration of the social and historical context in which programs operate.

Even if design problems could be solved, the question "Does it work?" still would not be helpful to practitioners. Conscientious practitioners do not approach their work as skeptics; they believe in what they do. It has been documented that people who believe in integration can develop programs that make it work (Biklen 1985; Bogdan 1983; Taylor 1982). There are practitioners in the field of special education and disability who are not asking whether integration is possible; they are attempting to accomplish it. To ask "Does it work?" is anachronistic here because, in our minds, and in the minds of many practitioners, the matter of whether people with severe disabilities should be integrated into society is a moral question rather than an empirical one. It is an issue similar to that of slavery. If social scientists had been around immediately before the Civil War would we have asked them to tell us whether freeing slaves was efficacious? Some policies are made regardless of the immediate implications for the people who experience them. They represent a change in consciousness. Implementation follows.

"Does integration of people with severe and profound disabilities work?" is not the right question to ask. It is a skeptical question rather than an optimistic one. Our research attempts to frame issues in ways that help people visualize the future rather than to see things the way we have in the past. Our interests are to discover how people are getting integration to work. "What does integration mean?" and "How can integration be accomplished?" are our questions.

SELECTING SITES

Given the nature of our research question, and the optimistic approach we use, we choose agencies to study in an unusual way. Because of the interests of policymakers and officials in the ability to generalize, most national evaluation studies, even those employing qualitative data-gathering and analysis procedures, use some variation of random sampling techniques to select programs to study.

In our research, we are not interested in learning about average or supposedly representative programs. We know that many "community programs" are as segregated from the community as from institutions. In fact, a random sample of community programs might tell us very little about integration. Rather than select a random sample of programs, we consciously try to find places that can teach us about how people with severe disabilities can be integrated into the community. We start with only a vague definition of integration. Since we have studied total institutions extensively in the past, we know what we are not looking for, places that cut people off from the wider society. However, we treat the concept of integration as problematic, something to be investigated rather than assumed. We want to learn about how agencies committed to reversing the historical pattern of exclusion of people with severe disabilities from society define and accomplish integration.

While we use a variety of strategies to solicit nominations of integrated programs, including announcements in professional newsletters, national mailings, and reviews of the professional literature, the most successful strategy is a variation of the "snowballing" technique often used in qualitative research. We start by identifying "key informants" and ask them to tell us about agencies that are doing a good job of integrating people with severe disabilities as well as other people who might know of programs. Our key informants have two characteristics: first, they share a philosophical commitment to integration; second, they are people who have the opportunity to travel around the country evaluating or consulting with programs and hence have first-hand knowledge of different agencies.

After compiling a list of nominated programs, we conduct in-depth phone interviews with each site in an attempt to further screen for positive examples. On the basis of these interviews, we select eight agencies to visit each year.

We have found tremendous differences in the nature and quality of life of the people served in the programs we have visited. Some meet our expectations of providing positive examples of integration; others do not. For example, some small group homes, though physically located in typical residential neighborhoods, are socially isolated from the community; others substitute institutional regimentation with behavioral programming that controls every aspect of people's lives. By comparing agencies we are able to develop a clearer understanding of what integration means and a deeper appreciation of innovative agencies.

No agency is perfect or without problems and dilemmas. What makes some stand out as successful is that they seem to be moving in the right direction and are struggling with the right issues. For example, some are trying to look past the client role to treat people as human beings; some are also actively trying to connect people with nondisabled community members; some direct their efforts not just to providing services to specific "clients" but also to bringing about changes that increase opportunity for all people with disabilities.

FIELD RELATIONS

In contrast to our research at institutions, we have experienced no problems gaining access to sites or obtaining the cooperation of agency officials and staff. People at the programs we visit have gone out of their way to accommodate us by arranging for visits to homes; scheduling interviews with staff, clients, family members, and other agencies; and providing us with reports and documents. The visits last from two to four days and often go from early in the morning to late at night.

Our approach also explains the cooperation provided to us. When we first contact agencies, and in subsequent contacts, we tell them that they have been nominated as innovative or exemplary. Most administrators are flattered, especially those in small agencies that have not previously received national visibility. All are positive and welcome us.

Ironically, our positive approach leads many officials and staff to be more candid about their dilemmas than they otherwise might be. Most are just as likely to talk about their problems and struggles as to boast of their successes.

ANALYSIS AND DISSEMINATION

On the basis of the visits, each researcher prepares a case study of the agency visited. The case studies provide an overview of the agency (e.g., history, size), a description of innovative approaches (e.g., adoption subsidies; strategies for increasing consumer control over staff), and, in some cases, a discussion of problems and dilemmas (e.g., fiscal or regulatory constraints) faced by the agency. Since the visits focus on the lives of at least two people served by each agency, the reports illustrate approaches and practices through their impact on people's lives.

After completing the case studies, short articles are prepared for publication in newsletters published by major professional and parent associations. The newsletter of The Association for Persons with Severe Handicaps regularly features our articles. These articles tell the "story" of the agencies.

Most of our reports and articles focus on the positive aspects of the agencies we visit. In addition to demonstrating that people with disabilities, even those with severe disabilities, can lead decent lives in the community, the reports and articles legitimate positive efforts. In several cases our reports have been used by agencies to defend themselves against state bureaucracies attempting to stifle their creativity. When the reports focus on negative aspects of less than exemplary agencies, we give agencies the choice of whether or not their names will be mentioned or whether they will be described anonymously.

As researchers, we are interested in patterns that transcend individual cases. Since the site visits yield not only reports and articles but also field notes and interview transcripts, we have thousands of pages of data that can be analyzed from different perspectives. Part of our analysis that has been helpful to practitioners has focused on describing the "state of the art" in serving people with severe disabilities in the community, for example, the movement away from group arrangements to supporting children in families and adults in their own homes.

Another part of our analysis has focused on the characteristics of "good" agencies. In contrast to much of the management literature, which has been adopted uncritically in the human services field, our data point to the importance of philosophical commitment, a belief in human potential, a broad commitment to social justice, a willingness to change in response to new ideas and challenges, and similar characteristics as critical to the creation of effective and responsive human service organizations. We also point practitioners to conceptual issues that needed to be thought through in order for effective community support programs to develop. For example, early formulations of deinstitutionalization and community living did not clearly distinguish between "being in the community" and "being part of the community." Being in the community points only to the physical presence; being part of the community means having the opportunity to interact and form relationships with other community members. We describe services where practitioners understand this distinction and are active in helping people with disabilities have meaningful relationships with other community members. In a similar way we have described the tendency for agencies supplying support to people with disabilities to become cocoons to their clients and have described approaches agencies have used to overcome this tendency.

THEORETICAL UNDERSTANDING

While our "optimistic approach" might be considered too intertwined with practitioners to even be called research, we are also developing sensitizing concepts and grounded theory that transcend the commonsense ideas of the people we study. We are seeing that what appears to be very practical and applied research is yielding basic findings that have a contribution to make to understanding and to the merging of theory with practice. By taking our "optimist approach," we have been guided to data that we might have overlooked, namely, the acceptance of people who are demonstrably different by those who are not.

Social work professionals are attempting to accomplish social integration of people with disabilities, but the emphasis on rejection does not provide a basis for them to formulate plans. The theoreticians of these plans tend to formulate strategies based on the labeling literature (Wolfensberger 1972). They develop plans of what not to do rather than on how acceptance is accomplished. Our work has pointed out how we need an emphasis on acceptance not only for practice but also for theory.

The positive approach we described here has implications for issues and populations beyond community integration and people with severe and profound disability. Many attempts to create more meaningful futures for people in a variety of oppressive situations and with a range of needs can be studied in the way we have outlined here. Too often our approach to research, the questions asked, the sample chosen, and the researchers' agenda and value base undermine social change rather than promote it. This need not be the case.

REFERENCES

Bercovici, S. M. 1983. *Barriers to Normalization.* Baltimore: University Park Press.
Biklen, D. 1985. *Achieving the Complete School.* New York: Teachers College Press.
Bogdan, R. 1983. A closer look at mainstreaming. *The Educational Forum* 48 (Summer): 425–34.
Bogdan, R. and S. J. Taylor. 1975. *Introduction to Qualitative Research.* New York: Wiley.
Bogdan, R. and S. J. Taylor. 1982. *Inside Out: The Social Meaning of Mental Retardation.* Toronto: University of Toronto Press.
Bogdan, R. and S. J. Taylor. 1987. Toward a sociology of acceptance: The other side of the study of deviance. *Social Policy* 18, no. 2 (Fall): 34–39.
Bogdan, R., S. J. Taylor, B. deGrandpre, and S. Haynes. 1974. Let them eat programs: Attendants' perspectives and programming on wards in state schools. *Journal of Health and Social Behavior* 15 (June): 142–51.
Braddock, D., R. Hemp, and G. Fujiura. 1987. *Public Expenditures for Mental Retardation and Developmental Disabilities in the United States: State Profiles.* 2d ed. Chicago: University of Illinois.
Conroy, J., J. Efthimiou, and J. Lemanowicz. 1982. A matched comparison of the developmental growth of institutionalized and deinstitutionalized mentally retarded clients. *American Journal of Mental Deficiency* 86: 581–87.
Emerson, R. M., E. B. Rochford, and L. L. Shaw. 1981. Economics and enterprise in board and care homes for the mentally ill. *American Behavioral Scientist* 24, no. 6 (July/August): 771–85.
Goffman, E. 1961. *Asylums.* Garden City, N.Y.: Doubleday.
Groce, N. 1985. *Everyone Here Spoke Sign Language.* Cambridge, Mass.: Harvard University Press.

Landesman-Dwyer, S. 1981. Living in the community. *American Journal of Mental Deficiency* 86, no. 3 (November): 223–34.

Scull, A. 1981. A new trade in lunacy. *American Behavioral Scientist* 24, no. 6 (July/ August): 741–54.

Taylor, S. J. 1977. The custodians: Attendants and their work at state institutions for the mentally retarded. Ann Arbor: University Microfilms.

Taylor, S. J. 1982. From segregation to integration. *The Journal of the Association for the Severely Handicapped* 8, no. 3: 42–49.

Taylor, S. J. 1987. Observing abuse: Professional ethics and personal morality in field research. *Qualitative Sociology* 10, no. 3: 288–302.

Taylor, S. J. and Bogdan, R. 1980. Defending illusions: The institutions' struggle for survival. *Human Organization* 39, no. 3: 209–13.

Taylor, S. J. and Bogdan, R. 1984. *Introduction to Qualitative Research Methods: The Search for Meanings.* 2d ed. New York: Wiley.

Warren, C. A. B. 1981. New forms of social control. *American Behavioral Scientist* 24, no. 6 (July/August): 724–40.

Wolfensberger, W. 1972. *The Principle of Normalization in Human Services.* Toronto: National Institute on Mental Retardation.

TWENTY-SIX

Qualitative Evaluation Methods in the Public Sector: Understanding and Working with Constituency Groups in the Evaluation Process

Richard T. Pulice

Changes in economic and political relationships among levels of government, program providers, and recipients of service have signaled a reshaping in approaches to the measurement of program success. These changes result in a new challenge for program evaluators who seek to understand the impact of the changes. Unlike program evaluators of the past, who needed only to have a one-dimensional look at services, evaluators in the 1990s must use a multidimensional approach responsive to the opinions and needs of those impacted by programs at a variety of levels.

Within each of these levels a number of constituencies exist, representing multiple, and sometimes conflicting, roles. Given the diversity of information sources, qualitative evaluation methods provide access to this abundance of data that cannot be ascertained through quantitative methods alone (Epstein 1985). The purpose of this paper is to examine the role that each of these "constituencies" has in assessing a program's effectiveness and the information that program evaluators need to understand about these groups as they proceed with the evaluation. Drawing upon work in fields such as education, the term *constituency* refers to any group that has a stake in program outcomes and ranges from the planners of services to the providers and recipients of such services (Sage and Burrello 1986). The emphasis is on understanding the roles that these constituency groups play and how qualitative approaches to evaluation, particularly "key informant" and related "needs assessment" approaches, can contribute to our understanding of program effectiveness. The focus is on systemwide approaches rather than on examining a single program. To illustrate the issues at hand, one aspect of the public service system, mental health services for the seriously mentally ill, is examined in greater detail.

CONSTITUENCY GROUPS

Unlike private-sector organizations, public social service agencies have a set of constituencies that seemingly approach the same stated goals. However, their definitions of these goals may vary widely. The power of each of these groups changes over time and is influenced by the political and economic dimensions that impact the public sector on at least an annual basis. These changes in power are driven most forcefully by budgetary demands but also by social policies that are influenced by the public perception of the "problem" relative to other competing "problems."

A taxonomy of the constituency groups and their roles and influences is helpful in considering the impact of each of these groups. One could examine these constituencies from a number of perspectives.

Insiders vs. Outsiders

First, is the identified group an "insider" or "outsider" in the system? Whether a group is viewed by others as inside the system or outside makes a significant difference in the amount of influence the group has and in what their opinions are regarding system success or failure. Further, the group's view of where it sees itself in the system has a major impact on its perceptions. For example, if the group sees itself as an "outsider" it may be more critical of system responses than if it views itself as an "insider" with a stake in program outcomes.

Professional or Layperson

Second, one can consider a professional vs. layperson approach. This is particularly important in social service organizations where roles determine place in the hierarchy, the ability to make decisions, and the ability to influence others to implement those decisions. For example, at a micro level, psychiatrists use their professional status to influence where a person lives, what drugs they take, and what the consequences of compliance vs. noncompliance to treatment will be. At a macro level, "laypersons" often defer to professionals in deciding what the policy will be that drives a set of social programs. In analysis of homelessness, for example, whether the homeless are really the mentally ill displaced from hospitals or persons who became mentally ill because of their homelessness has been the subject of numerous studies that have influenced federal, state, and municipal responses to this population.

Consumer or Provider

Third, a consumer vs. provider approach may be considered. In the past, this view would not have been very different than a professional vs. layperson approach. However, new definitions of "consumers" and their rights have differentiated this approach. Consumers in many parts of the public service system have organized (or have had groups organize on their behalf) and are questioning the services provided them. In addition, they use their influence to change the way in which the service system responds. In some cases, those previously viewed as consumers of the system take on a "provider role," substituting their peer "service" approaches for those of the traditional provider (Lord, Schnarr, and Hutchinson 1987).

Policymaker or Policy Implementor

Finally, one could examine a group's role from a policy perspective, i.e., at what level did this group become involved in the implementation of this program? Is the group viewed (or does it view itself) as a policy developer, policy influencer, or policy implementor? A legislature, for example, might view itself as the major force in policy development with a minimal role in implementation. A neighborhood or county level advocacy group may see itself involved as a policy influencer, while a state agency might view itself as having a stake in all three levels.

In assessing each of these approaches, the first, the insider vs. outsider, offers the most relevance in the service system, supported by the other three roles. The dichotomous relationship of insider or outside that many groups have within the service system seems to have the strongest influence on overall system perceptions. In addition, the insider vs. outsider role is supported by additional subroles that further support its response to program effectiveness.

Roles of the Insider vs. Outsider

Within the insider vs. outsider framework, groups identify themselves as having particular roles to play in ensuring that the program is fulfilling its

goals and in protecting against or advocating for the program in the larger service system.
Some of these roles are defined as follows:

Advocate.   Groups that take on the advocate role view themselves as supporting the goals and objectives of the program. They see themselves as both ensuring that the program is implemented as designed (i.e., not diluted by political and economic constraints) and that the designated target group receives services.

Facilitator.   Groups that take on the facilitator role view themselves as supportive of the goals and objectives of the program. Facilitators see themselves as helping the program meet its goals. This is accomplished by easing transitions into communities, ensuring additional resources are made available, or attempting to have regulations interpreted in a manner that helps the program meet its objectives.

Planners.   Planners assume the role of identifying needs in a community or client group. This role places heavy emphasis on the prediction of future need and tries to influence the system perceptions so that it allocates new resources or redistributes existing resources based on these assessments.

Monitors.   The monitor group views itself as providing a "watchdog" function. This includes monitoring for violation of program regulations (e.g., case load size) as well as protecting consumers from potential abuses.

Manager.   Those who identify themselves as managers see their role as influencing the overall (day-to-day) functioning of a program. Although they are most appropriately the direct program administrators, other groups at a more macro level also see themselves as being in the manager role.
A constituency group can play more than one role. Program evaluators should be aware of the conflicting roles that many groups identify themselves as playing. For example, groups that identify themselves as both a monitor and a manager are likely to use one of these roles inappropriately, in fact, leaving behind one in favor of another. Which role they abandon is often influenced by political and economic resource decisions and thereby impacts the ability of both the constituency group and the program to operate effectively. For example, when budgets are cut, more effort goes into the monitoring role (to ensure efficiencies in hard times) while less effort is expended in advocacy on behalf of client groups.

PUBLIC SECTOR EVALUATION

Data Collection Approach

Public sector, systemwide evaluations lend themselves to the use of qualitative techniques. As programs mature and constituencies develop, methodologies that were primarily quantitative lack the kind of detail and content that can be obtained only through more "hands on" qualitative methods. One approach is to utilize a technique termed evaluability assessment, a qualitative approach to examining programs' readiness for evaluation (Strosberg and Wholey 1983; Wholey 1983).

This approach requires the evaluator to carefully document the processes that are taking place across the system. First, relevant constituency groups must be identified at all levels. Choices about where to start are somewhat arbitrary; however, using a "snowball" technique that begins at the level requesting the evaluation and moving out to other levels is often most effective. For example, if a local government requests the evaluation, then the process begins at this point. Preliminary interviews are completed with key informants at the identified level to determine the reasons for the evaluation request, including the time frames in which it needs to be completed and the intended uses of the evaluation findings. Special emphasis is placed on developing a list of potential constituencies and what role the level requesting the evaluation believes each constituency plays.

Second, a thorough literature search should be completed, examining documents that include relevant legislation, committee reports, and agency-related documents, i.e., annual reports, etc., to determine the nature and content of documentation available relative to the evaluation questions. For example, if the evaluators are examining the impact of the addition of new services for clients, working documents such as regulations, policies, and procedures manuals, etc., that impacted the implementation of the new services should be examined.

Third, by use of the results of the preliminary interviews at the requesting level and the literature review, a taxonomy of the identified constituency groups is developed. On the basis of this taxonomy, the evaluators identify the expected role of each constituency; e.g., are they insiders or outsiders to the system? What insider or outsider role do they seem to play, i.e., advocate, facilitator, planner, monitor, or manager?

Fourth, based on the results of the preliminary interviews, literature search, and constituency taxonomy development, semistructured interviews are developed that address the evaluation questions. Usually composed of five to seven structured questions, the interviews are intended to verify the roles of each group and to gather each group's perspectives on the impact of the program.

Considerable flexibility in interview content allows the interviewer to expand beyond the original question, gathering additional evaluative information. Although threats to reliability can exist, it has been found that interrater reliability is very high, especially in those interviews where two raters are present during the same interview period. In addition, given resource constraints, a group interview process (similar to a focus group) may be employed to maximize interview time.

Analysis

Using the results of the literature review and interviews, the evaluators are able to develop conclusions about program impacts or to develop additional quantitative approaches to broaden their understanding of the program's impact.

The major approach to analysis is a text analysis, reviewing the results of the interviews for common themes between and among groups. At this point the understanding of the insider and outsider roles and subroles (manager, facilitator, etc.) is particularly central. Common themes across groups are particularly important, especially when it appears that the groups' conflicting roles should have produced opposite results. Contrasting themes between groups suggest areas for further analysis, either through additional qualitative approaches or through the development of quantitative approaches.

ONE SYSTEMWIDE EVALUATION

In order to apply some of the tenets previously described, the following presents a qualitative evaluation approach designed to identify constituencies in a statewide multilevel, geographically and socioeconomically diverse program for seriously mentally ill adults.

The Community Support Services Program

The Community Support Services Program (CSS) was instituted in New York State in 1978. During the period 1978–1988, the program enrolled more than 50,000 clients and was estimated to serve approximately 20,000 clients per month in 1988 (Pulice and Donahue 1989). Fifty of the sixty-two counties in New York State participated in the program. One hundred and seventy agencies provided CSS services, although considerable variation existed in the number of services available across counties. Combinations of service modalities were funded including the following: clinic treatment, day treatment, continuing treatment, on-site rehabilitation, day training, sheltered workshops, hospital admission, screening, homemaker and housekeeping services, transportation, outreach visits, psychosocial programs, and case management. Legislative changes over the years broadened the criteria for eligibility to the program and changed the funding structure to include administrative involvement from counties. This was important in that counties are strong governmental entities in New York State, often having health and social service systems that mirror state government.

In an effort to assess the ongoing impact of the CSS program in 1980, the New York State Office of Mental Health (NYSOMH) contracted with the Research Foundation for Mental Hygiene (RFMH) to provide staff to evaluate the program. The staff were a combination of doctoral, masters, and bachelor-trained evaluators whose primary professional affiliations were in fields including psychology, social work, education, and economics. Previous analyses of the CSS program relied heavily on quantitative approaches to evaluation (Intagliata 1982). Although well done, these studies lacked utility for those responsible for statewide program planning.

During the period under study, multiple annual evaluations were completed on a statewide basis to assess the impact that the CSS program was having on both the outcome of clients being served and on the delivery system (Huz and Taber 1988; Lannon and Banks 1988; Pulice and Donahue 1989).

The CSS Constituencies

Given the statewide nature of the CSS program, the evaluators charged with examining the services provided were required to take a systemwide rather than program/site-specific approach. This was exacerbated by New York State's diverse geographic, socioeconomic, and service availability issues. Because of this diversity, it was necessary, from an evaluation perspective, to develop a taxonomy of the service system that took into consideration the multilevel, and sometimes overlapping, areas of jurisdiction and concern.

Upon examination, four levels of the service system that mirrored the overall New York State health and social welfare system were readily apparent. These were

The central level. The central level included the legislature, governor's executive staff and a NYSOMH agency administration.

The regional level. In NYSOMH, five regional administrations existed that mirrored the central administration. In addition, more than thirty state psychiatric centers provided regional services usually on a multicounty basis.

The county level. Each of the fifty-seven counties (plus New York City) in
New York State had discrete governmental levels referred to as local government units (LGUs). These LGUs had their own legislative, executive,
and judicial branches and mirror the central administration. Many LGU's
were also service providers.

The agency level. Across New York State a very sophisticated system of not-
for-profit and for-profit organizations providing mental health services existed. These agencies provided services under contract to the NYSOMH
or with the LGU. It was possible for an agency to be under contract to
provide services at multiple levels. Most of these agencies were also Medicaid and Medicare certified and may have been reimbursed by private in-
surers.

Once identified, each level presented a challenge to evaluation. What
were the constituency groups within each level? Furthermore, how did
these groups overlap and/or integrate with each other to impact on the CSS
program's implementation? Finally, were there changes in the roles of
various groups as the CSS program itself mandated? Each level and its
constituencies were analyzed to determine the answers to these three questions.

The central level.   The central level, primarily located in Albany,
contained a diverse set of constituencies. First, the state legislature, which
passed the enabling legislation and produced the later requirements to the
program, had to be considered. The legislature viewed itself as an outsider
to the process, playing the role of policymaker as well as monitor. Provis-
ions placed in the law that enacted CSS and its later revisions indicated that
the legislature in its monitoring role required NYSOMH to respond on the
program level and impact changes on the service level.

Second, the governor's executive staff, most specifically the Division of
the Budget (DOB), played a major role in the CSS program. Active in an
insider role and as a monitor, DOB ensured the priority placement of CSS
in the state budget and monitored its annual progress via the contract
mechanism. In addition to the overall budget line item, all contracts issued
to providers of CSS service were approved by the DOB. In fact, a review
of DOB's role indicated that they not only reviewed the contracts but also,
as a condition of approval, modified the spending plans of the agencies to
comply with DOB guidelines (both formal and informal) (Governor's Budget Message, State of New York 1987, 1988, 1990).

Third, groups that were identified as more traditional constituencies
operated at the central level. For example, the NYS Mental Health Association (NYSMHA) acted on behalf of CSS. Operating primarily in an outsider
role, NYSMHA acted as an advocate and facilitator attempting to ensure

that the program was funded by the legislature, not cut by DOB, and implemented by NYSOMH. In addition, groups like the Alliance for the Mentally Ill (AMI) participate at the central level. Primarily composed of family members of the mentally ill, AMI has become more influential with the NYSOMH as pressure from the federal level to increase citizen participation has increased. Constituency groups like NYSMHA and AMI were also powerful in that they had affiliated organizations at the national and local levels. This enhanced their ability to network at all levels.

Regional levels. In the five regional areas set down by the NYSOMH administration, structures that paralleled the central level developed. Regional offices, with sometimes large and bureaucratic staffs, monitored the program activities that occurred in the counties comprising each region. They also acted as planners and managers within the system. Finally, they often acted as facilitators on behalf of programs with county governments that were sometimes reluctant participants in state-designed and state-mandated programs.

State psychiatric centers (PCs) made up the second constituency group found at the regional level. Historically, prior to regionalization, psychiatric centers operated as independent organizations with little to no direct input on the facilities functioning from the outside. Many of the program initiatives implemented under CSS called for a change in the way state PCs delivered services to clients. The resistance that the evaluators faced was found in how this program (CSS) was changing what was viewed by the PC's administration and staff as a well-functioning and orderly system. As managers, the PC administration stressed the tension between what they viewed as their primary role (manager) and the new roles they were being asked to play (monitor and facilitator). Finally, in addition to the mirror image administration that the regional office had with the central office, the same phenomenon occurred with other groups. The Mental Health Association, AMI, and related consumer groups all operated at the regional level with a similar set of priorities and demands that were being expressed at the central level.

County level. Perhaps the most difficult to assess, yet most important constituency in the CSS evaluation process, was the role of the counties. Unlike many states, county government in New York is extremely powerful, with bureaucracies that rival some state governments. For example, the number of county employees in Albany county (home of the state capital) exceeds the number of employees who administer the entire state of Maine.

What was the role of the counties in CSS? Originally, county government was, for the most part, excluded from any active role in CSS services.

Although they could opt to become a provider of services, they were given no priority to do so, and many contracts were written directly between the state and not-for-profit agencies, completely bypassing the county. Later revisions of the law made the county directly responsible for the administration of CSS within their boundaries. This change placed the county in a transitional role, going from an outside monitor of services to the role of manager.

The evaluators' difficulty in assessing the constituent role of counties was in understanding the point at which counties perceived themselves during the evaluation process. Did they see themselves as supportive insiders or antagonistic outsiders? If they chose a more active role via the new administrative mandates, how did their manager or planner role in mental health compare with the other management priorities in the county (e.g., health, social service, and public works)?

Given the changing role of the counties, their relationship to the provider organizations was very important. Prior to legislative changes, providers dealt only with the state on CSS issues with little involvement by the counties. With the legislative changes, counties could now impose new rules of operation, and new power relationships emerged. As evaluators assessed projects within CSS, this change needed to be well understood and integrated into the context and conclusions of the evaluation. Programs looked very different in counties that took on a facilitator or advocate role in contrast to those that approached their role in CSS from the manager viewpoint.

Finally, the role of constituencies like family and consumer groups also had to be considered at the county level. As with the other groups, the transitional nature of the counties' relationship influenced how these groups interacted with each other, in trying to understand what role county government was choosing to play. In those counties that took on strong manager or planner roles, family and consumer groups were forced to be actively involved in their county governmental process, while in those counties that continued with a more benign approach to CSS, these constituents continued to focus at the regional level to impact services.

Agency level.   The final level of concern was that of the agency level. Clearly, agencies viewed themselves as managers responsible for day-to-day operation. However, a number of other issues impacted the role of the agency and added to its managerial responsibilities. First, what was the role of CSS in the agency? Were CSS services the sole or primary mission of the organization or was this program one of many provided by the agency? For example, it was not unusual for an agency to provide mental health services to the serious mentally ill, to the developmentally disabled, and to substance-abusing populations all under the same administrative organization as well as to those clients whose disability/problems were mild and often transient. How closely knit these services were was an important aspect of the evaluative process.

Second, what was the role of consumers and families within the organization? Were they active participants in the planning process or were they viewed as passive recipients? Was the view that consumers and families had of their role different from the agency view? Where consumer and family groups were placed in the agency determined what constituent roles they had. For example, in those agencies where consumers may be in an employment relationship, they might have to give up their advocate role.

Third, what was the agency role vis-à-vis the other agencies in the county or region? Were they viewed as facilitators, planners, or monitors? Or were they so passive in their roles that other groups failed to identify them as having an impact on the system? Finally, what was the relationship of this constituency to constituencies at other levels, for example, county government, regional administration, or the state?

Using the results of this qualitative analysis on the role of program constituencies, the evaluators then designed qualitative and quantitative methodologies to assess program effectiveness and client outcomes. These constituency analyses were critical to the evaluation's effectiveness, particularly in preventing the types of errors that result in good programmatic approaches being overshadowed by politically influenced circumstances.

The whole process can be summarized pictorially as shown in figure 26.1.

This paper examined the evaluation of public sector programs at a statewide level. It focused on the understanding of constituency groups in the evalua-

FIGURE 26.1 *A Model for Qualitative Analysis in the Public Sector*

Taxonomy of Constituencies	*Roles*	*Service System Levels*	*Collection* Data	*Analysis*
Insider vs. outsider	Advocate	State/ central	Evaluability assessment	Text analysis — Between groups — Among groups
Professional vs. layperson	Facilitator	Regional	Literature search	Common themes
Consumer vs. provider	Planner	County/local	Constituency taxonomy	Contrasting themes
Policymaker vs. policy implementor	Monitor Manager	Agency	Semi-structured interviews	

tion process. The definition of constituency groups included a broad array of interested parties, from government officials to consumer groups. A taxonomy of constituencies was presented that was based on the role of the group as being an insider or outsider to the system. Furthermore, subroles in which constituencies engaged were described. These included the role of constituencies as advocates, facilitators, planners, monitors, and managers. Constituencies played multiple subroles that, in turn, impacted their influence on program implementation and their views of programs' successes or failures. A qualitative approach to data collection and analysis was suggested that allowed for the collection of information that was sensitive to the roles (perceived and real) of the constituent group and allowed for linkage for the development of quantitative techniques as needed. Utilizing the New York State Community Support Services as a case example, the role of constituents in a multilevel geographically and socially diverse state bureaucracy was analyzed, demonstrating the interactions of constituencies between and within these levels.

REFERENCES

Epstein, I. 1985. Quantitative and qualitative methods. In R. M. Grinnel, ed. *Social Work Research and Evaluation*. 2d ed. pp. 263–74. Itasca, Ill.: Peacock.

Governor's Budget Message, State of New York, 1987, 1988, 1990.

Huz, S. and T. Taber. 1988. *Evaluating the Implementation of the Statutory CSS Program*. Albany: New York State Office of Mental Health.

Intagliata, J. 1982. Improving the quality of community care for the chemically mentally disabled: The role of case management. *Schizophrenia Bulletin* 8, no. 4: 655–74.

Lannon, P. and S. Banks. 1988. *CSS Clients in New York: A Statewide Profile*. Albany: New York State Office of Mental Health.

Lord, J., A. Schnarr, and P. Hutchinson. 1987. The voice of the people: Qualitative research and the needs of consumers. *Canadian Journal of Community Mental Health* 6, no. 2: 25–36.

Pulice, R. and S. Donahue. 1989. *CSS Client Enumeration Study*. Albany: New York State Office of Mental Health.

Sage, D. and L. Burrello. 1986. *Policy and Management in Special Education*, pp. 202–12. Englewood Cliffs, N.J.: Prentice Hall.

Strosberg, M. and J. Wholey. 1983. Evaluability assessment: From theory to practice in the Department of Health and Human Services. *Public Administration Review* 43 (January–February): 66–71.

Wholey, J. 1983. *Evaluation and Effective Public Management*. Toronto: Little, Brown.

TWENTY-SEVEN

Constructivist Evaluation: The Policy/Practice Context

Mary K. Rodwell and David Woody, III

The notion of attentiveness to context and its importance in addressing research questions confronting social work practitioners and administrators is not new. The person/environment construct is an embodiment of the profession's long attention to the setting in which action or inaction occurs. Nor is the process of evaluators' ignoring context new. In fact, evaluability assessment, or the determination about whether or not an evaluation is practical, technically, feasible, or politically appropriate (Chambers, Wedel, and Rodwell 1992; Wholey 1979), is entirely dependent on the culture and context in which the evaluation should be occurring and is a largely overlooked aspect of evaluation practice, particularly evaluations gone awry.

What is new to social work inquiry is a constructivist approach to evaluation (Guba and Lincoln 1989; Rodwell 1990) that, in addition to other benefits of qualitative methods in the evolution or construction of contextual meaning, has the capacity to shed light on the dynamics of the evaluation process itself. Constructivism allows the evaluator to get some understanding about what happened when an evaluation does not go well. More importantly, an evaluation truly guided by constructivist assumptions will not go awry because the constructivist approach "embeds results in the context within which they are derived. The person-in-situation becomes inextricably intertwined" (Rodwell 1990:31). From this perspective, the agency political reality and its impact on evaluability assessment can never be an overlooked contextual reality of program evaluation. Constructivist evaluation done correctly never allows an overlooking of the context of our deeds.

UNDERLYING ASSUMPTIONS OF CONSTRUCTIVISM

Constructivist inquiry is predicated on the assumptions that the nature of reality is multiple, constructed, holistic, divergent; that generalizations are not possible or desirable owing to the context and time-bound nature of reality; and that interactive mutual shaping, not causality, can be discovered in a research process that recognizes the value-bound, interrelated nature of the inquirer and the object of inquiry (Guba and Lincoln 1989).

Though not without controversy, proponents of constructivism operate within a framework of very different assumptions for the evaluation process and product. Table 27.1 is a brief articulation of those (Guba and Lincoln 1989:44–45) that underscore the focus on multiple constructed realities, rather than a single reality, and that are studied holistically to gain understanding instead of prediction and control.

The mutual interaction of the inquirer and the respondents as well as the value basis of the inquiry influence the preferred methodological strategies for constructivist evaluation. These strategies, identified by Lincoln (1985), include data collection in a natural setting and reliance on an emergent research design, with the human inquirer as the primary research instrument. Qualitative methods, particularly interviewing and participant observation, are chosen to allow a probing of the tacit, or intuitive, knowledge of the respondent. Results are reported in a case study format with a focus on word rather than numerical data to provide a thick description of the phenomena under study.

Constructivist evaluation maintains a research rigor parallel to traditional scientific rigor of internal and external validity, reliability, and objectivity, through credibility, dependability, confirmability, and transferability (see Guba 1981; Lincoln and Guba 1985). In addition, there is a criterion for rigor, authenticity (Guba and Lincoln 1986, 1989), more directly implied by the constructivist assumptions. Authenticity builds on the interactive process of the constructivist evaluation itself, focusing on the integrity and quality of the inquiry process more than on its product.

To judge the authentic quality of the constructivist evaluation, the degree to which the following are present must be determined:

• evenhanded representation of all viewpoints (fairness)
• increased awareness of the complexity of the program's social environment (ontological authenticity)

TABLE 27.1
Constructivist Assumptions for the Evaluation Process

• "Truth" is a matter of consensus among informed and sophisticated constructors, not of correspondence with an objective reality.

• "Facts" have no meaning except within some value framework; hence there cannot be an "objective" assessment of any proposition.

• "Causes" and "effects" do not exist except by imputation, and hence, accountability is a relative matter and implicates all interacting parties equally.

• Phenomena can be understood only within the context in which they are studied; findings from one context cannot be generalized to another; neither problems nor their solutions can be generalized from one setting to another.

• Interventions are not stable; when they are introduced into a particular context they will be at least as much affected (changed) by that context as they are likely to affect the context.

• Change cannot be engineered; it is a nonlinear process that involves the introduction of new information, and increased sophistication in its use, into the constructions of the involved humans.

• Evaluation produces data in which facts and values are inextricably linked. Valuing is an essential part of the evaluation process, providing the basis for an attributed meaning.

• Accountability is a characteristic of a conglomerate of mutual and simultaneous shapers, no one of which nor one subset of which can be uniquely singled out for praise or blame.

• Evaluators are subjective partners with stakeholders in the literal creation of data.

• Evaluators are orchestrators of a negotiation process that attempts to culminate in consensus on better informed and more sophisticated constructions.

• Evaluation data derived from constructivist inquiry have neither special status nor legitimation; they represent simply another construction to be taken into account in the move toward consensus.

• increased understanding of and respect for the value systems of others and their impact on the other stakeholder constructions (educative authenticity)

• change (reshaping) of the program (catalytic authenticity)

• empowerment or redistribution of power among stakeholders (tactical authenticity) (Chambers, Wedel, Rodwell 1992:326).

Table 27.2 describes techniques for achieving the five aspects of authenticity. Note that all techniques are reflective of the very nature of the differences in constructivist evaluation: multiple constructions of reality heavily shaped by context and values; full participative involvement in the evaluation process by all stakeholders; and an action orientation of the teaching/

TABLE 27.2
Techniques for Achieving Authenticity

Criteria	Technique
Fairness	Identifying stakeholders of players in the context being evaluated
	Soliciting interpretations of context from within all stakeholding groups
	Open negotiation of recommendations
	Open negotiation of agenda for responding to the emergent nature of process
	Gathering fully informed consent from all participants
Ontological authenticity	Reflecting alternative views of other respondents while collecting data
	Providing feedback from other participants to increase alternative thoughts about phenomena under study
	Questioning procedures or positions to rethink what has happened over time
	Maintaining audit trail of individual constructions during the process
Educative authenticity	Gathering testimony about views of constructions different from their own
	Gathering evidence of developing understanding or appreciation of alternative views
	Gathering evidence of greater empathy respect for differing perspectives born out of differing responsibilities
Catalytic authenticity	Gathering testimony about interest in acting on the results
	Gathering evidence of willingness to be involved in rethinking or reshaping
	Reviewing resolutions that evolve from negotiations on results of evaluation
	Systematic follow-up assessing the extent of resultant change or action
Tactical authenticity	Assuring that all participants are equal partners in process
	Treating all with honesty and respect
	Avoiding conscious manipulation or diminishment
	Gathering testimony about the degree of empowerment experienced by participants
	Systematic follow-up assessing the degree to which all stakeholders participate

learning process that is the evaluation. This attention to the joint, collaborative, and shared constructions brings life to the constructivist evaluation process. And it is in an organization that is amenable to the unpredictable sociopolitical outcomes that will result from the emergent, uncontrollable power-redistributing nature of the constructivist process where such an evaluation is possible. Unfortunately, authenticity was not the focus of the case study of evaluability assessment presented here. (This evaluation was undertaken by Mr. David Woody, III, doctoral student at Virginia Commonwealth University, as a part of a directed research project under the direction of Mary K. Rodwell.)

DETERMINING AGENCY EVALUABILITY AND CONSTRUCTIVIST METHODOLOGY

The use of qualitative methodology allows for the emergence of knowledge about an agency reality, permitting the understanding of the "gestalt, the totality, and the unifying nature of particular settings" (Patton 1980:40). The constructivist evaluation process requires a pursuit of data that are rich and fluid, addressing the perspectives of those seeking services, noting the quandaries of those providing services, and demanding an interaction between the two within a context—the agency/program setting. But not all programs can or should be evaluated by use of constructivism.

Determining whether an agency or program is evaluable involves a process of deciding whether to conduct the evaluation, identifying what program or agency changes may be needed before completing an evaluation, and establishing what method or methods may be most appropriate in judging the performance of an agency or program (Chambers, Wedel, and Rodwell 1992). Evaluability assessment, according to these authors, includes the following:

- Clarifying purpose: What are the current informational needs of the program or agency?

- Identifying program reality information: How well is the program defined? Are goals and objectives detailed, and can the agency/program be expected to achieve specific goals?

- Technical feasibility: Is a methodology available for the evaluation of the program/agency, and what problems might arrive if one method is chosen over another?

- Internal organizational politics—human and political feasibility: Is the political atmosphere in the agency/program conducive to exploring how a context functions, or might such a process destabilize that context?

Constructivist methods to determine evaluability are very appropriate when the goal is to have all possible stakeholding groups involved in the process, while having problems emerge from observation, from experiences, and from the data (Rodwell 1990). Using authenticity as a guidepost reminds the evaluator to test the possibility for the collaboration necessary for addressing how effectively services are provided and what costs are incurred by these in the context as a result of service provision. As is shown in the following case study, authenticity did not inform the evaluability assessment.

THE CASE STUDY

The Agency Setting

The agency is a nonprofit child guidance clinic for evaluation and treatment of children with serious emotional disorders. A multidisciplinary team approach is used in the delivery of services. The clinic client population is more than 60% African American from single-parent families. The majority of these families have Medicaid in order to pay for services. Some United Way support is also available. The services are orchestrated through an organizational structure that includes a board of directors, executive director, clinical and administrative directors, and clinical, support, and accounting staffs. For constructivist evaluation purposes, all the funding sources, service recipients, and agency personnel could be considered stakeholders because all have a stake in the services of the clinic.

Just a few weeks prior to the introduction of the constructivist evaluation, clinical staff, exclusively clinical social workers, developed a list of concerns that they felt adversely affected their ability to establish treatment goals. These concerns, from their perspective, leave them unable to effectively respond to specific treatment issues inherent in the population served. They identified as problematic the internal obstacles in the clinic system related to interaction with other professional staff, such as lack of interdisciplinary respect and communication; having cost and reimbursement determine diagnosis; and having bill collection as a primary process in the clinical encounter. They noted how stress and burnout are the results. These concerns were sent in memo form to the administrators in the clinic. No response was received. At that point, enter the program evaluator, with tacit approval from the executive and program directors, to assess program evaluability with the goal of undertaking a constructivist evaluation of the clinic's programs.

Methodology in This Evaluability Assessment

Practical approaches, such as review of documents, interviews, and observation, are used to answer the basic evaluability questions. In this case the evaluator sought to identify the following:

- What are the current informational needs of the clinic?
- How well is the program is defined? Are goals and objectives detailed, and can the clinic realistically be expected to achieve specific goals?
- Is a methodology available for the evaluation of this clinic? What problems might arise if one method is chosen over another?
- Is the political atmosphere in the clinic conducive to exploring clinic functioning, or might such a process destabilize the system?

Historical documents such as annual reports, memos, and meeting notes were provided as well as clinic policies and procedures. Documents that were made available included the formal mission statements, by-laws, audit reports, brochures and bulletins that described the program, and working papers prepared by clinical staff. The evaluator also engaged in conversations with various stakeholders (representing clinical, administrative, and support staff) within the clinic and was a participant observer in various formal meetings. Both the interviews and the participant observations were purposive in that they were used to obtain here-and-now constructions of persons, events, activities, feelings, motivations, claims, and concerns (Lincoln and Guba 1985). For the interviews the format was nonstandardized because the goal was to surface the interviewee's definition, structure, and account of what was relevant because the evaluator was concerned with the unique, the idiosyncratic, and the wholly individual viewpoint (Guba and Lincoln 1981). During the participant observation the evaluator not only observed events within the clinic but also experienced first hand the emotions and concerns of the participants and the program. The evaluator then organized pertinent information in a usable format, and using the constant comparative method (Glaser and Strauss 1967; Lincoln and Guba 1985), completed a content analysis going from the specific raw units of information to subsuming categories that guided the construction of the evaluability report.

Evaluability Results

Table 27.3 shows the results of data collection in relation to the evaluability criteria described above. Though the quantitative data were available or could be collected, the qualitative or political data were less clear.

Little information appeared to be moving up within the organization. Various employees had what they felt to be useful information for administrative personnel in the agency, none of which was solicited or responded to when offered unsolicited. An assessment of good clinic functioning at the point of the evaluability analysis was dependent upon the number of

TABLE 27.3
Evaluability Results

Criteria	Clinic Indicator	Assessment
Clarifying purpose/need	Stakeholder conflict Identification of billing issues	Pattern of consistent description Differing views on conflict origins
Identifying program reality	Mission statement Program objectives Revenue view vs. staff/client satisfaction view	Differing views based on differing data related to agency functioning
Technical feasibility	Appropriate data available and • Ethical issues addressed • Confidentiality acceptable • Financial costs minimal • Liability issues addressed	Consent for participation Results reviewable by stakeholders
Internal organizational politics	Verbalized poor morale among stakeholders Administration rejection of role change proposal from clinical staff	Pattern of delayed response to memos to administration Acknowledged midmanager powerless on behalf of clinic staff

appointments scheduled by clinical staff. Little concern was experienced by clinical staff for the pressure and constraints that this production-oriented system imposed on staff.

The lack of professional autonomy experienced by the clinical, support, and finance department staffs appeared related to conflict among these stakeholding groups and to a lack of focus or clarity regarding how these groups interact in order to achieve the goals and objectives derived from the clinic mission statement. No identification of the constraint on the stakeholder by the larger administrative or funding system seemed present. Instead conflict was identified among the groups: clinical staff, support staff, finance departments staff, administration, and one funding source, United Way.

Concerns about fee setting and billing protocol appeared to affect every level of the organization. Many of those interviewed seemed to be searching not only for effective means of addressing the clinic's fiscal status but also for ways of remaining attentive to clients' needs. Most agreed it was important to be clear with clients about their financial responsibilities, but consensus was missing on how that should happen. The support staff saw hearing about, responding to, and clarifying client concerns about fees and billing as a part of their daily responsibility. Finance staff saw themselves as confronted with the results of the need for clients to renegotiate fee payment based on environmental issues affecting their families. These families make more work for them. It was also a concern to clinical staff who are expected to be more actively involved in the financial issues of clients in the clinic. This expectation that clinical staff also share in the responsibility of the other clinic staff who manage fee payments was seen to create additional interstakeholding group conflict.

Even with these different perspectives, the principal stakeholding groups, excluding administration and clients, appeared responsive to the notion of having their concerns elevated in a formal way via the evaluation process. It was felt by the evaluator and staff that the program evaluation could be adequately carried out with due regard for maintenance of personal rights and integrity. No harm could come to the program's client as a result of the evaluation process, and it was reasonable to expect the cooperation of clients.

In retrospect, the potential problems related to the human/political interaction were underestimated. The clinical and support stakeholders expressed concern that the formal discussion and analysis of structural and programmatic issues would result in a negative reaction from the administration and negative repercussions. The evaluator could not predict the results of the emerging political dynamics of the program evaluation. Because of this, the evaluator could not reasonably expect the cooperation of program personnel as the evaluation unfolded. The mere process of performing prior ethnography (Spradley 1979) in order to begin a constructivist evaluation had radically changed the principal stakeholders' relationship with their environment, and the evaluator acted as though the clinic environment had infinite capacity to absorb what eventually was seen by the executive director to be an evaluative assault.

In our defense, following Nay and Kay's suggestions (1982:177), we found the following:

1. Structure and operational relationships were defined and in place. Organizational roles and structure were clear.

2. Key expectations were plausible and attributable to the direct intervention. The clinic operated within a theoretical frame from which clinical activities were derived.

3. Potential measurements could be taken. Quantitative or qualitative processes were possible.

4. Users for the evaluation information were capable of acting or effectively

recommending action. Originally, the clinic administrator expressed full cooperation including interest and ability to use the results to shape clinic change.

5. Knowing various evaluation outcomes that were in excess of the costs of conducting the evaluation were of value to the users. The initial cost to staff involved only interview time. No additional documentation or data collection by them was deemed necessary. The evaluator's time was donated.

6. Administrative links to direct intervention were available through which action based upon evaluation information could come. Administrative and clinical staff structure allowed monitoring and supervision of clinical behavior if changes in clinical practice should be deemed necessary.

The evaluability decision was based on this. However, we ignored the context of our deeds.

The Research Proposal

In response to the five-year planning being completed by the administration in the clinic and as a result of the prior ethnography and the evaluability analysis, the evaluator prepared a final draft of the evaluation contract that proposed the research question: How well are clinic services meeting the needs of clients and at what cost to clinic staff?

The contract was developed based upon existing policy related to the completion of research in the clinic. Quantitative techniques proposed included a questionnaire to all stakeholders in the clinic system dealing with job satisfaction and a survey of current clients about satisfaction with clinic services. Qualitative research methodologies were outlined to further inform the descriptive quantitative research methodologies proposed. Qualitative techniques such as stakeholder interviews, using prearranged probe questions with specific key informants, and a review of case records of closed cases over the past three years were proposed to allow the evaluation hypotheses to emerge (Lincoln and Guba 1985). The hope was to allow the emergent design to further establish a clinic context that would shape the evaluation questions and how they would be addressed.

The clinic administrator rejected the proposed contract. An extended interview was undertaken to understand the basis of the rejection. A content analysis using unitizing and categorizing (Guba and Lincoln 1980:313) produced the following concerns.

Research policy. The clinic has an explicit policy concerning the initiation of a research project, and the proposed contract did not conform with the desired format: (1) statement of purpose of the study; (2) literature review; (3) clear research question; (4) hypotheses; (5) descriptions/copies of instruments to be used. (None of this format was explicitly stated in agency policy.)

Project/clinic conflict.   The proposed evaluation conflicted with current clinic homeostasis. Threats to homeostasis were recognized as follows: (1) too broad a focus with both client and staff satisfaction at issue, (2) time frame suggested too short for data collection, (3) primary stakeholders' (clinic staff) workload too overwhelming to permit their involvement in a data collection experience because of predicted difficulties in scheduling of interviews and completion of questionnaires, (4) research projects submitted by those associated with the agency as employees or consultants not accepted by the board of directors.

Clinic research needs.   Such a detailed internal evaluation is not needed now; instead comparison studies of this clinic's functioning with similar service providers in similar environments in other parts of the nation are needed in the following areas: client satisfaction with services and the relationship of funding base to service provision. In addition, to be truly scientific, quantitative research methods should be used.

It was clear that program evaluation of the type suggested in original negotiations with the administrator and explicated in the evaluation contract was not acceptable. From our perspective, the reasons provided by the administrator were not the real reasons for the contract's unacceptability. Instead, the reasons can be attributed to organizational power and the politics therein. The administrator had his own plans and timelines for change and was not willing to lose control of his change notions through such an uncontrollable, emergent process. The clinic administrator did not see the value of gaining information from clients and staff related to improving clinic functioning or adjusting parts of the organizational system in ways that might not conform to his own vision.

In developing the contract proposal, assumptions were made concerning the responsiveness of the clinic administrator to an evaluation process that in actuality he had not legitimized. In line with his own change notions the focus of administration at that time was outward. Effectiveness, based on comparison with the standards and performance of other service providers, was of more value and (less threat?) than an introspective look at the clinic system and how it meets its own criteria for both client and staff competence and satisfaction.

Weiss (1975) noted that the policies and programs with which evaluation deals are themselves the creatures of political decision. Evaluation reports can at times be viewed as competing with other factors in the political decision-making arena. In fact the evaluation itself has a political stance and makes implicit statements about issues such as the problematic nature of some programs and unchallengeability of others. All this was operant and unaddressed in the clinic. The evaluator could have had more power over the outcome if he had determined, beforehand, the extent of political imbalance that would be induced by the proposed evaluation (Guba and Lincoln 1981). Basic questions were not answered that should have been, as follows:

1. What kinds of political influence can be expected in the evaluation and from whom?
2. What does the program have to gain or lose from the evaluation?
3. What are the commitments to the evaluation methodology and report of the findings (Chambers, Wedel, and Rodwell 1992)?

Clearly, the administrator, in line with Guba and Lincoln's advice (1981), determined that the information likely to be derived from the evaluation either was not sufficiently weighty or was too uncontrollable to warrant the resulting political upset and decided against the risk. From our perspective, this occurred because we were inattentive to authenticity. Losing sight of the power-redistributing effects of authenticity in the evaluability assessment allowed the overlooking of the all-pervasive nature of the political context that should have been recognized and attended to in the development of the evaluation contract.

Constructivist researchers know that various stakeholding groups have criteria for evaluating effectiveness and that these criteria are likely to be from differing and in some instances conflicting value positions. Identifying ways of channeling energies into careful identification of agency reality is another way of addressing the need to evaluate the effectiveness of social work practice. But this effort is not without political consequences. Unless the profession can balance its need to identify practice outcomes with a fair assessment of agency sensitivity to client and worker satisfaction within the agency setting, alternative research strategies and traditional service values may be put aside by administrators as in this case example. This administrator rejected the evaluation "in order that the agency survive."

Evaluability assessment should create a referent in a not so rational program evaluation environment always present in social programming. This referent when combined with authenticity will inevitably represent a mix of rational and extrarational responses to evaluation to prepare for or to overcome the political forces of the context. Entering into an agency context as an evaluator is not a neutral act. Administrators do have the power to control the information used for evaluation. With serious attention to authenticity, constructivist evaluators should be able to identify and account for serious political barriers to dialogue and change in social service agencies. This is essential to ensure that the use of methodology that captures the essence of reality in agencies as experienced by both clients and service-providing staff is not only accepted by also embraced "in order that the agency survive."

REFERENCES

Chambers, D., K. Wedel, and M. K. Rodwell. 1992. *Evaluating Social Programs*. New York: Allyn and Bacon.

Glaser, B. G. and A. L. Strauss. 1967. *The Discovery of Grounded Theory*. Chicago, Ill.: Aldine.

Guba, E. G. 1981. Criteria for assessing the trustworthiness of naturalistic inquiries. *Educational Communications and Technology Journal* 29: 75–92.

Guba, E. G. and Y. S. Lincoln. 1980. The distinction between merit and worth in evaluation. *Educational Evaluation and Policy Analysis* 2: 61–71.

Guba, E. G. and Y. S. Lincoln. 1981. *Effective Evaluation*. San Francisco: Jossey-Bass.

Guba, E. G. and Y. S. Lincoln. 1986. The countenances of fourth generation evaluation: Description, judgment, and negotiation. *Evaluation Studies Review Annual* 11: 70–78.

Guba, E. G. and Y. S. Lincoln. 1989. *Fourth Generation Evaluation*. Newbury Park, Calif.: Sage.

Lincoln, Y. S., ed. 1985. *Organizational Theory and Inquiry: The Paradigm Revolution*. Beverly Hills: Sage.

Lincoln, Y. S. and E. G. Guba. 1985. *Naturalistic Inquiry*. Beverly Hills: Sage.

Nay, N. and P. Kay. 1982. *Government Oversight and Evaluability Assessment*. Lexington, Mass.: Lexington Books.

Patton, M. 1980. *Qualitative Evaluation Methods*. Newbury Park, Calif.: Sage.

Rodwell, M. K. 1990. Person/environment construct: Positivist versus naturalist, dilemma or opportunity for health social work research and practice? *Social Science Medicine* 31, no. 1: 27–34.

Spradley, J. P. 1979. *The Ethnographic Interview*. New York: Holt, Reinhart and Winston.

Weiss, C. H. 1975. Evaluation research in the political context. In E. L. Struening and M. Guttentag, eds., *Handbook of Evaluation Research*. Beverly Hills: Sage.

Wholey, J. S. 1979. *Evaluation: Promise and Performance*. Washington, D.C.: The Urban Institute.

TWENTY-EIGHT

Commentary: Evaluation in Context: Is There Any Other Way?

Stanley L. Witkin

In 1979 Harvard psychologist Elliot Mishler published an article entitled, "Meaning in Context: Is There Any Other Kind?" Mishler's thesis was straightforward: while all of us depend upon context to understand others as well as to be understood, conventional theory and research (and I would add, evaluation) have paid little attention to the contextual parameters of meaning. In contrast, the authors of the preceding papers (Pulice, Rodwell, and Bogdan and Taylor) demonstrate an appreciation of the importance of context. Each, in her or his own way, illustrates that evaluation, like all complex social activities, is "meaning-full" and, therefore, contextual. Forgetting or ignoring this axiom can lead to unintended and undesirable consequences ranging from alienating primary stakeholders to terminating an evaluation prematurely.

The complexity of evaluation results in multiple contexts within which it can be interpreted. Awareness of these contexts and their implications may be a crucial but little understood dimension of evaluation methodology. While qualitative methods cannot ensure that adequate attention is given to contextual issues, they at least can accommodate inquiry of this sort.

Evaluation contexts can be defined in different ways such as by level of abstraction (e.g., from the physical environment of an agency to its the organizational climate) or by type (e.g., historical and political contexts). Additionally, contexts may be identified with different stakeholder groups, including evaluators themselves. The contexts of these groups may or may not be similar or congruent. Since there are no absolute rules about how to determine context, evaluators may find themselves operating within the "wrong" context or ignoring the context of important stakeholders. As Rodwell poignantly illustrates, evaluation planning must include consideration of various contexts and their relationship to the larger evaluation task. For example, the "agency political reality," that Rodwell describes has sufficient generality to concern most evaluators. Similarly, Shadish, Cook, and Leviton (1991) use the term *program political impactedness* to describe the intransigence of social programs and their embeddedness within social policy. Both examples highlight how social programs are inextricably connected to some larger, more abstract (political) context. Thus, one evaluates, not simply a program, but a complex web of interrelationships in which the program is situated. Failure to identify and account for these more abstract contexts can, as Rodwell and her colleagues painfully learned, have unwanted effects on the conduct of an evaluation.

Pulice approaches contexts by identifying "constituencies" (stakeholders) and the roles they play in the evaluation process. Since each of these groups may hold a different view of what an effective program looks like, a comprehensive evaluation will attempt to account for these differences. Sometimes, however, the "political realities" of evaluation and the diversity of perspectives that exist among constituent groups conflict. In such cases, the more powerful stakeholders may attempt to shape the evaluation in ways that make it difficult to "hear" the less powerful. For instance, when evaluation goals are defined in advance by agency administrators, it may be difficult to identify what the agency should be doing but is not. Thus, social work evaluators may find themselves trying to accommodate powerful stakeholders who, if threatened, can derail the evaluation while, at the same time, trying to insure that the evaluation reflects the perspectives of less powerful, but important stakeholders (e.g., clients). Negotiating such difficult terrain requires skills that go well beyond the standard operating procedures of typical evaluation texts. In fact, one's training as a practitioner may be more useful in dealing with these contextual issues than the methodological armamentarium that has become the focus of evaluation training. An advantage of qualitative approaches is that they can often accommodate such maneuverings.

METHODOLOGY AS CONTEXT

Evaluators do not work within a neutral context. Rather, the conceptual models and methods used by evaluators often form a powerful context (the methodological context) that affects the implementation and interpretation of evaluation. This context is unique in that it is imposed by the evaluator. And because methodological contexts are pervasive and usually implicit, they are easily overlooked. For example, the use of standardized measures as the sole method of collecting information may be assumed by evaluators and stakeholders alike to be "context free." Neither group may be aware of how these measures are associated with a host of other assumptions or how they may restrict the range of what it is possible to say about a program.

Methodology should be distinguished from method. Methods refer to the techniques that are used in an evaluation such as an interview or a statistical analysis. Methodology refers to the overall guiding framework within which methods are employed, for example, constructivist or empiricist models (cf. Guba and Lincoln 1989). Unfortunately, discussion of quantitative versus qualitative evaluations often obscures this difference as is illustrated below.

Bogdan and Taylor's "positive approach to evaluation" represents a methodological context within which evaluation is understood and carried out. The significance of this context can be seen in its influence over which programs are selected as suitable candidates for evaluation. What is unique about Bogdan and Taylor's description of the positive approach is that their decision to work within this context was made because of its "biases." That is, they are quite explicit about the value assumptions that underlie this approach. Qualitative methods may be helpful in this approach since, unlike more conventional approaches, such biases are not necessarily considered detrimental to inquiry.

Bogdan and Taylor's paper also reminds us of a simple but powerful "truth": we usually find what we are looking for and, conversely, often miss what we are not prepared to see. Reality is equivocal and, therefore, open to multiple interpretations (Weick 1979). The methodological lenses evaluators wear may change how they interpret what they observe. This phenomenon was illustrated by Wikler, Wasow, and Hatfield (1981, 1983) in their study of mothers of children with mental handicaps. In their first report (1981), based on a problem-focused perspective, the authors described how the concept of "chronic sorrow" characterized the maternal experience of these women. Two years later, having shifted to a "strengths perspective," they revealed that in their earlier study many of the mothers also had expressed the belief that rearing a child with disabilities made them stronger people. At the time, this information was dismissed as a "methodological artifact" and not reported. Now, having adopted a different methodological framework, the "artifact" became "data."

Methodological contexts may affect the purpose of an evaluation. Bogdan and Taylor, for instance, contrast the objectives of the positive approach with that of an effectiveness approach. Within the positive framework, programs that appear successful are evaluated to learn how they achieve their success, while in effectiveness evaluations the objective is to learn whether programs are successful. This difference in perspective extends beyond issues of method (i.e., qualitative or quantitative). For example, Bogdan, Taylor, and Pulice use qualitative methods. However, whereas Pulice is concerned with "assessing a program's effectiveness" (1), Bogdan and Taylor focus on documenting how effective programs carry out their activities. The crux of this difference lies in the role of values within each framework. The positive approach is openly value based. Programs are assessed relative to their adherence to, and expression of, particular values such as the integration of people with disabilities into the community. The effectiveness approach attempts to be value neutral. While the values of stakeholder groups may be noted, the evaluation process itself attempts to avoid a particular value stance.

The methodological context also influences the degree to which evaluation is seen as a passive or active (i.e., change oriented) process. The value-neutral stance of effectiveness evaluation creates a context in which the evaluator records and analyzes the views, activities, and outcomes of a program. In contrast, the constructivist framework used by Rodwell views evaluation as a means of effecting change. Drawing upon the work of Guba and Lincoln (1989), Rodwell sees a minimal objective of evaluation as increasing awareness and understanding among stakeholders and helping to facilitate program change. Finally, within the positive context, evaluation is seen as a way to bring about social change. By presenting useful information about how exemplary programs function, Bogdan and Taylor hope to change perceptions and attitudes about people negatively labeled by society.

The issue of context is a critical one for evaluation. In different ways Bogdan, Taylor, Pulice, and Rodwell emphasize the need for evaluators to understand the various contexts within which evaluations occur. Less explicit is how evaluations, through the imposition of an overarching framework, *create* contexts. There is much yet to learn about these issues. Qualitative methods are not in themselves sufficient to address these issues. However, since qualitative methods are generally "context compatible," they can, if used judiciously, sensitize evaluators to contextual issues and encourage their explication and analysis.

REFERENCES

Guba, E. G. and Y. S. Lincoln. 1989. *Fourth Generation Evaluation*. Newbury Park, Calif.: Sage.

Mishler, E. G. 1979. Meaning in context: Is there any other kind? *Harvard Educational Review* 49: 1–19.

Shadish, W. R., Jr., T. D. Cook, and L. C. Leviton. 1991. *Foundations of Program Evaluation: Theories of Practice*. Newbury Park, Calif.: Sage.

Weick, K. E. 1979. *The Social Psychology of Organizing*. 2d ed. Reading, Mass.: Addison-Wesley.

Wikler, L., M. Wasow, and E. Hatfield. 1981. Chronic sorrow revisited: Parent vs. professional depiction of the adjustment of parents of mentally retarded children. *American Journal of Orthopsychiatry* 51: 63–70.

Wikler, L., M. Wasow, and E. Hatfield. 1983. Seeking strengths in families of developmentally disabled children. *Social Work* 28: 313–15.

III

Applications to Types of Practice, Settings, and Client Populations

CHILD AND FAMILY

TWENTY-NINE

Tidiness in an Untidy World: Research in Child Welfare

Anthony N. Maluccio and Edith Fein

Research in child welfare, particularly public child welfare, is an exciting, exhilarating, and effective enterprise that we trust leads to improvement in services to vulnerable children and families. This, at least, is what we would like to believe as we seek to apply our research expertise to the problems and needs evident in children's services.

The reality is, of course, quite different. Social work practice research, as with research in other settings in the "real world," more often than not can be accurately described as uninspiring, frustrating, time consuming, and inconsequential. In particular, the attempt to apply rigor and order and coherence to the research enterprise in the hurly-burly of the practice setting is a search for tidiness in an untidy world.

But if one can live with the lack of tidiness and appreciate the benefits of immersion in the clutter, the process of doing research holds potential for excitement, for having an impact on service delivery, for clarifying one's ideas, for learning, and for discovery. This is what we have found in nearly two decades of research using both qualitative and quantitative methods in public and voluntary child welfare settings.

On the basis of our experiences, in this paper we report some of what we have learned about the process, methods, and impact of doing research in child welfare. Rather than attempt the intellectually penetrating and erudite analysis that might be expected in a scholarly paper, we consider the nitty-gritty—some of the more practical, down-to-earth aspects of doing research that are not particularly exciting and that are rarely included in our literature. We address the following questions:

1. How do you get the commitment of the top administration as well as staff to do research?
2. What are the compromises in doing research in vivo?
3. How realistic is it to expect research and policy formulation to be connected?
4. How does the organizational culture affect the dynamic interaction between research and practice?

SERIES OF FOSTER CARE STUDIES

This paper is based on our experience with a series of studies on foster care that serve as examples of the kinds of research to which we are referring (Fein, et al. 1983; Fein, Maluccio, and Kluger 1990).

The studies were done under the auspices of the research department of a private, multifunction child welfare and mental health agency, in collaboration with the State of Connecticut's Department of Children and Youth Services (DCYS), and with funding from the U.S. Department of Health and Human Services. The state agency served as the site for data collection for the three studies in this series.

Study samples ranged from fewer than 100 cases to nearly 800, the total client population. In addition to quantitative measures, each study used qualitative methods, in particular the gathering of information from in-depth interviews with foster parents and biological parents.

THE AGENCY CONTEXT

Conducting research in the hurly-burly context of a public child welfare agency requires not only knowledge of quantitative and qualitative methodology but also appreciation of the organization's characteristics, especially the demands and challenges with which it must deal on a day-to-day basis (Shaffir and Stebbins 1991).

The Department of Children and Youth Services (DCYS), where the studies were carried out, is a statewide agency that combines child protection, child mental health, and juvenile justice programs. Services are provided through six community-based regional offices, with close coordination and monitoring from a central office. Although the agency had a large research and evaluation unit, the latter was involved primarily in gathering data and disseminating statistical reports rather than in engaging in formal research.

As with other public agencies, DCYS continually faced a number of pressures. Foremost among these was the need to act in the face of uncertainty, to respond to emergencies, and to cope with community pressures. Other pressures included concern about being evaluated, frequent turnover in management and staff during the research, staff perceptions of the research as imposed by the administration or as another example of "irrelevant" paperwork, and stereotyped perceptions of researchers as abstract thinkers with limited awareness of practice realities. As a result, despite its formal commitment to the various research projects in which it had agreed to participate, on many occasions the research did not matter, or did not seem to matter, or had to take a back seat.

Creating a Supportive Context

In light of the particular situation in which we worked, as well as what is known in general about the functioning of organizations such as a state agency, how do we create—and sustain—a context that is conducive to practice research? Preserving the original commitment to a project is perhaps as crucial as obtaining the agreement in the first place. How can we ensure that the support encompasses the contribution of all—from top administrators to line staff? In embarking on our work, we were guided by the following beliefs, which can be characterized as coping strategies for researchers in a practice setting.

Build and Maintain Rapport

Time and effort are required to establish relationships with agency representatives. Sometimes the effort is a long-term investment rather than one that has immediate results. For example, in our situation, we had served on committees and task forces with agency personnel for years. Whenever possible, we invited those people to participate in joint presentations at conferences and workshops to demonstrate our belief in our colleagueship.

None of these situations could be forced since success of the rapport-building effort depends on blending personalities that work well together. Nevertheless, energy needs to be expended on creating an environment in which compatible personalities flourish. Not much attention is usually paid to this requirement because research is supposed to be task oriented and objective, but the nurturing of relationships is crucial to the success of the research effort.

Be Sensitive to the Political Context

In all discussions about the research, during the entire process from project design to presentation of results, we always tried to communicate our understanding of the political realities within which the state system operated and the pressures faced by people in public agency work. In addition, we never represented ourselves as outside experts, particularly to the research and evaluation people. Instead, we considered ourselves as working with them, acknowledging that they did not have the time to produce the research we were involved in, but recognizing their expertise, particularly in the internal reports they characteristically produced.

Part of the political context in which we worked was the agency's sensitivity to yet another outside research study. Many studies in the past came to be seen as negative evaluations of the agency's services and competence, and we had to be aware of, and defuse, those attitudes, which were often justified by the staff's experience with research. Unanticipated events, such as the tragedy of a child's death, with the resultant press coverage reflecting negatively on the agency, also became part of our working environment that had to be acknowledged. Our attitudes became important indicators to staff about whether we could be trusted.

Sensitivity to the political context requires that commitment to the research be obtained from top administrators, but as much effort needs to be expended on the middle managers' commitment. The middle managers are the ones who make things happen in the district offices, so courting their allegiance is worth the time and energy required. By the same token, middle managers will not go against staff feelings on a project as peripheral to their interests as a research study, so appealing to line staff is also essential if the entire hierarchy is to feel comfortable.

Show Respect for the Multiplicity and Complexity of Demands and Pressures Faced by the Agency

The research task often becomes so important, particularly to the academicians among us, that we find it difficult to appreciate the stresses faced by those beyond the textbook. Public agencies typically face multiple and complex demands, for they operate with limited resources and unrealistic expectations from outsiders for perfect functioning. We must communicate openly and strongly a belief in the system with which we are working—that we understand that what the agency is doing is important, that they are doing the best they can under the circumstances, and that we do not share in the persistent criticism from various sources.

At the same time, we must maintain our belief in research despite the first-order need of direct service delivery. The potential for promoting data-based decision making becomes the basis for all our efforts, elevating our endeavors to the importance of the agency's day-to-day activities.

Gain Trust

Studies and contracts were steered our way because the state agency knew we could do the work. They did not need to monitor us, because of their experience with us. We always produced minutes of meetings, reports, and other helpful material—and always on time. Occasionally, when the bureaucracy delayed the signing of contracts, we worked without a contract and produced our reports so the agency could meet its internal deadlines. We always kept our promises to staff and never exceeded a deadline.

Demonstrate Technical Competence

All the goodwill in the world fades if a strong knowledge base is not demonstrated. The research team included members who were known to be experienced in child welfare practice and issues. They provided frequent progress reports on the research; the reports and findings were practice oriented; and the materials were designed to be easy to read, without busy tables and complicated statistical reporting.

Involve the Agency Actively in the Research Process

Other research teams have appreciated the importance of absorbing administration and staff into the research effort as much as possible and of not representing the team as the only research or child welfare experts. (McCroskey and Nelson 1989). In the "After Foster Care" study (Fein et al. 1983), for example, we devoted the first six months to that goal. We held numerous meetings with administrators and small groups of social workers to obtain their help in refining the research questions, developing various data collection instruments, and establishing research procedures. Once data were collected and analyzed, we met again with staff and administrators to get their reactions to our interpretations of the data and incorporated their insights into our findings. Less frequently, but as part of the process, we involved foster parent groups and associations for similar purposes.

Involvement of agency staff does not come automatically at the issuance of an invitation to a meeting. We found it important to "nurture" the staff. In order to maximize attendance at our meetings, we typically met at lunchtime in the various regional offices and brought sandwiches or pizza. This proved to be an effective strategy, as word spread that we not only knew what we were doing but also we also appreciated the workers' attendance. This reaction alerted us once again to how needy and unthanked public child welfare workers are, but that is another story.

IMPACT OF ORGANIZATION CONTEXT ON RESEARCH

As we carry out research in a public child welfare agency, what is the impact of the particular organizational context on the research process and outcome? Our experience with the series of DCYS studies suggests a variety of effects.

Impact on Research Protocal

Although scientific rigor is important, researchers must be ready to "compromise" certain standards or lower some of their expectations. For example, in the "After Foster Care" longitudinal study (Fein et al. 1983), the children's placements with permanent families were followed for seventeen months, when a longer period would have been desirable. In this study, as well as the others, it was not possible to obtain agency permission to interview the children, requiring us to gather information about their functioning through their caretakers. In each study, we were allowed to conduct only brief interviews with social workers, thus limiting the range and depth of data that we could gather on their perceptions of the foster care phenomenon.

As each study progressed, we realized that we had to be ready to provide preliminary information back to the agency. We regularly gave reports to field and administrative staff, to key decision makers, and to clients. Using simple language, we offered some data on early findings, highlighted issues that we encountered, and focused on themes and practice implications, not necessarily the findings per se. We could not wait until all findings were in and we had time for careful review, analysis, and neatly wrapped reports. The ongoing reports demonstrated the usefulness of research, kept participants interested, and maintained our responsiveness to the agency's need for help in coping with immediate, practical problems.

Through such a process, we were able to illustrate that research is most useful when it is seen as a joint enterprise between researchers and practitioners. This involves being ready to share control of the project with the agency and having the researcher become a part of—rather than apart from—the agency context.

Impact on Knowledge-Building Process

The contributions of agency administration and staff affected the knowledge-building process in direct as well as indirect ways. For example, there were numerous refinements in problem formulation, revisions in the research instruments, and increased use of qualitative research methodology. At a subtler level, our "immersion" into the agency's organizational context enabled us as researchers to better appreciate and conceptualize foster care and related phenomena. This led us to rethink some of our perspectives about child welfare practice and to be sensitive to a number of research implications and practice themes.

For example, one perception was of the need to apply to the study of child welfare various lessons from recent research in child development, human coping and adaptation, and heritability of intelligence. Such research shows that the growth, development, and functioning of human beings involve a complex, interactive process (Bronfenbrenner 1979; Chess and Alexander 1986; Lykken 1987; Rutter 1987). "An emergent trait is often drastically changed if the configuration of characteristics on which it depends is modified even slightly" (Lykken 1987).

In line with these thoughts, the findings from our series of foster care studies "suggest that the outcome of foster care placement, whether measured in terms of children's functioning or stability and permanency, depends on a complex set of factors that are interactive, rather than on a series of causal relationships" (Fein, Maluccio, and Kluger 1990:76).

Usefulness of Qualitative Approaches

Knowledge building as a consequence of research activity is enhanced by increasing the use of qualitative approaches in practice-oriented research. A qualitative approach encompasses more than qualitative methodology (Wells 1991a). In the studies discussed in this paper, much of the methodology was quantitative, but a qualitative approach—an immersion in the interview process with clients and with the practice of the social workers in the state agency—produced for us insights that informed the entire research process. These insights enriched our understanding of the quantitative material, thus demonstrating the value of flexible, ethnographic methods of interviewing "in vivo."

The qualitative approach helped, in particular, to bring us to an understanding of the complex, interactive phenomenon of foster care discussed above. For example, the concept of permanency planning, admirable in its purpose and clarity as a goal of child welfare, suffers in implementation from the complexities that human beings present. That is, a permanency plan to reunify a child in foster care within six months, for instance, can be derailed by the mother's entry into psychiatric care, a search for kinship caregivers, the social worker's leaving the agency and a new worker unfamiliar with the family being assigned to case management, the father's returning from jail and being willing to take the child, or the youngster's return to foster care after being abused. The status of the child at any of the intervening points may be difficult to specify quantitatively or may not fairly reflect the complexity of the situation. Only the qualitative approach in our interview experience alerted us to the richness hidden in the quantitative data.

Some of the interview vignettes from the long-term foster care study (Fein, Maluccio, and Kluger 1990) illustrated how complicated those data could be:

> I liked the social worker as a person and knew his job was hard. He was defensive about not being there as much as he should have been. His visits weren't well thought out; they needed more structure and planning.

> I've considered adopting him, but adoption would have to be "open" because he's still tied to his mother. I'm not sure I'd like to commit to open adoption.

> Don is twelve years old. I wanted to adopt him and his brother together but his brother wasn't ready. He lives with another family. Don doesn't know his mother. He came when he was thirteen months old; his mother wasn't responsible.

Meaning for Program Evaluation

The knowledge-building process is enhanced by program evaluation results as well as findings from "purer" research studies (Fein and Staff 1993; Turner 1993). "Practice-based research has the advantage of accumulating information on the real world of service delivery rather than a carefully controlled but then impossible-to-implement experimental condition" (Fein and Staff 1993). Service delivery contains a variety of unanticipated effects that a formal research study must ignore, but program evaluations can include them in the investigation; thus the connection between the study and reality is strengthened, reinforcing the foundation for utilization of results. The usefulness of findings is further enhanced when the studies are sensitive to the serendipity and flexibility that characterize human interactions (Wells 1991b).

IMPACT OF RESEARCH ON AGENCY

Practice-oriented research "in vivo" ideally also has an impact on the organizational context and on the agency's environment and its policies, programs, and practices. In other words, research can have practical consequences for the agency, some of which are unanticipated or flow from involvement in the research project itself rather than from a study's particular research findings. Some examples from our series of foster care studies follow.

Program/Practice

The findings reaffirmed the general importance of support services to foster and biological families and in particular the state agency's pivotal role as the principal agent in service delivery to families with children in foster care placement or at risk of such placement. As findings were shared with staff, specific practice implications were identified. For instance, the importance emerged of strengthening or expanding programs and practice strategies in such areas as aftercare services, use of recreational services for both children and biological parents, and advocacy with schools and other community resources.

Policy

Research experiences and findings were incorporated in the agency's five-year state plan for delivery of child welfare services, contributing to the agency's refinement of a "continuum of care" model and enhancement of its services to minority families. In addition, study findings were used immediately to support budget requests to the legislature for affirmative action programs, training of foster parents as well as social workers, and support for long-term foster care programs. In this connection, Junior League volunteers, who had served as interviewers, adopted study recommendations in their organization's social action committee and testified in the state legislature to support DCYS budget initiatives.

Participation in these studies also helped define the state agency as one committed to study and review of children in its care. Participation also helped the agency respond to pressure for accountability, especially in light of growing demands and expenditures. Finally, involvement in the various studies enabled agency administrators to appreciate better that certain research strategies could also be used internally by agency staff. They could see, for example, the value of gathering program and outcome data regularly and systematically to guide program development and address policy issues.

Our experience suggests that, while not giving up the search for tidiness, we need to appreciate the reality of practice when conducting research in a setting such as public child welfare. Excitement and rewards will follow, if we are ready to be flexible, anticipate frustration, and tolerate that research rarely proceeds in the orderly, planful way that we would wish. Additionally, we need to recognize that researchers and agency personnel share commitment to the same goal—improved lives for children and families. And the final report of a research study may not be the most important product but may be an important step in a dynamic process of change stimulated by the interaction between research and practice.

REFERENCES

Bronfenbrenner, U. 1979. *The Ecology of Human Development.* Cambridge, Mass.: Harvard University Press.

Chess, S. and T. Alexander. 1986. *Temperament in Clinical Practice.* New York: Guilford Press.

Fein, E., A. N. Maluccio, V. J. Hamilton, and D. E. Ward. 1983. After foster care: Outcomes of permanency planning for children. *Child Welfare* 62, no. 6: 485–562.

Fein, E., A. N. Maluccio, and M. Kluger. 1990. *No More Partings—An Examination of Long-Term Foster Family Care.* Washington, D.C.: Child Welfare League of America.

Fein, E. and I. Staff. 1993. The interaction of research and practice in family reunification. In B. A. Pine, R. Krieger, and A. N. Maluccio, eds., *Together Again: Family Reunification After Foster Care.* Washington, D.C.: Child Welfare League of America.

Lykken, D. T. 1987. Genes and the mind. *Harvard Medical School Mental Health Letter* 4 no. 2: 4–6.

McCroskey, J. and J. Nelson. 1989. Practice-based research in a family support program: The family connection project example. *Child Welfare* 68, no. 6: 573–87.

Rutter, M. 1987. Psychosocial resilience and protective mechanism. *American Journal of Orthopsychiatry* 57, no. 3: 316–31.

Shaffir, W. B. and R. A. Stebbins. eds. 1991. *Experiencing Fieldwork: An Inside View of Qualitative Research.* Newbury Park, Calif.: Sage.

Turner, J. 1993. Evaluating family reunification programs. In Pine, Krieger, and Maluccio, eds., *Together Again: Family Reunification After Foster Care.* Washington, D.C.: Child Welfare League of America.

Wells, K. 1991a. Eagerly awaiting a home: Severely emotionally disturbed youth lost in our systems of care. *Child and Youth Care Forum* 20, no. 1: 7–18.

Wells, K. 1991b. Placement of emotionally disturbed children in residential treatment: A review of placement criteria. *American Journal of Orthopsychiatry* 61, no. 3: 339–47.

THIRTY

Feminist Research Within a Battered Women's Shelter

Liane V. Davis and Meera Srinivasan

This paper is about feminist research and how women unwittingly recreate oppression within an organization designed to empower them.

DOING FEMINIST RESEARCH

Women passionately argue among themselves about feminist research and epistemology (see, for example, Harding 1991: Reinharz 1992). Some are content to adopt a feminist agenda, elaborating what areas need be studied to make women and their lives visible. These "just add women and stir" feminists want to achieve equality as directors, actors, and subjects in the research endeavor just as they want to achieve equality in other arenas of public life. Others, and we count ourselves among this second group, think it insufficient to correct merely the historical androcentric bias in knowledge making. We believe that the patriarchal "ideology of domination that permeates Western culture" (Hooks 1984:24) has produced a "framework concerning knowledge . . . (that is unique to) a highly particular group of men who give voice/text to the social world as seen, understood, and colonized by men like themselves" (Stanley and Wise 1990:39). We will be content only with a total transformation of the research agenda, the research paradigm, the epistemology, and the social political world as we know it.

We accept that feminist research can be done in multiple ways, and we do not intend this discussion to cut off others whose views of research are different. We also recognize that our perspective on feminist research comes from our more radical notions of ourselves as feminists. What we are talking about is our view of feminist research.

Feminist research is grounded in a politics of oppression and transformation. It is based on the belief that women, like people of color and gays and lesbians, have been forced to look on while white, heterosexual men have developed and run the social institutions and demanded adherence to their values and ethics. More insidious, because more subtle and far-reaching, has been patriarchy's control of knowledge making itself. Those in power have sought to define reality for the community as a whole. They have often succeeded. At the core of feminist research, therefore, is the commitment to give voice to previously marginalized and silenced people.

Feminist research is unabashedly political, openly acknowledging the impossibility and undesirability of a neutral research process and product and accepting the challenge to "search into all aspects of a society . . . for the expression and consequences of relations of domination" (Flax 1987:642). Feminist research holds out a vision of the future that eliminates privilege, hierarchy, and oppression.

FEMINIST RESEARCH AND QUALITATIVE METHOD

Just as diversity exists among feminists, diversity exists among feminist researchers and the methods they deem appropriate. For us, qualitative research is a rich and essential resource for feminist researchers. Qualitative methods have the potential to capture the contextual complexity of women's lives, to capture divergent perspectives among women, and to enable silenced women to tell their own stories in their own voices. But the potential can be realized only if the researcher sees the world through a feminist lens.

A Battered Women's Shelter: A Study of Domination and Oppression

Shelters, the only organizations uniquely devoted to the needs of women who are abused, have been strongly influenced by the feminist ideology and activism of the 1970s. Women are abused by individual men and their social institutions (see Dobash and Dobash 1979; Schechter 1982 for feminist analyses). Therefore, as they offered safe space to women, feminists sought to develop organizational environments that empowered residents and staff alike (Dixon et al. 1982; Ferraro 1983; Johnson 1981; Rodriguez 1988).

Many early shelters were conceived of as warm, nurturing environments where women could determine how to run their own lives. Many were run as feminist collectives, committed to nonhierarchical organizational structures and consensual decision making. The "residents," as the battered women were called, actively participated in developing policies and running programs (Schechter 1982). Egalitarian relationships among staff and residents were encouraged. Former residents were encouraged to return as workers in the belief that experience, not professional expertise, was the most effective resource. And men, the symbol of patriarchal oppression, were excluded.

Shelters have the potential to be quintessential feminist organizations. Whether the reality of shelters has conformed to feminist ideals has, however, been questioned. Evidence exists that many had been co-opted by traditional agencies by the early 1980s (Ferraro 1983; Johnson 1981) and that feminist shelters differed from professionally oriented ones in word, but not deed (Epstein, Russell, and Silvern 1988).

In the two decades since shelters for battered women first appeared many changes have occurred. Reliance on government funding has increased bureaucratization and professionalization of shelters (see Davis and Hagen 1988 for a discussion of these issues). And yet, most continue to identify the empowerment of women, a central feminist tenet, as their underlying philosophy (Davis 1987).

This study took another look at a battered women's shelter. Through observational research, it sought to understand how the organizational structure of a shelter, whose rhetoric was one of empowerment, actually affected the different members. Were *all* of its members empowered? Or was power and domination unwittingly recreated within the organization itself?

The "Researcher" as Volunteer

The study was conducted by a doctoral student, an Asian woman of Indian origin, who openly brought to the project a feminist awareness of personal and political abuse against women. Seeking to enter the organization as an equal she negotiated to serve as a volunteer. She was welcomed with open arms to assist an overworked staff. She was also free to talk informally to residents and staff members.

Most of the data were collected through informal interviews with both staff and residents. They were taped when an opportunity was available to plan the interviews. When interviews occurred more spontaneously, she asked and was granted permission to take notes.

Processing the Data

The data were processed in three stages. The first step involved dealing directly with the information obtained through interviews and observation. She read through the notes as soon as possible after she had taken them, making observations in the margins. She used the one-hour drive home from the shelter to tape her own observations and reflections. Then she transcribed all the tapes, both those from the interviews and her own observations. She then categorized all these data.

The second stage involved using colleagues to provide feedback on the research process itself and her role in it. Through dialogues with others, she was able to focus more directly on her role in the research process and reflect upon (and correct for, when possible and appropriate) the relevant and irrelevant biases that she brought to the project.

The third stage occurred after she had initially written up the research. During this stage, she continued to engage in dialogue and incorporated feedback to further organize and clarify the meaning of the material.

Entering the Organization as an Equal

Establishing egalitarian relationships with everyone was not easy. Staff readily accepted and treated her as another volunteer. From the beginning, however, some of the residents made it clear that they expected people, even within the shelter, to oppress them. One woman asked whether she was using them as guinea pigs for her study.

The Formal Organizational Hierarchy

A clear formal hierarchy was present within the shelter. The staff comprised fifteen paid employees and about forty to fifty volunteers. The executive director, like other agency executives, was responsible for fund raising, public relations, and the overall running of the shelter. She shared an office away from the shelter with the associate director, who managed both program and personnel, and the office manager. The shelter director, a counselor, a volunteer coordinator, and women's and children's advocates worked in the shelter itself as did the volunteers. Staff valued moving up the organizational ladder and valued the prestige that came with such advances.

A hierarchical pay structure existed also, albeit the differences were not large. At the top, the executive director's pay ranged from $26,000 to 35,000, while at the bottom, that of the advocates ranged from $13,000 to 18,000.

Some Evidence of Collectivism and Equality

Evidence of collectivism was also present among the staff. Major decisions about such things as funding, incidents involving residents, and the progress of program components were all made by consensus at weekly meetings attended by all employees. Residents were not, however, a part of this decision-making process.

Despite the absence of a rigid hierarchy among staff members, everyone knew who the boss was. Staff members were always informed of her visits. They sought her approval and subtly changed their behavior when she was at the shelter. For example, one of the staff, who had lain down in the office because she was not feeling well, expressed concern over how the executive director would react if she were to make a surprise visit.

Staff/Resident Hierarchy: A Recreation of Domination

The rules. All staff members had power over the residents. This was clearly seen in the formal and inflexible rules governing resident behavior. These rules included the following: (1) No alcohol or drugs in the shelter. (2) No violence will be used between residents and their children. Women gave their written consent to these rules upon entering the shelter and were expelled if they had accumulated more than three infractions of them.

The rules were the hardest thing for the residents to contend with. One resident, who had been at the shelter for two weeks, when asked whether she considered the shelter a home, said: "Honey, it's o.k., but if I had a home to go to, I'd go now." When asked how her experience differed from home she said: "Everything is different. I do what I like at home. I work late so I'd like to go some place after work, have a coffee or something but I can't do that here."

The sanctions. Staff members accepted their responsibility to enforce the rules. One staff member observed: "Sometimes I feel like a police, making sure they do this or they don't do this. But it is the only way to keep women who drink and take drugs away as that could cause problems."

Staff members also accepted their right to ask difficult residents to leave and to deny service to women who did not fit their perception of a deserving resident. They justified their power over residents by the need to keep out troubles. Yet they were not always comfortable exercising their authority. One staff member had written in the logbook: "I had to ask B to leave because she had not done her chores. When I confronted her she got verbally abusive. I asked her to leave. Not feeling nice."

The glass wall.   The most visible symbol of the staff/resident hierarchy was the glass wall that separated the office from the shelter living room. The shelter had recently moved into a newly renovated building. Much thought had gone into designing a physically attractive and homelike environment. And yet this glass partition strikingly illustrated the physical separation between residents and staff. Staff members had a noise-free work environment and a safe place to store their possessions. They also could observe the residents from a distance.

Residents and their children were not allowed to go beyond the glass partition without permission of staff. Yet staff members had free access to the living quarters (including bedrooms) of the residents. Some had reservations about using this right, not feeling comfortable walking into what they perceived as the private living quarters of the residents.

Who is the expert?   Staff members defined acceptable and unacceptable behavior. They subtly communicated to the residents that they, the staff, knew best. One of the ways this was demonstrated was telling the mothers how to discipline their children. As in many shelters, women were told they could not physically punish their children while in the shelter. Physical punishment was considered violent behavior and was a major ground for expulsion. This made little sense to many of the residents. As one resident said:

> I've been thinking about what the workers have been telling me. I am not sure about the time out bit. I don't think children would follow this very well at home. It would be hard to do this at home. I don't believe an occasional smack is bad. It is not hitting or slapping, but I guess I can't do that here.

While parent support services may be useful to some of the residents, the shelter sometimes forgot their primary reason for being: to address the violence in the lives of the women.

Woman-to-woman relationships.   Friendships developed among staff members. They babysat for and socialized with one another in non-work hours. They brought food to share with others. They expressed their appreciation of their colleagues' work with brief notes in the daily logbook. They were affectionate toward one another and readily responded when staff members were upset. For example, one volunteer, who had became upset after talking to an emotionally disturbed child of a ''difficult resident'' was held by another staff member until she had calmed down.

Staff members were more reserved with residents. They hugged and kissed the children. Some would provide respite to an upset resident by temporarily babysitting for her children. But it was rare for staff members to physically console or hug the residents, even when the residents were most upset. In three separate intake sessions, a staff member remained seated on the other side of a table while a resident cried.

Some staff members bridged the distance with residents by sharing their personal experiences of abuse. And though most residents did have a favorite staff member with whom they felt comfortable, by and large, relationships between residents and staff were formal and constrained.

Friendships blossomed among the residents. Women would go shopping or watch television together. Some visited their new friends in the shelter even after they themselves had left.

The residents recognized the power staff members had over them. Even while appearing to interact casually and sharing many of their personal concerns with staff members, they remained cautious about openly criticizing the shelter. Their concern with openness was realistic. Residents who challenged the staff's way of doing things risked being considered difficult.

The Ideology of Abuse Against Women

Staff members were taught that violence was a learned behavior, that an identifiable cycle of violence existed, and that the shelter could help break the cycle by empowering women. These beliefs were articulated by the executive director in group discussions with the staff, by the counselor in her work with individual residents, and by the staff as they casually talked with one another and the residents.

By focusing on the learned aspects of the behaviors and the need for individual women to change, staff members could wholeheartedly endorse the shelter's belief in empowerment while disassociating themselves from the politics of feminism. As one staff member said:

> No, I am not a feminist, but I do believe violence is cyclical. I believe that part of the role of the shelter is to provide good role models to the women and their children. We have to say violence is wrong and there are other ways of correcting the kids.

Shelters exist because women are oppressed. Women, not men, are battered in relationships, must leave their homes to find safety within formal organizations, and must turn to public funds to support themselves and their children when they have been battered.

When shelters first began, feminists hoped they could develop and maintain empowering organizational environments. They knew that achieving such an ideal would be difficult. As Dixon et al. (1982) observed:

> In rejecting traditional hierarchical forms of organization we are left with the question of what to put in their place. No group is structureless and in the

> absence of formal structure, informal structure will develop which can be
> even more exclusive as there is no way of challenging them. The answer is
> not simply to abandon structure but to create structures which enable every-
> one to participate.   (61–62)

This study suggests that, in one shelter, the hope has been partially realized. The informal structure of the organization enables the staff members to participate on an egalitarian basis with one another and be empowered by it. The organization recognizes and builds on the skills that women bring from their years of caring for others. The organization allows staff members to nurture and support one another.

The organization is not similarly empowering for the residents. The emphasis on rigid house rules and the threat of expulsion for failing to conform recreate the oppressive conditions from which they have come. The norms inhibit reciprocal relationships between staff and residents from which both could benefit.

The organization contrasts markedly with what Gutierrez (1990) has identified as the hallmarks of empowerment-based social work practice.

> The basis of empowering practice is a helping relationship based on collabo-
> ration, trust, and the sharing of power. To avoid replicating the powerlessness
> that the client experiences with other helpers or professionals, it is critical
> that the worker perceive himself or herself as an enabler, an organizer, a
> consultant, or a compatriot with the client.   (151)

Other shelters have had difficulty fulfilling their original aspirations. As shelters have grown older, they have become more bureaucratic (Epstein, Russell, and Silvern 1988). External pressures (from funding bodies, boards of directors) "make it difficult to experiment and take risks" with shelter services (Dixon et al. 1982:62). Frustration with the slowness of consensual processes and external pressures from funding sources constrain shelters from operating as collectives (Wharton 1987).

Other collectivist organizations have shared a similar experience and a similar fate. What is unique about shelters for battered women is that, as originally conceptualized, all aspects of the shelter experience were de-signed to empower all the women who came into contact with it, both residents and staff. The organizational structure was not merely designed to enhance the lives of those who worked within it. Equally important was its role in providing a new, empowering environment for the women who sought refuge from abuse.

What appears to have occurred, at least in one shelter, is that the organizational environment empowers those who work in it far more than it does those who seek refuge within it. While the implicit philosophy of the shelter is that of empowerment, an unspoken, even unrecognized, atmosphere exists in which the organizational structure continues the historic oppression of women.

This oppression was not intentional. Shelter staff members were, by and large, well-meaning people who expressed genuine concern for the residents. And yet, these personal concerns are not always visible or consistently supported by the structure of the organization.

We understand the difficulties in maintaining a feminist commitment in both word and deed. Yet we do believe it is possible to resist the pressure to be co-opted. Rodriguez (1988) provides an example of one such shelter that has managed, despite financial pressures and internal difficulties, to maintain its feminist commitment to empower women. It differs markedly from the shelter we have described. First, staff members remain committed to a cooperative, nonhierarchical organizational structure. All staff members are formerly battered women who work together to consensually make all administrative decisions. Furthermore, all staff members earn the same hourly wage. While there is a board, it plays a minimal role in the running of the shelter. Second, the residents are treated as responsible adults, allowed to set their own rules and make their own decisions. They are responsible for performing all household chores and for negotiating with one another for how they are to be carried out. While the shelter has a "no drugs and no violence" policy, women are rarely turned away unless they are seriously disruptive. Nor are limits set on the length of time a woman may stay at the shelter. Women are consistently supported in making their own decisions, even if those decisions are not thought to be in their best interests. As an example, residents are allowed to invite visitors to the shelter, even if the visitor is the man who abused them. Since staff members are formerly battered women, they provide powerful role models and develop strong relationships with the residents. And finally, the shelter itself clearly articulates its feminist philosophy, both to the residents (in ongoing consciousness-raising groups) and in the community, by serving as a locus for other feminist activities.

Although maintaining a commitment to feminist principles in an otherwise unsupportive environment is difficult, evidence exists that this is possible. It can only occur, however, only if structured opportunities are available for staff and residents to reaffirm what has brought them together. One shelter we know has multiple opportunities to do this. Residents and staff come together each day for "coffee mornings" where they can together deal with the ongoing issues of what it is like to live together and can reinforce ways in which the residents can live together nonviolently. Every month, former residents and staff members as well as other feminists in the community come to the shelter to talk with residents and staff about broader issues affecting women in the local community and larger society. Each month staff members from other shelters join together to reflect on how they are accomplishing the task of providing shelter for and empowering battered women. In this same shelter, a clear commitment exists to value the contributions that residents can make to the community itself.

This study supports the value of qualitative approaches to research. By our living within the shelter, listening to the contradictions between word and deed, hearing the subtleties in the verbal and nonverbal communications, the presence of a dual organizational structure emerged: one for the staff, the other for the residents. Qualitative research was valuable for another reason. By engaging in a dialogue with staff and residents, everybody began to ask questions about the organization and whether it was indeed operating as intended. Davis (1987) found that the dialogical nature of qualitative research provided a welcome opportunity for service providers to reflect on the ways in which they constructed the issue of wife abuse.

Davis and Hagen (1989) have observed that, if we are not to return to privatizing women's issues, we must continually assess how ideology affects both social policy and the models that guide our direct work with clients. This study further suggests the need to similarly assess how ideology affects the organizational environment in which services are delivered. When qualitative research is combined with a feminist standpoint, the many ways in which we may inadvertently fall back into traditional, patriarchal, organizational structures that oppress women are made visible.

REFERENCES

Davis. L. V. 1987. Serving Battered Women: A National Study. Unpublished.
Davis, L. V. 1987. Views of wife abuse: Does the research method make a difference? *Affilia: Journal of Women and Social Work* 2: 53–66.
Davis, L. V. and J. L. Hagen. 1988. Services for battered women: The public policy response. *Social Service Review* 62: 649–67.
Davis, L. V. and J. L. Hagen. 1989. The problem of wife abuse: The interrelationship of policy and practice. Paper presented at the 35th Annual Program Meeting of the Council on Social Work Education, March 3–7. Chicago.
Dixon, G., C. Johnson, J. Leigh, and N. Turnbull. 1982. Feminist perspectives and practice. In G. Craig, N. Derricourt, and M. Loney, eds., *Community Work and the State*. London: Routledge and Kegan.
Dobash, P. R. and E. R. Dobash. 1979. *Violence Against Wives: A Case Against the Patriarchy*. New York: Free Press.
Epstein, S., G. Russell, and L. Silvern. 1988. Structure and ideology of shelters for battered women. *American Journal of Community Psychology* 16: 343–67.
Ferraro, J. K. 1983. Negotiating trouble in a battered women's shelter. *Urban Life* 12: 287–306.

Flax, J. 1987. Postmodernism and gender relations in feminist theory. *Signs: Journal of Women in Culture and Society* 12: 621–43.

Gutierrez, M. L. 1990. Working with women of color: An empowerment perspective. *Social Work* 35: 149–53.

Harding, S. 1991. *Whose Science? Whose Knowledge? Thinking from Women's Lives.* Ithaca, N.Y.: Cornell University Press.

Hooks, B. 1984. *Feminist Theory: From Margin to Center.* Boston: South End Press.

Johnson, M. J. 1981. Program enterprise and official cooptation in the battered women's shelter movement. *American Behavioral Scientist* 24: 827–42.

Reinharz, S. 1992. *Feminist Methods in Social Research.* New York: Oxford University Press.

Rodriguez, N. M. 1988. A successful feminist shelter: A case study of the Family Crisis Shelter in Hawaii. *The Journal of Applied Behavioral Science* 24: 235–50.

Schechter, S. 1982. *Women and Male Violence: The Visions and Struggles of the Battered Women's Movement.* Boston: South End Press.

Stanley, L. and S. Wise, 1990. Method, methodology, and epistemology in feminist research process. In L. Stanley, ed., *Feminist Praxis: Research, Theory and Epistemology in Feminist Sociology,* pp. 20–60. London: Routledge.

THIRTY-ONE

Commentary: Managing the Organizational Context in Qualitative Research

Bonnie E. Carlson

Although much has been written about qualitative research, relatively little has been said in a systematic way about the organizational context of such research. This is an especially important issue for knowledge development in social work because so much of social work research is carried out within the context of organizational settings. In fact, undoubtedly social agencies can be said to be the major organizational contexts or settings where social work practice research, both quantitative and qualitative, is carried out. In that sense agencies are probably at least as influential as university settings in their impact on all aspects of the research process. This paper addresses neglected aspects of the organizational context that should be carefully considered by qualitative researchers, particularly those aspects of the "untidy world" found in child and family agencies.

One question that might be asked is whether organizational context issues are uniquely relevant to qualitative research in contrast to traditional quantitative research, and if so, how. Having done numerous quantitative studies using data obtained through social agencies and other human service organizations, I can say that organizational context issues exist any time a researcher enters such a setting with the hope of conducting a research study. Thus, all subsequent observations and suggestions are potentially relevant to any social scientist engaged in applied research in organizational settings.

Context is especially important in qualitative methodology, which assumes that human behavior is best studied in the settings where it occurs (Marshall and Rossman 1989). Thus, viewed within this paradigm, social work practice issues are best studied, not in the laboratory, but rather in the agency settings where they naturally manifest themselves. Likewise, clients are best studied in the natural environments where they interact or receive services, such as hospitals, schools, prisons, and so forth. What are the implications of these distinctive features of qualitative research for organizational context?

The greater salience of context for qualitative research demands that attention be paid to the organizational setting where the study is being conducted. By its very nature the research will affect both the setting and those who interact there and be affected by the setting despite efforts of the researchers and requests at the setting to be as unobtrusive as possible. However, this set of reciprocal influences does not necessarily have negative implications for the research process. In fact, in my view, qualitative research may have greater potential for being a positive experience for the host setting than quantitative research has. Two features in particular may make agencies and other organizations more receptive to a qualitative than to a traditional quantitative study: flexibility and the ability to analyze and interpret the data (and modify the study) as they are being collected. The latter enables the organization to obtain early feedback about what is being learned, while flexibility offers the possibility of the setting's having constructive input into the research process.

On the other hand, qualitative data collection sometimes lasts a long time since it does not entail performing a discrete experiment or administering a set of questionnaires. This can be disruptive to an organization and necessitates what Marshall and Rossman (1989) call "role management," as discussed below.

Having established the importance of attention to the organizational context within which one is conducting research, I now must identify the relevant dimensions of that environment. First, the type of organization and its primary goals are important. Is it a traditional social agency in which social work roles and functions are primary, such as the child welfare agency discussed by Maluccio and Fein? Or is it a setting where social work plays a secondary role, such as a hospital or school, or one where social work as a profession has little or no presence at all, such as the battered women's shelter studied by Davis?

Other dimensions of organizational context that should be considered are size, power structure and chain of command, and the broader political climate within which the agency operates. For example, to enter a battered women's shelter without specific knowledge of the politics of providing shelter services to this population, as well as the larger feminist political context within in such services are framed, would be foolhardy and naive. Likewise, conducting a research study in a relatively small organization like a shelter would bear only limited resemblance to studying inmates in a large, complex bureaucracy such as a state correctional facility or to discharge planning in a major urban hospital.

The remainder of this paper focuses on suggestions for how qualitative researchers can most effectively cope with or manage the organizational environment within which they are conducting research. Examples may be found in Shaffir and Stebbin's (1991) *Experiencing Fieldwork.*

Gaining entrée to a setting is the first important concern that must be addressed, since obtaining access to the setting is a prerequisite to being able to conduct the research (Marshall and Rossman 1989; Shaffir and Stebbins 1991). This is a particular concern for social work researchers in light of the long-standing suspicion many practitioners have about research. Generally it will involve a great deal of time- and energy-consuming negotiations and compromise, as Maluccio and Fein note. However, the personal relationships that are formed with institutional gatekeepers will be critical in determining whether access will be granted (Shaffir and Stebbins 1991). Becoming as familiar as possible with the different dimensions of the organization mentioned above is advisable before one attempts to negotiate entry (Gurney 1991). Self-presentation is extremely important, and Shaffir and Stebbins (1991) have observed that success at this stage is as much a function of one's interpersonal skills and organizational sensitivity or sophistication as it is of the nature and quality of the proposed project. If all goes well, these negotiations should eventuate in an informal agreement or understanding, or even a formal contract, that will spell out what both the researcher and the setting agree to do.

Once the researcher has gained entry into the organization and the project is initiated, attention must be devoted to maintaining relationships with contacts in the organizational setting, or what has been called role management (Marshall and Rossman 1989). The nature of those relationships will strongly influence both the quantity and quality of data gathered subsequently. Establishing rapport with all potential research participants is important because the researcher needs their cooperation, which is in turn dependent on their willingness to trust the researcher with sensitive, personal information (Shaffir and Stebbins 1991). The importance of building trust is addressed by Maluccio and Fein in their paper. Establishment of good relations is also important because data collection may continue over a lengthy period of time, and participants may experience frustration with the demands of the study or lose interest in what initially seemed like a promising idea.

This raises the issue of reciprocity, which appears to be more relevant to qualitative than it is to quantitative research. Because so much is being asked of participants in terms of sharing personal information and world views, it is important that the researcher acknowledge this and demonstrate a willingness to reciprocate (Marshall and Rossman 1989; Shaffir and Stebbins 1991). The nature of this reciprocation is difficult to specify because it will depend so much on the nature of the study and the setting. At the very least a commitment to share the findings in a formal way should be made, as well as acknowledgment of those who participated. Other forms of reciprocation include attendance at staff meetings and willingness to serve on agency committees, as mentioned by Fein and Maluccio; being a volunteer to the agency while serving as a participant observer, which Davis mentions; and offering to share one's professional expertise with organizational staff through pro bono in-service trainings or workshops.

Some final thoughts pertain to issues surrounding one's exit from the setting where the research has been carried out. Here again, some differences between qualitative and quantitative studies are apparent because of the kinds of relationships often formed between qualitative researchers and those they study. Being a participant-observer is quite different from administering a questionnaire, precisely because one has been a participant. When one interacts with research subjects over a period of time, a relationship develops (Taylor 1991). The researcher affects the life of the person being studied and may in turn be affected by the intimate and personal details learned about those being studied. In such cases leaving may bear more resemblance to terminating with a client than simply completing the data collection phase of a research study.

This paper has addressed the neglected issue of attending to the organizational context in conducting qualitative research. Some of the features that distinguish qualitative from traditional qualitative research, such as length of data collection and nature of the relationships formed between the researchers and subjects, and that have implications for managing the organizational context have been identified. At the same time, it was acknowledged that those carrying out quantitative research in agencies or other organizational settings could also benefit from attention to these concerns. Several dimensions of the organizational context were identified that qualitative researchers should attend to. Finally, suggestions were offered regarding gaining access to potential research settings and subsequent role management and regarding leaving qualitative research settings.

REFERENCES

Gurney, J. M. 1991. Female researchers in male-dominated settings. In W. B. Shaffir and R. A. Stebbins, eds., *Experiencing Fieldwork: An Inside View of Qualitative Research*, pp. 53–61. Newbury Park, Calif.: Sage.

Marshall, C. and G. B. Rossman. 1989. *Designing Qualitative Research.* Newbury Park, Calif.: Sage.

Shaffir, W. B. and R. A. Stebbins. 1991. In Shaffir and Stebbins, eds., *Experiencing Fieldwork:* Newbury Park, Calif.: Sage.

Taylor, S. J. 1991. Leaving the field: Research relationships and responsibilities. In W. B. Shaffer and R. A. Stebbins, eds., *Experiencing Fieldwork: An Inside View of Qualitative Research*, pp. 238–247. Newbury Park, Calif.: Sage.

MENTAL HEALTH

THIRTY-TWO

Paradigm for Research in Context: An Example from Mental Health

Peter J. Johnson

Many subjects of critical importance to social work must employ strictly quantitative methods and all the accompanying scientific conventions. For instance, to dramatize the effects of welfare cuts, the extent of child abuse, the effects of discrimination, and a myriad of other social problems, it is necessary to present the hard facts of malnutrition; increased hospital admissions, psychiatric diagnoses, or deaths; and lifetime earning potential, life expectancy rates, or infant mortality rates. This paper begins with the assumption that some other areas of social work, especially the nature of social agency practice and the person-in-environment interface, are not adequately captured by accepted scientific procedures.

Although some have called for the development of competing alternatives to accepted methodologies as though qualitative and quantitative approaches are incompatible, some rigorous integration of the two already exists. This has been demonstrated in Jules-Rosette's work (1978a, 1978b) in which she sought a rapprochement between empirical social sciences and folk inquiry. She placed the two systems of knowledge on equal ground and documented their similarities in shaping the decisions on which knowledge can be built.

TABLE 32.1
Jules-Rosette's Stages of Knowledge and Derived Research Principles

A. The conception of a theory
 1. Interactive theory development
 2. A theory's self-assessment
 3. Sociolinguistics
 4. Study in context

B. Encounter with another thought form
 1. "Going native"
 2. Recording
 3. Referring back to the initial model
 4. Explicating the other thought form

C. Interpretation and evaluation
 1. Return to an analytic stance
 2. Reestablish scientific criteria of adequacy
 3. Accept the legitimacy of alternative explanations

D. Communication
 1. Develop a lexicon that captures the experience
 2. Revise the initial model
 3. Shed the veil of objectivity
 4. Data display

THE STAGES OF KNOWLEDGE

Jules-Rosette explicated four stages of knowledge that form the basis of an epistemology for research in natural settings. She discussed how this epistemology could bridge the gap between science and folk inquiry. The same framework is applied in this paper to connect research and social work practice. The framework is briefly explicated and is applied to social work, and then strategies for research are developed. Jules-Rosette's epistemology and research principles derived for this paper are depicted in table 32.1.

The Conception of a Theory

Theoretical openness allows the investigator, as an intellectual detective, to follow up on leads suggested by serendipitous findings and to reformulate the conceptual model in the process. This is an ethnographic approach to producing knowledge, for it assumes an interaction between the culture of the researcher and the culture of the informant on equal grounds and thus reduces the usual social distance between researcher and "subject" (Mehan and Wood 1975). Four research principles are derived from the conception stage of knowledge.

Interactive theory development. Although the awareness that alternative theories are acceptable may be a hallmark of science, it is often difficult for the social scientist to reach such openness without the fear of having succumbed to subjectivity. Jules-Rosette advised that, at this stage, researchers view themselves as ''an apprentice in the topics investigated'' and that an ''intersubjective exchange'' would follow. This exchange ''can never be complete, nor should it be'' (1978a:565).

A theory's self-assessment. Self-assessment requires that the initial causal framework be open to reformulation in the process of the study based on the interaction of the researcher and prior conceptualization with informants and their construction of reality.

Sociolinguistics. Cross-cultural researchers are constrained for obvious reasons to learn the language of the people they plan to study. But semantic differences exist within cultures and subcultures as well.

Study in context. The meaning and utilization of knowledge depend on rapidly changing historical contexts and an inexhaustible multiplicity of social contexts. Human events can be understood only within their own socially grounded rules for defining, categorizing, doing, and interpreting. The challenge that emerges is to develop context-sensitive methods of observation, analysis, and reporting. A basic tenet here is to go to the site where events naturally occur rather than to simulate events or simply to survey peoples' recollections or orientations.

Encounter with Another Thought Form

The second state in an epistemology for research in context is discovery, or ''the full encounter of another thought form in an effort to understand it on its own grounds'' (Jules-Rosette 1978a:554). The stage of discovery and the principles of involvement implied by it allow for more thorough exposition, reexamination, and reformulation of the underlying principles in the original framework. In this epistemology, knowledge essentially is produced in experiences with informants.

Some specific research strategies and principles are implied by this stage of knowledge. They are: becoming immersed in the other culture or ''going native," recording, referring back to the initial model, and beginning an effort to explicate the other thought form.

"Going native."   As Jules-Rosette explained, "Discovery . . . embraces the dangerous, boundary-breaking process of 'going native,' that is, of attempting to exchange subjective positions with the other in order to experience a situation as he does" (1978a:554).

A continuum is present in this experiential strategy ranging from observation to participation and to provocation. Each strategy requires, however, a letting go of the myth of neutrality, an implicit or explicit presentation of the investigator's theory, and a detailed account of the physical, interpersonal, temporal, and political context of the study.

Recording.   Promptly recorded field notes, such as daily entries in a research journal, are indispensable. Audiotapes can be useful, especially when extensive factual information is being gathered, but the presence of the recorder changes the context of the interaction. Field notes are usually voluminous in qualitative research and are the "raw data" that are subjected later to analytic inductions. Data overload is often the bane of qualitative researchers.

Techniques to record the quality of field records and also to reduce the volume of data that are recorded can be found in Huberman and Miles (1983).

Referring back to the initial model.   The mutual evaluation across forms of thought can have a powerful effect on the initial conceptual framework, and unexpected findings tempt constant revision of the model. It is useful to preserve the essence of the original model in some form as a fixed point of reference to ground one's thinking in the midst of the experiential phase. The researcher could use the device of a standard set of questions and the standard presentation of visual aids at all sites. This also allows for more easily reduced comparisons within the study.

Explicating the other thought form.   Immersing oneself in the culture of others and repeated comparison with the initial conceptual model lead to tentative knowledge of the other thought structure. At this stage, the investigator makes beginning efforts to outline the thought structure of the informants, e.g., their explicit and tacit priorities and values, preferred types of evidence and reasoning, aspects of experience that are accepted on faith, and so forth.

Interpretation and Evaluation

The attempts to exchange subjective positions and to experience situations as informants do yield to evaluation or interpretation across the different forms of thought. The researcher must find ways to bridge scientific theory with the experience gained in the discovery phase. Jules-Rosette admonished:

> If the researcher becomes completely drawn into the doctrine, cosmology, or system studied, one may legitimately inquire about the line to be drawn between sheer advocacy of the new-found belief and investigation of it. Discovery does not ensure total understanding of an alternative thought form. It does not improve either appraisal or the ability to return to an analytic stance.   (1978a:555)

Return to an analytic stance. This cognitive step requires a less personal, if not impersonal, assessment of the data gathered in the encounter stage. The researcher poses the original questions from the new perspective gained. This principle fits under the hermeneutic concepts of translation and understanding. Translation is the interpretive process of "bringing to understanding." Palmer discussed this process as follows:

> One brings what is foreign, strange, or unintelligible (even from within same-language situations and ostensibly the same broader culture) into the medium of one's own language. . . . Translation, then, makes us conscious of the clash of our own world of understanding and that in which the work (here, the research context) is operating.   (1969:27, 30)

The analytical stance in this stage of research is ineluctably personal. The scrutiny thus may be more difficult than in the discussion of findings in more conventional research.

Reestablish scientific criteria of adequacy. Now that researchers consider their experiences and impressions and informants' statements as data, questions must be raised about their adequacy. How complete is the documentation? Is the evidence capable of public disconfirmation? Were unusual circumstances present that should be reported? Does the amount of information gathered warrant the partitioning of data or the ultimate conclusions? Do others agree with the partitioning of themes or conclusions?

Accept the legitimacy of alternative explanations.   Because the researcher encountered the worldview of informants in their natural context, the experience of an alternate interpretation is always present for the researcher. Jules-Rosette illustrated how a phenomenon, such as lightning, could be assessed in two different systems—witchcraft and atmospheric disturbance—without logical contradiction: "The label of natural occurrence may linger in the scientist's mind, but the experience of an alternate interpretation is always present" (1978a:566).

Communication

The final stage in an epistemology for research in context is communication to the larger audience of persons who have not been "immersed" in the experience. This requires a lexicon that captures both the ethnographic material and its subsequent conceptualization, "a translucent vocabulary through which all the layers of experience and thought become visible" (Jules-Rosette 1978a:555). In this epistemology, there is complete acceptance of the validity of the other form of thought and simultaneously a revision of the original conceptual model.

The communication state of knowledge implies four principles for research.

Develop a lexicon that captures the experience.   A lexicon requires a discussion of the conclusions of the research that captures the nuances of experience, is capable of verification by scientists and confirmation by the lay persons studied, and can be used as feedback to the initial sources.

Revise the initial model.   The interpreted experience can be considered as evidence for expanding, revising, or even rejecting the original model or conceptual framework.

Shedding the veil of objectivity.   This shedding involves the acceptance of critical self-analysis of the investigator's presence to and merging with the objects of description and a rejection of the unquestioned correspondence between "objective facts" and theory. This can be juxtaposed with the failure to report, or the alleged suppression of the influence to the investigator as a person in controlled trials, e.g., using symptom checklists or minimizing "Hawthorne effects" of the study situation.

Data display.   Huberman and Miles (1983) have developed several techniques for illustrating voluminous qualitative data in various matrices and figures from within-site and cross-site analyses in large studies.

ILLUSTRATIVE STUDY

I have been interested in learning more about how societal values and norms are reflected in the espoused and operative emphases of social agencies and in the attitudes and activities of program staff. Such knowledge could help refine theories of management of disability and illness. I have assumed elsewhere that there would be a direct reflection of societal values in agencies' and practitioners' goals (Johnson 1983). Much has been written about the low priority given to the 1.7 to 2.4 million chronically mentally ill (CMI) in this country (Goldman, Gattozzi, and Taube 1981). It is tempting to suspect that the low priority given to severely disabled psychiatric patients is an effect of the pervasive values in a reluctant welfare state toward persons who have no record or prognosis for economic productivity and of how those values affect programs and professional staff. The extent of a causal relation of general societal values to specific program or practitioner values was too unwieldy to be submitted to a controlled investigation. But it is known that the United States is a reluctant welfare state (Wilensky and Lebeaux 1965) by international standards and that CMI have a comparatively low quality of life and are not aggressively cared for in most programs (Lamb 1981; Rubin and Johnson 1982; Williams, Bellis, and Wellington 1980). Would the situation be different in a general societal

TABLE 32.2

Questions Asked to Patients in Community Programs in Sweden

---

1. Please describe your use of the program.

2. What do you like most about it?

3. What things don't you like about it?

4. Please describe your life outside the hospital compared to inside the hospital.

5. Where do you live? Is it comfortable? Do you live alone? With family or friends?

6. How do you pay the rent?

7. If you are lonely, do you have friends to call?

8. How are your meals? Where do you eat? With whom?

9. Do you feel comfortable in this town? *Everywhere*/here?

10. Which places do you go to the most?

11. How is your physical health? How do you get health care?

12. How is your economic situation?

13. Would you say that you're satisfied or happy? If not, what things keep you from being happy? What do you need more of or less of to be satisfied or happy?

TABLE 32.3
*Questions Asked to Program Management and Staff and to the Government
Planners and Patient Advocacy Group Representatives in Sweden*

1. Please describe your program(s) or intended programs(s).

2. What are/will be the auspices of the program(s)?

3. What are the things you want the program to achieve?

4. Which of these goals do you emphasize? Why?

5. Which of these goals are closest to what your patients seem to want?

6. Which of these goals are closest to what your sponsors (board of directors, legislators) seem to want?

7. Where do you stand on the cure vs. care issue? Where does psychotherapy fit, if at all? Where does chemotherapy fit, if at all?

8. Can you give examples of staff advocacy for better social conditions for your members?

9. Please explicitly discuss the place of employment training in your program.

10. Which social supports has (will) your program develop(ed)?

11. Describe the quality of life for your patients. What definitely facilitates their QOL?

12. Which chronic mental patients are you NOT able to serve?

13. Describe for me the ideal program, its components and processes.

environment that was generous in its social provision? Would policymakers, programs directors, and line staff emphasize quality of life (QOL) as a program goal for chronic patients, and would this be corroborated by patients' satisfaction with their care? To answer these questions, I went to Sweden, which has the highest expenditure per capita on health care in the world and a ranking of 7 on Estes's (1984) Index of Social Progress (compared with a ranking of 42 for the United States) and which was just beginning a large-scale deinstitutionalization effort.

The best research design remained elusive, but I went to Sweden in May 1983 with several questions in mind and certain conceptions of the topic I planned to study. A set of questions I planned to ask patients appears in table 32.2. They are drawn from the "life domains" framework of Baker and Intagliata (1982:77) and from a consensus of current literature about the needs of the CMI.

I planned a different set of questions to program staff, managers, government planners, and patients' advocacy group staff. These questions appear in table 32.3 and draw from a wide range of current literature about deinstitutionalization in the United States. I also planned to collect and examine as many existing materials, such as program descriptions and evaluations, as were available.

I decided to investigate all the institutional and community programs in one geographic area. I would observe and interview staff and patients in the geographic area of Stockholm and Uppsala (forty-five miles apart). This was where I had quickest access to informants because this area had the most programs in the country in numbers and diversity, allowing for relatively good saturation in the two months available for on-site data collection, and because the location of the central government there would facilitate interviews with officials. The informants and sites of interviews and observations were planned in advance to include, at a minimum, one psychosocial rehabilitation program, at least two other community support programs, and at least two psychiatric institutions. Although I planned questions and scheduled some sites in advance, I anticipated that many other questions and sites would emerge and that my understanding of the problem could change through the process of discovery.

Conception of a Theory

Some aspects of my conceptualization of comprehensive community-based care needed to be reconsidered almost immediately after I arrived in Sweden. In the United States, the deinstitutionalization movement has been incremental in the last three decades. Sweden, on the other hand, was considering widescale deinstitutionalization as a discrete choice. A phrase of a prominent social psychiatrist I interviewed was "10,000 tomorrow," which conveyed his belief that almost half of Sweden's institutional population of 21,000 could be discharged immediately with no adverse effects on the patients or society. The back-wards-to-back-alleys phenomenon in the United States would make such a suggestion seem ludicrous here. But on the basis of my observational research in Sweden this assumption had been rejected and my whole conceptual model needed quick adjustment.

Some major planks in my framework that I needed to realign were (1) the role of *work* (No patients reported any stigma for not working, yet most wanted very much to have a job. Competition for jobs was intense, but unemployment was very low at 2.8 percent); (2) hospitalization (Sweden's hospitalization rate has been high in all areas of illness and its psychiatric hospitalization rate of 4300 per 100,000 [Brinck and Östman 1982] is three times as high as that of the United States at 1400 per 100,000) (Kiesler 1982); (3) psychoanalysis and psychotherapy (Both play a very minor role in Sweden relative to the United States); and (4) the relationship of health and psychiatric care and social services (Health and social services are highly integrated at institutional levels. There is extensive outreach by social services, which perform the same case management services, though not titled as such, that have become part of mental health systems in the United States).

With respect to sociolinguistics, I developed a beginning proficiency in Swedish for this study. Because most Swedes speak some English, many interviews had elements of both languages. Even when the interview as mostly in English, the interviewee seemed more receptive to me because I had made the effort to learn the host country language. In addition to gaining respect, learning the language has merit for its sociolinguistic aspects. This had dramatic implications in my study. Ideas such as "hospital care" have special meaning in a country with the highest expenditures for capita on health care in the world. But even this notion had significantly different connotations for different groups. A liberal professor of social welfare whom I interviewed was proud of Sweden's hospitalization rate; a psychiatrist was pleased because it meant more opportunities for clinical research; for leaders of a patients' advocacy group (the Department for Social and Mental Health), the hospitalization rate meant a vile deprivation of liberty.

The importance of research in the context of the issues is obvious in my study. Survey responses, recidivism rates, and answers to my scheduled interview questions were not as rich in meaning as spending time at two hospitals in Dalarna and Uppsala were. Their beauty and comfort were like more expensive private hospitals in the United States. This made the charges of inhumane care by the patients' advocacy groups and social psychiatrists all the more striking.

Another example of research in context was to spend time with some deinstitutionalized patients in their apartments and favorite cafes, where I could get first-hand information about the high quality of public housing and the ease of sitting calmly in a public place for hours without feeling ridiculed for not working.

The fact that the sixty-four professionals and forty-six patients I spoke with unanimously told me that material resources were not a barrier to QOL in Sweden is impressive and in stark contrast to the situation in the United States, but its meaning or actuality is not as stunning when patients' lives in the community are observed and experienced.

Encounter with Another Thought Form

Encountering another thought form is more complex and intellectually and personally demanding than standard observational methods, no matter how exhaustive and detailed they are. I participated in 135 hours of discussions with forty-six patients and sixty-four professionals in two psychiatric institutions (Dalarna and Ulleråkers), a psychosocial rehabilitation program (Fountain House, Stockholm), two community support programs (Nacka Project and Club Lindormen), a halfway house (Dalarna), community apartments for patients (Uppsala), at government offices (Court of Social Insurance in Stockholm), and at the patients' advocacy group "RSMH," Riksforbundet for Social och Mental Halsa (the Swedish Association for Social and Mental Health). To the extent that I wanted a saturated exposure to all programs in one area, I succeeded.

Two aspects of my immersion experience are particularly illustrative. First, I participated in many exceedingly intense discussions among patients and staff in all my contacts over the issue of biological versus social psychiatry. With very few exceptions people took a definitive position in one camp or the other. The biological psychiatrists represented careful planning, insistence on experimental research for the basis of any changes in institutionalization policies, and, of course, the neurophysiological bases of mental illness. They have always dominated Swedish Psychiatry (Brinck and Östman 1982; Lachman 1970). The social psychiatry camp included many patients and RSMH members, social workers, psychologists, and a minority of psychiatrists. The discussions over these issues were fierce. The social psychiatry position was fervently ideological and included no specific strategies for community care. The "inmates" must be given their freedom and the rest will take care of itself, an official of RSMH told me. The titles of RSMH pamphlets convey the intensity of the social psychiatry camp: *Psychiatric Manifesto; Revenge!;* and *The Blessed Violence—About the Hypocrisy and the Brutality, About the Breaking-up and the Explosive Force in the Mental Ward. The Blessed Violence* has a picture on its cover of a building, presumably a psychiatric institution, being demolished.

In most of my contacts, including those with patients, the social versus biological psychiatry issue had been an ongoing discussion. In most of the contacts in which I was either interviewer or observer, and during four programs in which I lectured to professional groups, people sought to establish which side I was on. Because I did not have strong agreement with either position and because I thought it was none of my business, I demurred. But it was exceedingly difficult to remain neutral in the midst of the heated discussions. The social psychiatry proponents perceived my comprehensive list of questions, my review of the mixed success of deinstitutionalization, and my more provocative queries ("You say half the patients can be discharged right now. But en masse deinstitutionalization has failed elsewhere. What makes you think it will work here?") as being opposed to their point of view. The biological psychiatrists, when exposed to my comprehensive and data-based approach to the subject, thought I was closer to their point of view. I was told, "We (biological psychiatrists) can understand you. You take a scientific approach to this." The experience of being in the middle of the debate was an intellectual and personal strain. From the perspective as a researcher drilled in quantitative methods, I thought I was not getting enough specific information. Professionals could not retreat from the ideological fervor long enough to help me administer QOL scales to patients. But from the perspective of qualitative–ethnographic methods I was getting good data. Perhaps more was to be learned from the informants' inability to focus on, plan, and administer collaboratively the QOL scales than in the statistics that might have been generated by the scales.

A second example of experiential research was my visiting with patients in community coffee shops and their apartments. This was especially useful in getting a sense of the physical comfort in these patients' lives, the absence of rebuke from community members for being unemployed, and also their loneliness.

I made eighteen hours of audiotapes of interviews and meetings and filled 125 pages of handwritten field notes. This was a relatively small amount of recording for a field study. Below is a sample entry:

> Fernando is 40. He is articulate. Speaks five languages fluently. His lips are swollen, probably from medication. Unexpectedly threw a knife at his roommate prior to his last hospitalization. Visited him in his apartment. Very comfortable, spacious, new. Provided by the community government. Also gets a $400 disability pension each month. His four sisters were mutilated by a junta in Argentina. Four of his six girlfriends committed suicide. He conveys that he has been through hell, but he is hopeful about the future. He studies mathematics (free-of-charge) and paints. The ones of nude females are uninspired, like cartoons in "skin mags." The faces of the women do not appear in most of these.
>
> He spends his days visiting a sequence of coffee houses. He speaks eloquently of the ambiance in the various shops. He is surviving in comfort and safety. He is not even a Swede, but he is well cared for here.

I had two devices that permitted reference back to the initial model. The use of a standard set of questions with patients (table 32.2) and staff and planners (table 32.3) facilitated this. More specific statistical data regarding responses to these questions appear in Johnson (1991). Also, in the four presentations I made to professional groups about deinstitutionalization in the United States, I used many of the same visual aids (projected transparencies of definitions, outlines, figures, and tables). These promoted some continuity in the midst of the more spontaneous and serendipitous aspects of the study. The visual aids also could be thought of as a standard stimulus for comparison of responses among groups. One aspect of these that highlights the epistemological stage of "mutual evaluation across forms of thought" was my presentation of a definition of chronic mental illness that is widely referenced in the United States. This comprehensive definition includes reference to "functional incapacities which prevent or erode patients' abilities to work" (Goldman, Gattozzi, and Taube 1981:23). This was challenged everywhere I went. A group of neurophysiological researchers looked stunned when I presented the definition. One of them confronted me: "What is a patient's 'ability to work' doing in a scientific definition of a clinical syndrome?" We proceeded to discuss the social construction of scientific realities and how a country's value system may infiltrate its mental health practices.

Interpretation and Evaluation

The return to an analytic stance was a far more gradual and painstaking process than the writer's experience of retrieving survey data, preparing them for computerized statistical analysis, examining printouts, and setting up tables. There was a series of concentric circles as I moved from an experiential awareness based on my participation with informants through a rigorously subjective process of critically examining my own field notes to a data-based statement of findings.

I conducted a content analysis of my field notes and the available program documents and simple frequency counts of responses to the interview schedules. Upon inspecting these data, I concluded that I did not furnish as much detail as I would have liked for making more definitive statements about program operations and the practical aspects of the lives of the cohort of patients. There were many nonresponses to the interview schedules, usually because the respondents had not had to consider deinstitutionalization issues and because some informants were so polarized that they did not want to discuss details. With respect to establishing other scientific criteria of adequacy, I followed analytic induction procedures for setting up categories as prescribed by Kerlinger (1973:525–30) and by Selltiz, Wrightsman, and Cook (1976:458–73). After categories were set up, two research colleagues reviewed random samples of my field notes and audiotapes. The interrater agreement on the categorization of data was ninety percent.

An example of accepting the legitimacy of alternative explanations was in regard to the rhetoric of the social psychiatry proponents. Their goals, if enacted in the United States, could be disastrous here because no comprehensive system is in place to provide health and material supports for disabled persons in the community. Later I could accept their tactics as a way to challenge the hegemony of the biologically oriented psychiatrists. Then their epithets began to seem sensible and maybe necessary.

Communication

In developing a lexicon to merge my conceptual understanding of program tools in community-based care with my interpretation of encounters with my informants, five salient issues emerged in the content analysis of field notes and the frequency tabulation of interview responses. These are briefly summarized here:

1. *Polarization.* The exaggerated, dichotomous split within the mental health field over social and biological psychiatry in the early stages of deinstitutionalization in Sweden seemed to preclude methodical planning with a few exceptions.

2. *Civil libertarianism.* This was conspicuous in its absence as a device to resolve issues about commitment procedures, length of stay, use of chemotherapy, etc. Myrdal (1960) claimed, ''Americans need far more state legislation to lay down general rules for conduct in life and work than the more homogenous nations do'' (100).

3. *Social provision.* Lack of material resources was not viewed as a deterrent to QOL by anyone of the 110 people I met with, in sharp contrast to the United States, where inadequate food and shelter are the greatest deterrent to QOL of the CMI. The adequacy of material resources was so institutionalized as a right that it seemed to be assumed correctly by mental health planners that the physical survival of patients did not need to enter into program priorities.

4. *Lack of social support.* Of the forty-six patients I met, thirty-six reported that inadequate or nonexistent social support was their major problem in life. In a survey conducted by one community support program (Club Lindormen, Uppsala) of its members, the two most frequently mentioned benefits of the program (out of twenty-eight items) were *bryta isolering* (to break isolation) and *träffa människor i olika aldrar och med olika intressen* (to meet people of different ages and with different interests).

5. *The place of jobs.* Employment for members was viewed as the ultimate goal by one program, Fountain House in Stockholm. All my informants valued work for its psychological and social rewards, i.e., as a source of self-esteem and interpersonal relationships, not for its remuneration. There was not a feeling by any patient–informant that society expected him or her to hold a job. Tor-Bjorn, a thirty-five-year-old hospital patient, looked forward to resuming his avocation as a master chess player; Fernando painted, studied, and visited coffee shops; Sven-Erik was active as a member of the community support program and as a patient represen-

tative of RSMH. Work was not an issue for these "able-bodied" adult men. "Economic self-sufficiency" does not intrude into the socially constructed definition of pathology in Sweden and, with one exception, did not enter the program planning for community care.

Some will object to the mixture of phenomenological and positivist approaches outlined here. The case has been made that the exigencies of a human science require each posture. Pure phenomenological approaches capture the richness of historical, physical, and interactional context but can fail to develop the necessary social conventions for efficient dissemination of knowledge and the standards for the capability of public disconfirmability of findings. Positivistic approaches may detect systematic variance in social relations at the expense of accuracy about the dynamics of the person-in-environment interchange and the purposes, political powers, and mythical stories in which practice is based. Whether the field will shed its veil of objectivity and simultaneously expand its epistemology and make its science more open to alternative realities remains to be seen.

My findings forced me to reconsider the conceptual model of the role of the general societal environment in shaping the priorities in mental health programs. It is possible that there are other general environment features in Sweden directly reflected in priorities in the mental health programs in Stockholm and Uppsala. That possibility warrants further study. But on the basis of this study, I would have to reconsider the hypothesized relationship. Other factors that could possibly explain the finding were the sampling of available, and somewhat self-selected, patients; the interorganizational problems of the mix of programs in the geographical area I studied; and the early developmental stage of these programs.

Recent critiques of social work research have created the opportunity to examine the governing norms in the profession's epistemology. But the critiques have not explicated specific alternatives for a broader epistemology or for research methodology. It is hoped that the application of Jules-Rosette's stages of knowledge to social work and the writer's derivation of research principles will move the discussion forward.

REFERENCES

Baker, F. and J. Intagliata. 1982. Quality of life in the evaluation of community support systems. *Evaluation and Program Planning* 5: 69–79.

Brinck, U. and O. Östman. 1982. Psychiatric care in Sweden. *Svenska Institutet,* no. 291.

Estes, R. 1984. In quality of life, Denmark ranks first, Ethiopia last, U.S. in the middle.

Press release of summary of research. Philadelphia: *University of Pennsylvania News* (August 20).

Goldman, H. H., A. A. Gattozzi, and C. A. Taube. 1981. Defining and counting the chronically mentally ill. *Hospital and Community Psychiatry* 32, no. 1: 21–28.

Huberman, M. and M. D. Miles. 1983. Drawing valid meaning from qualitative data: Some techniques of data reduction and display. *Quality and Quantity* 17: 282–96.

Johnson, P. J. 1983. Community support systems for deinstitutionalized patients. In L. L. Bachrach, ed., *New Directions in Mental Health: Deinstitutionalization,* pp. 81–92. San Francisco: Jossey-Bass.

Johnson, P. J. 1991. Emphasis on quality of life of people with severe mental illness in community-based care in Sweden. Psychosocial Rehabilitation Journal 14, no. 4: 23–27.

Jules-Rosette, B. 1978a. The veil of objectivity. *American Anthropologist* 80: 549–70.

Jules-Rosette, B. 1978b. The politics of paradigms: Contrasting theories of consciousness and society. *Human Studies* 1: 92–110.

Kerlinger, F. 1973. *Foundations of Behavioral Research.* 2d ed. New York: Holt, Rinehart and Winston.

Kiesler, C. A. 1982. Public and professional myths about mental hospitalization. *American Psychologist* 37: 1323–39.

Lachman, J. H. 1970. Swedish and American Psychiatry: A comparative view. *American Journal of Psychiatry* 126: 119–23.

Lamb, H. R. 1981. What did we really expect from deinstitutionalization? *Hospital and Community Psychiatry* 32, no. 2: 105–09.

Mehan, H. B. and H. Wood. 1975. *The Reality of Ethno-methodology.* New York: Wiley.

Myrdal, G. 1960. *Beyond the Welfare State.* New Haven, Conn.: Yale University Press.

Palmer, R. E. 1969. *Hermeneutics.* Evanston, Ill.: Northwestern University Press.

Rubin, A.. and P. J. Johnson. 1982. Practitioner orientations to the chronically disabled: Prospects for policy implementation. *Administration in Mental Health* 10: 3–12.

Selltiz, C., L. S. Wrightsman, and S. W. Cook. 1976. *Research Methods in Social Relations.* 3d ed. New York: Holt, Rinehart and Winston.

Wilensky, N. L. and C. N. Lebeaux. 1965. *Industrial Society and Social Welfare.* New York: Free Press.

Williams, D. H., E. C. Bellis, and S. W. Wellington. 1980. Deinstitutionalization and social policy: Historic perspectives and present dilemmas. *American Journal of Orthopsychiatry* 50: 54–64.

THIRTY-THREE

Amplifying the Consumer Voice: Qualitative Methods, Empowerment, and Mental Health Research

Charles A. Rapp, Walter Kisthardt, Elizabeth Gowdy, and James Hanson

As if responding to Wintersteen's (1986) call for accepting a leadership role, social work is increasingly becoming the dominant profession in the community care and rehabilitation of people with severe mental illness. More social workers are employed by community support programs than any other profession. The last decade has witnessed a substantial growth in specialized course work in M.S.W. curriculums (Ewalt and Rapp 1987) and social work research in this area (Rubin 1984; Videka-Sherman 1988). Virtually all the reported research uses quantitative methods.

The thesis of this paper is that social work research and evaluation are not value neutral and that it should be conducted in a manner that supports the consumer empowerment social agenda. The paper describes how current research not only does not support consumer empowerment but actually does injustice to it. An initial framework for empowering research strategies is presented. In addition, three studies using qualitative methods are described and their role in fostering the empowerment social agenda highlighted.

RESEARCH STRATEGIES FOR CLIENT EMPOWERMENT

It is well established that research is a value-based enterprise. That requires no rehash here. Social work research and evaluation must not only be reflective of good science but must also contribute to the empowerment of those we seek to help. Empowerment is defined as "an intentional, ongoing process centered in the local community, involving mutual respect, critical reflection, caring, and group participation, through which people lacking an equal share of valued resources gain greater access to and control over those resources" (The Cornell Empowerment Group 1989). In other words, people with severe mental illness would be better served by research that is a function of and reflects the values of empowerment (Ecumenical Institute for the Development of Peoples 1981).

To accomplish this, the researcher must ask the following kinds of questions as suggested by Rappaport (1989):

Whom does the content of this research empower?

Whom does this method of research empower?

What voice does it amplify?

Whose point of view does it champion?

Research has been conceived as a series of decision points, from formulating the question through dissemination of the results (Runkel and McGrath 1972). The decisions that are made will determine the quality and the content of the science and manifest the values of the researchers. The framework contained in table 33.1 identifies considerations and strategies for using consumer empowerment as at least one set of decision guides.

The framework is divided into five decision points. Each decision point contains strategies that can enhance the possibility that the research will serve the interests of the empowerment social agenda. A more thorough description of the decision points and strategies has been reported elsewhere (Rapp, Shera, and Kisthardt 1991).

The framework suggests that empowerment research strategies can be employed in quantitative and qualitative investigations. There are features of qualitative research and certain protocols that come with it that allow such research to be particularly conducive to consumer empowerment. Ethnography is particularly well suited since the method is focused on learning from the respondents their "worldview" in their words. It automatically gives voice to that view; it assumes the respondents are respected informants and almost guarantees that respondent strengths and capacities will be explicitly or implicitly captured. Since feeding back the results of the data analysis as one validity check is often suggested, the subjects have input into the analysis and findings and are often queried about their implications. Some ethnographic studies use the data to formulate scale items that are used with a broader range of subjects. The words and

TABLE 33.1
Framework of Research Strategies for Consumer Empowerment

Research Strategies

1. Formulating research questions/phenomena to be investigated (e.g., intervention, environment, experience)
   a. Involvement of consumers/compatibility with consumer agenda
   b. Study strengths (what's right with people?)
   c. Study interventions at other than individual level (e.g., organizational, systems)
   d. Search for possible iatrogenic consequences of phenomenon of interest

2. Context of research (study phenomenon in the setting that it naturally occurs)

3. Consumer vantage point

4. Data collection
   a. Reflective of consumer priorities and interests
   b. Language of data collection (e.g., outcomes, questions, scales, interviews)
   c. Consumer input into the development and implementation
   d. Ethnographic interview
   e. Empowerment as measure

5. Analysis and dissemination of research results
   a. The data can be fed back to consumer groups who through discussion can help interpret the results and identify conclusions and implications from their perspectives
   b. From the data, consumers can contribute to and help formulate recommendations for policy and program changes and develop strategies for promoting such changes
   c. Research that highlights consumer success or achievement could warrant public or private recognition and celebration
   d. Research could be presented at consumer conferences and meetings
   e. Research products could include summaries written in layperson language and be made available to consumers

---

language as well as the dimensions selected are directly derived from the ethnographic interviews.

THE STATUS OF CURRENT RESEARCH

A sizable proportion of rehabilitation and community support program (CSP)-related research, however, does injustice to this value. In the typical case, intervention is designed to solve some problem experienced by consumers. But how that problem is defined can impede or support an empowerment perspective. Much of the existing research in mental health reflects a "blaming the victim" ideology whereby problems experienced by people suffering from severe mental illness are defined as lack of skills, of work histories, of interpersonal or daily living skills, of symptom control, of compliance with medication and treatment regimens, or of motivation. In the research that has focused on families, the overwhelming conditions under which families operate have often been reduced to lack of education, lack of communication or coping skills, excessive emotionality, and so forth. The definition of problems conducive to "blaming the victim" is descriptive not only of mental health research but also of much of the research in both social work and psychology (Caplan and Nelson 1973; Kagle and Cowger 1984). Once the problem has been defined as person centered, then interventions are developed to remedy the deficit, and research is undertaken to test its efficacy. Even when ecological interventions are implemented, the research undertaken does not shift its focus.

One of the reasons for the dominance of person-blaming interventions and research is that the people we seek to help have not been judged to be important informants or collaborators in the execution of the research. Entire areas of psychiatric rehabilitation exist in which little or no research has been undertaken querying consumers about their experiences, perspectives, and recommendations. For example, what published research has asked consumers for their view of obstacles to employment and successful strategies in obtaining meaningful work? A similar question can be asked for crisis intervention or rehabilitation services for people diagnosed with mental illness and substance abuse. A major reason that research on the role of families has moved from person blaming has been the recent literature and research based on the family's own perspective (Hatfield 1978, Hatfield, Fierstein, and Johnson 1982; Hatfield and Lefley 1987). The devaluing of the consumer vantage point can also be seen in the selection of research instruments. The most frequently used measures continue to tap the ratings and evaluations of professionals.

Testing the effectiveness of rehabilitation and CSP interventions is based on sets of dependent variables often derived from the problem definition. For example, lack of job skills leads to interventions directed at teaching job skills then measured by what degree such skills are now in the research subject's repertoire. In general, current research has used a fairly narrow range of desired outcomes, whose core includes a decreased level of symptomatology, reduced use of psychiatric hospitalization, development of functional skills and behavior, compliance with treatment regimens, and service use. These provider-driven outcomes reflect a focus on the illness, consumer deficits, and adherence to professional prescriptions.

Much of current research in mental health undermines the value of fostering client empowerment. It does so through the definition of the problem, the resultant interventions, the selection of outcome variables and measures, and the choice of vantage point, often excluding the people we seek to serve. The contribution that the context of research and the reporting of research results has on the empowerment social agenda has been discussed elsewhere (Rapp, Shera, and Kisthardt 1991; Rappaport 1989). This paper briefly describes three studies conducted by faculty and students at the University of Kansas School of Social Welfare that used qualitative methods of inquiry in a fashion that contributes to client empowerment.

FAMILY STUDY

As has been suggested, families of people with severe mental illness have been among the greatest victims of the deinstitutionalization movement. They have been asked to shoulder much of the responsibility for the community care of their relative including housing, crisis intervention, transportation, leisure time activities, finances, and case management. Despite their herculean efforts, much of the professional literature has focused on the pathological family elements that contribute to the mental illness, client functioning, and well-being: schizophrenicgenetic mother (Fromm-Reichmann 1948), double-bind (Bateson et al. 1956), family functioning as a cause of vulnerability and appearance of a mental illness (Howells and Guirguis 1985), dysfunctional family communication (Wynne 1963, 1981; and Wynne et al. 1977), and family isolation (Brown, Birley, and Wing 1972). Even the "expressed emotion" (Brown, Carstairs and Topping 1958; Leff 1976; Vaughn and Leff 1976) research has been criticized as a subtler form of blaming (Hatfield, Spaniol, and Zipple 1986).

The rationale for this study was developed after a dismally disappointing effort to combine case management services with an in-home psychoeducational effort. Both interventions are spoken of glowingly in the literature. To extend the case management model to include help for the family seemed natural, logical, and potentially beneficial. The families, however, did not seem to appreciate the outreach psychoeducational effort that had been designed. They reacted to the material in most cases with apathy and in some cases with hostility.

This response was particularly surprising in light of the fact that much of the work in developing psychoeducational approaches in this country has dealt with family members' satisfaction with this approach vs. traditional interventions (Anderson, Reiss, and Hogarty 1986; Falloon, Boyd, and McGill 1984; Reynolds and Hoult 1984). However, given our essential ignorance of the perspectives of families with severely mentally ill members, it seemed sensible to once again turn to the family members themselves. Given this stance, a qualitative form of investigation was both necessary and appropriate.

This study attempted to learn what factors and processes are important from the families' point of view. The initial set of informants were families with whom we worked for the passage of the Kansas Mental Health Reform

Act. Future informants were identified through word of mouth in both the Alliance for the Mentally Ill (AMI) and the professional community. Thirty-four family members were interviewed by use of the ethnographic interviewing strategies suggested by Spradley (1979).

Such interviewing and analysis in this type of research should continue until no new information is forthcoming with regard to major themes and patterns of meaning. Diversity of respondents increases the external validity of the data. Diversity in terms of relationship with the index client, location in the state, years since the onset of the illness, and membership in AMI was achieved. All interviews were tape recorded, transcribed, and analyzed. The subsequent analysis or cognitive map was reviewed by the informants for validation. The informants universally felt that the text accurately reflected significant parts of the family experience. A survey instrument was developed from the text and administered to ninety-eight members of AMI in Kansas with an eighty-four percent response rate. The results of the survey overwhelmingly concurred with the interview data.

The data suggest that both the families and the people with severe mental illnesses experience dramatically changing roles at different stages of the intervention process, that families remain very dissatisfied with major elements of service delivery, that they view their experience with early years of the illness very differently than what has been attributed to them, and that their needs and concerns are neither obtuse nor inappropriate. Finally, the data indicate that our knowledge of the family experience is indeed in its infancy. For example, it is possible that interventions such as psychoeducation will need to be more finely tuned to the families' particular stage within the larger intervention process. (Please see Hanson 1991a, b, 1993; Hanson and Rapp 1991, for a more thorough description.) The families' story suggests that engaging families with severely mentally ill members is, on one level, a much more complicated task than is recognized in a rather simplistic educational literature. This is especially true if professionals are not asked to abandon many of the notions gained from their formal and on-the-job education. Choosing ideas to replace the abandoned concepts has been difficult in part because we lack good information.

Fortunately, the families themselves can and will provide much of the information necessary if asked and listened to. They are quite clear with regard to what kinds of changes and help they would like. If we are willing to use their ideas, their perspective will serve us well. Their ideas can serve as a guide to forming a collaborative partnership with families and as an overarching map for acting in the best interests of people suffering from a severe mental illness.

In terms of the role of qualitative methods in fostering the empowerment social agenda, this study demonstrated several features. First, the entire study was designed to "amplify the family's voice." In fact, early drafts of the findings were distributed to legislators, mental health policymakers, and other constituency groups in support of the need for mental health reform. Second, families demonstrated their ability to act as collaborators in the research enterprise beyond their role as subjects. They helped design the study and locate subjects, reviewed the findings, read and understood the study, and helped shape the recommendations and conclusions. Third, they were helpful in disseminating the results in a fashion that increases the likelihood that they may make a difference.

MANAGERIAL STUDY

The inadequacies of community care have been well documented (Basuk and Gerson 1978; Chu and Trotter 1974; Goldman, Adams, and Taube 1983; Talbott 1979). The family study provided additional weight to this body of evidence by identifying families' needs and desires for inclusion and concrete services and by clarifying parts of their perceptions of their experience (Hanson and Rapp 1991). Despite this appraisal, there are programs making real differences in people's lives. The question, then, is what is different about these programs from the rest. It has been proposed that one way to foster the empowerment social agenda is to explore consumer and system's strengths (Rapp, Shera, and Kisthardt 1991). As Rappaport (1989: 12) states, "Empowering research attempts to identify what is right with people."

This study emerged from a failure much like the family study did. The School of Social Welfare operates a statewide client outcome data system for Kansas that allows us to know the agencies that are producing the best results in terms of hospitalizations, independent living status, and vocational status. We used these data to select the eight agencies producing the best results of the thirty-two programs in the state. Seven of the eight agencies provided a similar array of services under the community support program (CSP) banner: psychosocial day programs, case management, and medication clinic. The one program that did not conform to this was the Sedgwick County Compeer Program. This program matches consumers to community volunteers for companionship and support. We then collected data on the most frequently expressed reasons for success: size of budget, size of budget per client, program technology used, length of program operation, credentials and experiences of staff, supportiveness of the executive director, and urban vs. suburban vs. rural. We found no association between any of these variables. While programs doing "good work" with this population are "out there," we know surprisingly little about how the good work is being accomplished.

Since the questions pertained to discovery and description of certain initially unknown variables of organizational culture, ethnographic methods of qualitative research were employed. Field data were gathered through interviews with managers of community-based programs, staff, and consumers. The use of nondirective interviews to gather information was based on the principle that a culture's "cognitive map" is reflected in its language. Questions such as "What is a typical day like in the program?" and "What is a typical workday like for you?" and "Tell me about your clients" were used. Elaboration questions were asked based on earlier responses. By listening to what managers, staff, and consumers say and by observing what they do, inferences can be made about the underlying set of principles in operation. Ethnographic methods of inquiry challenge the researcher to gather information in ways that will form an unbiased "picture" of the work cultures under study. As much as possible, the questions used and observations made during data gathering were not based on preconceived ideas of what might comprise the cognitive map.

The data suggested four principles or sets of management behavior that were common to these eight programs (six of eight programs for each principle minimum).

Clients are people.   Managers play a key role in communicating the values of the program to those who use it, those who work for it, and to the community in which it operates. Managers whose community support programs show effective results are managers who create helping environments wherein consumers are seen and treated as human, as people with a future versus patients with an insurmountable past. The managers of even large programs were familiar with clients' stories, their histories, their families. They talk about people, not target populations or diagnoses; their stories are laced with respect and hope; they revere the clients as heroes and concern themselves with human needs for intimacy, contributing to others, and being a part of a community as well as with compliance with treatment plans.

Learning for a living.   Those managers whose programs show effective results in working with people with long-term mental illness are those who seem to "learn for a living" rather than "work for a living." They actively seek out input and feedback on program performance from participants and staff members to publications, performance reports, funders, and consultants. Their programs are open to visitors and observers; their offices are open to continual streams of clients and staff; their conversations are laced with stories about what they have learned from reflecting on their own practice. As a group, these managers evidence the critical skills of learning, including a total lack of defensiveness about evaluating their work, a drive to critically examine minute helping interventions and decisions to glean their impact, and the ability to brainstorm with others so truly creative ideas can be identified and pursued.

Making something from nothing.   A manager's daily work life is often typified by a continual stream of needs and demands from consumers, staff members, funders, providers, courts, regulatory agents, and advocates. There are deadlines to meet, reports and grants to be written, meetings to attend, phone calls to take, questions to be answered, and crises to be solved. In the face of such a chaotic milieu, managers seem to evidence two responses: surrender to such constraints and be satisfied maintaining the status quo or persist in finding opportunities to improve the program in the midst of chaos. Both groups work equally hard, it seems, but they work differently. The effective managers are those who take the second course of action. Rather than remain inactive behind excuses of "not enough money," "not enough time," or "not enough staff," managers who are "making something from nothing" for people are those who say, "This is needed. Let's make it happen." The results of this perspective are programs that are flexible and changing, sprouting innovations based on emerging consumer needs. The "making something from nothing" principle is composed of the following practice elements: (1) positive perception of self as powerful and responsible, (2) flexibility and invention based on people's needs, (3) step-by-step problem-solving skills, and (4) persistence.

Focus on client outcomes.   The manager ensures that program goals and activities mesh with what people say they need. Simply put, specific outcomes desired by clients become the centerpiece of program mission and activity. Practice experience and research with people with long-term mental illness indicate they both need and ask for assistance in getting housing, jobs, financial support, food, medical attention, friends, and social support (Ewalt and Honeyfield 1981; Lewis and Hugi 1981). Thus, effective managers clearly communicate and focus energy on these outcomes. They easily articulate such goals and find a variety of ways to help people reach them. One manager said, "If you don't know where you're going, how do you get there?" They see themselves as answerable to the people the program intends to help and are personally invested in working toward these outcomes. "My responsibility is to my clients. I have to look them in the eye every morning, so I have to be accountable to them above all else."

The results of this study were used to develop a forty-hour training program for supervisors and CSP directors that is the basis for certification in Kansas. The dissemination of the results in Kansas brought attention and recognition to these "excellent" programs, which have led to their becoming sources of consultation and training and something to emulate for others.

The qualitative methods used in the study allowed us to:

1. explore other than individual level interventions
2. investigate a phenomenon where little was known
3. focus on strengths
4. involve consumers as informants
5. use research results to highlight achievement warranting public recognition and attempts to emulate

CASE MANAGEMENT STUDY

Case management has become the proposed solution to a myriad of client and service system problems during the 1980s. Recently a spate of studies has appeared examining the efficacy of various models of case management. The results have been uneven and at times contradictory and contain a host of conceptual and methodological problems (Chamberlain and Rapp 1991). The concern here, however, is that the research does not contribute to the empowerment social agenda and in fact undermines it because measures rarely include the consumer vantage point and many of the outcomes (e.g., service usage, compliance with treatment plan, compliance with medication, and pathology-oriented measures) are based on adherence to professional prescriptions or are deficit based.

The University of Kansas School of Social Welfare has been implementing, testing, and refining the strengths model of case management for almost a decade. The results have demonstrated promise in terms of reduction in hospitalization, high levels of individual consumer goal attainment across life domains, and high levels of consumer satisfaction (Modrcin, Rapp, and Poertner 1988; Rapp and Chamberlain 1985; Rapp and Wintersteen 1989). Careful attention to monitoring the implementation of the strengths model across studies has shown great fidelity with the model in terms of the principles, functions, and specific methodologies. Despite this, we had never systematically explored the "consumer experience" with the strengths model. To what degree did they "notice" what we were doing? What contributed to the outcomes? What did not? What changes in the model were indicated? How should the training of case managers be changed?

In this study we combined quantitative outcome data with ethnographic methods. We operated four case management projects in four different community mental health centers. The fidelity with the model and the client outcomes were consistent with our past efforts. Of the sixty-six clients served, eighteen were selected for interviews by the researcher. The questioning was very nondirective (e.g., "You've been working with Harry as a case manager for eight months. Can you tell me about it?"). Other questions were used to probe for specifics of their comments (e.g., "Can you give me a specific example? What did you mean by. . . ?"). All interviews were taped, transcribed, and then analyzed to locate patterns, key concepts, and categories.

The results included the following:

1. The importance of the relationship was prominently mentioned by all but one informant (ninety-four percent).

2. Sixty-six percent specifically mentioned some aspect of the goal-planning process as being important to them.

3. Seventy-seven percent specifically mentioned the case manager's resource acquisition and advocacy efforts on their behalf.

4. Of some concern was the confusion between the role of the case manager and the consumer's therapist (if they had one).

5. The strengths assessment process was conspicuously excluded from their responses.

Based on their feedback, a number of changes and refinements were made in the model and its training. First, a great deal more attention is being devoted to the relationship and, particularly, the engagement process. This includes developing a wider range of engagement strategies and permitting more time, if necessary, to this stage prior to demanding that an assessment be "completed." We also have begun to see that for consumers, the relationship is an end in and of itself, as well as a vehicle for enhancing motivation, confidence, and goal achievement. Second, in our training, goal planning is described with much more vigor and imperative. While goal planning has always been central to the strengths model, actual quotes from consumers about its helpfulness and more varied ways of using it with consumers are now used.

Third, we have developed specific guidelines to help case managers and consumers decide and understand the role of counseling by case manager and that which is better served by a therapist. These guidelines help case managers be clearer about expectations and reduce ambiguity and confusion for clients.

Fourth, we were greatly surprised by the lack of mention of the strengths assessment methods since the process is so totally different from the usual process in which these clients have participated. In addition, ten years of discussions with case managers in thirty-six states have suggested that the elements of the model deemed most critical was the strengths assessment and strategies for resource acquisition. Yet, from the consumer's perspective, a very different order of priorities is suggested.

Two explanations were generated. First, the assessment was not seen as the work (i.e., the meat) of the case manager and consumer. It was merely information gathering that was needed to do the work and therefore seemed less pronounced. Second, the consumer was not sufficiently involved in the strengths assessment process. Although never our intention, it may have been perceived as being "done to them," like many other assessment methods, rather than "with them." We now require the strengths assessment and its update to be reviewed by the consumer and encourage the consumer to be the writer on the form. We encourage the case manager to give the consumer a copy and add items as the consumer thinks of them. We ask case managers to have the strengths assessment in front of the consumer and case manager while they are doing the goal planning and to demonstrate how it is being used.

The qualitative methods used in this study allow us to:

1. capture information about the models that had not been available for nine years

2. give voice to the client perspective and ensure that the model was consonant with the consumer agenda

3. locate weaknesses (i.e., iatrogenic consequences) of the model despite the overwhelming level of achievement reflected in the outcome measures

In identifiable ways, the three studies did contribute to the empowerment social agenda. The use of these strategies did not undermine "the science" of the research (unless one believes that data can only be in the form of numbers) and, in fact, made it better science. We simply learned more than we would have by not employing these strategies. Is not science but the pursuit of learning?

Empowerment as a philosophy and set of related strategies represents a concept that few social workers, researchers, program managers, and practitioners hesitate to embrace. Shifting the focus, however, from evaluating intervention impact by "controlling" predesignated variables deemed as relevant from the perspective of the professional to exploring the learning more about what holds value and meaning from the consumers' point of view requires the development and delivery of research protocols that place consumer-focused questions at the forefront of the research agenda. We must be willing to evaluate consumers from the role of client to the roles of teachers and partner in a collective learning enterprise.

References

Anderson, C. A., D. J. Reiss, and G. E. Hogarty. 1986. *Schizophrenia and the Family*. New York: Guilford Press.

Basuk, E. L. and S. Gerson. 1978. Deinstitutionalization and mental health services. *Scientific American* 238: 46–53.

Bateson, G., D. Jackson, J. Haley, and J. Weakland. 1956. Toward a theory of schizophrenia. *Behavioral Science* 1: 241–64.

Brown, G. W., J. L. T. Birley, and J. K. Wing. 1972. Influence of family life on the course of schizophrenic disorders: A replication. *British Journal of Psychiatry* 121: 241–58.

Brown, G. W., G. M. Carstairs, and G. G. Topping. 1958. Post-hospital adjustment of chronic mental patients. *Lancet* 2: 685–89.

Caplan, N. and S. D. Nelson. 1973. On being useful: The nature and consequences of psychological research on social problems. *American Psychologist* 28: 199–211.

Chu, F. O. and S. Trotter. 1974. *The Madness Establishment: Ralph Nader's Study Group Report on NIMH*. New York: Grossman.

Chamberlain, R. and C. A. Rapp. 1991. A decade of case management: A methodological review of outcome research. *Community Mental Health Journal* 27: 171–88.

The Cornell Empowerment Group. 1989. *Networking Bulletin* no. 1: 2.

Ecumenical Institute for the Development of Peoples 1981. *Conscientizing Research: A Methodological Guide*. Hong Kong: Plough.

Ewalt, P. L. and R. M. Honeyfield. 1981. Needs of persons in long term care. *Social Work* 26: 223–32.

Ewalt, P. L. and C. A. Rapp. 1987. Strategies for preparing social workers for practice with the chronically mentally ill. Paper prepared for the National Deans Conference on Severe Psychiatric Disabilities, Seattle, Wash.

Falloon, I. R. H., J. L. Boyd, and C. W. McGill. 1984. *Family Care of Schizophrenia*. New York: Guilford Press.

Fromm-Reichmann, F. 1948. Notes on the development of treatment of schizophrenics by psychoanalytic psychotherapy. *Psychiatry* 11, no. 3: 263–73.

Goldman, H. H., N. H. Adams, and C. A. Taube. 1983. Deinstitutionalization: The data demythologized. *Hospital and Community Psychiatry* 34, no. 2: 129–34.

Hanson, J. 1991a. *The Family Perspective of the Early Stages of Severe Mental Illness*. Lawrence, Kans.: The University of Kansas School of Social Welfare.

Hanson, J. 1991b. *Families' Perceptions of Psychiatric Hospitalization for Relatives with a Severe Mental Illness*. Lawrence, Kans.: The University of Kansas School of Social Welfare.

Hanson, J. G. 1993. Families of people with a severe mental illness: Role conflict, ambiguity and family burden. *Journal of Sociology and Social Welfare* 20: 110–18.

Hanson, J. and C. A. Rapp. 1991. *Families' Perceptions of Community Mental Health Programs for Their Relatives with a Severe Mental Illness*. Lawrence, Kans.: The University of Kansas School of Social Welfare.

Hatfield, A. B. 1978. Psychological costs of schizophrenia to the family. *Social Work* 23: 355–59.

Hatfield, A. B., R. Fierstein, and D. M. Johnson. 1982. Meeting the needs of families of the psychiatrically disabled. *Psychosocial Rehabilitation Journal* 6: 27–40.

Hatfield, A. B., L. Spaniol, and A. M. Zipple. 1986. Expressed emotion: A family perspective. *Schizophrenia Bulletin* 13, no. 2: 221–26.

Hatfield, A. G. and H. P. Lefley. 1987. *Families of the Mentally Ill: Coping and Adaptation*. New York: Guilford Press.

Howells, J. G. and W. R. Guirguis. 1985. Introduction. In J. G. Howells and W. R. Guirguis, eds., *The Family and Schizophrenia*. New York: International Universities Press.

Kagle, J. D. and C. D. Cowger 1984. Blaming the victim: Implicit assumptions of social work research? *Social Work* 19: 82–89.

Leff, J. P. 1976. Schizophrenia and sensitivity to the family environment. *Schizophrenia Bulletin* 2: 566–74.

Lewis, D. A. and R. Hugi. 1981. Therapeutic stations and the chronically treated mentally ill. *Social Service Review* (June) 57: 206–20.

Modrcin, M., C. Rapp, and J. Poertner. 1988. The evaluation of case management services with the chronically mentally ill. *Evaluation and Program Planning* 11: 307–14.

Patti, R. J. 1987. Managing for service effectiveness in social welfare organizations. *Social Work* 32, no. 5.

Rapp, C. A. and R. Chamberlain. 1985. Case management services for the chronically mentally ill. *Social Work* 30: 417–22.

Rapp, C. A. and R. Wintersteen. 1989. The strengths model of case management: Results from twelve demonstrations. *Psychosocial Rehabilitation Journal* 13: 23–32.

Rapp, C. A., W. Shera, and W. Kisthardt. 1991. *Research Strategies for Consumer Empowerment*. Lawrence, Kans.: The University of Kansas School of Social Welfare.

Rappaport, J. 1989. Research methods and the empowerment social agendas. In P. Tolan, C. Keys, F. Chertok, and L. Jason, eds., *Research Community Psychology: Integrating Theories with Methodologies*. Washington, D.C.: American Psychological Association.

Reynolds, I. and J. E. Hoult. 1984. The relatives of the mentally ill: A comparative trial of community-oriented psychiatric care. *Journal of Nervous Mental Disorders* 172: 480–89.

Rubin, A. 1984. Community-based care of the mentally ill: A research review. *Health and Social Work* 9, no. 3: 165–77.

Runkel, P. J. and J. E. McGrath. 1972. *Research on Human Behavior: A Systematic Guide to Method*. New York: Holt, Rinehart and Winston.

Spradley, J. P. 1979. *The Ethnographic Interview*. New York: Holt, Rinehart and Winston.

Talbott, J. A. 1979. Deinstitutionalization: Avoiding the disasters of the past. *Hospital and Community Psychiatry* 30, no. 9: 621–24.

Vaughn, C. E. and J. P. Leff. 1976. The influence of family and social factors on the course of psychiatric illness: A comparison of schizophrenic and depressed neurotic patients. *British Journal of Psychiatry* 129: 125–37.

Videka-Sherman, Z. 1988. Metaanalysis of research on social work practice in mental health. *Social Work* 33, no. 4: 325–38.

Wintersteen, R. T. 1986. Rehabilitating the chronically mentally ill: Social work's claim to leadership. *Social Work* 31, no. 5: 332–37.

Wynne, L. C. 1963. Thought disorder and family relations of schizophrenics. II. A classification of forms of thinking. *Archives of General Psychiatry* 9: 199–206.

Wynne, L. C. 1981. Current concepts about schizophrenics and family relationships. *Journal of Nervous and Mental Disease* 169: 82–89.

Wynne, L. C., M. T. Singer, J. J. Bartko, and M. L. Toohey. 1977. Schizophrenics and their families: Research on parental communication. In: J. M. Tanner, ed., *Developments in Psychiatric Research*, pp. 254–86. London: Hodder and Stoughton.

THIRTY-FOUR

Commentary: Can It Help Us Get There? A View of Qualitative Research in Mental Health in the 1990s

James B. Mullin

The mental health field in the 1990s is poised to finally fulfill the promise of community living for persons with mental illness. For almost three decades, the rhetoric of mental health leaders employed the term *community based* to represent a major shift in the approach to the treatment of mentally ill individuals. In fact, the fundamental aspect of this approach entailed a shift of services from institutional, hospital settings to programs offering similar treatments but located in communities. People thus went to outpatient clinics, day treatment programs, and the like that were located in community settings, but there they interacted with staff in much the same way that they did in the institutions—they "received" clinical services. As a result, the ability of persons to actually live in the community was little improved.

The emphasis on services and their location was reflective of an approach based on a continuing philosophy of treatment. The belief seemed to be that if clinical interventions and clinical services were provided in the community, persons receiving these services would be able to remain in the community and would prosper. This view ultimately worked to interfere with the implementation of the "community-based" ideal and impeded the realization of its promise.

By continuing to provide clinical services, though in a community setting, the mental health field virtually ignored the needs of people to be able to live in the community. The integration with health, social, and human services needed to provide persons not only with clinical services but also with the skills necessary to live in the community was long in coming.

At the initiation of the 1990s, there has been a decided paradigm shift, from the prevailing "treatment" approach, with its emphasis on impairment and intervention to alleviate clinical symptoms, to a new paradigm focused on recovery and rehabilitation. Recovery entails the active participation of persons in their treatment; it includes, in some instances, the individual's direct management of their disorder, and it promotes opportunities for persons to be active health care consumers. Rehabilitation involves the learning or restoration of skills needed for personal satisfaction in the living, learning, working, and social environments of one's choice.

Both recovery and rehabilitation reference the person as a worthy, active, and contributing member in any program of assistance. They are based on underlying assumptions that a psychiatric diagnosis is not an all-encompassing definition of a person and that individuals diagnosed with a mental disorder can learn about it, can come to understand how it affects their lives, and can directly participate in the management, treatment, and control of these effects. In short, recovery and rehabilitation both begin with a belief that persons with psychiatric diagnoses can get on with their lives and can live successfully in the community.

Recovery

In a process of recovery, the person moves from being treated as a dependent, noncontributing patient of whom compliance with prescribed interventions is expected to an equally valued partner with caregivers. This empowerment emphasizes that, with supports, persons with psychiatric diagnoses will lead productive lives. Empowerment occurs in their relationships with therapists, in their involvement with self-help techniques, and in the recognition that physical health is an essential ingredient in overall well-being.

Relationship with Therapists

There is a growing recognition that the most knowledgeable person about all aspects of their disorder, their symptoms, their pain, and even their treatment is the person who has experienced mental illness and mental health interventions. By becoming active members in the relationship with therapists, this knowledge regarding what treatments—including medications—have been most effective and what have not, and when the person has felt well, is sought out, albeit cautiously and slowly, by psychiatrists and other mental health professionals.

By being valued for their experiences and knowledge and validated by being included as active participants in the process, persons with a psychiatric disorder can assume more responsibility both for planning and engaging in their treatment.

Self-Help

New, and still developing, self-help is as yet neither a movement nor a method, but as employed by many individuals it appears to offer much promise in dealing with the effects of serious mental illness. The principal elements of self-help include an understanding of one's disorder, the ability to recognize the "triggers" (for the more traditionally oriented, "prodromal signs") that typically signal the onset of the illness, and the practice of one or more coping behaviors or strategies to limit the progression of the disturbance. Through self-help, people are reporting the ability to "ride out" the occurrence of serious symptoms, to minimize their effects on other areas of their lives, and even to prevent their rise. For example, a college professor listens to his wife when she tells him that ideas that he presents as breakthroughs are in fact somewhat global and bizarre; he then knows that it is time to adjust his medication or take a few days off. Another individual, who has a diagnosis of manic-depressive illness, knows she must begin to "wind down" at a certain hour, must avoid certain favored but too stimulating activities—"If I start to read a book after 9:00 I'll be at it all night, and I probably won't sleep for days"—and must engage in meditation to prepare her mind for sleep. A psychologist now recognizes when he becomes delusional—"I think that others are reading my mind"—and then utilizes techniques he has taught himself "to let the thoughts simply go." Still another individual utilizes a form of communication when he feels threatened or challenged—he hands the other person a card that says, "I have a disability which in some situations causes me great discomfort when addressed in a confrontational way. Please state your views in a more conciliatory way." It works for him.

In these examples, and many more like them, individuals are knowledgeable about the aspects of their illness. They rely on trusted individuals to help them recognize the implications of certain behaviors, and they are able to intervene effectively through techniques that they have developed and found are helpful for them. In almost all cases this knowledge was gained over a long period of time. Sometimes (rarely, in fact) their approach was developed with the assistance of mental health professionals. More commonly, these individuals turned to self-help because they believed they were not being helped, and in fact were being harmed, by the mental health "system."

As presently developed, persons who practice self-help and coping may do so in combination with other therapies, including medication, or not. (It is not axiomatic that self-help is antimedication or antipsychiatry). The key is that people make their own choices and do so after careful consideration of the consequences and effects. For example, the psychologist referenced previously acknowledges that "I would be very ill without medication, and I would be very ill without self-help. I need them both." On the other hand, the woman diagnosed as manic-depressive has had the experience of being "a rapid recycler" when taking medication and through self-help is able to manage her illness without medication.

Health Care

Persons who have serious mental illness, especially those who have experienced it over a long period of time, are used to seeking/receiving care for the specific attributes of their disorder, e.g., hallucinations, thought disorders, depression, etc. They are very aware of and accustomed to receiving attention for this aspect of their being. Conversely, many times these individuals are not as aware of, or used to seeking assistance for, their physical health. It is not uncommon for them to attribute feelings of discomfort, pain, etc. to that part of them they have had examined more frequently, their mental illness, even when these phenomena are actually symptoms of a physical disorder.

The integration of physical health care with mental health care is a fundamental aspect of living in the community. As many as half of the persons who receive community mental health services have been found to have a physical condition warranting medical care (Koran et al. 1989), while one in six may have a condition that can cause or exacerbate their mental disorder (Bartsch et al. 1990). At a minimum, physical illness can affect an individual's ability to participate in mental health programs and thus compromise or delay any beneficial effects.

An active promotion of health and health care must be adopted by persons with mental disorders as well as by mental health care providers. It is an indispensable part of recovery that, too frequently, neither has emphasized sufficiently.

REHABILITATION

Living in the community requires more than the alleviation of symptoms, and more than awareness of and opportunities for mental and physical wellness. People must be able, knowledgeably and skillfully, to meet the demands of a variety of situations that arise where they live, work, learn, or socialize.

The competency for successful community living does not come easily to persons whose life has been marked by major mental illness and mental health interventions. Through a process of rehabilitation, however, persons with a mental disorder can acquire the abilities they need. According to Anthony, Cohen, and Farkas (1990), psychiatric rehabilitation focuses on the person's ability to perform certain behaviors within certain environments. As with recovery, the individual's personal choice is a fundamental underpinning of rehabilitation and guides rehabilitative efforts in living, learning, working, and social environments.

Living

Having a place of one's own is an aspiration of all of us. A place to return to after the day, a place from which to branch out into the greater community, and a place to bring and enjoy friends and family is a fundamental value of all people.

Persons with mental disorders desire their own home and consider it a key to their recovery. Throughout the era of deinstitutionalization, however, many people received "placements" in community residences that usually had built-in time constraints (placements were typically of up to eighteen months), were located far from the individual's home community (placements were typically dependent on bed availability), and may not have provided the supports that the individual needed. Too often, individuals were unprepared for real community living and frequently returned to psychiatric centers when their disorders worsened.

A rehabilitation-based approach to housing seeks to secure apartments and homes within the existing housing stocks in communities; it assists persons with mental disorders to choose among available options, consistent with their rehabilitation goals; and it provides the support they need to maintain this valuable resource.

Persons who have chosen and received supported housing report that they blend into and become a part of the community, that neighbors are unaware that they have a mental illness, and that they thus do not feel the stigma that had been such a part of their lives.

Learning

For many persons with mental illness, learning has been a fragmented, often interrupted experience. The resulting gaps in knowledge and skills have seriously affected their abilities to successfully obtain homes, jobs, and friends.

Through a rehabilitation perspective, learning may mean completing an educational program interrupted by psychiatric hospitalization or initiating a program that an individual was unable to pursue because of a disorder. Learning may also mean a program to acquire specific job skills, information about employment opportunities, or job training. Through the provision of rehabilitation supports, the idea of "lifetime learning" has special meaning for persons with mental disorders.

Working

There is perhaps no more effective response to the stigma that persons with mental illness feel than having a meaningful job. A feeling of worth, a sense of identity, the satisfaction of contributing, and a sense of hope are all conveyed through a purposeful job.

For persons whose inner life becomes chaotic at times, the predictability of a workday can provide sufficient external structure to help them through a difficult period. For those who have a tendency to withdraw, having a job to go to can provide the reason to look forward to each day. For those whose self-confidence has eroded, being successful at work can convey the sense of competency they need to approach and surmount other demands of community living.

As beneficial as work can be for persons with mental disorders, however, it presents many pitfalls as well. For example, for persons who are acutely vulnerable to stress, the workplace introduces many demands that may be very stressful. The pressure to complete work within specified time periods, to perform work with other people, and to coordinate one's efforts with theirs and the requirement for accuracy, speed, and concentration may all become barriers that people must overcome.

None of these work ingredients, however, represents as much of a barrier to people's recovery than being told they are incapable of work or are able to perform only menial, low-paying, low-stress jobs. The expectation that people with a mental illness must be "sheltered" from the demands and stresses of real work are interpreted by the individuals as statements of no hope. An essential ingredient of a rehabilitative approach is that hope is necessary for recovery. This begins with respect for people's choice regarding what kind of work they want to pursue and continues with whatever assistance they need to obtain and retain their job. With this support, people with a psychiatric diagnosis can overcome barriers and can learn ways to be productive in a work setting. The benefits go far beyond the wages the people receive.

Social

People by nature are social beings. They must interact with others, e.g., family, friends, co-workers, employers, merchants, and other intimates in a variety of situations to meet social and emotional needs. In a very basic way, success in living in the community is dependent on the quality and extent of the relationships people establish with other community members.

According to Lieberman, DeRisi, and Mueser (1989), there are specific methods that "people naturally use to learn skills for dealing effectively with new situations: 1. observing another person competently use the skill ('modelling'), 2. practicing the skill in a simulated situation ('behavior rehearsal'), and 3. obtaining feedback and suggestions for improvement from others ('social reinforcement')." As "natural" as these methods may be for most people, they each pose difficulties for persons who have a mental disorder. As a result, their ability to initiate relationships and become comfortable in them is often substantially impaired.

These same methods, however, form the basis for a social skills training approach that can prepare individuals for successful social interaction in the environment of their choice.

The emergence of recipients of mental health services into active roles in their treatment, recovery, and rehabilitation has been a principal impetus for change within the mental health system. This change has been initiated because persons with mental disorders have begun to be listened to by clinicians, administrators and policymakers. It has been influenced very little by classically scientific or academic research.

CONTRIBUTION OF QUALITATIVE METHODS

In the papers by Rapp et al. and Johnson, succinct criticisms of the nature of current research and suggestions for a new research agenda are carefully presented. Within those proposals and within the new mental health paradigm there is ample room, and need, for research that focuses on consumer goals and choices and yet remains "scientific."

Qualitative methodology is particularly well suited to the study of the kind of programs found within the new paradigm. Indeed all the approaches presented in this volume have a role to play in such research. I shall comment briefly on some possible applications. If people with mental disorders are to be involved as true collaborators in recovery/rehabilitation programs, there is a need to learn as much as we can about their own perspectives. The ethnographic and narrative methods presented in earlier papers can serve us well here. Through participant observation and informal interviewing in such settings as supported housing, social clubs, work places, and self-help groups, we can learn about their needs and viewpoints concerning the service system as well as jobs, health care, and housing. Narratives in the form of life history interviews can give us insight into their long-term struggles to cope with their illness.

These methods can also be applied to consumers' social networks, e.g., family members and community caretakers. It is important to learn how these sources of support view the persons with whom they interact. For example, a good deal of study has been done of the role of "expressed emotion" in triggering relapses (Anderson, Reiss, and Hogarty 1986). From this research it seems clear that hostility and criticism from family members, instead of support, can contribute to relapses. However, there is need for a more penetrating and detailed look at how families actually see their affected member to understand the sources and shape of these negative reactions. In turn, how do the affected members themselves view such actions/reactions?

Although a great deal of literature on case management and other services for persons with mental illness has appeared (Rubin 1990), little knowledge has accrued about how these supports play themselves out in actual practice.

Methods of discourse analysis and change process research can shed light on what actually happens when consumers and service providers come together. An interesting example of this kind of research is Loneck's study of counseling processes in work with MICA clients, that is, persons afflicted with both a mental illness and chemical dependency.

Qualitative approaches can add critical dimensions to the evaluation of community services for persons with mental disorders. Quantitative evaluations that make use of questionnaire data from consumers of service can give quite distorted results. The problem is not so much clients' lack of competence to answer the questions but rather their dependent relationships vis-à-vis the services they are being asked to evaluate. The answers they give may be those they believe the evaluators, or providers, want to hear rather than those that reflect their true feelings. Qualitative methods can probe beneath such superficial and socially desirable responses.

Moreover, as the paper by Pulice illustrates, community programs are likely to be complex, multilayered organizational systems involving a variety of constituencies. Thoroughgoing evaluations of such systems need to give voice to these constituencies and to examine in rich detail the intricacies of the processes that make services happen—or not happen. While the knowledge they produce may be quite provisional, qualitative methods can achieve these goals in ways that are beyond the scope of quantitative approaches. Finally, new theoretical perspectives are needed as we move to the new recovery/rehabilitation paradigm. All the qualitative approaches just reviewed can be used to develop grounded theories about how persons move from illness to recovery, about how they cope, about their interactions with meaningful others, and about their relations to service systems. For example, many of the people who advocate self-help/coping turned to these devices after many years' experience with mental illness and mental health interventions. If self-help/coping, as they now promote it, had been available to them at another time, would they have been able to derive as much benefit as they later did? An understanding of their disorder and a conclusion that they were not being helped by traditional mental health methods are keys to the decisions of self-help/coping advocates to assume more responsibility for the management of their recovery. Is this understanding ("insight," if you will) possible during a person's earliest experiences with mental illness? In other words, is there a temporal dimension to self-help/coping that is yet to be recognized? Such questions could be fruitfully addressed through a grounded theory study of persons who have experienced mental illness for the first time.

Inquiry into these promising areas will be necessary both to evaluate and promote their effectiveness. Students, practitioners, and researchers will need to be exposed to these results as the quest continues to find ways to assist persons with serious mental disorders lead satisfying, productive lives. Many forms of research will need to be used in the discovery process, some that do not produce scientific results in the form of numbers but that, according to Rapp, "do not undermine the 'science' of the research, and in fact make it better." The practitioner's need for "what works" and the scholar's need for discipline and methodology can be combined for the benefit of those who care not whether something that helps them succeed at living was the result of a quantitative or qualitative research design. The field of mental health will continue to progress toward real community affiliation for persons with mental illness. The move has begun, the direction is clear, the need for new, effective, consumer-supportive approaches is great. The question is, Can research that combines the best that scholars and practitioners have to offer help get us there?

REFERENCES

Anderson, C. M., D. J. Reiss, and G. E. Hogarty. 1986. *Schizophrenia and the Family*. New York: Guilford Press.
Anthony, W., M. Cohen, and M. Farkas. 1990. *Psychiatric Rehabilitation*. Boston University: Center for Psychiatric Rehabilitation.
Bartsch, D. A., D. L. Shern, L. E. Feinberg, B. B. Fuller, and A. B. Willett. 1990. Screening CMHC outpatients for physical illness. *Hospital and Community Psychiatry* 4: 786.

Koran, L. M., Sox, H. C., Morton, K. I., Moltzen, S., Sox, C. H., Kraemer, H. C., Imai, K., Kelsey, T. G., Rose, T. G., Levin, L. C., and Chandra, S. 1989. Medical evaluation of psychiatric patients. Archives of General Psychiatry 46: 733.

Lieberman, R. P., DeRisi, W. J., and Mueser, K. T. 1989. *Social Skills Training for Psychiatric Patients*. New York: Pergamon Press.

Rubin, A. 1990. Is case management effective for persons with serious mental illness? A research review. Paper presented at annual meeting of National Association of Social Workers, New Orleans, November 16, 1990.

IV

Integration of Qualitative and Quantitative Methods

THIRTY-FIVE

The Inevitability of Integrated Methods

W. David Harrison

Thus far, social work research has led to fewer improvements in practice than one might have hoped for. The exceptions have been notable, but they represent the fruits of only a small fraction of the field's research effort. This is a problem. It is largely a result of the application of a conventional modernist view of science and research to social work practice. Social work practice defies the limits that make the scientific approach work smoothly, and we have not on the whole applied it very successfully. The application of the scientific approach was historically inevitable, because social work is part of the culture that developed and used the scientific world view. A hierarchy of research methods evolved within the researchers' community of discourse. The hierarchy was dictated by the assumptions of hypothesis-testing and statistical methods, including the ability to specify what a practice "intervention" would be like before the experimental situation occurred.

Researchers communicated more with other researchers than with practitioners. The methodological status hierarchy was related largely to the research community's allegiance to social science technologies, including both quantitative and qualitative ones that assumed objectivity and the independent existence of social work practice. It largely ignored the critical role of ideology (Beardsley 1980), its own or the practitioners'. The hierarchy was not related to the nature of practice or to the ways that practitioners use information (see Argyris 1985; Harrison 1987, 1991; Rein and White 1981). Practice, too, developed a hierarchy of methods, based, not on scientific logic, but on a set of moral beliefs, ideas about professionalism, and perceptions of effectiveness. The formation of what Bazerman and Paradis (1991) call discourse communities, applying and strengthening commitment to methods based on the literal application of paradigms, was the essential factor in the estrangement of practice and research, although there are many other facets of the problem. Multiple ontologies developed, and with them different notions of what the criteria were to certify "truth" (Ellis 1990). The application of conventional social science to social work was a good effort on the part of the profession, especially in recent attempts at "empirical practice," but it is an effort that is now facing the inevitable needs for redirection, expansion, and integration.

Toward Integration

Social workers now face the possibility of their field becoming a "science based profession." Yet social work shares much with the many other professions and disciplines that have begun to question the value of conventional research approaches. Gergen (1991) provides a wide-ranging account of this disillusionment and questioning. This phenomenon is a reflection of the organization of all practice professions in an increasingly technical society. It is especially problematic in social work, with our espoused canon of a "person in environment" outlook and our strong humanistic, utopian, and positivistic traditions. We are interested not only in the individual but also in the so called "social environment." We have never intellectually resolved problems about whether a so-called client is the subject or the object of our work. This situation has led us directly to a research mission of extraordinary complexity, ripe for competing perspectives and conflict, in both our ideas about practice and practice research. In trying to do good conventional research, the profession has done what most others have: looked to social science for its research methods, a movement that was inevitable but one that has contributed to the estrangement between practice and research. More recently, the field has looked to the humanities, but this movement is not so distinct or so widespread as the imprint of social science is.

Have the limited research-based advances in professions been due to inadequate operationalization of scientific methods? Is practitioners' inability to understand that research supposed to be good for them? I think that neither explanation will lead to more integrity and integration. The fundamental response to the problems of practice–research and qualitative–quantitative disintegration should be to incorporate two qualities shared by excellent practitioners into all our research. I have been fortunate to have the opportunity to talk with and "jointly construct meaning with" (Mischler 1986) many exemplary social workers using qualitative research methods (Harrison 1987, 1990, 1991). I have also done quantitative studies of students at different developmental points (Harrison and Atherton 1990; Harrison, Kwong, and Cheong 1989). Through my work using both research approaches I have concluded that two social worker attributes offer enormous potential for integrating research and practice and also for integrating qualitative and quantitative methods of research. These qualities are relativism and reflexivity.

By *relativism* I mean the ability to perceive the world from more than one frame of reference or "paradigm." I would not limit the term to the ability to understand several views abstractly, with "anything goes" or a "whatever works for you" being the rationalizations for what one does in practice. Instead I would include the dimension of commitment to a standard of ethical and capable practice. Many workers actively seek new frames of reference by engaging in the process that I have called "heuristic searching" (Harrison 1987, 1991), a form of relativism that social workers are likely to engage in, often with their colleagues and "clients" or constituents. By *reflexivity* I mean the ability to formulate an integrated understanding of one's own cognitive world, especially understanding one's influence or role in a set of human relations. It is a quality of metacognition, thinking about one's perceptions and ideas. These characteristics are related to the widely espoused social work qualities of "empathy" and "self-awareness."

As social work researchers, we have done too little to put these qualities into action either in interacting with practitioners or in developing our own research methodologies that integrate both qualitative and quantitative methods. However, a number of signs indicate that qualitative–quantitative integration is not only possible but also inevitable. In the process the integration of practice and research will probably be much more likely. The reason is that exemplary practitioners use information and paradigms (sets of assumptions and related guides to action) in an integrated, flexible, heuristic way. In looking for ways to change the social situation, they use research findings, theoretical formulations, past experience, current observations, and affective responses. Rarely do they use this information and these research perspectives literally, in the form that social science has stressed:

In situation type S, if I apply intervention type I, outcome O will occur with the probability P.

Instead, social workers, perhaps having given up on such cause-and-effect logic some time before, are more likely to use processes of seeking analogies, similarities, contrasts, and anomalies and to find ways to apply them in the current situation. They are quite happy to use research findings toward this end. They can be persuaded by almost any method, if it has this heuristic value, this utility. Quantitative and qualitative methods are both useful. As the philosophers Fuller (1988, 1991a,b) and Ellis (1990) point out, we must be careful not to overlook the power of methods intended to approximate objectivity, however imperfect they may be.

If a worker is reflexive and relativistic, the worker is the "site" or the "agent" of integration. Since relativism is not an end in itself, and it helps in practice only when it yields practical cognitive guidance through a process of reflective consideration, the worker builds the bridges between the paradigms and the information and the rhetorical and methodological strategies behind the research. "Research," meaning the process and public products of deliberate inquiry, is incorporated in these considerations. Thus, to some extent, practice and research are inevitably integrated in the consciousness of the practitioner who seeks new ways of understanding and practicing. This may happen to different degrees, depending especially on the worker's attributes and the nature of the information that the worker has to work with.

FOUR FORCES MAKING INTEGRATION INEVITABLE

Thus far, I have argued that research and practice and methods of research come from different paradigms that can be integrated. I have noted that one of the ways in which integration has come about is through the qualities of the relativistic and reflexive practitioner. But this is a rather individualistic way of looking at integration. It speaks to inevitability only at one level. There are also four interrelated social forces that are more generally applicable and that will all work toward the inevitable integration of our spheres of interest. These forces come from the inseparability of quantitative and qualitative research methods, the increasingly comprehensive scope of social work research and practice, the developmental course of researchers through their careers, and the increasing recognition and legitimacy of "postmodern" perspectives in social work.

The Inseparability of Quantitative and Qualitative Methods

Noted above was that researchers should take into account practitioners' ways of knowing. Likewise, we have to ask ourselves how the current proposal might take into account the researchers' mindsets. For a start, researchers must be reflexive and relativistic. We must learn to integrate methods by developing ways of seeing what is inherently integrated in them. Thus, by applying some of the best qualities of practice, social work researchers can peer into methodological cracks to see where the split turns into whole material.

It is important to recognize that technical quantitative and qualitative methods are inextricably intertwined. They are indeed two different perspectives (Ruckdeshel 1985), but each perspective exists only artificially—in a way that people manufacture—rather than as an independently existing natural entity (Simon 1969). Campbell, best known as an experimentalist, argues strongly that quantitative methods cannot exist without qualitative knowing of research conventions, of theories, of operationalization, of analysis, and of creative cognitive ways of drawing conclusions and making generalizations (Campbell 1978). And it is impossible to express qualitative perspectives, methods, perceptions, and conclusions without communications that are at least partially amenable to quantitative representation and, therefore, quantitative analysis. Words can be counted; language patterns can be studied quantitatively. Art and religion can be analyzed "scientifically," even though the result is not usually intended to be more art or religion.

Two examples of the interwoven qualitative and quantitative fibers of the research cloth come to mind from my own recent research projects. They serve as reminders of the value of relativism and reflexivity. First, consider the naming of factors in exploratory factor analysis, one of the most highly quantitative research methods or techniques we have. This method involves "data," which means "factual information." Let us make a leap of faith for the moment about how "factual" any data are, by assuming that representations on a Likert scale representing states of being are factual. (This leap and its consequences are thoroughly covered in Lipsey's [1988] splendid article on practice and malpractice in evaluation research.) Use your relativistic faculties to grant that these presentations of self are "variables." Assume that our subjective states and our "behaviors" can take on more than one value and that the appropriate value can be perceived and recorded in a way corresponding to a number.

So far we have transformed a behavior or a state qualitatively, making it into a datum. It has not only been represented; it has been changed, transformed into a numeric symbol. To do our analysis, a number, that is a quantity, of these modified data or numbers are further transformed according to prescriptive statistical formulae, which have been consented to and communicated by imprecise social, historical processes, to determine which data are correlated—that is, co-related—with which others, and to what degree. The data that are sufficiently related according to the formulae and rules are qualitatively transformed into new, synthetic variables called factors. Any errors of logic and measurement may have been multiplied along the way. If the first formulation does not yield something meaningful, the researcher has several different strategic and prescriptive tracks for finding a meaningful relation among data. For example, axes can be "rotated." Thus "massaged," the data yield a conclusion with more qualitative value to the researcher. The data are made into something new and different, just as almost anything else is constructed from other materials. Once the transformations of number have been interpreted as having meaning, the new entities are then named, becoming "real" for the researcher as they are qualitatively recognized and christened. At this point the synthetic entities and the names they have acquired assume the status of being real, a status that will hold in the researcher's logic and probably in that of the people who will read or hear about a publication (another transformation) as well.

How does one know what to call the factors discovered when doing an exploratory factor analysis? Ask your colleagues for guidance in the naming of factors. Look in all the factor analysis books you can find. If your search is like mine, you will find amused colleagues and many books and articles that work all around the subject, but you will probably find little help.

Reid and Smith (1989) provided one of the best treatments of the subject available in any discipline when they stated that

> Factors are constructs or abstractions without any inherent substantive meaning. . . . The grouping is based on solely statistical considerations—in the pattern of intercorrelation among the items. The factor labels . . . are designations devised by the researchers to capture the observed statistical "glue" which joins the items. The labels may or may not correspond to whatever organizing concepts the researchers had in mind in developing the instrument. . . . By grouping together measures that intercorrelate, factor analysis not only serves to reduce and organize the data, but can generate new measures for use in further data analysis.   (279)

The task of naming these factors is a qualitative one. A careful listener or reader will note a high proportion of metaphorical discussion of this point. There will be many terms similar to "statistical 'glue' " in discussions, and visual imagery will almost certainly be present. Only rarely is the qualitative effect of graphical, visual presentations of quantitative data discussed (e.g., Tufte 1983), but the rhetorical relations of language, image, and data are unavoidable. Thus, we have an example of methodological integration.

Expert statisticians and my limited experience with factor analysis lead me to think that the production of constructs by factor analysis is not necessarily a rigorous, convention-bound procedure. Factor analysis, in fact, is sometimes conducted in ways that could be criticized for many of the faults that have been noted about qualitative research. It appears that naming or labeling constructs in factor analysis ideally would be conducted in a method very similar to a constant comparative method, usually associated with qualitative analyses (e.g., see Strauss and Corbin 1990). Each component variable would be compared to those addressed before it for its contribution to the label, which should represent the substantive meaning that is being discovered. Contradiction and inconsistencies would be accounted for. At any rate, qualitative analysis takes the data as they come, rough and unstandardized, not very clearly ordered on the surface, just as we find with the odd assortments and commonsense correlations that characterize factors. Since the researcher has to "devise designations" in order to "capture the observed statistical 'glue' which joins the items" the researcher has constructed a qualitative reality from quantitative data that were originally based on qualitative experiences and ideas.

The problem with considering this approach as an example of the constant comparative method is that the data are too shallow and unidimensional to do "good" comparisons; many of the statistically correlated items are not very well correlated ontologically, and their relations are nonsensical. But the constant comparative method (by which each new datum is compared to others for similarity, difference, and meaning added to a concept or construct) could yield considerable rigor to factor analyses by confronting the meaning of the relations among numerical data more directly. For example, what if the verbal items "loading" quantitatively on a factor were compared qualitatively, that is, semantically, for the meaning that they contribute to a factor or construct? A researcher could document the evolution of the meaning and name of a factor through the qualitative technique of memorandum writing. One might ask "What has Item *C* got in common with Items *A* and *B?* Could they represent opposites on some aspect of the construct and thus be linked mathematically? Could they be two expressions of the same belief or feeling or state of mind? Is there a social phenomenon that could bind these psychological items?" A similar process occurs when new analyses with new samples are done in the scale development process. In one recent study by Harrison and Atherton (in press) the underlying construct was reframed by such a combination of quantitative and qualitative methods. It happens very often, but the qualitative dimension is seldom documented or presented as part of the evidence.

Systematically understanding the meaning of numbers is especially important if we are measuring the way we most often do in social work, with real, unidimensional numbers being assigned to multidimensional self-reports of feeling, recollections of behaviors, and similar cognitive representations. Dimensionality is reconstructed mathematically through statistics. "Depth" of emotion, for example, is a metaphor that may be replaced by a spatial, mathematical metaphor of depth. Thus, dimensionality is extremely speculative and hypothetical, yet it is reified. When ideas are so far removed from the world of practice and experience, they may thus be very weakly grounded.

Note too the idea that a factor can "generate new measures." When a factor gets a name, it is granted a life of its own, regardless of what the component variables were or what people meant when they contributed original data. It is a "real" representation of a "real" construct, and it can be represented by "real numbers." Multivariate analyses depend on grasping the ideas of vectors in space and three-dimensional data planes arranged at right angles. How empirical are the planes and vectors in space that the data are assumed to correspond with? Is this type of empirical study of complex phenomena a quantitative, scientific enterprise, subject to the rules that reducible, countable physical entities are? Or is this a metaphorical way to represent the world that might prove very useful to relativistic social workers who reflexively understand the metaphorical nature of the frame of reference they are adopting?

As another example of the inseparability or integration of quantitative and qualitative research, consider the idea of constructing a substantive conceptual framework or theory based on interviews and observations. This experience is no less humbling than trying to construct meaning from data that have already been made numerical and then "reduced" into more manageable forms and that, like nylon fibers, display synthetic reality. It is noteworthy that one of the most common verbs used in proposals for qualitative studies and in textbooks is "emerge." Although the term *emerge* is basically *verboten* in my own qualitative seminar and dissertations, it captures a sense of what occasionally happens, just as factor analysis sometimes "generates" new measures, but rarely does anything emerge without some active searching.

Qualitative studies require a good bit of speculative, intuitive searching for the "glue" that holds together constructs. But because something is speculative and intuitive is it exempt from examination by other methods? In my interview studies and those of my students, I have tried to do elementary textual analyses of the interviewer's role in shaping the interview and of the processes by which researchers come to conclusions. Dividing interviews into discrete units by classifying, counting, and diagramming the questions we ask, the observations we share in transcripts, and the participants' responses is worthwhile, especially when we are looking deductively for regularities by a content analysis focusing on specific, predetermined classes of activity, that is, factors or behaviors like long questions that lead to short answers on sensitive topics. Labov and Fanshel's (1977) study of therapeutic interviews illustrates the power of this type of research.

When we look for themes, regularities, recurring terms, words, events, or sensations among the phenomena we produce and study, we compare. Comparison is a simple technical research method. Yet as soon as we say that two of something share qualities, or that instance A is more like instance D than instance B is like D, or that instance C is more like D than B is, we have clearly entered the realm in which our qualitative project is also amenable to some forms of quantitative analysis. Qualitative researchers may not like this much, since we tend to think that our work is somehow devalued and misconstrued. The fact that devaluation and misunderstanding may happen is irrelevant; the same concerns hold for the qualitative study of quantitative work. But as soon as we put ideas into words we face the inescapable fact that our work is amenable to other forms of analysis. This fact is "necessary but not sufficient" for integrated methods.

One interesting example of how this type of integration can occur and appeal to the reflexive and relativistic qualities in us can be found in Brendstrup and Schmidt's (1990) study of "HIV risk behavior" in Danish homosexual and bisexual men. Interviewing a small group of men from a large, national survey, they described their finding that those men who were engaged in high-risk behavior were those who had experienced psychological trauma without engaging in remedial activities. The information in this study is potentially useful because the presentation engages both the scientific and the humanistic faculties of the social worker-reader. Numerical information and a direct, logical presentation are provided along with accounts of lives of people that one not only cares about but feels one knows about from practice. The scale of the study is small enough for the practitioner to identify with, too. It does not deal with large numbers of people and trivial but "statistically significant" differences among the groups. It may be that the studies that have had the most influence on practice have had this ability to engage the relativistic ability of the reader, by being logical and convincing and at the same time being personally moving on a level that allows one to see reflexively images of one's own practice in the research. Practitioner and researcher doubtless would share an interest in exploring further Brendstrup and Schmidt's finding.

The Increasing Scope of Social Work Research and Practice

This factor affecting integration occurs at a different level than the first one. It is related to Brendstrup and Schmidt's (1990) combination of epidemiological surveys and intensive interviews. Simply put, the social work research enterprise has grown enormously, especially when one considers the many overlaps with other fields. We now have available an accumulation of studies that have used multiple methods to "triangulate" findings, to "replicate" tests and explorations, and to "link" data and methods systematically (Fielding and Fielding 1986). The entire field, not just the individual, is the venue for integration.

In this regard, we integrate not methods so much as the "findings" and their methodological contexts. We integrate, or make whole, bodies of consensual understanding, both of the substance of the research and of the ways that people have gone about it. Likewise, we find that the results sometimes could be more meaningful or valuable with new methods. Social work has been fairly slow to develop research methods, and the ones it borrows have been relatively conventional qualitative and quantitative prescriptions for the most part. Many examples exist of methods that might be useful, such as the sociologist Ragin's (1987) approach to qualitative comparisons using Boolean, rather than linear, algebra. From the humanities, Durant and Fabb (1990) have recently produced a particularly promising set of integrated methods for literary analysis. And if we choose to look at ourselves in a study of group reflexivity, we might consider the overtly integrated methods described in Bazerman and Paradis's (1991) collection on the textual dynamics of the professions. The main point, which is crucial, is simply that we have grown large enough that each of the avenues opening up for integrated methods is now likely to have enough people involved to learn collectively.

The Developmental Course of Researchers Through Their Careers

In an earlier essay (Harrison 1990) I discussed my dissatisfaction with a principle that I had learned years before. The principle stated that the research method should be "dictated" by the problem or question. I understand and like the logic, but it is at best a heuristic device of the sort a reflexive researcher or practitioner might use as a starting point. It leaves out the problem of how the problem is originally formulated. Is there any research problem that has only one way of being defined and only one best corresponding way of being pursued? Do definitions and methods of inquiry really connect that clearly? I will come back to this point momentarily.

This matter became important to me when I once realized that I had used a method for essentially rhetorical, if not political, purposes. I had done a rather elaborate, methodologically well-received study (Harrison and Atherton 1990; Harrison, Kwong, and Cheong 1989), choosing my method mainly so that those disagreeing with my argument, which was consistent with but not dependent on the method or the data, would have to overcome my high-status method as well as my ideas. A qualitative study would not "do the trick," I thought, even though it might have produced at least as meaningful a set of findings.

Before and after this essay, as part of the work done for the NIMH Task Force on Social Work Research, I talked to a number of researchers about their careers. I learned that many of them had gotten past academic tenure decisions and were now feeling the academic freedom to pursue the subjects they wanted to, in the way they wanted to, without the demands of publishing a number of studies with higher status methods but apparently of less importance to the researchers. Likewise, some of the people to whom I talked spoke of their interest in using qualitative methods to complement their quantitative ones to get at the heart of important phenomena. They were "becoming social researchers" (Reinharz 1979), establishing identities as researchers and developing their own perspectives that integrated others and that allowed for reflexivity in research.

As we increasingly develop an appreciation of the contributions of the qualitative dimension of our methods, our future researchers will reach these levels of methodological integration that depend on two integrated identities: practitioner and researcher, out of which can come a new set of schemas to nourish relativistic thinking and out of which can come reflexivity based on one's awareness of oneself in both practice and research worlds. This is a long-term process.

The Increasing Recognition and Legitimacy of "Postmodern" Perspectives in Social Work

Perhaps too much has been written and said about something so amorphous as postmodernism, the ill-defined set of perspectives that we live with in the wake of our concerns about the inadequacies of science and romanticism (see, e.g., Gergen 1991). Despite my numerous statements implying causal relations and encouragement of conventional research, I know that social work is being affected deeply by this outlook. For our purposes, the important point is that the sort of relativism and reflexivity that I have been researching and that I have presented here are virtual hallmarks of postmodernism. Social workers need not make a commitment to the more obscure methods of deconstruction, for example, in order to recognize that our field shares perspectives and some methods of inquiry, with many other fields (see Orcutt 1990), including, as just one example "critical legal studies." Postmodernism reflects an integration of both perspectives and methods from across the intellectual spectrum.

Integrating methods and frames of reference means finding ways to build bridges among actions, sources of knowledge, and ways of inquiring. These are characteristics of this contemporary reckoning with the human predicament. The understanding that the world is incomprehensible, at least in any ultimate sense, is a hallmark of postmodernism and of relativistic social work. Postmodern inquiry shows an appreciation of contradictory ways of moving toward interpreting the world and even of contradictory ways of understanding and reporting "facts" (Atlas 1991). Contradictions are not necessarily disintegrating. Similarly, Hartman (1990) writes about our "many ways of knowing" in social work. We need to seek creative integrations of ways of knowing.

While we recognize that science is but one perspective, we recognize too that it is a crucially important one. It is the method, not only of the powerful and conservative (Unger, Draper, and Pendergrass 1986), but a method that can also reveal new perspectives upon which to act. I think that we are now free to add paradigms and that we need not lose others in the process. We certainly do not want to abandon a scientific approach, but instead we need to integrate humanistic perspectives with it, as has begun to happen (see, e.g., England et al. 1991). We are doubtless now developing our own "theory of method" by asking what we really do want to learn about and what kind of advice we do want from our organized methods (Sarkar 1983).

Gergen (1991) published a guide through some of the diverse methods and fields that constitute an integrated, postmodern outlook. Gergen is rather hopeful about postmodern consciousness as a nutrient for our sense of identity, since he finds that rather than collaborate in an enterprise of finding ultimate truths of science (modernism) or of moral character (romanticism), we find ourselves through the appreciation of human relationships. To the extent that we are open to these perspectives and open to our own relations to our colleagues, we will find compatibility with our profession and the inevitable integration of our methods.

REFERENCES

Argyris, C. 1985. Making knowledge more relevant to practice: Maps for action. In E. E. Lawler, A. M. Mohrman, S. A. Mohrman, G. E. Ledford, T. G. Cummings, and Associates, eds., *Doing Research That Is Useful for Theory and Practice*, pp. 79–106. San Francisco: Jossey-Bass.

Atlas, J. June 23, 1991. Stranger than fiction. *New York Times Magazine*, pp. 22, 41, 43.

Bazerman, C. and J. Paradis. 1991. *Textual Analysis of the Professions: Historical and Contemporary Studies of Writing in Professional Communities*. Madison: University of Wisconsin Press.

Beardsley, P. L. 1980. *Redefining Rigor: Ideology and Statistics in Political Inquiry*. Beverly Hills, Calif.: Sage.

Brendstrup, E. and K. Schmidt. 1990. Homosexual and bisexual men's coping with the AIDS epidemic: Qualitative interviews with 10 non-HIV-tested homosexual and bisexual men. *Social Science and Medicine* 30: 713–20.

Campbell, D. T. 1978. Qualitative knowing in action research. In M. Brenner, P. Marsh, and M. Brenner, eds., *The Social Contexts of Method*, pp. 184–209. London: Croom Helm.

Durant, A. and N. Fabb. 1990. *Literary Studies in Action*. London: Routledge.

Ellis, B. 1990. *Truth and Objectivity*. Oxford: Basil Blackwell.

England, S. E., S. Poirier, C. Mattingly, M. Bartlett, B. Miller, N. Linsk, J. Gorman, M. G. Henderson, B. Coats, M. Graham, R. Marder, and J. Robertson. 1991. Relationship, reasoning, and access to formal care: Accounts of care and dependency. Unpublished research grant proposal.

Fielding, N. G. and J. L. Fielding. 1986. *Linking Data*. Beverly Hills, Calif.: Sage.

Fuller, S. 1988. *Social Epistemology*. Bloomington: University of Indiana Press.

Fuller, S. 1991a. Is history and philosophy of science withering on the vine? *Philosophy of the Social Sciences* 21: 149–74.

Fuller, S. 1991b. Social epistemology and the brave new world of science and technology studies. *Philosophy of the Social Sciences* 21: 232–44.

Gergen, K. 1991. *The Saturated Self: Dilemmas of Identity in Contemporary Life*. New York: Basic Books.

Harrison, W. D. 1987. Reflective practice in social care. *Social Service Review* 61: 393–404.

Harrison, W. D. 1990. Going native in one's own land—or—Whither methodological pluralism? *Philosophical Issues in Social Work* 1: 3–8.

Harrison, W. D. 1991. *Seeking Common Ground: A Theory of Social Work in Social Care*. Aldershot, England: Avebury.

Harrison, W. D. and C. R. Atherton. 1990. Cognitive maturity and the "one foundation" controversy in social work education. *Journal of Social Work Education* 26: 87–94.

Harrison, W. D. and C. R. Atherton. In press. The Attitudes About Reality Scale: A note on the use of logical positivism as a construct. *Journal of Social Psychology* (June 1992).

Harrison, W. D., K. Kwong, and K. J. Cheong. 1989. Undergraduate education and cognitive development of MSW students: A follow-up to Specht, Britt, and Frost (1984). *Social Work Research and Abstracts* 25: 15–19.

Hartman, A. 1990. Many ways of knowing. *Social Work* 35: 3–4.

Labov, W. and D. Fanshel. 1977. *Therapeutic Discourse: Psychotherapy as Conversation.* New York: Academic Press.

Lipsey, M. W. 1988. Practice and malpractice in evaluation research. *Evaluation Practice* 9, no. 4: 5–24.

Mischler, E. 1986. *Research Interviewing: Context and Narrative.* Cambridge, Mass.: Harvard University Press.

Orcutt, B. A. 1990. *Science and Inquiry in Social Work Practice.* New York: Columbia University Press.

Ragin, C. C. 1987. *The Comparative Method: Moving Beyond Qualitative and Quantitative Approaches.* Berkeley: University of California Press.

Reid, W. J. and A. Smith. 1989. *Research in Social Work.* 2d ed. New York: Columbia University Press.

Rein, M. and S. H. White. 1981. Knowledge for practice. *Social Service Review* 55: 1–41.

Reinharz, S. 1979. *On Becoming a Social Scientist: From Survey Research and Participant Observation to Experimental Analysis.* San Francisco: Jossey-Bass.

Ruckdeshel, R. 1985. Qualitative research as a perspective. *Social Work Research and Abstracts* 21: 17–21.

Sarkar, H. 1983. *A Theory of Method.* Berkeley: University of California Press.

Simon, H. A. 1969. *The Sciences of the Artificial.* Cambridge, Mass.: Massachusetts Institute of Technology Press.

Strauss, A. and J. Corbin. 1990. *Basics of Qualitative Research: Grounded Theory Procedures and Techniques.* Newbury Park, Calif.: Sage.

Tufte, E. R. 1983. *The Visual Display of Quantitative Information.* Cheshire, Conn.: Graphics Press.

Unger, R. K., R. D. Draper, and M. L. Pendergrass. 1986. Personal epistemology and personal experience. *Journal of Social Issues* 42, no. 2: 67–79.

THIRTY-SIX

Integrating Qualitative and Quantitative Methods in Clinical Research

Inger P. Davis

This is a report of a comparative case analysis using combinations (triangulation) of qualitative and quantitative data to probe the pros and cons of involving children and adolescents in family-unit treatment. The extent of children's verbal participation is explored through comparison of four cases engaged in task-centered family problem-solving treatment with the same family practitioner. Two of these cases are further analyzed in search of answers to the question of the content and nature of the children's communications and of clues to why inclusion of children worked well in one case, and not in the other.

TRIANGULATION AND EXAMPLES OF ITS USE

The idea of combining research methodologies is not new but is lately voiced with increased frequency (Brewer and Hunter 1989; Combs-Orme 1990; Guba 1990).

Combining research methods is often referred to as *triangulation,* a term used with many connotations in the research literature. According to Knafl and Breitmayer (1991), triangulation, as a navigation technique of plotting the location of an unknown point from two known or visible points, was first used metaphorically by social scientists to designate the use of multiple methods of measurement of a single construct.

Triangulation serves two distinct purposes, as a means of strengthening the convergent validity of one's study by using multiple methods of measurement, data sources, or observers or as a means of creating as nearly complete a picture as possible of the contextual dimensions of the topic under study by a multiplicity of methods, sources, and theories, each adding a piece to the puzzle. In the former "convergence" function, triangulation counteracts threat to validity inherent in each method used by balancing strength and weaknesses of all measures, sources of data, etc. Quantitative researchers who develop instruments or study concrete constructs or events are particularly in need of establishing convergent validity, while qualitative researchers would tend to use triangulation to achieve completeness in portraying the context of the topic under study. Of course, all researchers, regardless of the qualitative/quantitative preference dimension, need and welcome the increased confidence that may result from consistent findings across multiple methods and sources (Jick 1983; Knafl and Breitemayer 1991; Patton 1980).

In their own study of how families define and manage a child's chronic illness, Knafl and Breitemayer (1991) and their collaborators use five types of triangulation: multiple investigators, data sources, methods (intensive interviews and five standardized child and family functioning measures), unit of analysis (individual and family), and theoretical triangulation (child and family developmental theories).

Another example is Blake's (1989) study of the impact of an educational program on level of morbidity of adults who were at high psychosocial risk because of recent stressful life events and weak social supports. Traditional quantitative methods were augmented by such qualitative measures as genograms and life-space drawings before and after participation in the educational program. Qualitative data were translated in quantifiable variables amenable to statistical comparisons. The third step was in-depth qualitative analysis of a small number of cases from those with the highest and lowest levels of morbidity. Blake argues that complex characteristics and processes, such as social support, coping, style of communication, and other family dynamics cry out for a synthesis of quantitative and qualitative approaches, not just one or the other.

CHILDREN'S PARTICIPATION IN FAMILY-UNIT TREATMENT

During the 1970s child therapists intensely challenged the assumption underlying family therapy, that all children's problems are symptomatic of parental or family system interactions and therefore can be treated only in the family context. This stance appears to have been softened somewhat in the 1980s by the acknowledgment that children can have problems of their own, even though the family matrix may be influenced by them (Grunebaum and Belfer 1986; McDermott and Char 1974). Thus child therapy without integration of family members in the therapeutic process runs the risk of bringing the parents' built-in power to influence the child to bear on the situation with the possible result of withdrawal of the child from therapy or blocking carryover of the child's therapeutic changes to the home environment.

Conversely Guerney and Guerney (1987) point out that family therapy without sufficient recognition of the child's intrapsychic problems may ignore these, or the young child with problems may not be accorded a genuine "voice" in the therapy session.

The general move away from an either/or position on children's inclusion in family treatment has led to greater attention to the need for an ongoing fit between the developmental needs of all family members as well as the family as a system and to experimentations with combinations of several modalities (Gordetsky and Zilbach 1989; Guerney and Guerney 1987; Zilbach 1989).

The task-centered family problem-solving model (TCFP) by Reid (1985) goes a long way in that direction. It generally favors inclusion of children in family sessions as active participants in problem exploration, task implementation, and problem-solving work, but it may work with parents alone (Reid and Donovan 1990) or use combinations of individual and family interviews. It also consistently seeks feedback from children about their experiences. Children twelve years and older are routinely asked to give written feedback and fill out standardized instruments. Thus the TCFP model, which was applied in the cases to be compared below, uses input from all family members for the dual purpose of further model development and answering research questions.

CASE COMPARISONS

This case comparison seeks answers to the following: How much did the children participate in the family sessions? What did they say? How engaged were they in the problem-solving work? Did the children appear to be better or worse off for having been included, or did it seem not to matter much? Do these cases offer any clues to contextual or other factors that may be indicators or contraindicators for including children in family sessions? Does the case comparison validate or disconfirm the importance that professional observations ascribe to seeing parents and children separately prior to joint sessions and to establishing rules for in-session and in-home behaviors?

Study Method

These questions, along with others, were addressed in the author's pilot study of TCFP treatment at San Diego County Family Service Agencies. The discussion here is limited to the topic of children's involvement in joint family problem-solving work.

The larger pilot study sample consisted of eleven family cases. Treatment was offered by five experienced MSW/LCSW social workers and three graduate social work students with extensive clinical experience. The families were selected by the social work practitioners on the basis of their request for help with parent–child problems and their potential receptivity to TCFP treatment.

The McMaster Family Assessment Device (Miller et al. 1985) was filled out by parents and children twelve years and older pretreatment and posttreatment. The family practitioners recorded tasks and task progress. Sessions were audiotaped.

Data have been analyzed by quantitative and qualitative procedures. Logging sheets were developed for in-depth content analysis of family sessions tapes, which were transcribed to provide greater descriptive accuracy. The logging sheet columns allow for accumulation of the number and content of session, home, and environmental tasks; levels of task achievement and problem alleviation; and listing of contextual changes and/or contextual factors (that is, individual, familial, or societal factors that may serve as resources or barriers to the family's problem-solving work). A final column gave space to "informative events," that is, unanticipated episodes or events of the therapeutic process that in the case analyst's mind have interest beyond the case itself in triggering novel approaches to problem solving, pinpointing successes or failures, and so on (see Davis and Reid 1988; Reid 1985 for further details).

The Stepwise Case Analysis

First, four cases (Families III, IX, X, and XI) were compared to discern possible patterns across cases of the extent to which the therapist and family members occupy the floor. Practitioner "A" worked with all four families, which provides some control of one of the major study variables.

The lower half of figure 36.1 depicts the percentage distribution of session responses of participants. As one would expect, the practitioner and parents together account for the major portions of responses. The children's combined total number of responses (as indicated by the black line cutting across the bars in figure 36.1) remain below 25% in all cases except in case IX, involving a single mother, her two talkative boys, and a

FIGURE 36.1   *Responses by Members of Four Families in Task-centered*
Family Problem Solving Treatment by Practicioner "A"

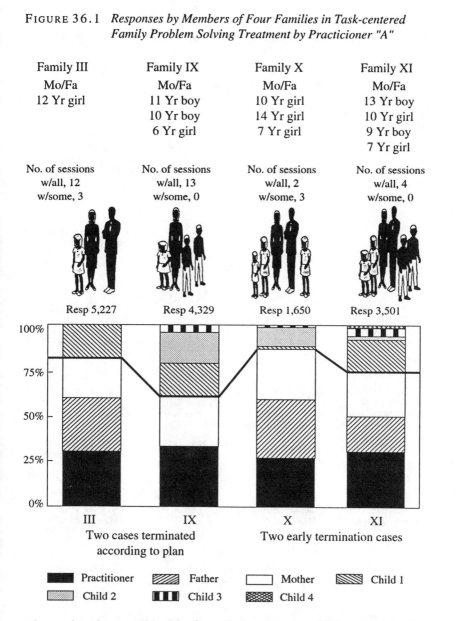

Family III	Family IX	Family X	Family XI
Mo/Fa	Mo/Fa	Mo/Fa	Mo/Fa
12 Yr girl	11 Yr boy	10 Yr girl	13 Yr boy
	10 Yr boy	14 Yr girl	10 Yr girl
	6 Yr girl	7 Yr girl	9 Yr boy
			7 Yr girl

No. of sessions	No. of sessions	No. of sessions	No. of sessions
w/all, 12	w/all, 13	w/all, 2	w/all, 4
w/some, 3	w/some, 0	w/some, 3	w/some, 0

Resp 5,227   Resp 4,329   Resp 1,650   Resp 3,501

III   IX   X   XI
Two cases terminated   Two early termination cases
according to plan

■ Practitioner   ▨ Father   □ Mother   ▧ Child 1
▨ Child 2   ▥ Child 3   ▨ Child 4

rather quiet six-year-old girl. Overall the younger children tend to be
"squeezed out."

From the four cases, Cases III and X were singled out for further
fine-grained comparisons. They were chosen because they, despite many

TABLE 36.1
Comparison of Two Task-centered Family Problem-solving Cases

Case III		Case X	
	Family Composition		
F (father)	31 yr	F (father)	38 yr
GF (5 yr live-in girl fr)	26 yr	GF (7 yr live-in girl fr)	34 yr
F's daughter "R":	12 yr	F's daughter G-1	10 yr
		GF's daughter G-2	14 yr
		F & GF's daughter G-3	7 yr
R's biomother refused to care for R 2 months ago. CPS placed R with F & GF		G-1 removed by CPS from biomother 5 yr ago; has lived with F & GF since	

Referral Source

Case III	Case X
Family friend	Principal of G-1's school. G-1 refused to go home because GF slapped her hand after taking G-1 to school. F brought G-1 to his parents to stay overnight

Target Problems

Case III	Case X
1. Deficits in communication: Talking by or interrupting one another; TV on all the time	1. G-1's impulsivity, hitting, and biting GF especially, but also G-2 & G-3
2. R's disobedience; R out of control (stealing and lying)	2. Poor communication patterns in family, blaming, yelling, and screaming by G-1 causing complaints from neighbors

Agreed-upon Case Goals

Case III	Case X
1. Somewhat vague. F & GF want R to stop lying; disobeying rules	1. Eliminate or at least reduce aggressiveness
2. F: Wants to learn to keep his temper GF: Wants to become comfortable with R in home R: Wants to gain F & GF's trust, and "to be able to let them know my feelings"	2. Develop listening skills, substitute verbal for nonverbal communication

Contract

Case III	Case X
10–12 TCFP sessions agreed upon Actual: 15 sessions (12 w. all three members, 3 sessions with some: F + GF/F/J)	8–10 TCFP sessions agreed upon Actual: 5 sessions (2 with all 5 members, 3 mixed: F + GF + G − 1 + G − 3/GF + G1 − 2 − 3/ F + GF)

Tasks

Case III	Case X
17 Session tasks + 18 home tasks	10 Session tasks + 7 home/environmental tasks

Task Achievement Level (0-highest Level: 4)

Case III		Case X	
All tasks addressing Pb.#1:	2.80	All tasks addressing Pb. # 1:	1.2
" " Pb.#2:	2.38	" " " Pb. # 2:	1.64
Tasks adr. Pb #1 & 2 combined:	2.26	1 Task addr. other matters:	4.00
" " other problems:	3.00		

Problem Alleviation Status (0-highest level: 10)

Case III		Case X
Problem # 1 (combined rating):	7.25	Problem # 1: 6 (minimal alleviation)
" # 2 " "	8	" # 2:4 (slight aggravation)

FAD Scores

Not available

F scored in clinical range on all seven dimensions at case opening, and all scores were increased by case closing, except "communication," which remained unchanged. GF's scores were all in healthy functioning range at case opening but fell into clinical range by case closing, except for "affective responsiveness," which improved. GF's statement "I finally felt listened to" confirms this change in score.

Outcomes

Contextual changes: Growing pos. relsh. btw. GF & R. R dreaded foster care, and when she accepted that F& biomother would never get together again, R became very involv. in pb. solv.& tasks. Did well in school throughout. F became depressed, yet pleased w. outcome. Contracted for indiv.treatm.to deal w. anger assoc. w. severe physical abuse in childhood. One yr.later F & GF married, which he had previously refused to do.

Tension, focusing on C-ls shortcomings, escalated in joint sessions to point of P requesting to see F + GF alone. They continued in parent counseling. G-1 was to paternal grandmother, who shortly thereafter separated from her husband, who moved in with F + GF. F & GF married 1 yr. later. G-1 did poorly in school throughout. She was strongly attached to her biomother, whose drug abuse resulted in G-1 original removal by CPS.

commonalities, differed in case outcome: Case III was completed according to plan, and in Case X the TCFP model did not seem to work, and the parents were shifted to parent counseling. Factors on which the two cases are contrasted appear in table 36.1.

In referring back to figure 36.1 for distribution of all responses in the four cases, the "identified" problem child (listed as C-1, except in case IX where both C-1 and C-2 were considered "problems") tends to occupy the highest percentage of responses among the children. G-1 from Case X, however, stands out by accounting for only 1.6% of all responses in the two sessions with all family members present, with her older stepsister occupying 7.8% of the responses.

G-1, who controls the homefront by loud verbal explosions, may paradoxically attempt to control the sessions by her reluctance to speak, which infuriated her parents and stepsister and started a barrage of verbal attacks, which the practitioner tried to stop with the result of being accused of letting herself be sucked into G-1's manipulations the same way the paternal grandmother does. Her parents together held the floor almost 60% of the time as compared with the parents in Case III, who were also very active, holding the floor for almost half the number of responses.

Table 36.2 indicates that G-1's stepsister, G-2, also tried to dominate the situation by initiating more than half of her responses, while G-1 initiated only one-fifth of the few utterances she did engage in. R in Case III, on the other hand took the initiative in 38% of her responses, although she also took advantage of the practitioner's invitation to speak (49% of R's responses). The two "problem" girls in Cases III and X were both exposed

TABLE 36.2
Comparison of Cases III and X: Children's Responses According
to Initiating vs. Responding to Others

N of Responses:	Case III		Case X	
	Girl (12 yr) (N = 919)	Girl#1 (10 yr) (N = 69)	Girl#2 (14 yr) (N = 182)	Girl#3 (7 yr) (N = 34)
	%	%	%	%
Child initiates responses	38	19	60	6
Child responds				
" Prac- titioner	49	52	22	82
" Father	8	3	5	0
" Mother	5	25	11	0
" Sibling	NA	1	2	12
	100	100	100	100

% per child of all responses in case X: Girl#1: 24% Girl#2: 64% Girl#3: 12%

to parental pressures in the sessions, but the practitioner in Case III was able to stop hostile escalation and bring an exchange back in compliance with rules for session behavior, while in Case X she was never able to even get the rules fully accepted. Thus to stop the verbal abuse in Case X, the practitioner decided to end the joint sessions and continued with the parents alone.

The extent to which children participate in family sessions may, however, have less meaning than what they say. The results of content analysis of children responses in Case III and X are presented in table 36.3. actively engaged in tasks and problem solving (48%), but G-1 and G-2 in Case X were almost as much involved proportionately. Much less child involvement is noted in problem identification and selection, which also was found in earlier studies comparing children's and adults' behavior in individual task-centered treatment (Fortune 1979).

Another indicator that G-1 was more "on the spot" than R can be found in the priority ranking of the target problems. In both cases family communication and child's behavior were chosen, but in reversed order. In Case III family communication was ranked above R's problematic behavior. In Case X G-1's acting-out behavior was first. The misery of G-1's session experience is also seen in her crying on three occasions and in the laughter of the stepsister and half-sister. G-1 first cried during problem identification when every family member vividly described her acting-out behaviors at home; the second occasion was during negotiation of consequences for wearing dirty clothes, which the father in particular resented to the point of threatening to dispose of the clothes; and the final

TABLE 36.3
Comparoson of Cases III and X: Content of Children's Responses

	Case III		Case X	
	Girl (12 yr)	Girl#1 (10 yr)	Girl#2 (14 yr)	Girl#3 (7 yr)
Total N of Responses:	(N = 919)	(N = 69)	(N = 182)	(N = 34)
Subject Matter of	%	%	%	%
Children's Responses				
"Simple" responses	28	19	20	56
Problem id/exploration	5	13	15	18
Target pb. determinat.	3	7	5	0
Session tasks*	6	22	18	21
Home tasks	16	2	1	0
Problem-solving	26	20	26	3
Contextual analysis	8	17	12	2
Treatm.sit.or pract.	3	0	3	0
Other	5	0	0	0
	100	100	100	100
Emotional				
expressions:				
laughter/crying	Mixture: 26	Crying: 3	Laughter: 5	Laughter:1

*Tasks done in session, usually involving structured face-to-face communication among family members.

example of crying occurred as G-1 proposed as a consequence that G-1 would not be allowed to talk with her biomother on the phone, if G-1 hit GF or anyone else in the family. Needless to say the practitioner did not go along with these proposals and requested the parents to meet with her alone.

G-1's episodes of crying seem in accord with the findings of Crits-Christoph et al. (1991). In their case study, family discussion of the child, and hostility directed toward the child in family sessions were found to be at higher levels prior to a child's crying spells. And a stepwise discriminant analysis indicated family discussion of the child to be strongest in signaling the onset of crying.

In Case III, R, while crying openly in several sessions, also burst into happy laughs as she evidenced acceptance in the family. Her crying was mostly associated with her little half-brother who still lived with her biomother. R missed her brother and was concerned about his safety as well.

The longer duration and greater severity of the conflict situation in Case X than in Case III are likely to represent a factor with some linkage to case outcome. Furthermore family structural variables obviously need to be considered in choice of modality. Sometimes prior family systems appear to be sufficiently alive to prevent a new, blended family to emerge and gel. In Case X, ten-year-old G-1 had tried for years to get her biological parents back together again, refusing to accept the stepmother with whom she was in almost constant warfare. This girl lost and was sent to the parental grandparents, and her father married his long-term girlfriend, the stepmother.

In case III twelve-year-old R attempted the same thing, but over the course of treatment R accepted the inevitable and opened herself to a relationship to her father's long-term girlfriend, who eventually married the father. A major difference in the two cases, however, is that G-1 had a stepsister and a half-sister to compete with, while R was an only child and likely to remain so because the father was unable to have another child. These family structural differences represent contextual factors with likely impact on case outcome. To state the obvious, family therapy presupposes a family, and if the household members do not experience themselves as a family unit, and only some of the members desire to become one, the outlook for a unit approach is likely to be dim.

A major purpose of seeing parents and children separately initially—and perhaps during later phases of treatment—is to gauge the strength and commitment to the family as a system so as to help the family members decide whether they want to use a family unit or other modality to vitalize the family unit or to facilitate disengagement.

The results of content analysis of children's responses in joint sessions across the eleven pilot cases indicate that it is difficult to accommodate more than three children in any one session. Problem identification becomes lengthy because it takes longer to draw out the children's perceptions of family problems. Some practitioners very skillfully employed children's drawings in this process and were creative in designing home and session tasks in accord with the children's level of interest and communication patterns. The younger children would frequently be seemingly preoccupied with play at the fringe of the circle of people, but from time to time a child would butt in with a very pointed remark showing that the child had been listening intently all along and was well aware of what was going on.

Another factor potentially worthy of further study is an observed link between parents' level of expressed satisfaction and the level of children's participation in the joint sessions. In the three cases with the highest rank of client satisfaction, parents' percentage participation in task activities exceed that of any of the children's. The pattern is reversed in the three cases with the lowest level of client satisfaction. Parents seem to welcome children's active participation in problem solving "up to a point" but are not as satisfied when children become more actively engaged than they are.

Finally, in chaotic family interactions it is almost impossible for practitioners to avoid getting trapped in the crossfire of unfinished sentences and attempts to draw them into the family's agenda of singling out one member as the culprit (as seemed to be the case in Case X). And this problem seems exarcerbated when many children are present in the family sessions.

In sum, case comparison of the four cases showed, as expected, that these children overall participated less in session interaction than parents and the practitioner; that children in their responses focus more on problem solving than on problem identification and exploration; that three of the four children in the two case comparisons initiated fewer responses than those triggered by the practitioner; that numerous contextual variables, such as family structure, number of children in the family, level of conflict, and duration of problem situation are worthy of future systematic examination to gain greater empirical weight as indicators or contraindicators of joint family sessions as the arena for parent–child problem work. Furthermore this case comparison gives some support to the practice observation that seeing parents and children separately may be necessary as preparation for joint sessions.

While triangulation of quantitative and qualitative research methods in this case comparison study produced observations with stronger empirical grounding than that usually gained from clinical trial and error, the need for replication and further work is self-evident. Many types of research designs using integrated methods are available; they are, however, extremely labor intensive and painfully slow. Hill (1989) took five years to study eight cases—and that was just of brief therapy cases! Thus the research tools for study of therapeutic process phenomena should be chosen with great care and with a narrower focus than in the current analysis. Event and context analysis, as used by Crits-Christoph et al. (1991), for example, in their study of a child's crying in family sessions, hold promise as next steps in the ongoing inquiry of how best to facilitate alleviation of parent–child problems.

REFERENCES

Blake, R. L. 1989. Integrating quantitative and qualitative methods in family research. *Family Systems Medicine* 7, no. 4: 411–27.

Brewer, J. and A. Hunter. 1989. *Multimethod Research. A Synthesis of Styles*. Newbury Park, Calif.: Sage.

Combs-Orme, T. 1990. The interface of qualitative and quantitative methods in social work research. In: L. Videka-Sherman and W. J. Reid, eds., *Advances in Clinical Social Work Research*. Silver Spring, Md: NASW Press.

Crits-Christoph, P., L. Luborsky, E. Gay, T. Todd, J. P. Barber, and E. Luborsky.

1991. What makes Susie cry? A symptom-context study of family therapy. *Family Therapy* 30, no. 3: 337–45.

Davis, I. P. and W. J. Reid. 1988. Event analysis in clinical practice and process research. *Social Casework* 69, no. 5: 298–306.

Fortune, A. E. 1979. Problem-solving processes in task-centered treatment with adults and children. *Journal of Social Service Research* 2, no. 4: 357–69.

Gordetsky, S. and J. J. Zilbach. 1989. Child and family therapy: An integrated approach. In: J. J. Zilbach, ed., *Children in Family Therapy: Treatment and Training*. New York: Haworth Press.

Grunebaum, H. and M. L. Belfer. 1986. What family therapists might learn from child psychiatry. *Journal of Marital and Family Therapy* 12, no. 4: 415–23.

Guba, E. G., ed. 1990. *The Paradigm Dialog*. Newbury Park, Calif.: Sage.

Guerney, L. and B. Guerney. 1987. Integrating child and family therapy. *Psychotherapy* 24 (Fall), 3 S: 609–14.

Hill, C. E. 1989. *Therapist Techniques and Client Outcomes. Eight Cases of Brief Psychotherapy*. Newbury Park, Calif.: Sage.

Jick, T. 1983. Mixing qualitative and quantitative methods. Triangulation in action. In: J. Van Manen, ed. *Qualitative Methodology*, pp. 135–48. Beverly Hills: Sage.

Knapfl, K. A. and B. J. Breitmayer. 1991. Triangulation in qualitative research: Issues of conceptual clarity and purpose. In: J. M. Morse, ed., *Qualitative Nursing Research*. Newbury Park, Calif.: Sage.

McDermott, J. F. and W. F. Char. 1974. The undeclared war between child and family therapy. *Journal of Child Psychiatry* 13, no. 3: 422–36.

Morse, J. M., ed. 1991. *Qualitative Nursing Research. A Contemporary Dialogue*. Rev. ed. Newbury Park, Calif.: Sage.

Patton, M. Q. 1980. *Qualitative Evaluation Methods*. Beverly Hills: Sage.

Reid, W. J. 1985. *Family Problem Solving*. New York: Columbia University Press.

Reid, W. J. and T. Donovan. 1990. Treating sibling violence *Family Therapy* 17, no. 1: 49–59.

THIRTY-SEVEN

Grounded Theory Meets the Reflective Practitioner: Integrating Qualitative and Quantitative Methods in Administrative Practice

Susan R. Bernstein and Irwin Epstein

Whether administrators see it this way or not, their work is in many ways analogous to that of researchers. Both are routinely engaged in collecting, analyzing, interpreting, and presenting information. Where they may differ involves: (1) the character of the information (qualitative, quantitative, or both); (2) the kind of analysis (formal or informal, statistical or nonstatistical); (3) the form of interpretation (descriptive, explanatory, or predictive); and (4) the presentation of information (verbal or written). Where administrators and researchers differ most, however, is that administrators continuously use information for making decisions and for taking actions with regard to program planning, implementation, and stabilization (Bielawski and Epstein 1984; Epstein and Tripodi 1977, 1978). Researchers do not.

Despite the striking similarities and likely instructive differences, little attention has been given to the administrative practice/research analogue or to research models that are especially congenial with models of administrative practice. In this paper, we propose that a "grounded theory" approach to research is especially compatible with a "reflective practitioner" approach to administration. Synthesized, they offer a compelling approach for dynamically integrating qualitative and quantitative methods in administrative practice.

In so doing, however, we hasten to point out that what is referred to as "grounded theory" has changed considerably since Glaser and Strauss announced its "discovery" in 1967. In our eyes, some of these changes are less than salutary. And the "reflective practitioner" model so attractively introduced by Schön in 1983 has yet to be fully articulated, particularly with regard to human service administration. Its lack of evolution in this practice context is equally troublesome.

GROUNDED THEORY AND REFLECTIVE MANAGEMENT

"Grounded theory" has come to mean a primarily inductive, qualitative, change-oriented system for generating and testing theory through the continuous interplay between data collection and data analysis (Corbin and Strauss 1990). Viewed in this manner, the generation of grounded theory is similar to what Schön refers to as "reflection in action," a process by which the professional "becomes a researcher in the practice context" (Schön 1983:68–69). However, our understanding of the original meaning of the term *grounded theory* diverges from its current usage.

The seminal feature of Glaser and Strauss's (1967) notion of "grounded theory" was that data could be used to generate, rather than just verify, theory. Their emphasis, and that of Strauss in his later work with Corbin (1990), was on procedures for the development of comprehensive theory. Just as most research to test theories is not conclusive, most grounded theory studies appear to fall short of this level of explanation for phenomena. However, the value of grounded theory is in its approach to data and to the relationship between data and theory. It is an illuminating "approach to conceptualization" (Rennie, Phillips, and Quartaro 1988), and that is the sense in which we use the term.

Glaser and Strauss (1967:15–18) were unequivocal in their assertion that both qualitative and quantitative data could and should be used in both the generation and verification of theory. In 1990, Strauss and Corbin (18–19) briefly say the same thing, while acknowledging that both are rarely used in the same study. Indeed, the very title of their book, *Basics of Qualitative Research: Grounded Theory Procedures and Techniques* seems a retreat from the earlier position. Others have noted the lack of multiple methods and data applied to the same problem, despite professional exhortations to do so (Glisson 1990:191). Consistent with the original conceptualization, however, we believe that the grounded theory approach in administrative practice offers a unique opportunity for demonstrating how qualitative and quantitative methods and data can be integrated.

Initially, Glaser and Strauss (1967:249) maintained that developing grounded theory required "professionally trained sociologists." In his later work with Corbin, Strauss (1990:25–26) maintains that "almost anyone" can do so as long as they study and practice the procedures and are open and flexible enough to adapt them as indicated. We suspect that effective use of the grounded theory approach, like skillful administrative practice, requires the "ability to learn from experience" (McCall and Kaplan 1985:83). Subsumed under this ability are a predisposition for handling and enjoying ambiguity, thinking inductively as well as deductively, and taking risks. The skills required for the approach will be discussed further; however, the extent to which they can be taught and learned seems an unresolved question.

POTENTIAL OF AN INTEGRATING APPROACH

The identification of an approach to integrate quantitative and qualitative methods and data is significant for administration where "Information is the core of the job" (McCall, Morrison, and Hannan 1978:36). Despite the increase in literature on social work administration, little is known empirically about these practitioners (Patti 1983:235). An approach that captures such an essential dimension of administrative work and provides an analog for it promises to stimulate study of what administrators actually do.

Administrators use diverse types of quantitative data concerning clients, staff, and budgets to manage their organizations and to coordinate service delivery (Slavin 1985:311). Some of the information managers need is most adequately acquired through explicit research methods, such as literature reviews, questionnaires, interviews, observational techniques, forms, sampling, and formative evaluation designs. Although they overlap in reality, the major information requirements of administrative practice and the corresponding techniques vary depending on the stage of practice—initiation, implementation, or assessment (Epstein and Tripodi 1977, 1978).

In these days of fiscal austerity, timely acquisition, analysis, dissemination, and utilization of information are becoming increasingly essential for the survival of organizations. The structures and interpersonal relationship patterns in an organization affect its "learning system," making it "more or less adaptable to new findings, more or less resistant to new tasks" (Schön 1983:242). From Drucker's imperatives for nonprofits (1990:115–16) to Kanter's (1983:160–62; 1989:353) description of the "new corporate ideal," the current administrative emphasis is on the free flow of information.

Little is known empirically about how social work administrators use information or information systems (Weirich 1985:326). In several conceptualizations, however, social workers are seen as researchers (Briar 1980:35–36; Grinnell 1985:20–22; Weissman, Epstein, and Savage 1983:262–99). Simon (1989:32) believes managers are experts in the blending of intuitive and analytical styles, as revealed in their "thinking-aloud protocols."

Schön's (1983:236–66, 308) conceptualization of the corporate manager as a "reflective practitioner" is the most comprehensive: "research is an activity of practitioners. It is triggered by features of the practice situation, undertaken on the spot, and immediately linked to action." While there has been considerable interest in Schön's work, perhaps because of the complexity of the associated methods, the "reflective practitioner" idea has not been developed in the investigation of administrative practice. Linking this concept with the grounded theory approach, however, has the potential to stimulate this development.

In the grounded theory approach, one takes as a premise that situations change and that people act on these changes (Corbin and Strauss 1990:5). This emphasis on process, on the interactive, is especially congenial for administrators. Their work requires managing multiple relationships with people who do not necessarily share their objectives.

Another premise of the approach is that it should be applicable in practice. Criteria for assessing the validity of grounded theory are that it "fit, be general enough, . . . be understandable," . . . and "be applicable *in* situations as well as *to* them" (Glaser and Strauss 1967:249). Administrators are involved in an ongoing, iterative process of trying to have what they do be valid for the situation. They seek information in multiple ways about all aspects of their work, determine its meaning, decide what to do, act, and seek information about the results of their actions.

A final premise of the grounded theory approach is its emphasis on the interplay of inductive and deductive thinking (Strauss and Corbin 1990:111–12). This is a crucial reason why the approach has so much potential as an integrating framework for the use of quantitative and qualitative methods and data in administrative practice. Curiously, however, in many discussions of grounded theory, only the inductive method is mentioned. Similarly, in discussions of "quantitative" methods, typically only deductive processes are noted. Reasoning both toward (deductive) and from (inductive) observations is usually involved in any scientific inquiry (Babbie 1989:44). Administrators, too, go from theories (cognitive maps, perspectives, perceptions, principles, values) to observations and from observations build theories of practice.

Despite their assertion that "almost anyone" can develop grounded theory, Glaser and Corbin (1990:25–26, 58) say development requires "a balance among the attributes of creativity, rigor, persistence, and above all, theoretical sensitivity." This sensitivity "refers to the attribute of having insight, the ability to give meaning to data, the capacity to understand, and capability to separate the pertinent from that which isn't" (42). Miles and Huberman (1984:251) add to their similar list of "core requisites for qualitative analysis," the requirement for "cognitive flexibility—the capacity to undo rapidly one's way of construing or transforming the data, and to try another, more promising tack." All these requisites are essential for the effective administrator.

In the grounded theory approach, data collection and analysis are concurrent procedures. This is achieved by constant refinement of the inquiry questions based on analysis of the most recently collected data, by theoretical sampling, and by the constant comparative method (Corbin and Strauss 1990:6–9). These processes parallel those administrators use daily.

Administrators, too, must simultaneously collect and analyze information about multiple issues. When they receive data inconsistent with previous data or their expectations, they search for more data for verification. They seek information from as many dimensions and people related to the problem as possible, and they compare what they learn to other, related phenomena.

In another, similar conceptualization, qualitative data analysis (or, we believe, the grounded theory approach) is a "continuous, iterative enterprise" requiring simultaneous data collection, reduction, display, and conclusion drawing and verification (Miles and Huberman 1984:21–23). For administrators, these processes are critical. The need to reduce data into manageable units, whether by literally coding it or intuitively labeling and sorting it, is constant. Increasingly, the ability to display data, both quantitative and qualitative, in ways that clarify issues and decisions is essential (Peters 1987:582–95). And administrators' efforts to understand the meaning of the information they receive and verify the validity of that meaning are continuous. Administrators, like Schön's (1983:269) reflective practitioners, have to be "open to the situation's back-talk."

GROUNDED ADMINISTRATORS

Perhaps most significantly, the grounded theory approach, in combination with reflection-in-action, is an apt analog for administrative practice because of its suitability for capturing the reality and complexity of that work. We propose that a fertile conceptualization is of administrators as discoverers of grounded theory, with effective ones being grounded administrators. We illustrate the concept here by using, appropriately, a study that had a grounded theory approach to understand how nonprofit agency administrators manage contracted services. Interviews were conducted with managers of diverse agencies, and transcripts of the interviews were analyzed with the assistance of a computer software program, The Ethnograph (Seidel, Kjolseth, and Seymour 1988), which facilitates the coding and conceptualization of the grounded theory approach (Bernstein 1991).

Consistent with the limited empirical research, these managers perceive their skills as "basic, 'not fancy' " (202). Their grounding is not in theories of management, research about what managers do, or in sophisticated managerial systems or tools. Instead, their grounding is in their values, experience, program/people knowledge, and reality.

Although their commitment to clients is repeatedly tested by a conflicting obligation to meet the regulatory requirements of funding sources, administrators are decisive.

> We're not going to do what we don't feel is in the best interests of the child—send the child home sooner than we really want to just to meet a particular deadline, a particular date.   (125)

Being grounded in the fundamental commitment of their jobs is critical to these managers.

> I think the most important thing is keeping in perspective what your job is. You could get so caught up in the forms they could overtake you. That could become your whole job—becoming a forms expert—and you lose sight of who the kids are, and the families, and the people who work in the system, and what the system's goal is, and what the system is responding to in terms of the larger social issues. If you lose sight of all of that, then most likely you're not going to do your job well, is the way I see it.   (203–04)

Effective administrators are also grounded in what they have learned from their own experience (56). They are adept at applying knowledge gained in one situation to others, often seemingly quite different from the first. For example, a manager who was a former engineering student describes how he developed forms to help staff comply with regulatory deadlines.

> I used a systems flow technique [used in designing an airplane] for plotting projects—what has to be built in what order, what gets attached to what in what order, how long does it take, and what are your required steps. That was basically the model that I was using. It worked perfectly, and people liked it.   (59)

Administrators are grounded not only in their values and experience but also in the nature of social work services. They understand the guts of the work they are trying to do. A manager describes an offensive and ineffective effort by nonsocial workers to train human service managers, in this instance "to say no."

If you're at your desk, and you're doing paperwork, and somebody comes to you with problems—they're assuming that their problem is more important than what you're doing, and you have to be able to say no to that. I raised my hand, and I said, "Have you ever had an office that was a storefront, and some little old lady comes up to you while you're doing paperwork and tells you that she's about to be thrown out of her apartment?" No, they've never dealt with a client.   (197)

In addition to being grounded in the work, these administrators consider it their responsibility to know, really know, the people with whom they work.

> The line workers are the key to the whole thing. [The executive director] and I know all of the one hundred employees so if they're doing a good job or if they're screwing up, we know about it.   (178)

This obligation to know people extends beyond the agency to those on whom administrators depend for funding.

> They began to know us. They knew our faces. They knew our names. We became very knowledgeable and viable, and they knew that we were up there. We kept writing. Those are the things that really set the stage, I think, for our getting funded.   (102)

By being grounded in their knowledge of funding organization staff, administrators create a reciprocal knowledge among these staff and thereby have leverage with them. A manager exercises this when she ignores a contractual requirement to maintain supervisory logs:

> But he doesn't challenge me. I think some of it is because they know me well enough and they know the agency well enough that they have some sense of what the quality of work is here.   (105)

In addition to their values, experience, and program/people knowledge, grounded administrators are consummate inductive learners. They are constantly striving to be grounded in reality. They "always try to go through a process of it."

> I feel like my job is to first take in and hear what the users need, the users being everyone in the agency. Interpret that, combined with what has to be, and then give back something that's relevant. So, I see myself as part of that circle really, as opposed to just somebody on top who sends things down.   (69–70)

When government funding agencies are not grounded in reality, administrators are committed to making them so. For managers of community residences for the mentally ill, "the first step" was to get the funding staff out of their offices and "around to see what the agencies did, because they really had no idea."

These grounded administrators learn, repeatedly, from the results of their actions. One describes how he finds out about the "semantics game" played by government funders and nonprofit agencies:

> Getting burned. Looking at my hand and wondering, "Okay, now the city slapped me or the state slapped me for doing that wrong. What did they cite? They cited this. What does that mean? What is the wording? Is there any other way around it? Okay, well, next time we'll word it this way and see what happens. Oh, they accepted it that way. Okay." (144)

To ground themselves in reality, managers must find ways to handle and communicate data. They create forms and charts to make the data visible to staff, to communicate as graphically and quickly as possible the status of the program in achieving contract requirements (77). Since their agencies have computer capability, their ability to monitor and evaluate services increases dramatically (78). They struggle with how "to aggregate things in a reasonable and useful way." (164)

The grounded theory method in combination with reflective administrative practice is proposed as an integrating approach for the use of quantitative and qualitative data in administrative practice. Identifying such an approach is significant because of the centrality of information in administrative work and the need to understand what administrators actually do. This integrating approach is compelling because it is an analog for administrative practice— in its premises, requisite personal qualities, and skills. From its potential to capture the reality of that practice, we propose the conceptualization of the grounded administrator.

Exploiting the potential of this integrating approach will require research, using the grounded theory method, to determine, especially, how administrators do use qualitative methods and data and how they integrate them with quantitative ones. How do administrators know when they are grounded? When they are not? How do they conceptualize the learning systems of their organizations? How do they try to affect or work within them? Schön (1983:337) suggests that reflective administrative practice is inherently in conflict with bureaucratic requirements, but is it?

Finally, the implications of this integrating approach for education in administrative practice need to be considered. It appears there are many parallels between the demands of using the grounded theory method and those of administrative decision making. The approach can model the integration of quantitative and qualitative methods and data for administrators and provide immersion in actual decision making. Most education in administrative practice emphasizes a deductive strategy. This integrating approach has the potential to give students crucial experience in recognizing, using, and integrating deductive and inductive thinking.

REFERENCES

Babbie, E. 1989. *The Practice of Social Research.* Belmont, Calif.: Wadsworth.

Bernstein, S. R. 1991. *Managing Contracted Services in the Nonprofit Agency: Administrative, Ethical, and Political Issues.* Philadelphia: Temple University Press.

Bielawski, B. and I. Epstein. 1984. Assessing program stabilization: An extension of the "differential evaluation" model. *Administration in Social Work* 8 (Winter): 13–23.

Briar, S. 1980. Toward the integration of practice and research. In D. Fanshel, ed., *Future of Social Work Research,* pp. 31–37. Washington, D.C.: NASW Press.

Corbin, J. and A. Strauss. 1990. Grounded theory research: Procedures, canons, and evaluative criteria. *Qualitative Sociology* 13, no. 1: 3–21.

Drucker, P. F. 1990. *Managing the Nonprofit Organization: Principles and Practices.* New York: Harper Collins.

Epstein, I. and T. Tripodi. 1977. *Research Techniques and Program Planning, Monitoring, and Evaluation.* New York: Columbia University Press.

Epstein, I. and T. Tripodi. 1978. Incorporating research into macro social work practice and education. *Administration in Social Work* 2 (Fall): 295–305.

Glaser, B. G. and A. L. Strauss. 1967. *The Discovery of Grounded Theory: Strategies for Qualitative Research.* New York: Aldine De Gruyter.

Glisson, C. 1990. Commentary: Distinguishing and combining qualitative and quantitative methods. In L. Videka-Sherman and W. J. Reid, eds., *Advances in Clinical Social Work Research.* Silver Spring, Md: NASW Press.

Grinnell, R. M., Jr. 1985. *Social Work Research and Evaluation.* Itasca, Ill.: F. E. Peacock.

Kanter, R. M. 1983. *The Change Masters: Innovation and Entrepreneurship in the American Corporation.* New York: Simon and Schuster.

Kanter, R. M. 1989. *When Giants Learn to Dance: Mastering the Challenges of Strategy, Management, and Careers in the 1990s.* New York: Simon and Schuster.

McCall, M. W., Jr. and R. E. Kaplan. 1985. *Whatever It Takes: Decision Makers at Work.* Englewood Cliffs, N.J.: Prentice Hall.

McCall, M. W., Jr., and A. Morrison, and R. L. Hannan. 1978. *Studies of Managerial Work: Results and Methods* (Technical Report no. 9). Greensboro, N.C.: Center for Creative Leadership.

Miles, M. B. and A. M. Huberman. 1984. *Qualitative Data Analysis: A Sourcebook of New Methods.* Beverly Hills: Sage.

Patti, R. J. 1983. *Social Welfare Administration: Managing Social Programs in a Developmental Context.* Englewood Cliffs, N.J.: Prentice-Hall.

Peters, T. 1987. *Thriving on Chaos: Handbook for a Management Revolution.* New York: Harper and Row.

Rennie, D. L., J. R. Phillips, and G. K. Quartaro. 1988. Grounded theory: A promising approach to conceptualization in psychology? *Canadian Psychology* 29, no. 2: 139–50.

Schön, D. A. 1983. *The Reflective Practitioner: How Professionals Think in Action.* New York: Basic Books.

Seidel, J. V., R. Kjolseth, and E. Seymour. 1988. *The Ethnograph* (Version 3.0) (Computer program). Corvallis, Oreg.: Qualis Research Associates.

Simon, H. A. 1989. Making management decisions: the role of intuition and emotion. In W. H. Agor, ed., *Intuition in Organizations: Leading and Managing Productively.* Newbury Park, Calif.: Sage.

Slavin, S., ed. 1985. *Social Administration: The Management of the Social Services.* 2d ed. New York: Haworth.

Strauss, A. and J. Corbin. 1990. *Basics of Qualitative Research: Grounded Theory Procedure and Techniques.* Newbury Park, Calif.: Sage.

Weirich, T. W. 1985. The design of information systems. In S. Slavin, ed., *Social Administration: The Management of the Social Services.* 2d ed., pp. 315–28. New York: Haworth.

Weissman, H., I. Epstein, and A. Savage. 1983. *Agency-Based Social Work: Neglected Aspects of Clinical Practice.* Philadelphia: Temple University Press.

THIRTY-EIGHT

Commentary: Practitioner-Researcher Perspective on the Integration of Qualitative and Quantitative Research Methods

Barry Loneck

When I worked in direct practice, it seemed that much of social work research, as embodied in books, monographs, and journal articles, was not particularly helpful in my clinical work. Following a move into academia and a review of the literature on the issue, I discovered that I was not alone. In this paper, I explore why I think this problem has occurred and what can be done to solve it. My premise is that social work research can be made more useful by integrating qualitative and quantitative methods, that qualitative methods can be used to ensure its relevance to practice, and that quantitative methods can support its validity.

THE PROBLEM

As suggested by Kirk (1990), I want to begin my discussion of this problem with the social work maxim, "start where the client is." But who are the clients of social work researchers? Because the major goals of social work research are to advance knowledge and develop practice methods in the profession (Reid and Smith 1989), it follows that their clients primarily include administrators and the direct practitioners.

I do not use the term *client* lightly. Rather, the word *client* implies a relationship with some provider and, further, this provider has a responsibility to serve the client. In the present discussion, I mean to say that the social work researchers have a responsibility to ensure that their work is of benefit to both administrators and direct practitioners.

The problem is, however, that the benefits of social work research have not been distributed uniformly across these groups. Administrators seem to have benefited the most. This is in large part due to the applicability of quantitative methods to their practice problems. Although there is a movement toward the integration of qualitative and quantitative methods in the study of administrative practice, as Epstein and Bernstein have indicated in their paper, most administrators are usually interested in finding out about client characteristics and needs, in seeing whether or not a program or policy has achieved its goals, or in comparing some new program to a standard intervention. These problems are resolved with relative ease through the use of quantitative approaches such as survey research, evaluation research, and experimental research.

However, despite the fact that social work has increased its use of scientific method (Fischer 1981), direct practitioners have been deprived of the benefits of social work research. Rosen and Mutschler (1982) found that direct practitioners viewed research as less important and less useful than both master of social work (M.S.W.) students and doctoral students. Comparing social work students, faculty, and direct practitioners, Lazar (1991) found that direct practitioners rated research less important than faculty did and less useful than both faculty and students did.

As potential consumers of social work research, direct practitioners have become disenfranchised from its benefits because it yields little in the way of practical application (Kirk 1990). In other words, the results of most social work research have little bearing on what direct practitioners do for or with their clients. But why has this occurred? I would propose that, when it comes to direct practice, a fundamental error has been made in social work research—an error in problem selection and formulation. This error revolves around four major issues.

First, social work researchers tend to select problems that are of more interest to administrators than to direct practitioners. Second, in available practice research, the critical factors of direct practice, factors that are associated with change, have not been fully identified. Instead, practice research has focused on the efficacy of entire procedures. While quantitative approaches have supported the validity of this research, direct practice within these procedural "black boxes" has not been adequately defined. Third, the concepts used to name these factors tend to be obscure terms. Frequently, these terms are better known to the researchers and their colleagues than to direct practitioners. Fourth, the ways in which these factors interrelate to define the actual process of direct practice have not been specified. In other words, although practice research may have specified what is to be done, it has not specified how it is to be done, at least not on the level of day-to-day or session-to-session practice.

To determine what is relevant for the direct practitioner, we must return to the maxim, "start where the client is." Social workers in direct practice want to know how to best conduct their practice. What could be more valuable to direct practitioners than evaluating what goes on in their interaction with clients? Unfortunately, social work research has not examined this area in a way required by those on the front line.

A SOLUTION

Harrison has stated in his paper that the integration of qualitative and quantitative methods is inevitable. To this I would add that, in the study of direct practice, integration of these methods is a necessity.

How can this integration occur? As a way of integrating methods, I propose using another social work maxim, "partialize the problem." As a first step in integrating these methods, social work research must jump into the "black box" of direct practice and examine it using qualitative methods (Kirk 1990). In this way, qualitative methods can be used to address each of the aforementioned issues in problem selection and formulation. First, we must use qualitative methods to identify problems encountered in direct practice by listening to and observing the work of direct practitioners. Certainly, this would not prohibit the researcher from formulating a direct practice research problem. However, qualitative methods can help to confirm the existence of such problems, as well as develop and refine them in a way most needed by direct practitioners.

Second, qualitative methods can be used to help researchers identify possible factors that have a direct impact on the problem. Third, these methods can help them to frame the research question by using the terms and concepts of direct practitioners. Fourth, qualitative methods can help researchers identify possible relationships between and among those concepts and to describe the process of direct practice.

Thus, by using qualitative methods in these ways, the research questions studied will be aimed at direct practice, potential factors that have a bearing on the problem will be identified, the concepts used will be ecologically valid, and the researcher will be able to formulate some tentative hypotheses. As a result, qualitative methods will ensure that subsequent research will be relevant to our clients, the direct practitioners.

As a second step in integrating qualitative and quantitative methods, we must use descriptive statistical techniques to test the associations between concepts postulated in the qualitative work. This would include statistical modeling of the direct practice process, in order to validate the links between and among concepts. This process can identify those methods that appear to be effective, as well as those that have no apparent effect or are possibly detrimental.

Once successful methods have been tentatively identified within a particular problem area, specific treatments or interventions can be developed that incorporate apparently successful methods and eliminate those that are apparently ineffective. Thus, in this third, and final, step of integrating qualitative and quantitative research methods, experimental and quasi-experimental designs can be used to test the effectiveness of these interventions on clinical outcome.

Partializing the research process is not a new idea (e.g., Reid 1990). Nevertheless, by using this three-step approach of qualitative exploration, descriptive analysis, and experimental testing, social work research can be valuable in helping to define a set of practice principles that are empirically valid and that have value and relevance for the direct practitioner.

EXAMPLE

In my own work, I am examining the relationship between therapeutic process and outcome with mentally ill chemical abusing (MICA) clients who enter a psychiatric emergency room. MICA clients are sometimes called dual diagnosed because they have a psychiatric diagnosis, such as schizophrenia, and a psychoactive substance disorder, such as alcohol dependence. Treatment of these clients is difficult for several reasons (Way and McCormick 1990). Like other substance abusers, they tend to deny their problems and, consequently, are resistant to therapy (e.g., Drake et al. 1990). Also, as researcher-clinicians Hellerstein and Meehan (1987) have noted, because mental health treatment tends to be supportive and substance abuse treatment tends to be confrontive, the clinician is faced with the dilemma of mixing the two approaches in an appropriate way.

One of the major goals of the psychiatric emergency room is successful referral of clients to appropriate services in the community. Unfortunately, only about half of the MICA clients follow through with such referrals (Solomon and Gordon 1988). As a result, I wanted to know what therapeutic process, that is, what mix of confrontation and support over time, is associated with MICA clients lowering their resistance and engaging in recommended treatment following their visits to the psychiatric emergency room.

To approach this problem, a framework developed by Greenberg (1986) makes clinical sense. Greenberg stated that three major levels of therapeutic process exist. The first is the speech act, which refers to the types of statements made by the clinician and the client; on this level a client's statement would be considered resistance and a clinician's statement would be considered support or confrontation. The next level is episode; an episode is a series of statements (speech acts) between the clinician and client that focus on a particular problem or issue. The third level is the relationship and is the quality of the therapeutic alliance between the clinician and client.

To assess the viability of this framework and to search for other factors that might impact outcome, I conducted a focus group with clinicians at a psychiatric emergency room in New York City. A focus group (Krueger 1988; Morgan 1988) is a qualitative research technique in which a moderator leads a planned group discussion that focuses on one or more topics selected by the researcher. In the focus group at the psychiatric emergency room, I asked the clinicians what clinical factors affected outcome of MICA clients, that is, whether or not MICA clients followed through with their referral to recommended treatment in the community. In a preliminary analysis of the focus group data, the clinicians validated the importance of client resistance and the impact of support and confrontation on outcome, as well as the effect of the therapeutic alliance on outcome.

Meeting with the clinicians in the focus group had the additional benefit of engaging them in the research at a fundamental level—formulating the problem and generating hypotheses. From my perspective, as a researcher, the clinicians confirmed the importance of several key elements of Greenberg's framework, using their own words. From the clinicians' perspective, they helped to generate a set of hypotheses for further study. In this way, these clinicians became part of the research process and now have a stake in its successful completion.

In the next phase of my research, I am conducting an in-depth study of sessions with MICA clients in that same psychiatric emergency room. Sessions are being audiotaped by the practitioners and will be transcribed. I am using the Hill (1986) Counselor Response Category System and the Client Behavior System (Hill et al. 1991) to categorize each therapist and client statement in each session. The counselor system includes the categories of support and confrontation, and the client system includes the category of resistance—terms used by the clinicians themselves in the focus group. Once each statement has been categorized, client behaviors and therapist responses will be plotted over time in an effort to discern therapeutic patterns.

In addition, I plan to use the Working Alliance Inventory (Horvath and Greenberg 1986) to assess the quality of the therapeutic relationship. It contains three scales: agreement on goals, agreement on tasks, and clinician–client bond. Again, in the focus group, practitioners specifically mentioned the importance of agreement on goals and clinician-client bond in obtaining a successful outcome.

Obviously, this is a data-intensive procedure and it prohibits a large sample. As a result, a qualitative comparison of patterns in twenty successful and twenty unsuccessful cases serves as a starting point for the analysis. This will be followed by an attempt to construct statistical models of successful and unsuccessful therapeutic processes. Finally, an intervention protocol, based on these models, will be developed. The goal of this protocol is to increase the number of successful referrals of MICA clients seen in a psychiatric emergency room. The effectiveness of this clinically based intervention protocol will be assessed by use of a standard experimental design.

In conclusion, I believe that social work research has neglected the needs of direct practitioners through the almost exclusive use of quantitative methods. Although a model of practice or clinical procedure can be easily defined, how a direct practitioner implements it, brings it to life, can be extremely complex. It is here that qualitative methods can help the social work researcher define key concepts and practice principles, which then can be tested through quantitative methods.

REFERENCES

Drake, R. E., F. C. Osher, D. L. Noordsy, S. C. Hurlbut, G. B. Teague, and M. S. Beaudett. 1990. Diagnosis of alcohol use disorders in schizophrenia. *Schizophrenia Bulletin* 16: 57–67.

Fischer, J. 1981. The social work revolution. *Social Work* 26: 199–207.

Greenberg, L. S. 1986. Change process research. *Journal of Consulting and Clinical Psychology* 54: 4–9.

Hellerstein, D. J. and B. Meehan. 1987. Outpatient group therapy for schizophrenic substance abusers. *American Journal of Psychiatry* 144: 1337–39.

Hill, C. 1986. An overview of the Hill Counselor and Client Verbal Response Mode Category Systems. In L. S. Greenberg and W. M. Pinsof, eds., *Psychotherapeutic Process: A Research Handbook*, pp. 131–59. New York: Guilford Press.

Hill, C., M. M. Corbett, B. Kanitz, P. Rios, R. Lightsey, and M. Gomez. 1991. Client behavior in psychotherapy sessions: Development of a measure. Manuscript submitted for publication.

Horvath, A. O. and L. Greenberg. 1986. The development of the Working Alliance Inventory. In Greenberg and Pinsof, eds., *Psychotherapeutic Process: A Research Handbook*, pp. 529–56. New York: Guilford Press.

Kirk, S. A. 1990. Research utilization: The substructure of belief. In L. Videka-Sherman and W. J. Reid, eds., *Advances in Clinical Social Work Research,* pp. 233–50. Silver Spring, Md: NASW Press.

Krueger, R. A. 1988. *Focus Groups: A Practical Guide for Applied Research.* Newbury Park, Calif.: Sage.

Lazar, A. 1991. Faculty, practitioner, and student attitudes toward research. *Journal of Social Work Education* 27: 34–40.

Morgan, D. L. 1988. *Focus Groups as Qualitative Research.* Newbury Park, Calif.: Sage.

Reid, W. J. 1990. Change-process research: A new paradigm. In Videka-Sherman and Reid, eds., *Advances in Clinical Social Work Research,* pp. 130–48. Silver Spring, Md: NASW Press.

Reid, W. J. and A. D. Smith. 1989. *Research in Social Work.* 2d ed. New York: Columbia University Press.

Rosen, A. and E. Mutschler. 1982. Social work students' and practitioners' orientation to research. *Journal of Education for Social Work* 18, no.: 62–68.

Solomon, P. and B. Gordon. 1988. Outpatient compliance of psychiatric emergency room patients by presenting problems. *Psychiatric Quarterly* 59: 271–83.

Way, B. and L. L. McCormick. 1990. *The Mentally Ill Chemical Abusing Population: A Review of the Literature.* Albany: Bureau of Evaluation and Services Research, New York State Office of Mental Health.

THIRTY-NINE

Commentary: The Qualitative/ Quantitative Debate: Moving Beyond Acrimony to Meaningful Dialogue

Ronald W. Toseland

I am a bit puzzled and, sometimes, even a bit shocked by the tone of the debate between those who advocate qualitative or quantitative methods of data collection and analysis. At a recent conference, I stopped on a large stairwell to talk with a colleague known for his staunch quantitative approach. When a second colleague joined us, the conversation switched to what sessions he was going to attend that morning. In a rather disparaging tone, he kidded about attending a workshop about the importance of qualitative methods in social work. It was clear to me that both he and my other colleague could see no value in the qualitative workshop. I continued down the stairs and ran into a group of individuals on the very next landing who are known for their criticism of quantitative approaches and for championing qualitative approaches. When I stopped to say hello to these individuals whom I also respect and admire, I found that they were talking about how much they were looking forward to the workshop on the importance of qualitative methods, and how "worthless" and "useless" the recent emphasis on empiricism, single-subject designs, and becoming a practitioner/ researcher was for clinical social work students.

I was, therefore, refreshed by the perspectives of the preceding authors who have given their perspectives on the integration of qualitative and quantitative methods. They clearly understand and respect the inextricable link between quantitative and qualitative approaches to the collection and analysis of data. They described and demonstrated how one approach enhances the other and how an exclusive reliance on either a quantitative or a qualitative approach can be limiting.

My own experiences conducting large and small research projects over the past twenty years confirms their perspective. Three recent examples from my own research may help to illustrate how qualitative and quantitative approaches can enhance each other and how they are inextricably interwoven and blended together in many research projects.

Example 1. The first project was an evaluation of the efficacy of short-term individual counseling for caregivers of cancer patients in which I conducted some preliminary data analyses on participants who had completed both preintervention and postintervention interview protocols. Although there were some open-ended questions requiring qualitative responses, much of the protocol consisted of standardized instruments, and our analyses utilized multivariate, repeated measures, analysis of variance (MANOVA)—clearly a quantitative approach. We found, to our dismay, that, as compared with participants receiving usual treatment, the short-term counseling produced few statistically significant improvements on the measures included in our interview protocol. We decided to listen to some of the tapes of the counseling sessions and to read participants' open-ended responses to our questions about the helpfulness of the intervention program. It became clear from this qualitative analysis that many of the participants were coping very well with their spouses' cancer and that they had agreed to participate in the research because they wanted to be helpful and to make a contribution to improving services for cancer patients and their families, rather than because they were very distressed and felt a pressing need for counseling. However, we also discovered that there was a subgroup of participants who were quite distressed. We then went back and reanalyzed the data separately for subjects who were very distressed and for subjects who were only moderately distressed. We found that the intervention was effective with the distressed group but not with the nondistressed group. Clearly, our combined use of qualitative and quantitative data enhanced our overall ability to interpret the results of our study.

Example 2. The second project evaluated the effectiveness and efficiency of an interdisciplinary team approach to the managed care of frail elderly veteran outpatients. One-hundred sixty frail veterans were randomly assigned to the team approach or to usual primary care by a physician. The blending of quantitative and qualitative research approaches in this project can be seen both in the data collection methods and in the analysis and interpretation of the data. For example, quantitative data collection included a trained rater observing frail veterans and recording their functional abilities on a standardized functional assessment measure. It also included two research nurses abstracting data from medical records to get a rating of the quality of the health care provided and the severity of each veteran's illnesses over the course of the intervention. However, data collection also included asking the veterans about their perceptions of different aspects of the care they were receiving and asking members of the clinical team and some of the participating primary care physicians about their perceptions of the outpatient health care that was delivered to frail aging veterans.

Data collection about the efficiency of the team approach was based on a quantitative analysis of the inpatient and outpatient health care utilization of the veterans in the study. The quantitative analyses revealed a complex pattern of usage rather than a clear-cut finding that one approach resulted in veteran's using fewer services. For example, it was found that veterans in the team approach used more rehabilitation services and more of the services of certain specialty clinics such as podiatry but fewer emergency room services and fewer of the services of certain other specialty clinics. To interpret patterns in the quantitative data we employed a qualitative approach, consulting both with the clinical team and some of the primary physicians who took part in the study. Clearly, the use of quantitative and qualitative approaches enhanced our ability to assess both the effectiveness and the efficiency of team care as compared with primary care.

Example 3.   The third project evaluated the comparative effectiveness of individual and group counseling for caregivers of the frail elderly. A quantitative analysis of the data revealed that the individual counseling had more impact on psychological well-being of participants, whereas group counseling had more impact on the social well-being of participants. We could not ascertain from the quantitative data analyses what it was about the two intervention approaches that caused their differential effectiveness. To interpret the results, my colleagues and I analyzed segments of the audiotaped recording of the group and individual sessions using the Vanderbilt Psychotherapy Process Scales and a measure of advice giving developed by a doctoral student for her dissertation (Smith, Tobin, and Toseland 1992). The findings of this latter study contributed to our understanding of the patterns of data we had obtained from our quantitative analyses of the effects of individual and group counseling for caregivers of frail older adults.

These three examples, and the preceding papers, clearly suggest that it is time to move beyond the long-standing, acrimonious debate between those who advocate an exclusive reliance on quantitative methods and those who advocate an exclusive reliance on qualitative approaches. Instead of hurling accusations at each other, it would be much more productive if both sides of the debate would instead concentrate on how to combine and make the best use of quantitative and qualitative methodologies. Such a change would go a long way toward strengthening our inevitably imperfect comprehension of the phenomena we study in our research endeavors.

REFERENCES

Smith, M., S. Tobin, and R. Toseland. 1992. Therapeutic processes in professional and peer counseling of family caregivers of frail elderly people. *Social Work* 37, no. 4: 289–384.

V

Qualitative Research and Epistemological Issues

FORTY

Setting the Theme: Many Ways of Knowing

Ann Hartman

Nothing is more crucial in shaping and defining the social work profession and its practice than that profession's definition of "the truth" and the selection of preferred strategies for knowledge building. Further, the process through which truth is defined and the methods of truth seeking chosen is highly political. As French philosopher Michael Foucault has taught us, knowledge is power and power is knowledge. He writes, "We are subjected to the production of truth through power and we cannot exercise power except through the production of truth" (1980:93). Although some truths are privileged and some are not, Foucault points out that it is not the priviledging of specific ideologies in that process that is most important but the "production of effective instruments for the formulation and accumulation of knowledge—methods of observation, techniques of registration, procedures for investigation and research, apparatuses of control. All this means that power, when it is exercised through these subtle mechanisms, cannot but evolve, organize, and put into circulation a knowledge or rather apparatuses of knowledge which are not ideological constructs" (1980:102).

This volume brings together a varied group of searchers after knowledge who share a common theme, an interest in qualitative research. Of course qualitative exploration is not new to social work. In the early years, our professional journals were filled with statements of practice wisdom, illustrated or supported by two or three case narratives. Much of the knowledge base of social work was thus painstakingly constructed of the experience-near reports of those deeply immersed in practice with individuals, families, groups, and communities.

With the coming of the scientific approach and the struggle of social work scholars and academics to gain recognition and validation in the universities, the old ways of knowing were discredited and social work embarked on its romance with empiricism.

In the last decade a return to qualitative research has occurred and a lively debate about the proper approach to knowledge development has ensued. The authors in this book have been a part of the reexamination of qualitative methods of knowledge building and a part of that debate. It has often been a lonely or embattled position. Most of these authors have probably felt silenced at times, their contributions defined as trivial, fuzzy headed, or unscientific. It is important that these writers' voices be heard, that their work be added to the fund of social work knowledge.

Also important is that the profession be aware of the utility and the appropriateness of different research methodologies. But the ongoing discussion raises much more than methodological issues. It surfaces the major epistimological, ontological, and value questions that are a continuous challenge in any human enterprise, in any practice, and certainly in any search for knowledge. The questions are explicitly or implicitly asked: What is truth? How may we know it? Or, even, is there such a thing as truth and may we ever know it?

We are not alone in asking these questions. Intellectual leaders in the sciences and the social sciences, as well as in the other helping professions, are challenging each other over similar issues. The discussions have spawned a new set of "isms": constructivism, deconstructionism, modernism, postmodernism, and even feminist postmodernism, which join the more familiar "isms" often rediscussed and evaluated: pragmatism, utilitarianism, relativism, positivism, and empiricism.

It is essential that all who teach, who do research, who serve on editorial boards, who publish articles and prepare papers published in books such as this one struggle with these questions and identify their epistomologies, their worldviews, their biases, their convictions about the nature of knowledge and knowledge seeking.

Znaniecki (1965), in his classic study, *The Social Role of the Man of Knowledge,* explored the social processes involved in the definitions of knowledge and in the boundary maintenance and gatekeeping functions of those "men," and now, it is hoped, women too, who select materials for publication and presentation. In our own profession, Karger (1983), very much in the spirit of Foucault, reminds us that at the heart of the debate about research and the nature of knowledge is a struggle for "the political control of the direction, leadership, and the future of the profession" (202). He writes "Those who define the questions to be asked define the parameters of the answers, and it is the parameters of the questions and the ensuing answers that function as the lens by which people view reality" (203).

Recently, an executive committee of a major school of social work challenged the qualitative research completed by a young scholar in her tenure review process. The study in question consisted of extensive and carefully analyzed interviews done in the field, interviews that had been recorded and fully transcribed. The interviews explored the subjects' perception of some major events in their lives. The members of the committee stated that they had difficulty evaluating the reliability and validity of the findings. Even though three papers based on the study had been accepted for publication in peer-reviewed journals, the committee continued to question the work based on the small sample size, the use of retrospective data, and the failure to establish a causal relationship among variables—criteria inappropriate to the design of her study.

We must not limit our profession by limiting our searches, by embracing a narrow epistemology, by failing to take advantage of the many ways of knowing. This volume expands our vision of truth seeking. Each discovery contributes to our knowledge and each way of knowing deepens our understanding and adds another dimension to our view of the world.

Of course we need large-scale studies in which variables can be reduced to measurable units and the results translated into the language of statistical significance, but we also need in-depth "thick descriptions," grounded in context, of a single case, a single instance, or even a brief exchange. For example, large-scale studies of trends in marriage today furnish helpful information about a rapidly changing social institution. But getting inside one marriage, as in *Who's Afraid of Virginia Woolf?*, richly displays the complexities of one relationship, leading us to new insights about the pain, the joys, the expectations, the disappointments, the intimacy, and the ultimate aloneness in relationships. Both the scientific and the artistic provide us with ways of knowing, and, in fact, as Geertz (1983) has pointed out, innovative thinkers in many fields are blurring the genres, finding art in science and science in art and social theory in all human creation and activity.

There are indeed many ways of knowing and many kinds of knowers: researchers, practitioners, clients. Some seekers of truth may take a path that demands distance and objectivity, while others rely on deeply personal and empathic knowing. Some will find the validation of their findings through statistical analysis and probability tests. Others will find it through the intensity and authenticity of "being there" (Geertz 1988) or through public and shared consensus in what has been called "practice wisdom" (Siporin 1989). Some truth seekers will strive to predict while other turn to the past for an enhanced understanding of the present. We must not turn our backs on any opportunities to enhance our knowledge, whether they be through the examination of correlations or the explications of myths, which, according to Rein and White (1981) align "rational action with normative ideals and historical commitments" (16). We must attend to the theoretical advances presented by our scholars and academicians but also gather and listen to the "stories that rise up out of practice" which "confront, challenge, confirm, or deny the stories that 'come down' from the distal citadels of the profession" (19).

We must listen to our clients and bring forth their wisdom, their lived experience, their visions of the world. As many of our clients have been powerless and oppressed, their knowledge has been subjugated, their insights have been excluded from the discourse by those empowered to define the "truth": experts, professionals, editorial boards.

We welcome survey research, large-scale studies that discover trends and identify needs. We welcome program evaluations that we may know more about what seems to "work." We need outcome studies that may call upon a range of ways of knowing through a single case study, experimental designs, or longitudinal reviews that reflect upon the consequences of events or conditions or interventions. We must also welcome phenomenological studies that may lead the explorer on uncharted paths, naturalistic and ethnographic studies that are familiar but more disciplined extensions of the practitioner's case study (Rodwell 1987). We should embrace heuristic approaches where the goal is utility rather than certainty as well as hermeneutic and interpretive investigations that lead us to decipher the meaning of events to clients, to significant others, and to ourselves (Scott 1989).

We can enhance our understanding by listening to and reporting the narratives, the stories that make order and sense of human experience and "organize it into temporarily meaningful episodes" (Polkinghorne 1988:7). We must attend to the myths that link value and action and we must respect the tacit knowledge and practice wisdom that is "inductively derived from experience and shapes the practitioners' cognitive schema" (Scott 1989:40).

And as the profession is more open to exploring and receiving many ways of knowing, we must be ever aware that each is grounded in and an expression of certain ontological, epistemological, and value assumptions. These assumptions must be made explicit, for knowledge and truths can be understood and evaluated only in the context of the framing assumptions. Theories can both illuminate and obscure our vision (Scott 1989:48). They also "constitute moral intervention in the social life whose conditions of existence they seek to clarify'' (Giddens 1976:8). We must be clear about the nature of these interventions.

The boundaries of our profession are wide and deep and our literature must reflect this extensive territory. We are concerned about the nature of our society, about social policy, social justice, and social programs. We are concerned about human associations, about communities, neighborhoods, organizations, and families. We are concerned about the life stories and the inner experiences of the people we serve and about the meaning to them of their experiences. No one way of knowing can explore this vast and varied territory. In the papers that follow, several ways of knowing, several paths to knowledge development are presented. We hope that this volume may be useful to those wishing to contribute to the profession's knowledge-building efforts. We hope the materials presented here will stimulate further discussion about the multiple ways of knowing and that out of this discussion will come even more ways to search, to discover, to enrich our understanding of our clients, ourselves, and our world.

References

Foucault, M. 1980. *Power/Knowledge: Selected Interviews and Other Writings.* New York: Pantheon.
Geertz, C. 1983. Blurred genres: The refiguration of social thought. *Local Knowledge: Further Essays in Interpretive Anthropology.* New York: Basic Books.
Geertz, C. 1988. *Works and Lives.* Stanford, Calif.: Stanford University Press.
Giddens, A. 1976. *New Rules of Sociological Method.* London: Hutchinson.
Karger, H. J. 1983. Science, research and social work: Who controls the profession? *Social Work* 28 (May–June): 200–5.
Polkinghorne, D. E. 1988. *Narrative Knowing and the Human Sciences.* Albany: State University of New York Press.
Rein, M. and S. H. White. 1981. Knowledge for practice. *Social Service Review* 55 (March): 1–41.
Rodwell, M. K. 1987. Naturalistic inquiry: An alternative model for social work assessment. *Social Service Review* 61, no. 2 (June): 231–46.
Scott, D. 1989. Meaning construction and social work practice. *Social Service Review* (March): 39–51.
Siporin, M. 1989. Metamodels, models, and basics: An essay review. *Social Service Review* 63, no. 3: 474–80.
Znaniecki, F. 1965. *The Social Role of the Man of Knowledge.* New York: Harper Row, Torch Books.

FORTY-ONE

Reframing the Epistemological Debate

William J. Reid

During the past decade the human service professions have been caught up in a growing debate over their epistemologies. The debate has been fueled by dissatisfactions with "mainstream" research approaches, those that tend to use preplanned designs, structured instruments, and largely quantitative data to examine frequencies and relationships within specific sets of variables. Mainstream research has been criticized for its adherence to inappropriately quantitative, reductionistic, context-stripping modes of inquiry that are based on an outmoded logical positivist epistemology; further, mainstream researchers may even impede development of professional knowledge by downplaying the intuitive insights of practitioners and foreclosing alternative research approaches (Gergen 1985; Haworth 1984; Heineman 1981; Lather 1987; Lincoln and Guba 1985; Tyson 1992; Witkin 1989).

The critics have proposed alternative paradigms that, they claim, offer research strategies better suited to the study of social phenomena or better designed to meet the interests of oppressed and other groups. These paradigms, which place much greater emphasis on qualitative methodology than one finds in mainstream research, include constructivism (Gergen 1985; Lincoln 1990), heuristic approaches (Pieper 1989, Tyson 1993), critical theory (Lather 1987; Popkewitz 1990), naturalist inquiry (Lincoln and Guba 1985), and "new paradigm" research (Reason and Rowan 1981).

Mainstream research has had its defenders (Fraser et al. 1991; Hudson 1982). It has been argued that the fundamentals of this research model were well established before logical positivism (Schuerman 1982) and that they can be justified by works of philosophers outside the logical positivist tradition—for example, Dewey, Popper, and Lakatos (Phillips 1987b). Recently, efforts have been made to construct postpositivist paradigms for social inquiry that can answer criticisms of logical positivism yet still provide justification for mainstream research—for example, the postpositivist philosophy of Phillips (1987a), the pragmatic behaviorism of Fishman (1988), and the temperate rationality of Newton-Smith (1981). Aside from agreeing that logical positivism is passé, critics and defenders have articulated few points of consensus.

The debate has taken the shape of a clash of paradigms—those of mainstream research versus the alternatives. The result has often been the generation of more heat than light (Brekke 1986) or the apposition of unfruitful dichotomies (Berlin 1990).

Speaking now (and henceforth) of social work, I would argue that the debate should be cast in other terms, that we should move away from arguments about epistemological worldviews and devote our energies instead to clarifying and resolving the specific issues imbedded in these arguments. These issues need to be addressed within a social work context. Further the issues need to be discussed in a vocabulary that social workers, both practitioners and researchers, can connect to their own professional experience.

Although philosophers can make valuable contributions to this discourse they should be used as guides, not authorities. As Rorty (1979), himself a philosopher of some repute, has pointed out, the presumption that philosophers "have a special knowledge about knowledge" is a dubious post-Kantian invention of philosophers themselves." The epistemologies of philosophers offer no " 'foundations or justifications' for scientific practice or for anything else in our culture" (393).

To practice what I have just preached, I attempt in this paper to deal with some issues that are a part of this debate. I have selected three that appear to be of central importance: (1) the appraisal of knowledge, (2) the relative importance of research and practice wisdom in knowledge building, (3) the interface between qualitative and quantitative methodologies in scientific inquiry. For each issue I offer what I consider to be some possible, and partial, resolutions, drawing on points of view that many social work practitioners and researchers share, as well as on contributions of philosophers, methodologists, and social work scholars.

APPRAISING KNOWLEDGE

We all have ways of evaluating the truth claims of knowledge. We are constantly sorting out the streams of information that come our way into what we regard as true, probably true, probably false, false, or uncertain. In this process we inevitably employ evaluative criteria.

In social work, as a practice profession, such criteria are best seen as based in the professional community at large rather than as the province of a particular elite, such as researchers or academicians. These criteria are fallible, correctable, and variously interpreted. But acceptance of such criteria to evaluate knowledge provides the basis for what Bloom (1990:348) has called a "social epistemological contract in which individuals surrender (agree) to common assumptions about the nature of knowledge and work within these assumptions."

Even if a relativistic, multiepistemological perspective is adopted (Harrison, this volume, Reamer 1992), standards are needed to evaluate knowledge claims emanating from diverse and conflicting epistemologies. Although devising criteria that would be universally accepted is not possible, proposing some that the majority of social work practitioners, scholars, and researchers would find acceptable may be possible. Below are presented some considerations that might form a basis for the development of such criteria.

Corroboration

Obtaining corroborative evidence bearing on the truth of a belief is generally seen as critical in establishing knowledge. Following Pepper (1970) one can distinguish between two types of corroborative evidence. "Multiplicative corroboration" involves person-to-person agreement or intersubjectivity. Do observers concur that a belief is warranted by the evidence? Do they concur that it has, in Dewey's (1938) terms, "warranted assertibility?" "Structural corroboration" requires a logical convergence of factual evidence. Do the facts add up to provide sufficient evidential warrant? For example, in accepting as knowledge that prenatal cocaine exposure can lead to behavior problems in children, one might require consistent agreement among clinicians and researchers that the evidence pointed in this direction. One might also demand evidence from convergent facts delineating the mechanisms by which prenatal cocaine exposure might lead to behavior problems.

In social work, intersubjective corroboration is particularly important given our lack of an extensive research base. As we know, much of our knowledge is built from agreements among practitioners. However, this knowledge still has an empirical foundation since it is derived from the experiences of practitioners.

An important extension of the nature of corroboration may be found in the principle of *"multiplism"* (Cook 1987). In essence, multiplism makes use of multiple methods and perspectives in knowledge building. Within a given study, multiple measures and modes of analysis are used to cross-validate findings. Multiple studies are concentrated on given research questions.

Such studies make use of different designs within the same or different projects. In multiplism, no single design, method of measurement, or analytic technique is seen as inherently superior. For example, experiments and quantitative analysis have their strengths and limitations and are better suited to certain questions than others. What is needed is not reliance on any particular methodology but rather the use of methods in combination, so that the weaknesses of one are offset by the strengths of another.

What is more, multiplism argues for "use of multiple stakeholders to formulate research questions and the use of multiple theoretical and value frameworks to interpret research questions and findings" (Cook 1987:459). In social work practice this notion can be extended to multiple applications of ideas and methods in diverse client populations and settings. Knowledge becomes credible as it becomes reaffirmed in these multiple contexts by researchers, theorists, and practitioners. From this perspective, research findings are less likely to be taken as definitive knowledge and more likely to be viewed as offering direction for analysis, application, and eventual synthesis with other forms of knowledge.

Bias and Truth

Bias refers to any of a multitude of factors that can interfere with the appraisal of the truth claims of knowledge. Because standards for appraising are seldom clear-cut, the presence of bias is difficult to determine. Yet its occurrence as a threat to the validity of social work knowledge has always been recognized, as has been the importance of its identification and control.

For example, in *Social Diagnosis* (1917), Richmond discussed the importance of recognizing and correcting for numerous sources of bias, such as false analogy, that might interfere with drawing valid inferences from case evidence. In more recent times, practitioners have been taught the importance of becoming aware of misperceptions of clients resulting from countertransference or from ethnic or cultural stereotyping. Used in a broad sense to include not only perceptual bias but also bias in sampling, measurement, interpretation, and so on, bias becomes virtually tantamount to error.

But the identification and control of even the most obvious biases—for example, researchers construing ambiguous data to justify their cherished hypotheses—are not possible without some standard of truth, even though, as Rorty (1979:385) puts it, " 'objective truth' is no more and no less than the best idea we have about how to explain what is going on." This "best idea" is not, however, wholly arbitrary. As Beach has argued,

> These principles of [objective knowledge] may contain errors or half-truths and they may never attain to a fixed and final form. Yet insofar as (a) their consistency is publicly verifiable, (b) their development is rational, and (c) their truth-content is demonstrably greater than that of rival contenders, they do constitute reliable criteria by which to evaluate subsidiary beliefs and hypotheses.   (1984:101)

Siegel (1987:167) makes a similar argument in proposing a "nonvulgar" [nondogmatic] absolutism: "All that is required . . . is the possibility of objective, fair, neutral, non-question-begging evaluation of rival claims in accordance with criteria which themselves admit of critical assessment and improvement." Thus, to argue for the existence of objective standards by which to assess bias and other shortcomings in the warrants of knowledge claims is not to argue for a dogmatic, elitist position. The argument is rather for guidelines to make the most rational decisions possible under conditions in which uncertainty and error are more the rule than the exception.

Although standards of objective truth are hard to define and open to criticism, they are very much a part of the fabric of professional life. For example, consider a principle of practice for working with families of delinquents formulated by Wood (1990b):

"Family relationships are supported, not eroded—unless there is clear *evidence* that these relationships are fundamentally destructive" (Wood 1990b:313) (emphasis in the original). Although values are involved in the notion that destructive relationships are bad, it is assumed that once that position is taken, destructiveness in family relationships can be adequately defined and that evidence about its occurrence can be obtained. We further expect that this evidence will be objective in the sense of being free of such biases as the practitioner's dislike of the family. Certainly the judge who may hear this evidence would have this expectation.

But is just a single truth at issue here? Consider the following observation by Guba and Lincoln (1982:13): "Phenomena do not converge into a single form, a single 'truth' but diverge into many forms, multiple 'truths.' " As Phillips (1987c) has pointed out, few would quarrel with such statements in the sense that multiple perspectives on a situation are always possible. One can examine a destructive family interaction from the vantage points of the child, parents, and social worker and come up with different views, but these "multiple truths" are not necessarily in conflict and may indeed reveal a more accurate picture of the situation than, say, just the viewpoint of the social worker. But using "truth" in this sense is quite different from the sense of "truth" versus error or falseness. The assertion that the parents are addicted to drugs and punish their children by locking them in a closet for several hours at a time purports to be a statement of fact based on evidence. The assertion may be true, partly true or false. It is not one truth among multiple truths.

The notion of objective truth, at least as a goal to strive for, appears to guide practical decisions in the world of social work. Data are obtained by practitioners to determine the extent of a client's depression or of street crime in a neighborhood. Data on the performance of students in the field are gathered by educators and used as the basis for presumably unbiased evaluations.

The practitioners and educators in the examples assume their purpose is to arrive at some approximation of the truth in such matters. Study of notions of bias, error, mistakes, and truth as used in ordinary practice might be a profitable way to gain a sense of the actual epistemologies used by social workers. These unrefined epistemologies from the world of practice might also provide an interesting challenge to formal epistemologies that eschew such notions as truth and objectivity.

Generalization

Despite the importance of case-specific and other forms of ideographic knowledge, knowledge development in both research and practice emphasizes propositions that have general application. Indeed, general knowledge pertaining to the course and dynamics of human development, the nature of psychosocial problems, principles of intervention, and so on provide guidance for work with specific situations.

In social work both practitioner and researcher appear to build generalizations in a similar way—by extending what has been learned from a given situation to others that are similar to it while keeping in mind how the situations differ. The process yields at best tentative propositions. As Cronbach (1975:125) put it: "When we give proper weight to local conditions any generalization is a working hypotheses, not a conclusion." Such hypotheses may suggest what is likely or possible in a given situation. Whether or not it does occur needs to be determined in the situation itself.

In research, generalization is largely a logical process (Reid and Smith 1989). Even in the minority of studies that use representative samples, generalizations, if they are to be meaningful, must usually be extended beyond the population from which the samples were drawn. That is, a study that draws a random sample of cases from an agency may provide a representative picture of the cases in that agency at that point in time, but that knowledge may be of quite limited value.

In respect to actual practice, the place of generalization in social work research is closer to the constructivist, naturalistic orientation of Lincoln and Guba (1985) than to the position of the logical positivists that generalizations should yield universal laws. Many social work researchers, as well as practitioners, would be comfortable with Lincoln and Guba's (1985) principle that the *"transferability* [of findings] is a direct function of the similarity between . . . contexts. If Context A and Context B are sufficiently congruent then working hypotheses from the sending originating context *may* be applicable in the receiving context" (124).

As Lincoln and Guba (1985) suggest, the role of context is especially important. In social work, few propositions hold across all situations. To say that a program has been found to be "effective" is to say very little unless one specifies what the program consisted of, for whom it made a difference, under what conditions, and so on.

Theory Testing

Thus far, appraisal of knowledge has been discussed in terms of discrete propositions. I now consider the evaluation of more complex organizations of knowledge, or theories. Theories are systems of concepts and hypotheses designed to understand, explain, and predict phenomena.

Theories can be systematically evaluated through tests of their hypotheses in research studies. This is admittedly a daunting process rife with conceptual and methodological problems. It is well recognized that theories are "underdetermined" by facts (Hesse 1980). Thus, if a hypothesis of a theory is not supported by evidence, other hypotheses from the theory can often be found to explain the contrary facts.

Although a theory may be able to survive a number of failed tests, it cannot prevail indefinitely if empirical support is lacking. This notion has been well developed by Lakatos (1972) a postpositivist philosopher, who has suggested (and illustrated with examples from the history of science) specific criteria for appraising the long-term success of a theory over a course of repeated testing. Although refuting a theory may still be difficult, deciding between a theory and a rival is quite possible. For example, suppose a theory repeatedly predicts x but x does not occur. Furthermore, the theory is not capable of predicting y and z. A new theory proves capable of predicting not only x but also y and z and at the same time can explain the successful predictions of the older theory. With such an outcome, the newer theory presents itself as a rational choice. The process takes time. As Lakatos (1972) has said, no "instant rationality," no "crucial experiments" can decide the issue right now and once and for all.

I agree with Brekke (1986) that Lakatos's ideas are applicable to knowledge testing in social work, but these formulations, developed in the realm of the natural sciences, need to be adapted to our field with its relative dearth of empirically tested theories and, indeed, of any empirical testing. Comparing theories in terms of outcomes of tests of their hypotheses should, however, be possible.

A good example of the application of these ideas to knowledge relating to social work can be found in the rise and fall of the "double-bind" theory of schizophrenia, originally proposed by Bateson et al. (1956). To put it simply, the double-bind theory posited that paradoxical and confusing communication sequences involving parents and offspring were influential in the subsequent development of schizophrenia in the offspring. The theory attracted considerable interest, and a substantial literature on double-bind communication soon developed (Watzlawick 1963). Hypotheses generated by the theory were tested in a number of studies. These tests generally failed to support the hypothesis; moreover, serious difficulties were encountered in making key concepts operational in the theory (Olson 1972). As a result, the theory gradually "lost ground," as Lakatos (1972) would put it, to rival explanations of the etiology of schizophrenia. The process took more than a decade.

Task Relevance

Knowledge may meet all the forgoing criteria yet may still lack a critical ingredient—relevance to the tasks of the social worker. I do not elaborate on this criterion here but consider it subsequently in the context of the roles of research and practice wisdom in building knowledge.

In the present formulation, notions of corroboration, bias, truth, generalization, theory validity, and task relevance are used to assess knowledge. The concepts (to which others can be added) are inherently "fuzzy," and we cannot be expected to agree on how they should be defined. Yet, they contain useful criteria for practical decision making.

The ways of evaluating knowledge that I have reviewed are those that social workers have traditionally employed in their efforts to understand human problems and to help people cope with them. Such criteria (to which others can be added) determine how knowledge is appraised in not only social work but also in society as a whole. We use them to evaluate the effects of smoking or exercise. We use them in our legal processes: corroboration of testimony is sought, judges and jurors should be unbiased, and witnesses should tell the truth.

In social work such criteria can provide a framework, as they do in other endeavors, for working out disagreements about specific issues. We may disagree on how particular criteria are to be conceptualized, defined, or applied in given cases. But this kind of framework, I would agree, provides the basis for an epistemology. As Rorty (1979:316) has said: "The dominating notion of epistemology is that to be rational . . . we need to find agreement with other human beings. To construct an epistemology is to find the maximum amount of common ground with others."

Such a Rortian epistemology, one that provides a vocabulary for continuing conversation, will take us further, I think, than grand epistemologies that trade in abstract assertions about Truth, Reality, and so on. Disputes at the grand epistemological level are likely to have few practical consequences, and for social work the practical consequences matter.

My position falls within the tradition of American pragmatism, especially as it has been set forth in the writings of Pierce, James, Dewey, and Rorty. Although it incorporates contributions of postpositivist philosophers of science (e.g., Lakatos 1972; Phillips 1987b; Siegal 1987), it is essentially pragmatic in its rejection of the utility of epistemological worldviews—logical positivist or whatever. Although this position presents a rational view of social work practice, whether that practice is with data or with people, it eschews a mechanistic view of such practice.

I would agree with Schoen (1983) that professional practice should be based, not on "technical rationality," but rather on "reflection-in-action." In technical rationality, research creates knowledge, and practitioners implement it "by the book."

In "reflection-in-action" on the other hand,

"the practitioner draws on multiple resources (research-based knowledge, practice wisdom, intuition, familiar examples), in continually reflective problem solving. In effect practice is a kind of research. Here the [practitioner] tries to control variables for the sake of a hypothesis-testing experiment. He [sic] produces knowledge that is objective in the sense that he can disconfirm it. He can discover that he has not achieved satisfactory change or that he ought to undertake change of a different order." (166)

The professional epistemology suggested by Schoen incorporates an approach to knowledge appraisal not dissimilar from mine but applies it in a complex model of reflection-in-action well suited to the sort of practice that typifies social work. I shall not consider how different kinds of social work knowledge can be incorporated into this kind of reflective practice.

RESEARCH AND PRACTICE WISDOM AS SOURCES OF BEST ATTAINABLE KNOWLEDGE

The criteria for knowledge evaluation that have been outlined guide the task of knowledge building. Research and practice wisdom have often been viewed as alternative, if not antithetical, ways of achieving this task. In this section I try to show that research and practice wisdom are in fact mutually reinforcing means of building social work knowledge.

Building Knowledge from Research

In research, knowledge evaluation criteria are refined and extended in an effort to produce the best evidence possible bearing on knowledge claims. Methods of testing the reliability and validity of measurement, systematic procedures for controlling bias in data collection, and approaches to design and statistical analysis to rule out alternative explanation are well-known examples of such elaborations. But they are extrapolations of ways of assessing knowledge common to rational problem solving in everyday life. As Dewey (1938:66) put it, "Scientific subject-matter and procedures grows out of the direct problems and methods of common sense—but enormously refines, expands, and liberates the contents and the agencies at the disposal of common sense."

As a means of rational problem solving, research has contributed substantially to the knowledge base of practice, as will be discussed subsequently. As yet, however, it has not proved to be a dominant factor in the knowledge that guides practice. Reasons are not hard to find. Practitioners want knowledge informing them of the dynamics and outlooks for the situations they face and the kinds of interactions that may be effective in changing them. Such situations, which Wood (1990a) (following Ackoff 1979) has appropriately called "messes," abound with interacting variables and are embedded in contexts that contain even more variables. Most of these variables are difficult to measure with available techniques. Determination of causal connections is an extraordinary challenge, especially in view of the constraints on experimental methods in the study of behavior and intervention. Inquiry has traditionally proceeded by creating and studying simplified representations of these elusive phenomena—with complexities and contexts often ignored. Development of multivariate analytic methods and greater sophistication in experimental design have increased the potency of such approaches. Still the findings they yield are usually limited in descriptive and explanatory scope and power. They often lack task relevance. As a result they may not strike practitioners as especially useful.

More directly useful to practitioners are research-based practice models, but as shall be shown, such models are by no means a straightforward application of research to practice.

Building Knowledge from Practice Wisdom

Although the practitioners who work with clients may share with researchers basic standards of knowledge appraisal, they implement them differently in their attempts to acquire knowledge from practice experience. The knowledge they create is primarily ad hoc, situation specific, intended to get a job done. The exigencies and structure of practice force a far more flexible and pragmatic application to knowledge generation than is possible in research, as social workers who move to and from the worlds of practice and research can readily attest. Despite these constraints, considerable amounts of knowledge have accumulated as the result of practice activities. Indeed the dominant form of knowledge used to guide practice has been generated in practice. I refer to this knowledge as "practice wisdom," in perhaps an extended sense of that common term. I am referring not only to the insights gained by practitioners in their work with people but also to the elaboration of such insights by practitioner/scholars into theories and methods of practice.

Practice wisdom is usually task relevant since it grows directly from practice questions. It grows, however, without the benefit of consistent use of the error-protecting devices well established in research procedures— reliability checks, control of bias, care in selecting (and generalizing from) samples, systematic hypothesis testing with original data, and so on. As a result, practice wisdom suffers from problems of bias, overgeneralization, and lack of rigorous testing. For example, speculative theories may be developed on the basis of a few situations and then "confirmed" by focusing on supportive examples and ignoring others. Moreover, these theories and their terms are often global and imprecise; as descriptive and explanatory tools their usefulness is often greater in perception than in reality.

Research and Practice Wisdom

The limitations of both research and practice wisdom as tools for generating truly useful knowledge for social work practice are so severe, in my view, that neither by itself is adequate to the task. However, to contrast practice-generated knowledge with research-based knowledge, as is often done, and as I have just done, creates a false dichotomy in my view. It makes more sense to view social work knowledge as a network of propositions with origins both in practice experience and research. Many examples can be used to illustrate this point. For example, consider the development of knowledge relating to planned short-term treatment, including the well-documented proposition that it is at least as efficacious, and most likely more efficient, than long-term treatment for many types of clients and problems (Gelso and Johnson 1983; Koss and Butcher 1986; Wells 1981).

Planned short-term treatment was developed from the practice wisdom of clinicians and theorists (Alexander and French 1946; Lowry 1957; Reynolds 1932; Taft 1933). Controlled experimental tests of this form of practice model did not occur until the 1960s. For example, the short-term model evaluated by Reid and Shyne (1969) was the creation of practice staff at the Community Service Society of New York. This study as well as others confirmed the promise of short-term treatment and added to its knowledge base. Favorable research results stimulated increased use of short-term methods, leading in turn to more research.

A second set of examples comes from applications of research-based "empirical practice" models—e.g., behavioral, task-centered. These models are highly structured and proceduralized and have been tested and developed through research programs. Although they can be applied in the mechanistic style of "technical rationality" discussed earlier, their actual (and in my view) best applications tend to be those in which the framework and procedures of the model are integrated with many other sources of knowledge relating to the clients and their situations, other intervention methods, and so on. The practitioner is (or should be) "reflective" in Schoen's (1983) sense of the term.

A third example comes from work with schizophrenic clients. Clinicians had long been aware of the unstabilizing effects of excessive stimuli on the schizophrenic individual. However, research on expressed emotion helped to identify specific factors in the family environment (e.g., criticism, hostility, and overinvolvement) that might contribute to relapse. (Brown, Birley, and Wing 1972; Leff and Vaughn 1981; Vaughn and Leff 1976). These studies led to the development of psychoeducational approaches to work with schizophrenics and their families (Anderson, Reiss, and Hogarty 1986; Leff et al. 1982). These approaches, stimulated by research, have been implemented and elaborated with a considerable amount of practitioner-generated knowledge.

Examples such as those given are becoming more frequent because of several factors. Practice-relevant research continues to accumulate. Social workers sophisticated in both practice and research are growing in numbers and are becoming increasingly involved in the development and testing of practice approaches. Finally, we have increased our understanding about the many processes by which research results are combined with practice wisdom and similar forms of knowledge. Thus, it has become apparent that research findings and practice wisdom are used together by theorists and practitioners in forming beliefs in a process referred to as "conceptual utilization" of research (Rich 1977). Moreover, research studies need not be read by everyone they influence. Probably research exerts its major influence on practitioners indirectly—for example, through courses, workshops, books, and articles that have been shaped to some extent by scientific findings.

Even so, research results and practice wisdom will usually fall short of what complex practice situations demand. There should be no pretense that we have the knowledge that is needed. It is more realistic to strive to attain the "best attainable knowledge" to inform our practice—that is, the best knowledge that is currently possible to secure, as limited as it may be.

The principle of using the best attainable knowledge would call first for defining types of intervention targets (e.g., client needs or problems in given contexts). Knowledge needed to assess and intervene effectively, that is, relevant knowledge, would be appraised in relation to its evidential warrants. The knowledge backed by the best evidence would be given priority.

This should ideally be knowledge from research given its well-developed methods for generating knowledge, but one cannot assume that research results are inherently superior to other forms of knowledge. How much credence we place in research depends on the quality of the research and its reporting, among other things. At the same time, flawed research may provide better evidence than "low grade" practice wisdom—e.g., the uncorroborated impressions of lone practitioners. In searching for the best knowledge available one should use a common standard for research and practice wisdom. That is, one should not reject the findings of a study because it fails to meet strict scientific criteria while crediting practice wisdom whose evidential base is even more problematic. Much of the criticism of the contribution of mainstream research to social work knowledge reflects this double standard. A common practice is to point out the shortcomings of accepted research methods with the implication that some "nonempirical" approach would be as good if not better, without a clear explanation of that alternative approach or application of the same standards of criticism to it. But a double standard may be used in the opposite way. Research findings may be given less searching criticism than knowledge based on practice wisdom. For example, deficiencies of studies, or contradictory results, may be glossed over when an attempt is made to marshal evidence against a particular piece of practice wisdom.

QUANTITATIVE AND
QUALITATIVE METHODOLOGIES

There is no denying that mainstream researchers have been guilty of treating qualitative methodology as second class. They are not so likely to criticize this methodology as to minimize its importance and avoid its cultivation. A need exists to redefine the nature of the mainstream so that qualitative methodology is a part of it, and not apart from it.

From my perspective, a new paradigm is not necessary to rationalize qualitative methodology. Such methodology should be seen as an essential tool of inquiry available to all researchers. The same epistemology can encompass both qualitative and conventional quantitative methodologies. If so, issues of whether or not to use qualitative methods and how to use them become largely methodological. In the present framework, such issues are decided on the basis of which type of method or combination of them is most likely to produce, not the most rigorous knowledge, but the best knowledge attainable.

Not only are quantitative and qualitative approaches eminently compatible, they also serve complementary functions in knowledge building. The strengths of one tend to be the weaknesses of the other.

Quantitative methodology can provide more exact statements of the degree of linkage between specific variables, better control over alternative explanations for these relations, more precise measures of phenomena that lend themselves to quantification, and larger data bases for purposes of generalization. Qualitative methodology is better able to depict the workings of social systems in holistic ways, to take into account contextual factors, to detect elusive phenomena, and to generate more thorough descriptions as a base for generalization.

Neither method is inherently superior to the other, but rather each provides the researcher with different tools of inquiry. The function of qualitative methodology should not be viewed as simply feeding or embellishing quantitative research, as exploring unknown areas, or as providing descriptive word pictures. Qualitative research can offer new perspectives in areas well studied through quantitative methods. It can also generate and provisionally test explanatory hypotheses that may constitute the best knowledge attainable.

But the contributions of each need to be examined in relation to a single set of standards in order to evaluate their relative knowledge yields and to facilitate their differential use. The measures obtained from an objective test may be distorted by the respondent's social desirability bias. Participant observation may be able to avoid this form of bias but may be susceptible to observer bias. The shortcomings of a study using either quantitative or qualitative methods need to be made clear, not as a basis for discarding its findings, but in order to know how much confidence to place in the knowledge produced.

I have argued that the "epistemological debate" in social work and related helping professions has been unfruitfully cast as a clash of paradigms for which "either–or" solutions are proposed. Irreconcilable conflicts may indeed exist in the discourse of philosophers, but their perspectives are not essential to the task of resolving differences and building consensus in the practical world of social work.

Fundamental to any ecumenical effort is a common vocabulary for defining and evaluating knowledge. Such a vocabulary exists, in my view, in considerations for knowledge assessment that social work practitioners and researchers use and find acceptable in their everyday practice. Although dialogues carried on with this vocabulary will be contentious and fall far short of unanimity, they are likely to produce more productive interchanges than arguments about realism, naturalism, positivism, and so on. Thus, as I have tried to show, it may be possible with a more pragmatic view to suggest ways of resolving issues about how different sources (research and practice wisdom) and different methods of inquiry (qualitative and quantitative) can be used to enhance social work knowledge. If these ideas have merit they will, I hope, contribute to conversations that will enable us to identify common ground when that is possible and, when it is not, to clarify issues about which we disagree.

References

Ackoff, R. 1979. The future of operational research is past. *Journal of the Operational Research Society* 30: 93–104.

Alexander, F. and T. M. French. 1946. *Psychoanalytic Therapy*. New York: Ronald Press.

Anderson, C. M., D. J. Reiss, and G. E. Hogarty. 1986. *Schizophrenia and the Family*. New York: Guilford Press.

Bateson, G., D. D. Jackson, J. Haley, and J. H. Weakland. 1956. Toward a theory of schizophrenia. *Behavior Science* 1: 251–64.

Berlin, S. B. 1990. Dichotomous and complex thinking. *Social Service Review* 64: 46–59.

Bloom, M. 1990. Symposium 2: On the epistemology of social work practice knowledge (with apologies to Plato's symposium). In L. Videka-Sherman and W. J. Reid, eds., *Advances in Clinical Social Work Research*. Silver Spring, Md: NASW Press.

Brekke, J. S. 1986. Scientific imperatives in social work research: Pluralism is not skepticism. *Social Service Review* 50: 538–55.

Brown, G. W., J. L. T. Birley, and J. F. Wing. 1972. Influence of family life on the course of schizophrenic disorders: A replication. *British Journal of Psychiatry* 121: 241–58.

Cook, T. D. 1987. Positivist critical multiplism. In W. R. Shadish, Jr. and C. S. Reichardt, eds., *Evaluation Studies, 12.* Newbury Park, Calif.: Sage.

Cronbach, L. 1975. Beyond the two disciplines of scientific psychology. *American Psychologist* 30: 116–27.

Dewey, J. 1938. Logic: *The Theory of Inquiry.* New York: Holt, Rinehart and Winston.

Fishman, D. B. 1988. Pragmatic behaviorism. Saving and nurturing the baby. In D. B. Fishman, E. Rotgers, and C. M. Franks, eds., *Paradigms in Behavior Therapy: Present and Promise.* New York: Springer.

Fraser, M., M. J. Taylor, R. Jackson, and J. O'Jack. 1991. Social work and science: Many ways of knowing? *Social Work Research and Abstracts* 27, no. 4.

Geertz, C. 1973. Thick description: Toward an interpretive theory of culture. In C. Gertz, ed., *The Interpretation of Cultures.* New York: Basic Books.

Gelso, C. J. and D. H. Johnson. 1983. *Explorations in Time-Limited Counseling and Psychotherapy.* New York: Teachers College Press.

Gergen, K. J. 1985. The social constructionist movement in modern psychology. *American Psychologist* 40: 260–75.

Guba, E. and Lincoln, Y. 1982. *Effective Evaluation.* San Francisco: Jossey-Bass.

Haworth, G. O. 1984. Social work research, practice, and paradigms. *Social Service Review* 58: 343–57.

Heineman, M. B. 1981. The obsolete imperative in social work research. *Social Service Review* 55: 371–97.

Hesse, M. 1980. *Revolutions and Reconstructions in the Philosophy of Science.* Bloomington, Ind.: Indiana University Press.

Hudson, W. W. 1982. Scientific imperatives in social work research and practice. *Social Service Review* 56: 246–58.

Koss, M. P. and J. N. Butcher. 1986. Research on brief psychotherapy. In S. L. Garfield and A. E. Bergin, eds., *Handbook of Psychotherapy and Behavior Change.* New York: Wiley.

Lakatos, I. 1972. Falsification and the methodology of scientific research programs. In I. Lakatos and A. Musgrave, eds., *Criticisms and the Growth of Knowledge.* Cambridge, England: Cambridge University Press.

Lather, P. 1987. Research as praxis. In Shadish and Reichardt, eds., *Evaluation Studies, 12.* Newbury Park, Calif.: Sage.

Leff, J., L. Kuipers, R. Berkowitz, R. Eberlein-Vries, and D. Sturgeon. 1982. A controlled trial of social intervention in the families of schizophrenic patients. *British Journal of Psychiatry* 141: 121–34.

Leff, J. P. and C. E. Vaughn. 1981. The role of maintenance therapy and relative's expressed emotion in relapse of schizophrenia: A two-year follow-up. *British Journal of Psychiatry* 139: 102–4.

Levitron, L. C. and E. F. Hughes. 1981. Research on the utilization of evaluations: A review and synthesis. *Evaluation Review* 5: 525–48.

Lincoln, Y. S. 1990. The making of a constructivist: A remembrance of transformations past. In E. G. Guba, ed., *The Paradigm Dialog.* Newbury Park, Calif.: Sage.

Lincoln, Y. and E. Guba. 1985. *Naturalistic Inquiry.* Beverly Hills: Sage.

Lowry, F. 1957. The caseworker in short contact services. *Social Work* 2: 53–58.

Newton-Smith, W. 1981. *The Rationality of Science.* Oxford: Routledge and Kegan Paul.

Olson, D. H. 1972. Empirically unbinding the double bind: Review of research and conceptual reformulations. *Family Process* 2: 69–94.

Pepper, S. 1970. *World Hypotheses.* Berkeley: University of California Press.

Phillips, D. C. 1987. Validity in qualitative research: Why the worry about warrant will not wane. *Education and Urban Society* 20: 9–24.

Phillips, D. 1987a. On what scientists know and how they know it. In Shadish and Reichardt, eds., *Evaluation Studies Reviews Annual, 12,* pp. 377–99. Newbury Park, Calif.: Sage.

Phillips, D. C. 1987b. *Philosophy, Science and Social Inquiry.* New York: Pergamon.

Pieper, M. H. 1989. The heuristic paradigm: A unifying and comprehensive approach to social work research. *Smith College Studies in Social Work* 60: 8–34.

Popkewitz, T. S. 1990. Whose future? Whose past? Notes on critical theory and methodology. In Guba, ed., *The Paradigm Dialog.* Newbury Park, Calif.: Sage.

Reamer, F. G. 1992. *Philosophical Foundations of Social Work.* New York: Columbia University Press.

Reason, P. and J. Rowan. eds. 1981. *Human Inquiry.* New York: Wiley.

Reid, W. J. and A. Shyne. 1969. *Brief and Extended Casework.* New York: Columbia University Press.

Reid, W. J. and A. D. Smith. 1989. *Research in Social Work.* New York: Columbia University Press.

Reynolds, B. 1932. An experiment in short contract interviewing. *Smith College Studies in Social Work* 3: 1–107.

Rich, R. F. 1977. Uses of social science information by federal bureaucrats: Knowledge for action versus knowledge for understanding. In C. H. Weiss, ed., *Using Social Research in Public Policy Making.* Lexington, Mass.: Lexington Books.

Richmond, M. 1917. *Social Diagnosis.* New York: Russell Sage Foundation.

Rorty, R. 1979. *Philosophy and the Mirror of Nature.* Princeton, N.J.: Princeton University Press.

Schoen, D. 1983. *The Reflective Practitioner.* New York: Basic Books.

Schuerman, J. R. 1982. Debate with authors: The scientific imperative in social work research. *Social Service Review* 56: 144–46.

Siegel, H. 1987. *Relativism Refuted.* Dordrecht, The Netherlands: Reidel.

Taft, J. 1933. *The Dynamics of Therapy in a Controlled Relationship.* New York: Mac-Millan.

Tyson, K. B. 1992. A new approach to relevant scientific research for practitioners: The heuristic paradigm. *Social Work* 37: 541–57.

Vaughn, C. and J. Leff. 1976. The measurement of expressed emotion in the families of psychiatric patients. *British Journal of Social and Clinical Psychology* 15: 157–65.

Watzlawick, P. 1963. A review of the double bind theory. *Family Process* 2: 132–53.

Wells, R. 1981. The empirical base of family therapy: Practice implications. In E. R. Tolson and W. J. Reid, eds., *Models of Family Treatment.* New York: Columbia University Press.

Witkin, S. 1989. Towards a scientific social work. *Journal of Social Service Research* 12: 83–98.

Wood, K. M. 1990a. Epistemological issues in the development of social work practice knowledge. In Videka-Sherman and Reid, eds., *Advances in Clinical Social Work Research*. Silver Spring, Md: NASW Press.

Wood, K. M. 1990b. The family of the juvenile delinquent. *Juvenile and Family Court Journal* 11: 19–37.

FORTY-TWO

Commentary on Reid's "Reframing the Epistemological Debate"

Ben A. Orcutt

The epistemological debate in social work that places logical positivism in opposition to alternative paradigms for scientific inquiry has tended to polarize research scholars and to foster antagonism and misrepresentation. Reid argues eloquently for reframing the debate. The need is rejected for the epistemologies of philosophers to undergird with authority the scientific inquiries in social work. A pragmatic approach to empiricism is taken, wherein attention is refocused from the epistemological worldview of logical positivism–empiricism to the level of clarifying and resolving issues that are embedded in these arguments. Peile (1988) suggests that a pragmatic approach to empiricism can provide common ground. The issues refer to the nature and source of knowledge in social work (research and practice wisdom) and methods of scientific inquiry (qualitative and quantitative methods). These issues relate to what constitutes social work knowledge, both explicit and implicit, including tacit (Polanyi 1966), and how it can be known.

The issues, along with possible or partial solutions that embrace the major themes of Reid's presentation, are illuminated in the following synthesis.

PRINCIPLE FOR APPRAISAL OF KNOWLEDGE

A principle is established for appraising and establishing knowledge that requires corroboration by evidence for the truth of beliefs. The larger philosophical issues of what is truth and reality are circumvented with a pragmatic focus on truth of a belief that must be subject to confirmation by rational evidence.

Social work knowledge is considered by Reid to be credible if it is reaffirmed in "multiple contexts" and by "multiple methods" in combination by researchers, theorists, and practitioners. The belief would seem to be endorsed that the strongest evidence derives from multiple strategies (Reinherz 1990), and it offers opportunity for practitioner judgment and wisdom. Interestingly, in this progressive and broadened view of credible evidence, research findings are seen as less definitive knowledge and more as direction for application, analysis, and synthesis with other knowledge. The liberalized view can narrow the gulf between knowledge-building and value-laden practice (Weick 1987), wherein the goal Reid strives for is the best attainable knowledge.

It is also interesting to consider this goal in relation to science defined as: "Observation and classification of fact; accumulated knowledge systematized and formulated with reference to discovery of general truths" (Webster's 1947:890). Newton-Smith (1981), philosopher, defines science more broadly as institutionalized justification. Thus, scientific inquiry in Reid's position as stated would require credible evidence (facts) for the truth of practice beliefs, which may precede more general truths. His goal is for the best attainable knowledge. It is consistent with what we know about the nature of certainty in knowledge. New evidence over time may supersede confirmed beliefs and even suggest new paradigms (Kuhn 1970, 1977). Actually, Carnap, an early positivist who liberalized positivism, in 1937 rejected the notion of hypotheses being verified and argued that they were only confirmed, since observations can never be infinite and may be disconfirmed with later findings; thus there is probability in confirmation of hypothesis and truth.

GUIDE TO KNOWLEDGE APPRAISAL

Since rational evidence in Reid's proposal is basic to accepting the truth of beliefs, appraisal of evidence is of vital concern.

Reid's proposal to define a guide and a standard for expressing objective truth is consistent with scientific inquiry and central to appraisal of knowledge. The guide would distinguish between corroborative evidence that is multiplicative and that which is structural. The former involves person-to-person agreement or intersubjectivity, whereas the latter refers to the convergence of factual evidence. Thus, the guide allows for multiple approaches in methods, measures, analyses, and cross-validation. It reflects responsiveness to the complexity of social data that is indigenous to practice and counters the criticism of empiricism as context stripping, reductionistic, and operationally overrestrictive (Heineman 1981; Pieper 1985, 1989, among others).

Standards for recognizing bias and for determining objective truth are admittedly difficult to define, especially since human observation and subjective experience are fraught with perceptual, cultural, and contextual biases that must be taken into account. Guidelines are critical to making the most rational decisions possible under conditions of uncertainty. Reid draws on Beach (1984), who proposes criteria for objective knowledge as including: (1) consistent public verifiability, (2) rational development, and (3) truth content demonstrated as greater than its rivals. Each of these criteria can be the subject of dispute, but each offers a base for determining agreement/disagreement regarding beliefs that underlie knowledge.

Reid considers criteria for generalization of findings to support practice truths to be similar for both practice and research, and he accepts theory building and validity in the empiricist tradition based on hypotheses of causal or associative relationships. He admits that the tenets he has proposed as guides: corroboration, bias and truth, generalization, theory validity, and task relevance lack definitiveness, but they do offer a framework for development of more definitive criteria. The aim for objective truth in knowledge that is generated by using multiple research strategies and practice wisdom as mutual reinforcers provides for specificity appropriate for the latitude needed to understand complex systems. It is clear that a course is charted that embraces pragmatic empiricism with an expansion in methods of inquiry to include practice judgments and descriptive, introspective, and interpretive evidence regarding practice problems, values, and experience.

INTEGRATION OF QUALITATIVE AND QUANTITATIVE METHODS

The proposal to reframe the debate clearly rejects hierarchy in research methods and recognizes compatibility, strengths, equality, and complementary functions of both qualitative and quantitative research methods. Sharp controversy does exist with regard to their compatibility, especially regarding objectivity/subjectivity; linear causation versus holistic, circular, interactional patterning; and reliability and validity (Lincoln and Guba 1985).

However, the position is taken that qualitative and quantitative methods can be used singly and in combination at the level of inquiry. The methods used would depend on the research question or problem for investigation. Reid proposes that conventional mainstream research be redefined so that "qualitative methodology is a part of it and not apart from it." This position is consistent with the "compatibility thesis" (Howe 1988).

Considerable literature in the field supports the assumption that differences between worldview or "paradigms" underlying conventional and qualitative approaches can either be accommodated or bypassed at the level of scientific inquiry (Davis and Reid 1988; Orcutt 1990; Miles and Huberman 1984; Patton 1986; Reid 1985; Reid and Davis 1987; Strauss and Corbin 1990). Actually, mixed methodology within a study is in current use (Fortune 1990). This point of view differs from the current call for a unifying approach that would offer a different world view or "heuristic paradigm" (Pieper 1989) but supports rigor and relevance in expanded conventional inquiry.

In summary, the epistemological debate has been enlightening, but as Reid has cogently proposed, it will be more productive to reframe the debate with attention focused at the level of scientific inquiry to include clarification and resolution of the basic issues in epistemology regarding the sources and appraisal of knowledge for social work and to consider, without prejudice, qualitative as well as quantitative research methods within the mainstream. I believe that this approach can substantially advance practice research since hierarchy in methods has been a contentious issue. I believe also that if we could clarify and resolve the fundamental issues of criteria and standards for credible knowledge that Reid has raised, knowledge generated at the level of scientific inquiry might subsequently lead toward a synthesis in worldview.

REFERENCES

Beach, E. 1984. The paradox of cognitive relativism revisited: A reply to Jack W. Weiland. *Metaphilosophy* 15: 1–15.

Carnap, 1937. Testability and meaning, *Philosophy of science* 4: 1–40.

Davis, I. and W. J. Reid. 1988. Event analysis in clinical practice and process research. *Social Casework* 69: 298–306.

Fortune, A. 1990. Problems and uses of qualitative methodologies. In L. Videka-Sherman and W. J. Reid, eds., *Advances in Clinical Social Work Research*. Silver Spring, Md.: NASW Press.

Heineman, M. 1981. Social work's obsolete philosophy of research. *Social Service Review* 55: 371–97.

Howe, K. 1988. Against the qualitative–quantitative incompatibility: A diagnosis die-hard. *Educational Researcher* 17: 10–16.

Imre, R. 1991. What do we need to know for good practice? *Social Work* 36: 198–200.

Kuhn, T. 1970. *The Structure of Scientific Revolution.* Chicago: University of Chicago Press.

Kuhn, T. 1977. *The Essential Tension: Selected Studies on Scientific Tradition and Change.* Chicago: University of Chicago Press.

Lincoln, Y. and E. Guba. 1985. *Naturalistic Inquiry.* Beverly Hills: Sage.

Miles, M. and A. Huberman. 1984. *Qualitative Data Analysis.* Beverly Hills: Sage.

Newton-Smith, W. H. 1981. *The Rationality of Science,* p. 1. London: Routledge and Kegan Paul.

Orcutt, B. 1990. *Science and Inquiry in Social Work Practice.* New York, Columbia University Press.

Patton, M. 1986. *Utilization-Focused Evaluation.* Newbury Park, Calif.: Sage.

Peile, C. 1988. Research paradigms in social work: From stalemate to creative synthesis. *Social Service Review* 62: 2–19.

Pieper, M. H. 1985. The future of social work research. *Social Work Research and Abstracts* 21: 3–11.

Pieper, M. H. 1989. The heuristic paradigm: A unifying and comprehensive approach to social work research. *Smith College Studies in Social Work* 60: 8–34.

Polanyi, M. 1966. *The Tacit Dimension.* Garden City, N.Y.: Doubleday.

Reid, W. J. 1985. *Family Problem Solving.* New York, Columoia University Press.

Reid, W. J. and Davis, I. 1987. Qualitative methods in single case research. In N. Gottlieb, ed., *Proceedings of Conference on Practitioners as Evaluators of Direct Practice.* Seattle: School of Social Work, University of Washington.

Reinherz, H. 1990. Beyond regret: Single-case evaluations and their place in social work education and practice. In Videka-Sherman and Reid, eds., *Advances in Clinical Social Work Research.* Silver Spring, Md.: NASW Press.

Strauss, A. and J. Corbin. 1990. *Basics of Qualitative Research.* Newbury Park, Calif.: Sage.

Webster's Collegiate Dictionary. 1947. Springfield, Mass.: Merriam-Webster.

Weick, A. 1987. Reconceptualizing the philosophical perspective of social work. *Social Service Review* 61: 218–30.

FORTY-THREE

Commentary: Epistemological Disagreements and the Search for Understanding

Roberta Wells Imre

In light of the need to integrate ideas from so many papers on qualitative research in social work, the question of synthesis arises. Synthesis in this context refers to bringing together, to seeing how things are related to each other. An *Oxford Dictionary* definition suggests that it is "the putting together of parts or elements so as to make up a complex whole." When looking for synthesis in a potentially contentious area like research and social work practice, it is useful to consider words like *conversation, listening,* and *resonances,* particularly unexpected resonances from different sources. The complex whole is social work. The goal is understanding of a variety of perspectives, and the end result may or may not include agreement.

In social work, particularly in the academic environment, our discussions are often arguments in which we defend our own perspectives. This conventional form of discourse, however, is not the best approach to an effort at synthesis or understanding. Lakoff and Johnson (1980) note that in our culture an argument, seen metaphorically, is a form of going to war. It is an adversarial procedure such that one wins or loses, thereby gaining or losing power. The end result is often to drive the participants apart. People are seldom, if ever, convinced of the superiority of another point of view by arguments or debates. Haworth (1991) illustrates how this works in his article, "My Paradigm Can Beat Your Paradigm: Some Reflections on

Knowledge Conflicts.'' I suggest that instead of arguing about paradigms and their relative merits, we focus on our common concerns and return to the theme suggested by Hartman that there are indeed many ways of knowing and many truths. And, I would add, it is possible to understand one another's truths if we can allow ourselves to listen and converse without having to prejudge the outcome.

Human beings are incredibly complex and have a way of resisting and escaping the most sophisticated efforts to define, categorize, or even to help them. Our need as social workers is for coherence and understanding, and we require disciplined studies as a way of focusing our efforts. Such studies are presented in abundance in this book. It seems clear, as Heineman Pieper emphasizes in her paper, that all points of view have limitations. Social philosophers throughout history demonstrate an apparently incurable human tendency to try to construct an all-encompassing "Grand Theory" (Skinner 1985), while at the same time decrying the efforts of others to do the same. Nevertheless, the contingent and limited nature of any human life precludes the possibility that any individual, or particular group, will ever be in possession of all the answers. This recognition should foster, not preclude, our learning from each other. Reading the papers in this book with this perspective in mind can be a very rewarding experience indeed.

A recent personal incident taught me something about what is needed. In the 1970s I was assigned as a mental health consultant to the local Jewish Community Center. Last year at a social occasion I met the former director of the center, Joe Harris, a friend and colleague whom I had not seen for years. As we were discussing my current writing on "good practice," he surprised me by saying that he thought that listening had been what counted most in my work at the center. My surprise was a measure of the degree to which immersion in the academic world had distanced me from the recognition of such a simple, basic truth. In preparing this paper I thought about his comment and what it meant and its relationship to how the content of this book might be approached.

One may safely say that listening is not what academics do best, and that may be one of the unacknowledged obstacles to our understanding each other. Weissman has suggested that when we listen to others, we tend to think about why they are wrong, instead of focusing on what they are saying. Yet, in practice surely, as well as in much research, listening is prerequisite to informed knowing. In practice it is basically an effort to understand, an openness to hearing what other people are saying about what it is like for them. Such listening requires a suspension of the need to formulate in advance, to plan an intervention before hearing the story. It requires a slowing down long enough to really be there, to provide what Marcel (1960) would have called ''a presence.'' While practice seen in this way is incompatible with some forms of research, it is congruent with a variety of qualitative approaches demonstrated in these papers.

The listening required in practice situations, and also in much qualitative research, often involves processes not visible to the outside observer. In fact, sometimes the meaning of what has happened is discovered by the participants themselves only in the course of later reflection. Cooperative efforts between researchers and practitioners to understand and improve practice require listening in ways that demonstrate a willingness to hear, to reflect on, and respond to what is heard. The purpose is understanding, and the results cannot be prejudged.

By itself of course listening is not sufficient for either practice or research. Our situation is immensely complicated by the inescapable fact that we live in a world of technology with its tendency to breed bureaucracies as a kind of social engineering. Whatever its drawbacks and limitations, technology is very much a part of our world, and understanding of the sophisticated research tools that belong to this milieu is vital. If we are to survive, we must be able to use the coin of the realm. But we must also be alert to the dangers of selling our souls or bartering those of our clients in the process. We would do well to keep in mind Ruchdeschel's point regarding current interest in research techniques for the evaluation of practice. He reminds us that evaluation is essentially a process of "finding the value"—another of those seemingly simple, and easily forgotten, insights. Our methods should be such that important qualities and meanings are preserved. Listening and acting upon what we hear are essential to this process.

Many of the good research approaches that have been developed and described in this book have been based on someone's listening, hearing, and wanting to understand what would really help. One of the basic strengths of the heuristic paradigm and its naturalistic methods, as described by Heineman Pieper, seems to me to be the built-in expectation that therapists must be free to listen and to be guided by what they learn. In Heineman Pieper's study, practice research is retrospective, based on reports of what was done and what informed the doing. The governing value is explicit; the welfare of the client must have priority over the research technique. The skill of the therapist is accredited, and study of treatment becomes an effort in which clinical judgment is enlisted in understanding what happened, what went right, and what went wrong. The knowledge thus acquired comes from the inside—from where the action really is. Such a study utilizes both scientific perspectives and practice wisdom. It recognizes that the participant observer has access to vital content unavailable to the outsider.

This perspective finds common ground with the observations of Dean that, in addition to the verbal exchanges in a practice situation, the worker can be guided by nonverbal clues as, for example, by internal resonances arising out of the effort to understand. Lang notes that the social worker can be described as a "participant actor," a phrase that gives priority to action over observation and highlights a common problem area in communication between researchers and practitioners. Heineman Pieper's study brings practice and research together in ways that surmount these difficulties. Her approach incorporates long-valued aspects of practice, such as the case study method, but her work has also been greatly enriched by the use of sophisticated qualitative research approaches not available to the pioneers in our field.

It is relevant to the purpose for which these papers were written that the research that Heineman-Pieper describes was not considered acceptable for a doctoral dissertation, and she was required to do something else for that purpose. It is not uncommon in a doctoral program to encounter such a prejudice against what experienced practitioners know. For some of us such confrontations have led to our own intellectual journeys, often in an effort to understand the origins and reasons for this attitude and to utilize the resources of other disciplines in calling attention to the missing content. It is fortunate for us that, when she encountered this academic bias, Heineman Pieper's research project was already underway, and she neither could nor would abandon it. It should not, however, be necessary to overcome such obstacles from within our profession in order to pursue research in this way. We cannot afford to waste our resources, personal or institutional, in such fruitless battles. There are too many people needing help and the resources never keep pace with the need.

It seems to me that a hermeneutic approach also provides a perspective for studying ways of helping people that allows us to learn from each other, without requiring that we all necessarily accept the same premises. Hermeneutics is concerned with understanding meanings—and in our work meanings are really what we know, or think we know, about what is important in human lives. Rorty (1979) uses the word *conversation* in discussing hermeneutics. In fact, traditionally hermeneutic inquiry can be seen to involve a series of ongoing conversations—between past and present, different cultures, different lives, you and me, and the worlds we represent or embody.

Cohler suggests that the semantic origin of the word *hermeneutics,* associated with Hermes as the messenger of the gods, is problematic, and he prefers the term *human studies.* Our work is full of linguistic pitfalls like this, and they reinforce the need for listening for the resonances in our ongoing conversations. The perspective generally meant by the use of words like *hermeneutic, interpretive,* or *human studies,* is increasingly evident in our literature. For some years now Sherman (1991a,b) has been explicating this approach and using it in his research studies. Recently another voice has entered the discussion (Borden 1992) calling attention to the usefulness of narrative perspectives in short-term treatment and suggesting ways of researching this method of practice.

Recent study of hermeneutics combined with some of the discussions in this book have led me into the complexities of the commensurability issue. This word reflects basic underlying philosophical concerns about the defense of knowledge and truth claims. In the literature of epistemology a strong tradition exists in which knowledge claims are settled by recourse to accepted rules of rationality and logic. Discourse takes the form of stating and rationally defending positions according to these agreed-on rules. An underlying assumption is that this method of discourse provides the way to Truth. Although the word itself is rarely used in our discussions in social work, commensurability issues are often implicitly present. Reid's insistence on the necessity for agreement about criteria and methods for settling knowledge claims in social work reflects such a concern. This problem often plagues our discussions of research methods particularly, because our different approaches to the subject are in fact incommensurable. We do not all agree on the basic premises of our work in ways that would permit the establishment of rules for determining what is true or what constitutes good knowing in our work.

Like Rorty, Bernstein (1983), and various others, I think it better not to cling tenaciously to a need for commensurability, or even to some kind of uneasy integration of divergent points of view, but to focus instead on understanding and how it is possible. And to do that we do indeed have to listen, to let ourselves really hear what others are trying to communicate, either orally or through the written word. My friend was right about listening; it is basic. It is required for understanding clients, ourselves, and each other. It is also the beginning of understanding of our need for many ways of knowing. Such a perspective can contribute to research that will further responsive and responsible work with other human beings—which is after all a purpose on which we can agree.

REFERENCES

Bernstein, R. J. 1983. *Beyond Objectivism and Relativism: Science, Hermeneutics, and Praxis*. Philadelphia: University of Pennsylvania.

Borden, W. 1992. Narrative perspectives in psychosocial intervention following adverse life events. *Social Work* 37: 135–41.

Haworth, G. 1991. My paradigm can beat your paradigm: Some reflections on knowledge conflicts. *Journal of Sociology and Social Welfare* 18: 35–50.

Lakoff, G. and M. Johnson. 1980. *Metaphors We Live By.* Chicago: University of Chicago.

Marcel, G. 1960. *Mystery of Being.* Chicago: Henry Regnery Co.

Rorty, R. 1979. *Philosophy and the Mirror of Nature.* Princeton, N.J.: Princeton University.

Sherman, E. 1991a. Interpretive methods for social work practice and research. *Journal of Sociology and Social Welfare* 18: 69–81.

Sherman, E. 1991b. *Reminiscence and the Self in Old Age.* New York: Springer.

Skinner, Q., ed. 1985. *The Return of Grand Theory in the Human Sciences.* New York: Cambridge University Press.

Glossary

ANALYTIC INDUCTION: a procedure for verifying theories and propositions based on qualitative data. A hypothesis is tested, revised, and retested case by case across a broad range of cases until the hypothesis adequately explains in all cases the phenomenon being studied.

AUTHENTICITY ASSESSMENT: an assessment of the interactive result of the evaluative process, not the product of the evaluation, in constructivist research.

CASE STUDY: an in-depth form of research that may focus on a person, a group, a program, an organization, a time period, a cultural incident, or a community.

CHANGE PROCESS RESEARCH: a form of clinical research that focuses on the processes of change that occur during psychosocial treatment. It interrelates process (in-treatment activities of client and worker) with intermediate (within- and between-session) outcomes.

CONSTANT COMPARATIVE METHOD: a grounded theory method in which the researcher simultaneously codes and analyzes data in order to develop concepts. By continually comparing specific incidents in the data, the researcher refines these concepts, identifies their properties, explores their relationships to one another, and integrates them into a coherent theory.

CONSTRUCTIVISM: the view that entities or objects exist within socially and personally constructed forms and contexts and that any knowledge or "truths" about these entities cannot be adequately known independently of these constructions or contexts. It is opposed to any view that sees entities and truths existing or being true independently of (our) apprehension.

CONSTRUCTIVIST EVALUATION: an evaluation that is holistically sensitive to the context of the study setting, to the views or "constructions" of the key parties, and to the interactional effects of the evaluation process itself.

CONTENT ANALYSIS: a research technique for the objective, systematic classification and description of the manifest content of communication in written (records, transcripts, etc.) or oral (taped) form.

CONTEXTUALIZING: relocating the essential features of the processes back into the total preexisting context or study setting.

DECONSTRUCTION: critical analysis and interpretation of prior studies and representations of the phenomenon in question.

DECONTEXTUALIZING: isolating the key, essential features of the processes under investigation from the total context or study setting.

DISCOURSE ANALYSIS: in linguistics, discourse analysis is the formal and systematic study of conversation or verbal interaction and dialogue. In social work research it is most likely to be an analysis of the client—worker dialogue.

EMIC: refers to the folk or indigenous and internal perspective of the people being studied by ethnographic methods. The emic approach is "domestic" or "internal" because what is discovered about a particular culture is related to that culture as a whole, rather than related cross-culturally.

EPISTEMOLOGY: The branch of philosophy concerned with the theory of knowledge. It deals with the nature and derivation of knowledge, the scope of knowledge, and the reliability of claims to knowledge.

ETHNOGRAPHY: the systematic study of human cultures and the similarities and dissimilarities between them.

ETIC: refers to the professional or external perspective of the researcher based upon a preexisting system of knowledge, e.g., the anthropologist studying an "alien" culture on the basis of knowledge of prior cross-cultural studies.

EVALUABILITY ASSESSMENT: a means of determining whether to conduct a program evaluation, whether program changes are needed before an evaluation is conducted, and which method or methods of program evaluation are most appropriate to judge program performance from a constructivist perspective.

FAMILY STUDIES METHOD: a form of participant observation of families based on the work of the anthropologist Oscar Lewis.

FOCUS GROUPS: as a form of qualitative research, focus groups are basically group interviews based on topics that are supplied by the researcher, who typically takes the role of moderator. The information arising from interaction within the group is the primary focus of attention, and the fundamental data produced are transcripts of the group discussions.

GROUNDED THEORY APPROACH: a qualitative research methodology for discovering theories, concepts, hypotheses, and propositions directly from data, rather than from a priori assumptions, other research, or existing theoretical frameworks.

HEURISTIC RESEARCH: a form of systematic inquiry that serves to guide, discover, or reveal, in which the primary concern is the discovery process and not the issues of verification and corroboration.

IDIOGRAPHIC RESEARCH: in-depth study of the unique individual, case, or situation. Its objective is individualization and the holistic understanding of the singular.

MEANING: what an experience means to a person, defined in terms of intentions and consequences; meaning is always triadic, involving interaction among a person, an object, and action taken toward the object; meaning is interactional, interpretive, open-ended, often ambiguous, inconclusive, and conflictual.

NARRATIVE: a story that has a plot: a beginning, a middle, and an end.

NATURALISTIC RESEARCH: the systematic study of phenomena in their natural context without alteration of the phenomena or the context for research purposes.

NOMOTHETIC RESEARCH: "nomothetic" means lawmaking, and the basic purpose of such research is to discover general laws by studying representative cases, samples, and situations so as to generalize about them.

ONTOLOGY: a branch of philosophy concerned with the nature of being (i.e., existence itself). It differentiates between "real existence" and "appearance" and investigates the different ways in which entities belonging to various logical categories (physical objects, numbers, universals, abstractions, etc.) may be said to exist.

ORAL HISTORY METHOD: a way of taking down reminiscences by means of a tape recorder through planned interviews on a subject of historical interest about which the narrator can speak with authority.

PARTICIPANT OBSERVATION: observing and participating in the worlds of lived experience that one is studying; involves learning how to listen, see, and talk within the worlds being studied.

PHENOMENOLOGICAL METHODS: research approaches that attempt to go directly to the empirical data without preconceptions or procedures based on prior theory or research.

POSITIVISM: the view that all genuine human knowledge is contained within the boundaries of science, i.e., the systematic study of phenomena and the explication of the laws embodied therein. Questions that cannot be answered by scientific methods are, in effect, unanswerable.

PROXEMICS: the study of people's use of space and its relationship to culture. Proxemics is concerned with nonverbal behavior with a focus on space, ranging from interpersonal distance to the arrangement of furniture and architecture.

QUALITATIVE METHODS: procedures for identifying the presence or absence of something, in contrast to quantitative methods, which involve numerically measuring the degree to which some feature is present. Thus, qualitative methods can be described as "procedures for counting to one."

QUALITATIVE RESEARCH: research that produces descriptive data based on spoken or written words and observable behavior.

SCIENTISM: the proposition that the methods of the natural sciences should be used in all areas of investigation.

SELF-NARRATIVE: a narrative that creates and interprets a structure of experience that is being told about; the self of the teller is at the center of the story.

SEMIOTIC ANALYSIS: a method of reading the meaning of words and signs within narrative and interactional texts; it directs attention to the codes, metaphors, and metonymies that organize the text; it suggests that texts are structured in terms of oppositions (e.g., male versus female). Any text contains multiple, often contradictory meanings and messages that a semiotic analysis helps to disclose.

SYMBOLIC INTERACTION: human interactional experience mediated by language and symbols.

TEXT: any printed, visual, oral, or auditory statement that is available for reading, viewing, or hearing; readers create texts as they read them.

THEORETICAL SAMPLING: a sampling method in which the researcher selects new cases to study according to their potential to expand on or refine the concepts and theory that have already been developed. Data collection and analysis proceed together.

THEORETICAL SATURATION: the point at which the researcher is not discovering new information from the theoretical sampling of cases.

THICK DESCRIPTION: capturing the meanings and experiences that have occurred in a problematic situation; reports meanings, intentions, history, biography, and relevant relational, interactional, and situational processes in a rich, dense, detailed manner; creates the conditions for interpretation and understanding; contrasted to thin description, which is factual.

THIN DESCRIPTION: a description lacking detail; a simple reporting of acts, independent of intentions or the circumstances that organize an action; a gloss

TRIANGULATION: the use of multiple research methods and sources of data to study the same problem and to enhance validity

Contributors

Julie S. Abramson: is an associate professor, School of Social Welfare, University at Albany, State University of New York. Her publications have related to collaboration between physicians and social workers, team work, program development in medical settings, and discharge planning.

John R. Belcher: is an assistant professor at the University of Maryland School of Social Work. He has published widely on homelessness, mental health, and poverty.

Susan R. Bernstein: is assistant director for administrative operations in the Department of Social Work Services of The Mount Sinai Hospital in New York City. Her publications reflect her professional experience in the use of qualitative methods to understand the management of human services.

Robert Bogdan: is a senior research associate at the Center on Human Policy at Syracuse University and a professor of special education, sociology, and cultural foundations of education. His books include *Qualitative Research for Education* (with Sari Biklen), *Introduction to Qualitative Research* (with Steven Taylor), and *Freakshow*.

Bonnie E. Carlson: is an associate professor in the School of Social Welfare at the State University of New York, Albany. She has published in the areas of family violence and corrections.

Adrienne S. Chambon: is assistant professor at the University of Toronto, Faculty of Social Work, where she teaches interpretive research methods and conducts research based on narrative/discourse analysis of clinical exchanges.

Bertram J. Cohler: is William Rainey Harper Professor of Social Sciences at The University of Chicago and a member of the faculty, The Institute for Psychoanalysis, Chicago. His publications have integrated psychoanalysis and the human sciences and analysis of narrative in the study of mental health and aging.

Inger P. Davis: is a professor at San Diego State University School of Social Work. Her publications have related to research in clinical social work practice and child and family welfare.

Liane V. Davis: is associate professor at the University of Kansas School of Social Welfare. She has published extensively in the area of battered women and feminist issues in social work.

Ruth G. Dean: is an associate professor at Simmons College School of Social Work teaching clinical practice at the master's and doctoral levels. Her recent publications have applied a constructivist perspective to clinical practice.

Pat Earnshaw: is a Saint Louis University M.S.W. student.

Irwin Epstein: is a professor of social work research at Hunter College School of Social Work. He is the author of several books and articles concerning research utilization in social work practice and the integration of qualitative and quantitative research methods.

Edith Fein: is a research director at Casey Family Services. She has recently coauthored *No More Partings: An Examination of Long-Term Foster Care* and *Permanency Planning for Children.*

Andrea Firrek: is an M.S.W. student at Saint Louis University.

Anne E. Fortune: is associate professor and associate dean at the School of Social Welfare, The University at Albany, State University of New York. Recent publications include research on termination of treatment and on field education in social work.

Jane F. Gilgun: is associate professor, School of Social Work, University of Minnesota. She is the author of many articles and book chapters, all based on her qualitative research on families.

Howard Goldstein: is professor emeritus, Mandel School of Applied Social Sciences, Case Western Reserve University. Prior publications include texts and articles on a unitary and cognitive approaches to practice, humanistic philosophies of practice, and the history and the artistic foundations of practice.

Julie Goodson-Lawes: is a candidate for the Ph.D. in sociocultural anthropology at the State University of New York, Albany. She has written on cultural issues in social work practice with Latino and Asian immigrant families.

Elizabeth Gowdy: is employed as evaluation specialist with the Women's Employment Network, Kansas City, Missouri, and is completing her Ph.D. in social work at the University of Kansas School of Social Welfare.

James Hanson: is assistant professor at the Northern Iowa University Social Work Department.

W. David Harrison: is professor of social work and chair of the Ph.D. program at the University of Alabama. His recent book, *Seeking Common Ground: A Theory of Social Work in Social Care,* reports on a study of innovative community social workers in Britain.

Ann Hartman: is dean and Elizabeth Marting Truehaft Professor at the Smith College School for Social Work. Currently editor of *Social Work,* she is the coauthor of *Family-centered Social Work Practice* as well as author of numerous books, articles, and chapters.

Roberta Wells Imre: has been coordinator of the Study Group for Philosophical Issues in Social Work since its inception in 1985, and she has written widely on the subject of philosophical issues in social work. She was visiting research associate at the Rutgers University Institute for Research on Women.

Peter J. Johnson: is regional director, Connecticut Department of Mental Health. He has written extensively in the areas of mental health administration and case management.

Walter Kisthardt: is coordinator of case management training for the University of Kansas School of Social Welfare and is completing his Ph.D. there.

Joan Laird: is professor at the Smith College School for Social Work, where she teaches family theory, family therapy, and sociocultural concepts. Co-author of *Family-centered Social Work Practice,* she is the author of many articles in the social work and family therapy fields.

Norma C. Lang: is a professor, Faculty of Social Work, University of Toronto. She has published in the areas of qualitative research and social work practice with groups.

Barry Loneck: is an assistant professor at the State University of New York at Albany and is a National Association of State Mental Health Program Directors' research fellow.

Anthony N. Maluccio: is professor at Boston College, Graduate School of Social Work. Most recently he coauthored *Adolescents in Foster Families* (1989); *Together Again: Family Reunification in Foster Care* (1992); and *The Child Welfare Challenge: Policy, Practice, and Research* (1992).

Ruth R. Martin: is associate professor, associate dean, at the University of Connecticut, School of Social Work. She has published on the use of oral history in chronicling the black experience in America.

Marleen McClelland: is assistant professor, Ohio University School of Physical Therapy, Athens, Ohio. She has published on the discourse of interdisciplinary teams.

Terry Mizrahi: is a professor at the Hunter College School of Social Work—C.U.N.Y. where she is chairperson of the social health concentration and director of the Education Center for Community Organizing. She has authored numerous books and articles on health advocacy, patients' rights, health policy, physician training and practice, community organizing, and collaboration and coalition building. She is author of *Getting Rid of Patients: Contradictions in the Socialization of Physicians* and coeditor of *Community Organization and Social Administration: Advances, Trends and Issues.*

James B. Mullin: is assistant director of staff development and training in the New York State Office of Mental Health. He also teaches community mental health at the School of Social Welfare, State University of New York at Albany.

Catherine Nye: is assistant professor at Smith College School for Social Work. She has published on the use of narrative and discourse analysis in clinical practice.

Ben A. Orcutt: is professor emerita, University of Alabama, where she was professor and director of the doctoral program in social work. She is the author of *Science and Inquiry in Social Work Practice* and an editor and contributor to books and journals for practice.

Martha Heineman Pieper: serves on the editorial board of *Social Work*. She is an adjunct professor of research at Smith College School for Social Work and is coauthor of *Intrapsychic Humanism: An Introduction to a Comprehensive Psychology and Philosophy of Mind.*

Richard T. Pulice: is an assistant professor in the School of Social Welfare, State University of New York at Albany. He has published extensively on service systems in mental health.

Charles A. Rapp: is professor and associate dean at the University of Kansas School of Social Welfare. He has published extensively in the field of mental health.

William J. Reid: is a professor at the School of Social Welfare, University at Albany, State University of New York, where he teaches clinical practice and research and chairs the Ph.D. program. He is the author of 125 published works, including six books on brief treatment. His most recent book is *Task Strategies,* published by Columbia University Press.

Mary K. Rodwell: is an assistant professor at the School of Social Work at Virginia Commonwealth University. She has published in the areas of child abuse and neglect, constructivist research and evaluation, and ethnically sensitive social work practice.

Roy Ruckdeschel: is a professor of social work at the School of Social Service at Saint Louis University. He has written various articles advocating the use of qualitative research methods.

Roberta G. Sands: is an associate professor at the University of Pennsylvania School of Social Work where she teaches practice and individual and social processes. She has written numerous articles on health, mental health, and women's issues and the volume *Clinical Social Work Practice in Community Mental Health.*

Edmund Sherman: is professor, School of Social Welfare, State University of New York at Albany, where he teaches M.S.W. and Ph.D. courses in clinical practice methods and theory. His recent books include *Counseling the Aging* and *Reminiscence and the Self in Old Age.*

Susan R. Sherman: is a professor of social welfare and of health policy and management at the State University of New York at Albany. Among her publications are *The Environment for Aging: Interpersonal, Social, and Spatial Contexts,* and *Foster Families for Adults: A Community Alternative in Long-Term Care.*

Max Siporin: is professor emeritus of the School of Social Welfare, State University of New York at Albany. He is the author of a widely used text *Introduction to Social Work Practice* and has published many papers on practice theory and methods, as well as on morality and ethics.

Meera Srinivasan: is a Ph.D. student at the University of Kansas School of Social Welfare.

Susan B. Stern: is associate professor and director of family studies and of the family therapy certificate program at Boston University School of Social Work. She has published on single—system designs in family-centered social work practice.

Steven J. Taylor: is the director of the Center on Human Policy and professor of special education at Syracuse University where he teaches courses in social policy and qualitative research. He has written extensively on public policy and disability as well as the application of qualitative research to decision making.

Ronald W. Toseland: is director and professor, Ringel Institute of Gerontology, School of Social Welfare, State University of New York at Albany. He serves on a number of editorial boards, including *Gerontological Social Work, Social Work With Groups,* and *Small Group Research.* He has written several books and more than fifty articles and book chapters. His most recent book is *Group Work with Older Adults.*

Sheldon S. Tobin: is a professor in the School of Social Welfare at the State University of New York at Albany, has published seven books and more than one hundred other publications focused primarily on psychosocial aspects of aging and on services for the elderly.

Katherine Tyson: is assistant professor at the Loyola University Chicago School of Social Work. Her publications have focused on applications of intrapsychic humanism to the diagnosis and treatment of children and also on social work's philosophy of research.

Harold H. Weissman: is the executive officer of the doctor of social welfare program at Hunter College School of Social Work. He is the author of numerous articles and books on social work administration and the design of social programs. His most recent book is entitled *Serious Play: Creativity and Innovation in Social Work.*

Stanley L. Witkin: is professor and chair of the Department of Social Work at the University of Vermont. Some of his recent publications include a chapter in *Restructuring for Caring and Effective Education* and papers in the *Journal of Sociology and Social Welfare* and *Social Work*.

David Woody III: teaches social work practice and cultural sensitivity courses at Baylor University. He is a doctoral candidate at Virginia Commonwealth University.

Author Index

Subject Index

Designer: Linda Secondari
Text: 10/12 Times Roman
Composition: Maple-Vail
Binder: Maple-Vail